CATHOLIC BIOET
A NEW MILLEN

CW00816356

Can the Hippocratic and Judeo-Christian traditions be synthesized with contemporary thought about practical reason, virtue and community to provide real-life answers to the dilemmas of healthcare today? Bishop Anthony Fisher discusses conscience, relationships and law in relation to the modern-day controversies surrounding stem cell research, abortion, transplants, artificial feeding and euthanasia, using case studies to offer insight and illumination. What emerges is a reason-based bioethics for the twenty-first century; a bioethics that treats faith and reason with equal seriousness, that shows the relevance of ancient wisdom to the complexities of modern healthcare scenarios and that offers new suggestions for social policy and regulation. Philosophical argument is complemented by Catholic theology and analysis of social and biomedical trends, to make this an auspicious example of a new generation of Catholic bioethical writing which has relevance for people of all faiths and none.

ANTHONY FISHER is a Dominican friar and the Bishop of Parramatta, in Western Sydney. He is a Member of the Pontifical Academy for Life, Professor of Moral Theology and Bioethics in the John Paul II Institute for Marriage and the Family, Melbourne, and Adjunct Professor of Bioethics in the University of Notre Dame, Sydney.

CATHOLIC BIOETHICS FOR A NEW MILLENNIUM

ANTHONY FISHER

CAMBRIDGE
UNIVERSITY PRESS

CAMBRIDGE UNIVERSITY PRESS
Cambridge, New York, Melbourne, Madrid, Cape Town,
Singapore, São Paulo, Delhi, Mexico City

Cambridge University Press
The Edinburgh Building, Cambridge CB2 8RU, UK

Published in the United States of America by Cambridge University Press, New York

www.cambridge.org
Information on this title: www.cambridge.org/9781107009585

First published 2012
3rd printing 2012

Printed and bound by CPI Group (UK) Ltd, Croydon CR0 4YY

A catalogue record for this publication is available from the British Library

Library of Congress Cataloguing in Publication data
Fisher, Anthony.
Catholic bioethics for a new millennium / Anthony Fisher.
p.   cm.
Includes bibliographical references and index.
ISBN 978-1-107-00958-5 (hardback) – ISBN 978-0-521-25324-6 (paperback)
1. Medical ethics–Religious aspects–Catholic Church.   2. Bioethics–
Religious aspects–Catholic Church.   3. Catholic Church–Doctrines.   I. Title.
R725.56.F57   2011
174.2–dc23
2011029844

ISBN 978-1-107-00958-5 Hardback
ISBN 978-0-521-25324-6 Paperback

Contents

Foreword by John Finnis viii
List of abbreviations xi

Introduction 1

PART I HOW ARE WE TO DO BIOETHICS?

1 Context: challenges and resources of a new millennium 13
 Sex and life in post-modernity 13
 Catholic engagement with the culture of modernity 21
 Promising developments 27
 Conclusion 37

2 Conscience: the crisis of authority 38
 The voice of conscience 38
 The voice of the magisterium 52
 Conscience in post-modernity 59
 Where to from here? 66

3 Cooperation: should we ever collaborate with wrongdoing? 69
 Traditional examples 69
 Five modern examples 74
 Some fundamental issues raised by these examples 86
 Why it matters so much 94
 Conclusion 97

PART II BEGINNING OF LIFE

4 Beginnings: when do people begin? 101
 Method, thesis and implications 101
 A closer look at the science 104
 A closer look at the philosophy 112

Individuality criteria 119
Conclusion 130

5   Stem cells: what's all the fuss about? 131
    Scientific potential and concerns about stem cells 131
    Ethical concerns about embryonic stem cells 138
    Social concerns about embryonic stem cells 148

6   Abortion: the new eugenics? 152
    The perennial debate about abortion 152
    Pre-natal testing: a search-and-destroy mission? 160
    The new abortion debate 169

PART III   LATER LIFE

7   Transplants: bodies, relationships and ethics 185
    Love beyond death 185
    Conceptions of the body and relationships in tissue transplantation 186
    Fashionable bioethical approaches to tissue procurement 191
    Better bioethical approaches to tissue procurement 202
    Ethical issues in tissue reception 209
    Conclusion 212

8   Artificial nutrition: why do unresponsive patients matter? 213
    Civilization after Schiavo 213
    Why the unresponsive still matter: a philosophical account 218
    Why the unresponsive still matter: a theological account 228
    Some final questions 241

9   Endings: suicide and euthanasia in the Bible 248
    The problem of suicide and euthanasia in the Bible 248
    Suicides and euthanasias in the Bible 255
    The scriptural basis of Judeo-Christian opposition to suicide
        and euthanasia 265

PART IV   PROTECTING LIFE

10 Identity: what role for a Catholic hospital? 275
    A tale of two hospitals 275
    Current challenges for Catholic hospitals 279
    Catholic hospitals as *diakonia* 286
    Catholic hospitals as *martyria* 290
    Catholic hospitals as *leitourgia* 296
    Conclusion: six tasks for a new century 299

11 Regulation: what kinds of laws and social policies? 302
    A tale of three politicians 302
    Catholic principles for politicians 304
    Reasonable stances for a pro-life politician 320
    Some virtues of a pro-life politician 324

Index 328

Foreword

The responsibility of one who undertakes to hand on faith, as a pastor or theologian, and the responsibility of one who undertakes to reflect and discourse philosophically are distinct responsibilities. The disciplines, each with its own criteria of soundness in argument and warrant in affirmation, are distinct. But they are responsibilities that can be united in a single lived vocation, by one who accepts and honours the distinctions but shows that each discipline can be pursued authentically, without compromise or commingling of criteria, but with complementarity, and some convergence of conclusions. That is the sort of vocation that I see being pursued by Anthony Fisher, and this book is one of its fruits. The primacy of the episcopal and theological in his personal calling does not suppress the philosophical in the method and reflective, argumentative grip of the book's core chapters.

They concern human life. But that abstract category can mask a reality which the book never forgets: to speak of such life is to speak of the very existence and reality of a human person, of each of us. For each of us, this existence and reality began in earliest embryonic form, when all our capacities were already given us, but as potentialities which, although they already were present and distinguished us already from embryonic mice, we could not yet exercise. Already, it now seems clear, that all-embracing, distinctively human capacity we call spirit had been bestowed on each of us as the organizing principle informing all the biochemical and biological processes of our individual formation, development and activity. Each of us was already an individual and a person. The difference in origins between most of us and those quite few of us who are monozygotic twins you will find discussed in these pages, and does not alter the essentials which I have just recalled. The dignity of being at once bodily and spiritual distinguishes us from all other creatures, so far as we can know and investigate them. The worth which that dignity entails is what this book explores and elaborates, and celebrates in its title.

Bishop Fisher expresses his sense of the significance, for his own generation of believers, of the late pope, John Paul II. So it will not be out of place to recall that great bishop's personal sense of the importance not only of the person, and thus of people, but also of the peoples within which human persons flourish by acquiring the language and indeed the whole patrimony of memory, culture and capital that a people – paradigmatically a nation – can accumulate for its members and from which it can draw to benefit other peoples in their need. To think of human life as something to be disposed of by choice – to be 'pro-choice' – is not only to violate those disposed of, and their most basic right, but also to betray one's own people. For a people lives, and carries itself into the future, only by a kind of deep solidarity which is eviscerated in one way by abortion, and in other ways by the various forms of euthanasia, suicide and assisting suicide.

And also by detaching sex from marriage (or approving non-marital forms of sex-act) – a theme which the author intimates in his introductory chapters. The philosophical and theological argumentation deployed in the book – and in the tradition from which it draws – is much more concerned with the way our choices (that is, our intentions, whether more ultimate or more close-in) bear on the persons they intentionally affect than with long-term overall consequences. But the intelligible patterns and structures of our human makeup mean that specific types of intentional choice tend predictably enough to have broadly specifiable types of social consequence. Our generation is witnessing, and the generations soon to come will experience all the more keenly, the consequences of that loss of the marital. In itself, and all the more so in combination with the loss of solidarity manifested in killings, including self-killing, this unwillingness to hand on life in the incomparably appropriate milieu of marital commitment is resulting in the accelerating decline of whole peoples – ours. Though the Church is universal and transcends all peoples, its own culture – at once universal and very specific – is rooted in the cultures of the peoples it has evangelized, and it cannot be indifferent to the collapse and overwhelming of specific cultures, least of all those in which its own tradition and life has been centred.

For the present, the author concentrates his reflective energies and zeal on the threats now commonplace to lives just begun, or wounded or debilitated or ageing towards death, rather than on the institution and acts by which life is transmitted and nurtured fittingly well. That focus is sufficient, and very important for us all, and I commend the outcome to readers of every opinion.

JOHN FINNIS

Abbreviations

AA	Vatican II, *Apostolicam Actuositatem: Decree on the Apostolate of the Laity* (1965)
CCC	*Catechism of the Catholic Church* (1993; revised 1997)
CDF	(Vatican) Congregation for the Doctrine of the Faith
CIC	*Code of Canon Law of the Latin (Western) Church* (1983)
CMQ	*Catholic Medical Quarterly*
DH	Vatican II, *Dignitatis Humanae: Declaration on Religious Freedom* (1965)
DV	Vatican II, *Dei Verbum: Dogmatic Constitution on Divine Revelation* (1965)
ES cells	embryonic stem cells
EV	Pope John Paul II, *Evangelium Vitae: Encyclical Letter on the Value and Inviolability of Human Life* (1995)
FC	Pope John Paul II, *Familiaris Consortio: Apostolic Exhortation on the Role of the Christian Family in the Modern World* (1981)
GE	Vatican II, *Gravissimum Educationis: Declaration on Christian Education* (1965)
GS	Vatican II, *Gaudium et Spes: Pastoral Constitution on the Church in the Modern World* (1965)
HV	Pope Paul VI, *Humanae Vitae: Encyclical Letter on Birth Control* (1968)
IM	Vatican II, *Inter Mirifica: Decree on the Means of Social Communication* (1963)
iPS cells	induced pluripotent stem cells
JAMA	*Journal of the American Medical Association*
JME	*Journal of Medical Ethics*
LG	Vatican II, *Lumen Gentium: Dogmatic Constitution on the Church* (1964)

xii| List of abbreviations

LQ	Linacre Quarterly
NCBQ	National Catholic Bioethics Quarterly
OT	Vatican II, Optatam Totius: Decree on Priestly Training (1965)
PO	Vatican II, Presbyterorum Ordinis: Decree on the Ministry and Life of Priests (1965)
ST	St Thomas Aquinas, Summa Theologiae
UR	Vatican II, Unitatis Redintegratio: Decree on Ecumenism (1964)
VS	Pope John Paul II, Veritatis Splendor: Encyclical Letter on Certain Fundamental Questions of the Church's Moral Teaching (1993)

The numbers following Church documents refer to paragraph numbers. All Vatican documents are published in Vatican City by Libreria Editrice Vaticana and on the Internet at www.vatican.va.

Introduction

'Speaking the truth in love' – so St Paul described the lived words of those who attain 'the unity of the faith and knowledge of the Son of God', those who grow up to be as fully human and close to divine as it is possible for human persons to be. Others, he warns, behave immaturely, 'like children tossed to and fro', carried about by the latest ideas, the spin of popular opinion-makers. That we might be assisted to take the first course, God graces 'some to be apostles, prophets or evangelists, some to be pastors or teachers', together building up the Church (Eph. 4:10–16).

I write as a Catholic moral theologian and bishop – as one of those Paul says are charged to build up God's people to maturity and unity. It is a serious responsibility. Without reliable teachers, Paul continues, people may be dim-witted, hard-hearted, alienated from God, callous, licentious and greedy. Charity requires that 'everyone speak the truth with his neighbour', that they might be converted from their old lusts and habits, and become the very image and likeness of God (Eph. 4:17–25).

Catholic theologians and pastors have no monopoly on moral wisdom. Today as in Paul's day the Church operates in a pluralist environment and cannot expect states or professions to conform to all her teachings. The Church, as Pope Benedict XVI so often says, *proposes* rather than imposes her ideas: people are free in practice to accept or reject them. Christians hope to be given a fair hearing even by non-believers and judged on the basis of their arguments, so the essays in this book are generally framed in the language of the age, of philosophy and healthcare, of ideals common to people of all religions and none. But the Church also speaks with the authority of her master, and so readers will from time to time encounter a more distinctively Christian argumentation, including appeal to the Sacred Scriptures and tradition.

I write also as one of the 'John Paul II generation' especially graced to receive his *Theology of the Body* and *Gospel of Life*. One of John Paul's goals was undoubtedly to prepare the Church for the challenges of the new millennium in the areas of life and love. As a young adult, religious, priest and then bishop, I welcomed his great teaching and example. With so many others I delight in the Holy Father's recent proclamation as a Blessed and prayerfully look forward to that day when 'John Paul the Great' is known as a saint.

Of course the wisdom of the *Theology of the Body* and the *Gospel of Life* came ultimately from Christ and had already been articulated in various ways before John Paul came upon the world stage. In his collaborator and successor Benedict XVI this wisdom is being spoken again, for he too has proved to be a great champion of the unborn, the family, the sick and the suffering. His particular interests in conscience and truth, in Christian culture and identity, are further enriching our understanding in these areas. Each apostle, prophet, evangelist, pastor and teacher has his own idiom and insights.

In *Novo Millennio Ineunte: Apostolic Letter at the Close of the Great Jubilee 2000* (2001) John Paul II renewed Christ's invitation to 'Put out into the deep' (Luke 5:4). 'These words', he explained 'still ring out for us today and they invite us to remember the past with gratitude, to live the present with enthusiasm and to look forward to the future with confidence. *Jesus Christ is the same yesterday and today and forever!*' (*Novo Millennio Ineunte* 1). If we are to live with enthusiasm and confidence, he argued, we must be aware of the particular challenges we face as a Church and a culture: secularization, economic uncertainty, environmental damage, wars and terrorism, contempt for fundamental rights. The field for these great battles is often the individual person, his or her conscience and body, together with the family and local community.

In the face of such big challenges it is easy to lose hope. So the Pope reminded us of Jesus' promise, 'I am with you always, to the close of the age' (Matt. 28:20). 'This assurance has accompanied the Church for two thousand years.' So when we ask, as we must, how to engage in the great contests of our day, we can do so 'with trusting optimism, but without underestimating the problems we face. We are certainly not seduced by the naïve expectation that, faced with the great challenges of our time, we shall find some magic formula. No, we shall not be saved by a formula but by a Person, and the assurance which he gives us: I am with you!' So, the Pope continued, 'It is not a matter of inventing a new programme. The programme already exists: it is the plan found in the Gospel and in the living Tradition ... it has its centre in Christ himself, who is to be known, loved and imitated, so that in him we may live the life of the Trinity, and with him transform history until its fulfilment ... But it must be translated into pastoral initiatives adapted to the circumstances of each community' (*Novo Millennio Ineunte* 29). For Christian witness to be effective, especially in the areas of bioethics and family life, where the Church's teaching may be unpopular or misunderstood, 'it is important that special efforts be made *to explain properly the reasons* for the Church's position' (*Novo Millennio Ineunte* 51). This book is one such effort at this third millennial project.

There is much about contemporary healthcare and bioresearch worthy of celebration. Lives are saved. People are cured of debilitating diseases or prevented ever from suffering them. Others have the advance of sickness limited or symptoms relieved. Many more are well cared for while they are sick, recovering or dying. At least in the more developed economies, people can now expect to live to 'a ripe old age'. Of course there are limits to the technology and art of healthcare – the limits of the possible and also of the moral. Medicine can be misused. Yet as the fourth-century doctor of the Church Saint Basil the Great observed: 'As regards medicine, it would not be right to reject this gift of God, just because some people misuse it … We should, instead, throw light on what they have corrupted, so that medicine might be used rightly.'[1]

In medicine today ethics often bumps up against *the technological imperative*: the idea that if a thing can be done it should be (or inevitably will be) done. Proponents of this view often caricature their opponents as 'Luddites' or 'fundamentalists', fearful of progress and seeking always to obstruct it; meanwhile they present themselves as benefactors of humanity as it marches into a glorious future. They resent 'interference' from outside the profession and brush aside ethical questions such as those raised in this book. But no technology – medical technology included – is self-justifying or beyond criticism. Leon Kass, a leading Jewish bioethicist and former chair of the US President's Commission on Bioethics, puts it well: 'We must all get used to the idea that biomedical technology makes possible many things we should *never* do.'[2]

A similar imperative to the technological one is *the rescue imperative*: the very natural desire to save those at risk of damage or death. This is, of course, what drives medicine and is a very important starting point for a 'pro-life' ethic. Yet the Good Samaritan norm of intervening to rescue

---

[1] St Basil the Great, *Regola lunga* 55:3.
[2] L. Kass, 'The wisdom of repugnance: why we should ban the cloning of humans', *New Republic* 216(22) (2 June 1997), 17–26.

is not absolute: there is no duty to preserve life *at all costs*, by every possible means, no matter what is required or forgone in the process. On the
contrary, a single-minded focus on preserving life (or improving health)
can be just as dangerous as any other fanaticism that ignores other goods,
norms and responsibilities, and the downsides of any choice. While there
is always cause to care, there will be times when some and perhaps all
treatments are no longer warranted. Sometimes the rescue imperative is
driven not just by a refusal to let go but also by a fear of disappoint-
ing relatives or ending up in court; it may even be driven by research or
financial goals. *Over-treatment* is common in some places and can be as
morally problematical as under-treatment.

Another tendency, also common in contemporary healthcare, is a *pragmatism* which masquerades as a proper concern for efficiency, effectiveness or quality of life, but which plays out in discharging people from
hospitals before time or denying them appropriate care or even abandoning them altogether. Once certain people are identified as expensive, difficult or having a low quality of life, as 'vegetables' or 'dying', there is a risk
that they will suffer *under-treatment* or a denial of basic care.

In the face of these and other contemporary tendencies the wisdom of
the Catholic bioethical tradition offers important points of guidance and
criticism. Here I list seven propositions from that tradition, articulated
especially in John Paul's bioethical charter *Evangelium Vitae*, and elsewhere in the Scriptures and the magisterium (authoritative and official
teachings) of the Catholic Church.

- There are objective philosophical and theological truths about the
  nature of the human person, relationships and actions, accessible to
  faith and reason, and these must inform the Christian conscience; to
  act morally and to flourish persons must act in accordance with such
  principles.
- Human beings are a unity of physical, emotional, intellectual and spiritual dimensions; like all animals 'we are our bodies', but unlike other
  animals our bodies make concrete a spiritual reality as free, rational,
  loving beings; we are created as children of God the Father, redeemed as
  siblings of God the Son, inspired as temples of God the Holy Spirit and
  destined to eternal bodily life with the Blessed Trinity and the saints.
- Nothing can diminish the intrinsic dignity and inviolability of the
  human person: God is the Author and Lord of life and he commands
  reverence for every human life.

- A direct attack upon an innocent human being is always gravely immoral, whether it is an end in itself or a means to some other end; such lethal attacks include murder, surgical abortion, abortifacient drug use, human embryo destruction, some reproductive technologies, search-and-destroy genetic testing, infanticide, suicide, active euthanasia (voluntary or not) and euthanasia by neglect of basic care (such as denial of feeding); so also non-lethal attacks such as direct torture, maiming, sterilization and substance abuse.
- Responsibility in this area is complex and thus the objective evil of killing does not necessarily indicate grave sin on the part of every perpetrator: those who are suffering from stress (e.g. in pregnancy) or depression, the terminally ill and the frail elderly, and those around them, often have very limited freedom, as do those who may cooperate in evils; but the Church must continue to preach 'the Gospel of Life' and to champion the victims of 'the culture of death' by seeking conversion of hearts and of cultures, and good laws, policies and practices.
- Human acts in this area are also complex, and so we must clarify our intended ends and the foreseen but unwilled side-effects of our proposals; hence we distinguish direct from indirect abortion, euthanasia from appropriate withdrawals of treatment and palliative care, and formal from material cooperation in evil.
- People should take reasonable measures to protect and promote life and health for themselves, dependants and others. Christians engage in healthcare ministry in pursuit of the common good and as a continuation of the healing mission of Christ; they must be conscious of the challenges today in maintaining Catholic identity and in justly allocating resources. They support healthy lifestyles, therapeutic procedures, some organ donation and all ethical research.

Here too we might note seven propositions from Catholic sexual teaching, also widely contested today, which have been articulated in the Scriptures and tradition, especially in John Paul II's exhortation *Familiaris Consortio* and his series of catecheses popularly known as the *Theology of the Body*:

- Sexuality is a fundamental aspect of our bodiliness, personality, relationships and activity, so that maleness and femaleness are fundamental in a way that race and tastes, for instance, are not; the male and female ways of being human are different but of equal dignity, complementing each other and grounding a reciprocity most perfectly expressed in marital communion.

- Sexual activity expresses a total self-giving and receiving which is marital and so is reserved to spouses; non-marital sexual activity is wrong.
- Marriage is the free commitment of a man and a woman to unite as husband and wife exclusively and for life – for the sake of their mutual fulfilment, for begetting and educating children within a stable family, for the building up of the social and ecclesial community and for the salvation of all concerned.
- Married couples have responsibilities to guard their own and each other's vocations and to fulfil them by loving, honouring and serving each other as faithful companions for the whole of life.
- The unitive and procreative dimensions of 'the marital act' are intrinsic and cannot be separated; neither should be deliberately excluded when a couple make love; couples should therefore engage in marital intercourse generously and responsibly, taking into consideration the times of fertility and their capacity to bring up a new child. Children should be conceived from an act of love rather than a laboratory procedure.
- Parents should raise their children justly and lovingly, promoting their growth according to Christian principles, so that their family is 'a school of deeper humanity' and 'a domestic church'.
- Everyone should cultivate chastity, courage, hope and love in their relationships, integrating sexuality into their vocation; particular challenges arise today in living a Catholic sexual and marital ethic because of false views of the human person, freedom and relationships.

There are many other propositions in the Catholic ethics of life and love, and it will be evident that 'bioethics' here overlaps with sexual ethics and social ethics in contemporary contests and responses. We must resist compartmentalizing the 'bio' from other parts of morality.[3] But my fourteen propositions are probably enough to start with! They will be elaborated and qualified in the course of this collection of essays. A number of these claims are as much contested within the contemporary Church as outside it; some of these assertions are supported by people outside the Church as much as by those within. In any case, these issues touch many people, often quite deeply, and require to be explored honestly and with

---

[3] See A. Fisher, 'Christian ethics, Roman Catholic', *Encyclopaedia of Applied Ethics* (San Diego: Academic Press, 1998), vol. I, pp. 471–92.

compassion. In this book I will try my best to do this, 'speaking the truth in love'.

Many people have affected the thinking I present in these chapters. My Dominican brothers saw to my education in moral theology and bioethics and supported me while I undertook much of this research. Professor John Finnis of the University of Oxford supervised my doctorate and has been a great influence on my thinking, as has his distinguished collaborator Germain Grisez. The staff and students of the John Paul II Institute for Marriage and the Family in Melbourne, Australia, have been my companions in these investigations. Professor Hayden Ramsay, deputy vice-chancellor of the University of Notre Dame Australia, Sydney, has been a constant intellectual and personal support. For most of the years that I have served as a member of the Pontifical Academy for Life – and for several years before – Bishop (now Cardinal) Elio Sgreccia gave sterling leadership to the academy and encouragement to its younger members: I thank him for this, as I do my colleagues in that academy.

I also record my gratitude to the Dominican community of Blackfriars Oxford, especially the Regent, the Revd Dr Richard Finn OP, to Mr Christopher Flynn and family and to George Cardinal Pell, Archbishop of Sydney, who gave me the ease of a sabbatical in Oxford to draw these chapters together and rework them. I also thank my secretaries, Mr Ben Lucas, Ms Alison Bell and Mrs Helen Howard, for their assistance and patience throughout.

Some of the chapters in this volume have been published previously in some form but all have been revised, some very significantly. Part I explores some fundamental questions under the umbrella of 'How are we to do bioethics?' The origins of Chapter 1 are in A. Schmitz (ed.), *A Garland of Silver: A Jubilee Anthology in Honour of Archbishop Mario Conti* (Aberdeen: Ogilvie Press, 2002), pp. 99–143. Chapter 2 was given at the 2007 Congress of the Pontifical Academy for Life in Vatican City and published in E. Sgreccia and J. Laffitte (eds.), *Christian Conscience in Support of the Right to Life* (Libreria Editrice Vaticana, 2008), pp. 37–70. Chapter 3 is largely drawn from a paper given in 2003 at an international conference of the Linacre Centre for Healthcare Ethics, at the University of Cambridge, England, and appeared in H. Watt (ed.), *Cooperation, Complicity and Conscience: Moral Problems in Healthcare, Science, Law and Public Policy* (London: Linacre Centre, 2005), pp. 27–64.

Part II examines some beginning-of-life issues. Chapter 4 considers the question that underlies all of this part – when does life begin? – by revisiting and updating a paper from *Anthropotes* 7(2) (December 1991), 199–244. Chapter 5 then examines death almost immediately after life begins – in the embryo laboratory – and a range of issues in the stem cell debate. It has evolved from conference papers at the University of Melbourne (Australia, 2002), the University of Brno (Czech Republic, 2004), the University of Santo Tomas, Manila (Philippines, 2005), the University of Notre Dame Australia (Australia, 2009) and the University of Toronto (Canada, 2010). Parts have appeared in the *Journal of the Royal Australian and New Zealand College of Obstetricians and Gynaecologists* 4(4) (2002), 276–7, and in F. Gomez (ed.), *Celebrating the Gospel of Life: Basic Issues in Bioethics* (Manila: UST, 2006), pp. 191–206. Chapter 6 looks at life-issues later in gestation and amplifies papers given to the Australian Theological Forum in the University of Melbourne in 1995 and at the Fifteenth International Conference of the Pontifical Council for the Pastoral Care of Health Professionals in the Vatican in 2000. These were published in H. Regan *et al.* (eds.), *Beyond Mere Health: Theology and Health Care in a Secular Society* (Melbourne: ATF, 1996), pp. 145–68, and in *Dolentium Hominum* 46(1) (2001), 85–95.

Part III treats some bioethical questions that arise at the other end of life. Chapter 7 substantially reworks a lecture given in 1999 in the Faculty of Medicine of the University of Santo Tomas, Manila, which appeared in F. Gomez and A. Yu-Soliven (eds.), *Love and Life-Making, Confidentiality, Xenotransplants and Aging* (Manila: UST, 2000), pp. 75–110. Chapter 8 is a shortened version of a paper delivered at the 2005 conference of the International Association of Catholic Bioethicists and published in C. Tollefsen (ed.), *Artificial Nutrition and Hydration: The New Catholic Debate* (Dordrecht: Springer, 2008), pp. 3–38. Chapter 9 has not previously been published but reworks papers presented in the Faculty of Theology of the University of Oxford and in the School of Theology of the Australian Catholic University, Melbourne.

Part IV explores some questions around nurturing and protecting human life. The identity of Catholic healthcare institutions is a major challenge for owners, sponsors, managers and professionals of those institutions – as well as outsiders looking in. Chapter 10 was delivered at Queens' College in the University of Cambridge for the Twentieth Anniversary Conference of the Linacre Centre for Healthcare Ethics, and published in L. Gormally (ed.), *Issues for a Catholic Bioethic* (London: Linacre Centre, 1999), pp. 200–30. The final chapter – on the responsibilities of politicians – began its life at another Linacre Centre conference at Cambridge and was published in L. Gormally (ed.), *Culture of Life – Culture of Death* (London: Linacre Centre, 2002), pp. 195–226.

Many people assisted with updating and editing these chapters, including Mr Jonathan Baker, Ms Georgina Meyer, the Revd Vincent Magat OP, Ms Thérèse Buck, Mr Brett Doyle and Ms Lisa Garland. Mrs Susan Holmes provided the index. I thank the publishers of some earlier pieces for permission to rework and republish them. I also thank Laura Morris, Anna Lowe, the referees and the rest of the team at Cambridge University Press for all their help. For this book I have not only updated and integrated the earlier articles in various ways but also cut back on the number and length of references in some chapters; readers who are interested in fuller references might check the original publications.

PART I

How are we to do bioethics?

CHAPTER I

Context: challenges and resources
of a new millennium

SEX AND LIFE IN POST-MODERNITY

Consumer bodies and recreational sex

Elizabeth Knox's novel *The Vintner's Luck* (Picador, 2000) was described
in *The Times* as 'an all-too-human chronicle of burning desire, violence,
murderousness, bitter jealousy, curiosity, sexual deviation, shame and
fidelity of a sort'. It is interesting what we regard today as 'all-too-human'.
The tale pivots on the annual meeting between Sobran, a nineteenth-
century Burgundian vigneron, and Xas, a fallen angel. Along the way
Knox elaborates the sexual adventures of the central characters: Sobran
marries his childhood sweetheart Céleste only after impregnating her, but
also continues his sexual affair with his brother-at-arms Baptiste, following him to the Napoleonic campaign in Russia. As the soldiers queue for
prostitutes, Sobran penetrates one nine months pregnant, inducing her
labour. After Baptiste's death Sobran returns to his vineyard and has two
affairs parallel to his marriage, one with Xas, an angel with the beautiful
man's body, and the other with Aurora, a local countess. Céleste gives
him many children but has her own affair with his brother Léon, a sado-
masochist who has his mistresses strangle him. The angel Xas roams the
earth, looking for bodies rather than souls to devour, including not only
Sobran but his son.

There is much more to this story and some of it admirable. But it is
striking how seductively *undisturbing* it all is, despite all the violence and
perversion. In the post-modern era people choose their own sexuality(s),
more or less at whim. Nothing is natural or unnatural. Sex and sexuality,
life-giving, even life-taking, are 'privatized', matters of taste – and tastes
are changeable. Physiology, psychology, ethics, all are irrelevant to sex
and life choices. What matters is the freedom to fulfil preferences. Liberal
autonomy as freedom from *nature* – freedom from God and his order in

13

the cosmos, or from the requirements of practical reason and the common good, indeed from any limit to the human will – has also become
freedom from our own *natures*. In his excellent recent treatment of *Life in
the Flesh* Adam Cooper observes that in modernity the body

has suffered a terrible fate. A fate not dissimilar, I would suggest, to that suffered by the literary text under Derrida, or by human nature under Nietzsche.
The body has been destabilized and emptied of intrinsic meaning. It no longer
speaks for itself. Whatever native voice it had has been silenced. Instead it now
says what we want it to say.[1]

Who are we to get in the way if people want to have sex with any other
human being or even with non-human beings, or if they want to enter
into a 'gay marriage', or if men want to be mothers? If medical practitioners or researchers want to clone human embryos, or create them from the
gametes of dead persons or help people be rid of their unwanted babies,
why not, as long as there is consent from the living? If people want to
design their children genetically, or pay someone else for the use of their
gametes or womb, or do genetic tests to exclude children with undesirable
characteristics, what is to stop them?

To keep extending their markets leading providers of reproductive technologies such as *in vitro* fertilization and the anti-reproductive technologies such as contraception and abortion, must sweep away any lingering
taboos against separating sex, reproduction, love and commitment.[2] As
the contraceptive pill allowed the development of 'recreational sex', so IVF
increasingly enables 'made-to-order babies' not just for infertile couples,
but for single people, same-sex couples and others. The future promises a
whole panoply of sexual options including 'virtual sex' with a computer-
generated 3D image and a similar range of fertility options such as designer
babies with qualities chosen from a catalogue. Caution in these matters is
quickly dismissed as 'religious' or 'narrow' and not to be taken seriously
in a progressive community. The marriage-based natural family, so long
recognized as the basic cell of society, will no longer be normative, and to
privilege it in any way is increasingly regarded as discriminatory.

Thus the consumer mentality has profoundly affected not only the way
the body, sex and relationships are viewed in modernity, but also our very

---

[1] A. Cooper, *Life in the Flesh: An Anti-Gnostic Spiritual Philosophy* (Oxford University Press, 2008),
p. 2.
[2] See, e.g., R. Jansen, 'Evidence-based ethics and the regulation of reproduction', *Human
Reproduction* 12 (1997), 2068–75, and 'Sex, reproduction and impregnation: by 2099 let's not con-
fuse them', *Medical Journal of Australia* 171 (1999), 666–7; C. Wood, 'Future change in sexual
behaviour?', *Medical Journal of Australia* 171 (1999), 662–4.

conception of children. Ownership, patents, quantity and quality control, 'take-home baby rates': the language and mentality of the free market have colonized the womb and nursery. After four decades of fertility and infertility technologies we now have as few children as we want, if any, as and when convenient, carefully spaced and increasingly according to our genetic preferences. Children have become the last big consumer item for the person who has everything. Hence the ease with which our society disposes of so many children by abortion while at the same time engaging in frenzied efforts to create them: it is the logic of the market.

An example of just how far we have come is bioethicist Peter Singer, Princeton's Professor of Human Values. Long an influential promoter of consequentialism, abortion, infanticide, euthanasia and animal liberation, he delights in 'stretching the boundaries' of the ethically permissible:

> Not so long ago, any form of sexuality not leading to the conception of children was seen as, at best, wanton lust, or worse, a perversion. One by one, the taboos have fallen. The idea that it could be wrong to use contraception in order to separate sex from reproduction is now merely quaint. If some religions still teach that masturbation is 'self-abuse', that just shows how out of touch they have become. Sodomy? That's all part of the joy of sex, recommended for couples seeking erotic variety. In many of the world's great cities, gays and lesbians can be open about their sexual preferences to an extent unimaginable a century ago. You can even do it in the U.S. Armed Forces, as long as you don't talk about it. Oral sex? Some objected to President Clinton's choice of place and partner, and others thought he should have been more honest about what he had done, but no one dared suggest that he was unfit to be President simply because he had taken part in a sexual activity that was, in many jurisdictions, a crime. But not every taboo has crumbled.

The last taboo is bestiality, and Singer thinks there is nothing special about humans or their sexual acts that makes bestiality problematic. 'Mutually satisfying' sexual relationships with household pets is fine, as long as the animal is not caused unnecessary suffering. While he deplores the suffering a hen might endure if penetrated by a man, he wonders if it is any 'worse than what egg producers do to their hens all the time'.[3]

Much could be said about such ideas and their authors, as well as the cultures, academies and media that foster them. *Reductio ad absurdum* – showing how false a position is by drawing out its manifestly absurd

---

[3] P. Singer, 'Heavy petting', www.nerve.com/content/heavy-petting (accessed 1 January 2011), reviewing M. Dekkers, *Dearest Pet: On Bestiality*, trans. Paul Vincent (London: Verso, 1994); interview in 'The beast and the bees', *Weekend Australian*, 21 April 2001, R1; cf. K. Lopez, 'Peter Singer strikes again: this could be your kid's teacher', *National Review*, 5 March 2001; J. Goldberg, 'Taking Singer seriously: don't do it', *National Review*, 14 March 2001.

logical conclusions – no longer works in bioethics and sexual ethics because there is nothing so unnatural or unreasonable that it is without its academic and journalistic advocates. After decades of disconnecting our conceptions of the human person, sexuality, fertility and relationships from human nature, community, culture and tradition, we are now hard put to resist anything, no matter how perverse.

Commitment-free relationships

Despite praise in *The Times* for 'fidelity of a sort', another thoroughly postmodern aspect of *The Vintner's Luck* is the fickleness of the relationships. Many secular social commentators concur with religious ones in identifying a crisis of understanding of freedom and authority in contemporary Western societies which undermines friendship. Thus Christopher Lasch observed that in America:

'Freedom of choice' means 'keeping your options open' … Identities can be adopted and discarded like a change of costume. Ideally, choices of friends, lovers and careers should all be subject to immediate cancellation: such is the open-ended, experimental conception of the good life upheld by the propaganda of commodities, which surrounds the consumer with images of unlimited possibility.[4]

This consumerist obsession with freedom plays out in various ways in marriage and family life and in attitudes to dependent human life. Surveys show that people are less inclined than they were a generation ago to make sexual fidelity, lifelong marriage, parenthood and care for children and the elderly their personal goals. Motherhood is no longer seen as even partly constitutive of womanhood, or fatherhood of masculinity. The proportion of people who regard marriage and children as burdensome and restrictive has more than doubled in a generation. The same surveys show that the proportion of people who regard sacrifice as a positive moral virtue has more than halved.[5]

---

[4] C. Lasch, *The Minimal Self* (London: Norton, 1984), p. 38. Other recent commentators on misunderstandings of freedom include Allan Bloom, Robert Bellah, Stanley Hauerwas, Christopher Lasch, Joyce Little, Alasdair MacIntyre, Michael Novak, Servais Pinckaers, Jeffrey Stout and Charles Taylor. See also John Paul II, *Veritatis Splendor: Encyclical Letter on Certain Fundamental Questions of the Church's Moral Teaching* (1993) 10, 28–83, etc.

[5] Recent commentators on contemporary challenges to married and family life include: Philip Abbott, Brenda Almond, William Bennett, David Blankenhorn, Bryce Christensen, Mary Eberstadt, William Gairdner, Robert George and Jean Elshtain, George Grant, Sylvia Ann Hewlett and Cornell West, Rita Kramer, Christopher Lasch, Dana Mack, Bill Muehlenberg and James Wilson. See also Pew Research Center, 'As marriage and parenthood drift apart, public

Self-sacrifice and obligation have fallen out of the vocabulary of modern liberal societies, being replaced by talk of autonomy, lifestyle choices, rights and preferences. People live in a moral universe of half-remembered and half-understood moral bric-à-brac: words, phrases and ideas inherited from various moral systems. At best a thin consensus regarding moral side-constraints is achieved between individuals who otherwise relate as friendly strangers or out-and-out rivals. If this is true of *the world*, it is also true among *religious* people. Vague recollections of stories and commandments, custom and religious vocabulary are commonly thrown together with bits of secular liberalism, consequentialism, feminism and cultural studies, as well as morsels of pop psychology, new age spirituality and other religions, to produce a 'user-friendly' ethic which bears little relation to Christian faith and practice.

In most developed nations, the decline in commitment and self-sacrifice has spelt a crisis of vocations not just to priesthood and religious life but also to marriage and parenthood. Fewer people are marrying at all. Of those who do, most cohabit before marriage despite the evidence that this radically reduces marital 'sticking power'.[6] In many countries most weddings are now only civil (non-church) ceremonies. Couples marry much later and are much less likely to stay together. Most will have only one or two children and many of these children will grow up in 'broken' or 'blended' families. Of course many of those involved in these situations love deeply and sacrifice themselves in various ways for the sake of their relationships and especially their children, but they do so against a backdrop of a civilization that is in many ways giving up on marriage, family, commitment and self-sacrifice, a civilization in which their sacrifices no longer make public sense. Later in this chapter I will return to the social effects of these changes.

The castration of a civilization

Set as it is in the nineteenth century, *The Vintner's Luck* unavoidably contains stories of childbirth and children. Yet the central character's most crucial emotional and sexual relationship – with a fallen angel – is, by

is concerned about social impact' (Washington, DC: Pew Research Center, July 2007), http://pewresearch.org/pubs/526/marriage-parenthood (accessed 1 January 2011).

[6] For example, L. Bumpass and J. Sweet, *Cohabitation, Marriage and Union Stability* (Madison, WS: Center for Demography and Ecology, 1995); D. Popenoe and B. Dafoe Whitehead, *Should We Live Together? What Young Adults Need to Know about Cohabitation before Marriage* (Washington, DC: National Marriage Project, 2002).

contrast, sterile. You might say our culture is just like that. We no longer value children as we did in the past; nor do we even take them for granted as part of life. They are, rather, an optional extra. As Bloom says of people today:

> They can be anything they want to be, but they have no particular reason to want to be anything in particular. Not only are they free to decide their place, but they are also free to decide whether to believe in God or be atheists, or leave their options open by being agnostic; whether they will be straight or gay or, again, keep their options open; whether they will marry and whether they will stay married; whether they will have children – and so on endlessly.[7]

Bloom's listing of the free-for-all in beliefs, sexuality, marital commitment and child-bearing is no accident: they come as a package in liberal modernity.

Yet it is not quite a free-for-all. Human beings are inveterate finger-pointers. Try as it may to manufacture a non-judgmental humanity, liberalism has its own list of 'sins', such as smoking, high-cholesterol food, gender-exclusive language, over-heating the planet – and child-bearing. The notion that multiple child-bearing is somehow irresponsible – even when spread over several years by those with plenty of time, money and affection to spend, but especially when done by poor people – is conveyed in many ways in modernity. In some Third World nations the propaganda against child-bearing has been backed up with various rewards, sanctions, even force. In the West subtler pressures are in place: ordinary cars take at most two children; people look askance if you have several children with you; children are often unwelcome in restaurants, people's homes, even churches; people whisper quietly to the mothers of more than two, 'Are you Catholic or something?' or 'Don't you know how to prevent that?'

In the modern world, 'safe sex' is sex with a condom. Elsewhere I have written more about the condomization of sex in response to HIV-AIDS.[8] But here we should note that 'safe' sex is not just sex without fear of AIDS: it is also sex safe from babies. The sterilization of sex and the demonization of children often go hand in hand. In a 'contra-*ceptive*' or 'contra-*life*' culture we are socialized not to love our bodies, life and children but rather to fear our fertility, withhold it even from our spouses, cauterize it temporarily or permanently. In the process our civilization is becoming literally sterile.

---

[7] A. Bloom, *The Closing of the American Mind* (New York: Simon & Schuster, 1987), p. 87.
[8] A. Fisher, 'HIV and condoms within marriage', *Communio* 36(2) (2009), 329–59.

The culture of death before birth

As well as sex there is plenty of violence in *The Vintner's Luck*, which very effectively evokes the blood and gore of Napoleon's Eastern front. Céleste feeds Léon's sadomasochism and together they engage in murder. Xas also kills, but only after he is first wounded by the Archangels Michael and Lucifer. Aurora kills animals to offer them in sacrifice to Lucifer. Though the story is set in the nineteenth century, the sexual-consumer revolution that it reflects took place in that bloodiest of centuries, the twentieth, a century unparalleled for the scale and brutality of its violence.[9]

The links between violence and sexual licentiousness in the twentieth century were complex and cannot be explored here. One, however, is worth highlighting. At no time in history was there more abortion and less shame about it. Though reliable figures are unavailable for many countries, each year there are probably more than 10 million abortions in Asia, 5 million in Europe and Russia, 4 million in both Africa and Latin America, a million in Northern America and over 100,000 in the Pacific.[10] While abortion is now the most common surgical procedure in the world, a whole new generation of 'morning-after pills', 'emergency contraceptives' and abortifacient drugs are taking a growing share of the before-birth deaths. New drugs are being developed which further blur the lines between genuine contraception (stopping conception), contragestion (stopping implantation) and abortion.

The abortion holocaust – as some have called it – involving now hundreds of millions of children and their mothers in recent decades would have been unthinkable without the sexual-consumer revolution of the post-war period. It is all of a piece with so much else in that violent century. Now that so many have had abortions and have so much invested emotionally, financially or politically in abortion, the pressure to 'mainstream' this activity and to suppress any dissent is unremitting. Indeed several First World countries have moved recently to deny health professionals the right conscientiously to abstain from providing or referring for abortion, and to force nations with very low abortion rates to increase abortion availability.

Such abortion rates, combined with high contraceptive rates, will exacerbate the Northern hemisphere's demographic decline and leave new generations of women suffering the physical, psychological and spiritual

[9] J. Glover, *Humanity: A Moral History of the Twentieth Century* (London: Jonathan Cape, 1999).
[10] See Chapter 6.

aftershocks. The practice of abortion will continue to desensitize the medical profession and the community to the evils of harming and killing. Hardly anyone outside the world of the World Health Organization, Planned Parenthood and some NGOs is happy with the current abortion numbers, yet hardly anything is done about it. Instead more and more value-free sex education and access to contraception are offered, despite forty years' experience that this only raises sexual activity rates and then, with or without contraception, pregnancy and abortion rates as well.

At the same time as witnessing historically very high abortion rates, Western nations have embraced a virtual free-for-all in the laboratory with early human life. It is estimated that 4 million lab children have been born to date, at the expense of 50 million or more embryos, manufactured but never brought to term. The new genetics is allowing more and more conditions and qualities to be tested for, and thus pre-implantation embryos in the lab and post-implantation children in the womb with the wrong qualities can be disposed of. I say more about this in Chapter 6, but for now we might note that, for all its much vaunted therapeutic potential, the new genetics presently contributes more to death than to life. The womb and the laboratory are now very dangerous places for young human beings to live.

The culture of death before time

So in the contemporary world, as in *The Vintner's Luck*, there is plenty of violence along with the sex. Several of Knox's characters meet a violent end. Céleste kills one of Léon's mistresses and Léon kills the others and himself. Aurora also attempts suicide while Xas eventually euthanizes Sobran as his last act of love-making. Campaigns for euthanasia are unrelenting in the West and may well be successful in the future. So far they have had only limited success. Only the Netherlands, Belgium and Luxembourg have legalized the practice; Switzerland and the US states of Oregon and Washington allow physician-assisted suicide. In other jurisdictions there has been some chipping away at the edges, especially with respect to feeding the persistently unresponsive, to which I return in Chapter 8. The task of caring well for the elderly, disabled and dying is especially challenging in a world increasingly inclined to discriminate against or even kill such people, all dressed up as 'respect for rights', 'mercy' for incurables and efficient use of resources.

Anarchy in 'private life' is tolerated as long as it does not impinge too much on 'public life'. Here we find a kind of split moral personality that is at the very heart of liberalism. My thought is that liberalism actually promotes perversion and violence, though within the limits of political harmony. The rhetoric of human rights, upon which liberal polities are founded, is increasingly vacuous and used as a weapon against ethics and against persons whose rights are not acknowledged. UN Declarations and Conventions, expressions of high ideals for human cooperation and flourishing, are now used against developing nations to impose the liberal 'sexual and reproductive rights' agendas. The message is: either contracept and abort your nation's future or we'll starve you out by cutting all aid. The US Supreme Court, supposedly the defender of human rights in the leading democracy, has time and again declared that some people – whether slaves in Knox's nineteenth century or the unborn in the twentieth – have no legal protection and may be freely subjected to violence, even death. Showing their subjectivist petticoats the judges declared in *Planned Parenthood* v. *Casey*: 'At the heart of liberty is the right to define one's own concept of existence, of meaning, of the universe and of the mystery of human life.'[11] Not only is the relativity of truth an epistemological postulate in modernity, it is now a legal and moral dogma.

CATHOLIC ENGAGEMENT WITH THE
CULTURE OF MODERNITY

First faltering attempts

Against this background the past century has seen a flowering of Catholic thinking on sexuality, marriage and family life, from married lay theologians as much as popes.[12] The Second Vatican Council celebrated this late blossoming, while recognizing that the most pressing problems for the Church in the modern world could well be in this area. The Council

[11] *Planned Parenthood* v. *Casey* 505 US 833 (1992); cf. R. Hittinger, 'What really happened in the Casey decision: et tu, Justice Kennedy?', *Crisis* 10(8) (September 1992), 16–22. Behind the court's rhetoric is R. Dworkin's ideology in *Life's Dominion: An Argument about Abortion, Euthanasia, and Individual Freedom* (New York: Knopf, 1993).
[12] Recent contributors to Catholic-Christian thought on marriage and sexuality, including the theology of the body, include: Donald Asci, G. E. M. Anscombe, Benedict Ashley, Erika Bachiochi, Joseph Boyle, Adam Cooper, Ramon de Haro, Peter Elliott, Jorge Cardinal Medina Estévez, John Ford, Germain Grisez, Benedict Guevin, Scott and Kimberly Hahn, Nona Harrison, Mary Healy, Richard Hogan, Dennis Hollinger, John Kippley, Dale Kuehne, Ronald Lawler, John LeVoir, William E. May, Dale O'Leary, Marc Cardinal Ouellet, Anthony Percy, Mary Prokes, Kenneth Schmitz, Walter Schu, Angelo Cardinal Scola, Mary Shivanandan, Paul Quay, Dietrich von Hildebrand, Vincent Walsh, Christopher West and Lauren Winner.

demonstrated remarkable prescience when in 1965 it identified among the emerging threats to marriage and family: divorce, promiscuity, self-obsession, hedonism, contraception, abortion, economic, social and psychological pressures and the campaign against over-population (*GS* 46–7). But rather than simply forecasting doom the Council gave greater impetus to the theology and pastoral care of marriages and families. It also called for an urgent renewal of moral theology (e.g. *OT* 16).

The first post-conciliar foray by the magisterium into this area was Paul VI's encyclical *Humanae Vitae*. This document re-presented traditional Christian wisdom on birth control and responsible parenthood in a new rhetoric. It proposed a beautiful vision of the place of sexuality and fertility in the vocation of marriage. It warned prophetically of the consequences for individuals and societies of embracing a contraceptive mentality. It came, of course, at a particularly difficult time. Despite the Council's insistence on the importance of authority and tradition in Christian life, many took up what they believed to be its views (and those of the secular world) on the dignity of conscience and the liberties of the person with greater enthusiasm than they did Church teaching on moral absolutes, such as the positive norms of respect for sexuality and marriage and negative precepts against contraception, abortion and divorce.

Thus *Humanae Vitae* met with incomprehension or hostility in many quarters, not least in academies and seminaries where scholars were creating a more permissive morality, in keeping with the fashions of the day. Catholic moral theology had long recognized the importance of human freedom and conscience. It knew the relevance of context in assessing a moral act; there was a long casuistry of 'the lesser evil' and 'due proportion' in self-defence and double effect. Writers such as Peter Knauer, Louis Janssens, Bruno Schüller, Josef Fuchs, Joseph Fletcher, Charles Curran and Richard McCormick now sought to develop these parts of Christian moral thinking by synthesizing them with strands of contemporary secular thought, such as *individualism* in the case of 'situationism' or *utilitarianism* in the case of 'proportionalism'. Taking up the more modern exaltation of freedom and rejection of appeals to nature, authority or any other universals, these writers denied that norms could ever spell out answers to moral questions *in advance*. Instead of the restrictions and 'fixations' of traditional morality, the moral life should be seen as a creative and self-expressive project in which the only absolutes are freedom, authenticity or benevolently seeking the greatest net good. Accordingly, the mature Christian would consider the well-established 'rules of thumb' found in the Bible or Church teaching but must also be willing to set these aside in particular circumstances. What matters, in the end, is whether one is genuinely committed to love of God and neighbour, considers honestly all the 'pre-moral' effects of each choice and then follows one's 'conscience'.

With what the late Servais Pinckaers described as 'an allergy to traditional positions' these writers proposed a new kind of *moral multiculturalism* marked by 'a taste for novelty, variety, relativity, adaptation'.[13] In time a number of Christian writers abandoned the idea that the human body, relationships and actions have any natural or God-given meaning: we make these things mean what we please. The claim that sex 'says' marriage was replaced with 'sex says love' and increasingly replaced with 'sex says recreation'. The ethical contention that other kinds of genital activity are objectively wrong was flatly denied. Contraception and masturbation – the early exceptions to the general rules of chastity and reverence for life – were soon joined by fornication, adultery and homosexual acts. All were permissible in certain circumstances. Likewise in bioethics, moral absolutes against practices such as abortion and euthanasia were gradually relaxed or abandoned; in due course human embryo experimentation and neglecting patients to death were also condoned by many ethicists. Oversimplifying already problematic theological positions and seeking to apply this new morality in pastoral practice, some preachers and moral advisers translated 'follow an informed conscience' into 'do whatever seems most loving in the circumstances'. 'Follow the truth' and 'serve others' became 'be true to yourself' and 'fulfil yourself'. 'Accept responsibility for your actions' became 'do whatever seems best on balance'.

The response of Pope John Paul II and his allies

This kind of thinking was devastating for the moral life of many individuals. It also left the Church ill-prepared to face up to the growing challenges of secular liberalism and post-modernity. Situationism and proportionalism effectively acquiesced in the 'me generation' culture. Though philosophically and humanly untenable,[14] these new moralities

---

[13] S. Pinckaers, *The Sources of Christian Ethics* (Washington, DC: Catholic University of America Press, 1995), pp. 304–5.

[14] Many critiques of individualism and consequentialism apply to situationism and proportionalism, and I need not rehearse those criticisms here. Suffice it to say that we need some objective values and absolute principles if we are to have a standard of self-criticism of our preferences, feelings, intuitions, past conduct, present proposals; if we are to be prudent and otherwise virtuous in making any situation-specific or proportion-specific judgments; if we are to serve the common good, respect people's rights and fulfil their reasonable expectations of us; and if we are

captured most seminaries and theology schools around the world and within a generation other voices were being systematically excluded from priesthood, academia, church bureaucracies, journals, even booklists. The new moralities were already waning when Pope John Paul's 1993 encyclical letter *Veritatis Splendor* (The Splendour of Truth) dealt them a lethal blow. The goal of conscience, John Paul II explained, is not to invent moral reality, but rather to recognize it accurately and respond to it appropriately. Autonomy and sincerity are not enough. No matter how 'loving', helpful 'on balance' or otherwise well intentioned, certain kinds of behaviour are objectively wrong and sincerity will not make them right. In the next chapter I examine the role of subjective conscience in more detail.

In the last two decades of the second millennium and the first decade of the third, John Paul II and Joseph Ratzinger, who eventually succeeded him as Benedict XVI, engaged in a powerful critique of the individualism, moral subjectivism, cultural relativism and values disorientation of modernity. Increasingly they found supporters not just in ecclesiastical circles but among secular social commentators. A range of social problems were partly or wholly attributed to the values revolution just described.[15] The numbers continue to climb, but a decade ago Philip Lawler was already commenting that 'The public consequences of "private" sexual behaviour now threaten to destroy American society. In the past thirty-five years the federal government has spent four trillion dollars ... on a variety of social programmes designed to remedy ills which can be attributed, directly or indirectly, to the misuse of human sexuality.'[16]

Similarly, Australian social commentator Anne Manne surveyed a number of recent writers about what she calls 'the shadowland of moral chaos' in which people float 'without a map on a raft of different choices, rudderless and alone in the sea of freedom, in the absence of God or tradition'. This is the downside of the contemporary obsession with autonomy, a social lottery that pays out as

to be genuinely *fulfilled* (rather than merely gratified) as human persons. Useful commentaries include D. Oderberg and J. Laing, *Human Lives: Critical Essays on Consequentialist Bioethics* (London: Macmillan, 1997).

[15] D. Blankenhorn, *Fatherless America: Confronting Our Most Urgent Social Problem* (New York: Basic Books, 1995) and *The Future of Marriage* (New York: Encounter, 2009); and M. Eberstadt, *Home-Alone America: The Hidden Toll of Day Care, Behavioral Drugs, and Other Parent Substitutes* (New York: Sentinel, 2004) summarize some of the now considerable literature on the ill-effects of family breakdown on children and adolescents. See also other works by Brenda Almond, David Blankenhorn, George Elshtain, Maggie Gallagher, Linda Waite and James O. Wilson.

[16] P. Lawler, 'The price of virtue', *Catholic World Report*, July 1997, 58.

record family breakdown, suicide, rising depression among children, drug abuse on an unprecedented scale. A world where the explosion of rights talk has ushered in what some critics call a 'duty-free' society ... Travelling upstream from the contemporary culture wars on euthanasia, abortion, divorce or institutional childcare ... one usually comes to a fundamental clash between an ideal of a sovereign, autonomous self, which is expressive of the individual's rights to freedom, choice and self-determination, and an ideal of an obligated self, which emphasises interdependence, connectedness and limits to freedom, where actions are constrained by the consequences for others.[17]

While the modern emphasis upon autonomy may have had some good effects such as encouraging personal initiative, respect for liberty and so on, it has also had very real costs: relationships are fractured, the young are disoriented and confused about what is worth valuing and committing to, governments are unable to act against even gross inhumanities like partial-birth abortions, fundamental institutions such as marriage and the family are under grave stress – and for all their freedom people feel powerless and resentful.

The vices and virtues of each age are inextricably intertwined ... The virtues of the *ancien regime* – family stability, security, a sense of community – were not easily separable from its vices – coercion, stigma and prejudice. The virtues of our age are also tied intimately to its vices – a tendency for the deepest human relationships to be commodified and have meaning emptied from them, where people seek fleeting connection in a society of strangers, where the heart becomes a lonely hunter ... suffering ... the absence of meaning, the anxiety and anguish that comes with post-modernity's unbearable lightness of being.[18]

Thus Manne asks: 'In post-modernity, in this sea of freedom, what islands of obligation, moral constraint and restraint still exist?' She argues that there is emerging 'a new position on the moral and political map', peopled as much by erstwhile supporters of the new morality as by its traditional opponents. Many of these writers are now proposing the 'voluntary renunciation of a measure of autonomy and the acceptance of limits'. Well, that's a start. The difficult tasks are to know where these limits come from and, once we know what we *cannot* do, how we decide what we *should* do.

In the decades after Vatican II, the curia of the Catholic Church published important correctives on various moral questions including those

---

[17] A. Manne, 'In freedom's shadow', *Australian Review of Books*, 4 July 1998, 12–15.
[18] *Ibid.*, following R. Gaita, *Good and Evil: An Absolute Conception* (London: Macmillan, 1991).

in the area of bioethics, sexuality and family life,[19] but these documents considered underlying anthropology and moral methodology only in passing. John Paul II taught at both levels, elaborating a fundamental vision of the human person and his or her vocation and stating some crucial moral principles, before applying them to particular questions. This was especially true of *Veritatis Splendor*.[20] The first ever encyclical on moral theory, it represented the climax of a lifetime's engagement with modernity and its challenges, especially in the areas of life and love. This engagement included ground-breaking works such as *Love and Responsibility*, written before John Paul II was pope, and *Familiaris Consortio*, written soon afterwards, the long series of catecheses now collected together as *The Theology of the Body* and his remarkable encyclical *Evangelium Vitae*, as well as his various letters and addresses.[21] In addition to his own enormous philosophical, theological and pastoral endeavour, John Paul II also initiated and inspired many others, catalysing the bishops of the world to be engaged in family and pro-life ministry, convoking the Synod on the Family and many meetings with families, establishing the Pontifical Council for the Family and the John Paul II Institute for Marriage and the Family, which now has campuses all around the world. Meanwhile his great ally Cardinal Ratzinger kept a watching brief on these matters in the Congregation of the Doctrine of the Faith. As pope he has explored

---

[19] From the Congregation for the Doctrine of the Faith: *On Abortion* (1974), *On Sterilization in Catholic Hospitals* (1976), *On Sexual Ethics* (1976), *On Euthanasia* (1980), *On the Pastoral Care of Homosexual Persons* (1986), *On Respect for Human Life and Procreation* (1987), *On Uterine Isolation and Related Matters* (1993), *On Proposals to Give Legal Recognition to Homosexual Unions* (2003), *On Artificial Nutrition and Hydration* (2007), *On Certain Bioethical Questions* (2008). From the Pontifical Council for the Family: *Vademecum for Confessors on Some Aspects of the Morality of Conjugal Life* (1997), *The Truth and Meaning of Human Sexuality* (1995), *The Family and Human Rights* (1999), *On Embryo Reduction* (2000), *On De Facto and Same Sex Unions* (2000), *Family, Marriage and 'De Facto' Unions* (2000). From the Pontifical Council for Health: *Charter for Healthworkers* (1994; English trans. 1995). From the Pontifical Academy for Life: *On Cloning* (1997), *On the Production and Use of Human Embryonic Stem Cells* (2000), *On Respect for the Dignity of the Dying* (2000), *On the 'Morning-After Pill'* (2000), *Prospects for Xenotransplantation* (2001), *On the So-Called 'Vegetative State'* (with the World Federation of Catholic Medical Associations, 2004).

[20] John Paul II, *VS* ch. 2. More recently: Benedict XVI, *Address to an International Congress on Natural Moral Law*, 12 February 2007; International Theological Commission, *The Search for Universal Ethics: A New Look at Natural Law* (2009); John Paul II, *Address to the Pontifical Academy for Life*, 27 February 2002.

[21] K. Wojtyła, *Love and Responsibility*, rev. edn, trans. H. T. Willetts (San Francisco: Ignatius, 1981); John Paul II, *Familiaris Consortio: Apostolic Exhortation on the Role of the Christian Family in the Modern World* (1981), *Man and Woman He Created Them: A Theology of the Body*, new trans. M. Waldstein (Boston: Pauline, 2006) and *Evangelium Vitae: Encyclical Letter on the Value and Inviolability of Human Life* (1995).

some of these same pastoral and theological issues in his encyclicals and his various discourses on conscience, relativism and modernity.

What then is in store for Catholic moral theology as the Church's leaders and flock confront the challenges of (post-)modernity to bioethics, sexual ethics and marital and family life? Individuals and communities are yearning for some more reliable moral compass than that offered by the autonomy culture. I now explore four especially promising directions that Catholic thought is presently taking in this difficult but vital area Where each will lead and whether the four can be synthesized is yet to be seen.

PROMISING DEVELOPMENTS

Greater emphasis on Scripture in moral theology

One of the principal gains of the Second Vatican Council was undoubtedly its insistence that Catholics give more attention to the Bible.[22] The 2008 Synod on the Word of God, a document from the Pontifical Biblical Commission of the same year and the subsequent papal exhortation *Verbum Domini* (2010) re-emphasized the importance of Scripture for Christian living.[23] Yet in *The Sources of Christian Ethics* Pinckaers pointed to the great irony that 'hardly has Scripture been restored to the Christian faithful than it is taken away from them to become the property of specialists. The current, confusing idea is that one can no longer understand Scripture today without having studied exegesis'.[24] Like John Wayne declaring 'this town ain't big enough for the two of us', the ordinary faithful and even moral theologians are warned off the exegetes' patch while being taunted for not being scriptural enough.

Few moralists are Scripture scholars, and there is rarely available any intelligible consensus of exegetical opinion on the content of particular texts to which non-professionals might refer. Pinckaers' solution was to insist on the priority of a direct reading of the texts over any type of commentary. This was not to deny the importance of an exact translation, an explanation of terms, some historical and religious background. But

---

[22] This had begun in moral theology before the Council: see Pinckaers, 'The return to Biblical themes', in *Sources*, pp. 300–2.

[23] Pontifical Biblical Commission, *The Bible and Morality: Biblical Roots of Christian Conduct* (2008); Benedict XVI, *Dei Verbum: Post-Synodal Apostolic Exhortation on the Word of God in the Life and Mission of the Church* (2010).

[24] Pinckaers, *Sources*, p. 316.

at least as important is 'an appropriate setting, such as that of private prayer or liturgy'. In this Pinckaers echoed von Balthasar's call for less 'theology on our bottoms' and more 'theology on our knees'. Reading commentaries is never a substitute for reading texts themselves, and professionals have no monopoly on 'authentic' interpretation. The Bible is a special case of a text which Christians believe offers an inspired word to every faithful reader. To Pinckaers' plea for a 'personal, direct reading of Scripture' I would add the importance of the post-biblical Christian tradition, including the councils, Fathers, scholastics and the magisterium, as offering some authoritative readings of scriptural texts.[25]

Around the time of the Council, Bernard Häring and others attempted a more scriptural moral theology but they soon found its conclusions uncomfortable and turned to other approaches. Others persevered.[26] The encyclicals and addresses of both John Paul II and Benedict XVI are examples of theology arising from *lectio divina* and offer a spirituality along with a profound anthropology and moral theology. In 2008 the Pontifical Biblical Commission issued *The Bible and Morality: Biblical Roots of Christian Conduct*. It treated the anthropology(s) articulated in the Old and New Testaments and suggested six specific criteria for Scripture-based moral reflection: convergence, contrast, advance, community, finality and discernment. In *Living the Truth in Love: A Biblical Introduction to Moral Theology* Benedict Ashley attempted a scriptural anthropology and moral theology with a strong Thomist flavour. His was a remarkably successful attempt to bring together a deeply personal love for the Scriptures and tradition, contemporary exegetical commentary and a scholastic methodology.[27] Ashley has shown how biblical theology supports the now much-contested claims about the preciousness of life and love and the norms that govern them. In our new century the challenge is to carry forward the enthusiasm of Vatican II for biblical renewal and the gifts of modern scriptural scholarship into the ethics of everyday

---

[25] Cf. T. Kennedy, *Doers of the Word*, vol. I, *Tracing Humanity's Ascent to the Living God* (Slough: St Paul's, 1996), pp. 93–111.

[26] Some of this history is told in W. Spohn, *What Are They Saying about Scripture and Ethics?*, rev. edn (New York: Paulist, 1995), and Pinckaers, *Sources*.

[27] See B. Ashley, *Living the Truth in Love: A Biblical Introduction to Moral Theology* (New York: Alba, 1996); C. Bartholomew (ed.), *A Royal Priesthood? The Use of the Bible Ethically and Politically* (Carlisle: Paternoster, 2002); S. Fowl and L. G. Jones, *Reading in Communion: Scripture and Ethics in Christian Life* (Grand Rapids, MI: Eerdmans, 1991); S. Hauerwas, *Christian Existence Today: Essays on Church, World and Living In-Between* (Grand Rapid, MI: Brazos, 2001); O. O'Donovan, *Resurrection and Moral Order*, 2nd edn (Grand Rapids, MI: Eerdmans, 1994); S. Pinckaers, *The Pursuit of Happiness God's Way: Living the Beatitudes*, trans. M. Noble (New York: Alba, 1998).

life. In Chapters 6, 9 and 10, in particular, I offer some examples of how scriptural scholarship can inform Catholic bioethics. We are yet to see a similar turn towards patristic scholarship in moral matters, but clearly this is also in order.

The renewal of natural law theory

The Thomist revival promoted by Pope Leo XIII in the late nineteenth century was carried forward into the twentieth century by such greats as Dominic Prümmer, Jacques Maritain, Étienne Gilson, Josef Pieper, Henry Veatch, Elizabeth Anscombe and Herbert McCabe.[28] In the later part of the century they were joined by Ralph McInerney, Servais Pinckaers, Romanus Cessario and many others,[29] not least of whom was John Paul II, both as philosopher and pope. Thomism offers a theory of practical reason by which moral principles are naturally known ('natural law'), an anthropology which elucidates the nature of human persons and what fulfils them, a moral psychology of virtues both natural and infused which integrate, moderate and direct character and a theology of grace and beatitude which build on these natural powers and moves agents towards their final good.

Overlapping with this Thomist movement was the work of writers such as Germain Grisez, John Finnis, William E. May, Joseph Boyle, Robert George and Patrick Lee, articulating an important new natural law approach.[30] They were also, however, responding to developments in modern philosophy, to Vatican II's call to renewal and to the fallout of

---

[28] Pinckaers, *Sources*, pp. 298–300.

[29] Other recent contributors to the Thomist revival in moral theology include: Denis Bradley, Lawrence Dewan, Kevin Flannery, Luke Gormally, John Goyette, Pamela Hall, Russell Hittinger, José Noriega, Hayden Ramsay, Martin Rhonheimer, Michael Sherwin, Paul Wadell and Daniel Westberg.

[30] Examples of the very rich contribution of these writers include: John Finnis, *Natural Law and Natural Rights* (Oxford University Press, 1980), *Moral Absolutes: Tradition, Revision and Truth* (Washington, DC: Catholic University of America Press, 1991) and his recently published five volumes of *Collected Essays* (Oxford University Press, 2011); Robert George, *In Defense of Natural Law Theory* (Oxford University Press, 2001), *Making Men Moral: Civil Liberties and Public Morality* (Oxford University Press, 1993); Germain Grisez, *The Way of Our Lord Jesus*, vol. I, *Christian Moral Principles* (Chicago: Franciscan Herald, 1983), vol. II, *Living a Christian Life* (Quincy, IL: Franciscan, 1993), vol. III, *Difficult Moral Questions* (Quincy, IL: Franciscan, 1997); William E. May, *Introduction to Moral Theology*, rev. edn (Huntington, IN: Our Sunday Visitor, 1994). Some interesting writers who might be called 'fellow-travellers' with much (but not all) of the natural law tradition and its 'new' expressions include: Robert Audi, Nigel Biggar, Gerard Bradley, David Brink, Cora Diamond, Alfonso Gómez-Lobo, Leon Kass, Mary Midgley, Thomas Nagel, Martha Nussbaum, Anthony O'Hear, Amartya Sen, Nancy Sherman, Michael Smith, Jenny Teichman and Christopher Wolfe. See also J. Vial Correa and E. Sgreccia (eds.), *The Nature and Dignity of the Human Person as the Foundation of the Right to Life* (Libreria Editrice Vaticana, 2003).

1968. Their methodology is continuous with mainstream Catholic tradition, especially Thomism, but offers some important refinements that have won it a place among the principal contenders not only in Christian ethics but in secular moral and political philosophy. These authors – all married with children – have argued that life (and health) and marriage (and family) are among the 'basic human goods' or reasons for human action, along with friendship, creativity, leisure, beauty, knowledge, religion and integrity. Equally fundamental and intrinsically good, each good should be reverenced in every life; none should ever be directly chosen against. We may reasonably forgo some participation in some good in pursuit of another good or another way of partaking in that same good. Not everyone, for instance, is bound to get married or to have a family, though all are bound to reverence and support marriage and family life. Richly experienced, these goods constitute genuine happiness or flourishing, a happiness or 'beatitude' perfected only in heaven. The fundamental maxim of morality – 'the good is to be sought and done and the evil avoided' – can thus be specified as a series of moral first principles, such as: preserve, transmit but never directly attack human life; cultivate friendship, marriage, family and social life; seek, tell and live the truth; create and contemplate beauty; and so on.

With further reflection a series of intermediate principles and thus the content of our 'common morality' can be derived. These include both positive norms such as 'follow the Golden Rule', 'help those in need' and 'foster the common good' and negative norms such as 'never harm the innocent' and 'thou shalt not commit adultery'. Some negative norms are absolute (exceptionless) and this is ultimately the basis of inviolable human rights.[31] The derivation and permanence of such natural law principles presumes and helps fill out a certain philosophical anthropology and theory of practical reason. But it is ultimately guaranteed by the Word having taken flesh and dwelt among us, sharing in the common nature of every human person, coming once-for-all as teacher and saviour and clarifying and supplementing ordinary human morality with his sublime divine law.[32] For the Christian, therefore, a life based upon natural morality will be integrated with that 'higher' calling revealed by Christ and with the life of worship, prayer and contemplation.

---

[31] Cf. Finnis, *Moral Absolutes*; W. E. May, *Moral Absolutes: Catholic Tradition, Current Trends, and the Truth* (Milwaukee: Marquette University Press, 1989).

[32] Cf. J. Finnis and A. Fisher, 'Theology and the four principles: a Roman Catholic view', in R. Gillon (ed.), *Principles of Health Care Ethics* (Chichester: Wiley, 1993), pp. 31–44.

The scriptural and natural law approaches offer, I think, the most thoroughgoing justification and exposition of the propositions which underlie this book, such as the objective meaning of human action, the marital significance of sexuality and the reverence appropriate to every human life. Natural law also offers common ground with people of other faiths or none and so some basis for discussion. In the century ahead the challenge of developing natural law ideas further will be all the more urgent as Christians seek to engage with others who do not share their scriptural faith. In the chapters that follow, the Thomist and New Natural Law influence on my own thought in these areas will sometimes be obvious.

The recovery of virtue, community, tradition and culture

Recent years have seen the advent of 'communitarianism'[33] and the revival of 'virtue ethics'[34] in secular moral philosophy. Despite a long Catholic pedigree, virtue, community, tradition and culture had all been neglected themes in modern ethical theory – with a few important exceptions such as Foot and Geach. In *Veritatis Splendor* John Paul II noted that the 'conversion of heart' necessary for a reliable conscience requires more than knowledge of moral principles. 'What is essential is a sort of *connaturality* between the person and their true good. Such a connaturality is rooted in and develops through the virtuous attitudes of the individual himself: prudence and the other cardinal virtues, and even before these the theological virtues of faith, hope and charity' (*VS* 64; cf. *GS* 30). Thus fidelity to the covenant and its commandments is not 'blind obedience' but an expression of virtuous compliance and love, of human fraternity and ecclesial communion. In the final part of the encyclical, the Pope recommended the martyrs and saints as models of Christian *character* and considered the importance of a united Catholic *community* and a rich Catholic *culture* transmitting sound Christian morality and supporting people in understanding and living moral truth. In the late twentieth

---

[33] Recent contributors to the recovery of community, tradition and culture in ethics include: Shlomo Avineri and Avner de-Shalit, Amitai Etzioni, David Fergusson, Kenneth Grasso, Stanley Hauerwas, Robert Hunt, Leon Kass, Mary Keys, Christopher Lutz, Alasdair MacIntyre, Earl Müller, Nancey Murphy, Oliver O'Donovan, Tracey Rowland, Thomas Schindler, Brian Stiltner and Charles Taylor.

[34] Recent contributors to virtue ethics include: David Beauregard, Romanus Cessario, Timothy Chappell, Fulvio Di Blasi *et al.*, Phillippa Foot, Raimond Gaita, Stephen Gardiner, Peter Geach, G. Simon Harak, Stanley Hauerwas, Russell Hittinger, Rosalind Hursthouse, Christopher Kaczor, Alasdair MacIntyre, Daniel Nelson, Herbert McCabe, Martha Nussbaum, Justin Oakley, Charles Pinches, Edmund Pincoffs, Jean Porter, Nancy Sherman, R. Scott Smith, Richard Taylor, Brad K. Wilburn and Allen W. Wood.

century writers such as Gaita, Hauerwas, MacIntyre, Nussbaum, Pincoffs, Sherman and Taylor, from very different angles drew attention to the psychology of moral feeling, commitment and character and the place of custom, community and culture in human flourishing. Not all of these thinkers were Catholics and some would be at odds with the Church at important points, yet much in their writing is deeply consonant with the Catholic moral tradition. Now that virtue ethics and communitarianism are all the rage in secular philosophy departments where utilitarianism once ruled, some scholars in Catholic theology departments are also taking up such themes with gusto.

In contemporary virtue ethics, virtues are constitutive aspects of the 'character' in 'the personal narrative' of every human life. They are relatively stable dispositions or sensibilities which integrate emotions and desires with rational responses to human goods. They socialize people appropriately for a common life with others. They help them not only to act well but to do so more readily and consistently. Vices do the opposite. Virtues and vices are residues of past acts and dispositions to engage in similar future acts. The seven classical virtues are being explored anew in contemporary moral theory. Other virtues, no longer necessarily strait-jacketed with the big seven, are also being rediscovered (e.g. compassion, respectfulness, truthfulness, humility, gratitude, modesty, hospitality). It is increasingly recognized that moral formation, counselling and spiritual direction require the cultivation of virtue and the correction of vice through imitation, habituation, role-modelling, storytelling and so on. It is also recognized that different roles in life require different virtues. Being a spouse, for instance, requires love, fidelity and marital chastity, a willingness to communicate, to give and forgive, to persevere; parenting requires all the marital virtues (for it is properly a fulfilment of spousing), as well as generosity, playfulness, devotion, patience and hope.

We cannot simply choose to be virtuous. Only immersion in a morally sound culture and tradition will develop good character traits while communicating sound principles of living. The communitarians rightly complain of liberalism, secular or religious, that it fails to take seriously the fact that we are *social* animals, highly interdependent and complementary, and that much of our lives involves shared interests, goals, identities. One of the functions of communities such as family and church is to call people of diverse temper into virtuous relationships. Here they can draw certain things from the group and give back in their own way. Affective bonds (of blood, friendship, loyalty, faith), joint projects (such as the upbringing of children and working out salvation together), common role-models (from the Holy Family to one's own grandparents), shared traditions and practices (such as family meals and acts of worship): all these knit the members of the group together, shape them with certain virtues and give them their identity, values and destiny.

With such bonds come mutual expectations. The group has its customs and beliefs. If you are unwilling to be self-sacrificing or don't like children, marriage isn't for you. If you believe in multiple gods or child sacrifice, neither is the Church. If it's Christianity you want, commit yourself to things like the Decalogue and the Beatitudes, to self-donation as spouse, parent, disciple and even martyr.[35] The roles of marriage and family life in cultivating humanity have long been appreciated but should gain new impetus in the face of the recovery of virtue, community and tradition in contemporary moral theory. Leon Kass has written of 'the household, that nest and nursery of humanity – private, intimate, and vulnerable':

Though its roots are the needs of bodily life – nurture, protection, reproduction, and then protection and nurture of the young – the household provides for more than the body. A richly woven fabric of nature and convention, it is established by law to nurture our nature. It is sustained by customs that humanize the human animal, engendering love and friendship, speech and education, choice and awareness, and shared beliefs and feelings.[36]

Here Kass echoes the thought developed by John Paul II in *Familiaris Consortio* and elsewhere that marriage and family life not only require certain character traits such as self-sacrifice and fidelity if they are to succeed but that they in turn *civilize* people in very particular ways. The lack of these family-given character traits helps to explain a great many contemporary social and personal ills. Likewise in *Evangelium Vitae* John Paul called not merely for an individual response but for building together a 'culture' or 'civilization' of life and love. Study of the internal ends, necessary character traits, customary thought patterns and traditional behaviours of institutions such as marriage, family, profession or hospital is another promising direction for Catholic morality in the

---

[35] The common good of any community requires not just a certain minimum etiquette, but a collective lifestyle founded on a shared vision. One of the functions of documents like book 3 of the *Catechism of the Catholic Church* (1994) – the ethics book – is to 'unpack' that vision and lifestyle in an authoritative way.
[36] L. Kass, *Toward a More Natural Science: Biology and Human Affairs* (New York: Free Press, 1985), p. 273. See also his groundbreaking 'The Wisdom of Repugnance', *New Republic* 216(22) (2 June 1997), 17–26.

century ahead. The influence of these strands of contemporary ethics will, I hope, be especially apparent in Chapters 2 and 7, which bring into question individualistic liberal approaches to conscience and organ procurement.

The specifically Catholic-Christian contribution

In *Ethics after Babel*, Jeffrey Stout – a non-believer – deplores the 'nearly complete breakdown of fruitful dialogue between secular philosophical thought and the religious traditions', suggesting that this impoverishes both. This results not only from secular moral philosophers adopting 'tropes and fetishes' that virtually preclude such conversation but also from the fault of theology failing to offer anything that might make an educated public sit up and listen.

> To gain a hearing in our culture, theology has often assumed a voice not its own and found itself merely repeating the bromides of secular intellectuals in transparently figurative speech ... Meanwhile, secular intellectuals have largely stopped paying attention. They don't need to be told, *by theologians*, that Genesis is mythical, that nobody knows much about the historical Jesus, that it's morally imperative to side with the oppressed, or that birth control is morally permissible. The explanation for the eclipse of religious ethics in recent secular moral philosophy may therefore be ... that academic theologians have increasingly given the impression of saying nothing atheists don't already know.[37]

Thus when the Second Vatican Council called for the renewal of moral theology it prescribed 'livelier contact with the mystery of Christ and the history of salvation', a firmer grounding in Scripture and tradition, and a clearer recognition that the Christian calling is heavenward in direction but earthly in its temporal enactment (e.g. *DV* 12; *OT* 16; *PO* 19). The response to this call was uneven. Von Balthasar, Ratzinger and other Catholic theologians joined leading Protestant scholars in bemoaning the fact that much of 'the new morality' after the Council was really the ethics of 'the world' dressed up in some religious poetry, an ethic of 'middle-class respectability', 'a series of platitudes ranging from the inane to the incoherent', a mixture of the trivial and the sentimental, a picture of God not as a moral law-giver but as a 'therapeutic nice-guy' who is comfortable with our little compromises and double standards. They called for

---

[37] J. Stout, *Ethics after Babel: The Languages of Morals and Their Discontents* (Boston: Beacon, 1988), p. 164. See also: S. Joseph Tham, 'The secularisation of bioethics', *NCBQ* 8(3) (2008), 443–54.

a radical recommitment to the *distinctively Christian* in ethics, and for Christians to be willing to be 'prophetic', 'counter-cultural', the advocates of a genuinely *alternative* lifestyle.[38]

Christian life begins with the call to repent, to (re)turn to God and to love Him with all our minds and wills (Mark 1:14; Matt. 22:35–38). Such union with God should make us God-like, holy, lights to the world, more and more conformed to Christ, living stones of God's house, temples of his Holy Spirit, perfect like our Heavenly Father (Matt. ch. 5; Luke 6:36, etc.; Rom. 12:1–2, 11–14; ch. 6; 1 Cor. 2:16; 3:10, 16–17; 6:19–20; 12:27; 2 Cor. 6:3–10; Eph. 2:19–22; Phil.1:27; 3:17–21; Col. 3:12–17; 1 Thess. 5:5–11; 2 Thess. 3:13; cf. *LG* ch. v). As John Paul II wrote in *Veritatis Splendor*:

> The new evangelization will show its authenticity and unleash all its missionary force when it is carried out through the gift not only of the Word proclaimed but also of the Word lived. In particular, the life of holiness which is resplendent in so many members of the People of God, humble and often unseen, constitutes the simplest and most attractive way to perceive at once the beauty of truth, the liberating force of God's love, and the value of unconditional fidelity to all the demands of the Lord's law, even in the most difficult situations. For this reason, the Church, as a wise teacher of morality, has always invited believers to seek and to find in the Saints, and above all in the Virgin Mother of God 'full of grace' and 'all-holy', the model, strength and joy needed to live a life in accordance with God's commandments and the Beatitudes of the Gospel … The life of holiness thus brings to full expression and effectiveness the threefold and unitary *munus propheticum, sacerdotale et regale* which every Christian receives as a gift by being born again 'of water and the Spirit' in Baptism. (*VS* 107)

John Paul II led by example in making his moral encyclicals deeply scriptural and Christological, and in using a distinctively Christian register to explore the mysteries of life and love. Thus in his more speculative works he talked of the 'horizon' and 'ground' of beings in Being, the 'the identity-difference' and 'subjectivity-alterity' of the person, the 'theodrama' of each moral 'actor', 'the nuptial significance of the body' and its 'language', the self-donation of marriage, the family as 'a school of virtue' and 'site and vehicle of evangelization', the 'covenant between the generations', the struggle between the 'culture of death' and the 'civilization of life' and so

---

[38] Recent contributors to the distinctively Catholic-Christian in moral theology include: Romanus Cessario, Benedict Guevin, Stanley Hauerwas, Terence Kennedy, Livio Melina, José Noriega, Aidan Nichols, Juan Péres-Soba, Servais Pinckaers, Marc Cardinal Ouellet, Joseph Cardinal Ratzinger, David Schindler, Heinz Schürmann, Hans Urs von Balthasar and Jozef Zalot.

on.[39] Benedict XVI has likewise made his own writings more patristic and soteriological than much recent moral theology, as he reflects on dualism, the ascent and purification of *eros* in *agape*, the significance of such 'ecstasy', the horizon of hope in *communio* with God and the saints, the importance of 'relationality' and the hopelessness of the contemporary commodification of the body, sexuality and fertility, such that 'unutterable violence' can take place in the 'most sacred human space of the womb'.[40] By elaborating an anthropology that is unashamedly Christian in its foundations, contemporary in its language and orthopractical in its conclusions, the two popes have pointed a way forward for those engaged in the task of theological understanding and catechetical renewal.

The liturgical turn in contemporary theology, led by Ratzinger and others, suggests reconceiving the moral life of the individual believer and of the believing community as offertory gifts which Christ the High Priest 'transfigures' as he does the Bread of Life, presenting it to the Father. The moral life might also be seen as an extension of divine service beyond the sacred liturgy and a preparation for return to it. The 'new evangelization' championed by various new ecclesial movements as well as traditional preaching orders also offers new pointers to a distinctively Catholic ethic. Thus morality can be seen both as the fruit of and as the motivation for a life of worship. Likewise morality is the field and engine for a life of mission *ad gentes*, especially to formerly Christian cultures experiencing radical secularization.

The project of recovering what is distinctively Catholic in moral theology has barely started and will be much more fully elaborated in the century ahead. Much of it is in a specialized language that requires translation into a more accessible idiom, and it must continue in partnership with the more philosophical work necessary if Catholics are to engage pluralist and increasingly secular societies. However, the task of elaborating a renewed moral theology in response to the call of Vatican II has, after some false starts, at last decisively begun. In its articulation in the new millennium it will bring a new energy to the contest over the central Christian claims made in the introduction to this book and considered

[39] For example, K. Wojtyła, *The Acting Person*, trans. A. Potocki (Boston: Reidel, 1979); John Paul II, *FC*, *VS* and *EV*.
[40] For example, H. Schürmann, J. Ratzinger and H. U. von Balthasar, *Principles of Christian Morality* (San Francisco: Ignatius, 1986); Benedict XVI, *Deus Caritas Est: Encyclical Letter on Christian Love* (2005), *Spe Salvi: Encyclical Letter on Christian Hope* (2007) and *Caritas in Veritate: Encyclical Letter on Integral Human Development in Charity and Truth* (2009).

in the chapters that follow. It will be crucial for the identity of Catholic institutions and apostolates, such as those considered in Chapter 10.

Chapter 10

CONCLUSION

Contemporary ethics is moving beyond the two ascendant models of the previous generation: the *buffet bioethic* where autonomous agents choose according to taste from a range of principles so that they get the conclusions they want and the *ledger bioethic* that purports to balance 'pre-moral' debits and credits. The best of twenty-first-century healthcare ethics will involve a much more richly textured morality of human goods, norms and commitments, natural and supernatural virtues, narratives, communities and traditions. The old liberal-individualist and utilitarian-consequentialist wolves have not yet altogether given up: sometimes they now dress up in neo-Aristotelian, neo-Kantian or other rather traditional-ist-looking sheep's clothing. Proportionalism, for instance, has re-emerged in some places dressed up as practical wisdom or casuistry. We are now less likely to be duped by such disguises and much better resourced, theologically and philosophically, to choose between what John Paul II called a civilization of life and love and a culture of lies and of death.

Do Christians believe and are they willing to live the creative and hopeful teachings of their tradition about life, sexuality, marriage and family – reformulated and developed appropriately with the aid of the best of contemporary moral thinking? Or do we prefer to acquiesce in the wholesale commodification and destruction of the early human life, the disintegration of marriage and the marriage-based family, the consumerization of sex, the blanket sterilization of individuals and societies and the abandonment of the disabled and the elderly? How we respond to such questions will literally be a matter of life and death not just for many individuals but for our civilization.

CHAPTER 2

Conscience: the crisis of authority

THE VOICE OF CONSCIENCE

Some wrong turns

I keep a lady in my car. From the dashboard she instructs me on which way I should go in life. 'In three kilometres turn left', she commands. 'Turn around', she pleads. 'Coming up, on your right, you have arrived', she advises. She is, of course, a global positioning satellite navigator and I would be lost without her calm voice telling me where to go. She can be wrong at times, because of mechanical faults or wrong information, especially about new developments on the roads. Sometimes I ignore her or switch her off. Usually I obey her, and I have found that when I fail to do so, through inattention or a belief that I know better, I am usually sorry later.

Conscience is sometimes thought of as our inbuilt satellite navigator, though I argue in this chapter that in important respects conscience is *not* like that. Many people talk as if conscience were a sort of angelic voice distinct from our own reasoning that comes, as it were, from outside us, even if we hear it inside our head or heart. On this view it is generally trustworthy, but we must decide whether to obey it, nonetheless. Cardinal Newman, whose life and work has been described by Pope Benedict XVI as 'one great commentary on the question of conscience,'[1]

---

[1] J. Ratzinger, 'Conscience and truth', in *Values in a Time of Upheaval*, trans. Brian McNeil (New York: Crossroad/Ignatius, 2006), pp. 75–100 at 84. Other texts of Ratzinger's on conscience include: 'Conscience in its age', in *Church, Ecumenism and Politics* (New York: Crossroads, 1987), pp. 165–79, *The Nature and Mission of Theology* (San Francisco: Ignatius, 1995), *Without Roots: Europe, Relativism, Christianity, Islam*, with M. Pera (New York: Basic Books, 2006), pp. 51–80, *On Conscience* (San Francisco: Ignatius, 2007). Cf. V. Twomey, *Pope Benedict XVI: The Conscience of Our Age* (San Francisco: Ignatius, 2007); T. Rowland, *Ratzinger's Faith: The Theology of Pope Benedict XVI* (Oxford University Press, 2008), pp. 39–40 and 81–3. In the present chapter references in [square brackets] are to page numbers in Ratzinger's 'Conscience and truth'.

might have encouraged such a view when he called conscience a messenger of God, 'the aboriginal Vicar of Christ'.² Newman's influence at Vatican II is evident in the citation of this text in the *Catechism* of the Council and in the Council's poetic description of conscience as a 'voice' of God, echoing in the depths of the person.

In the depths of his conscience, man detects a law which he does not impose upon himself, but which holds him to obedience. Always summoning him to love good and avoid evil, the voice of conscience when necessary speaks to his heart: do this, shun that. For man has in his heart a law written by God; to obey it is his very dignity; according to it he will be judged. Conscience is the most secret core and sanctuary of a man. There he is alone with God, whose voice echoes in his depths. (*GS* 16; cf. *VS* 54; *CCC* 1778)³

Whatever such passages mean, they clearly do not mean that conscience is a divine or diabolical voice that intrudes into our ordinary reasoning processes, commanding or complaining and acting as a rival of our own moral thinking and a possible substitute for it. If we experience such voices we should probably see a doctor or an exorcist! Were conscience really a voice from *outside* our reasoning it would play no part in philosophical ethics and there might be some kind of double truth in moral theology: my merely human practical reasoning tells me to do X, but my 'divine voice' says to do Y, not X.⁴

---

² J. H. Newman, 'A Letter addressed to His Grace the Duke of Norfolk on the occasion of Mr Gladstone's recent expostulation', in *Certain Difficulties Felt by Anglicans in Catholic Teaching Considered* (1875; Westminster: Christian Classics, 1969), vol. II, p. 246: 'Conscience is not a long-sighted selfishness, nor a desire to be consistent with oneself; but it is a messenger from Him, Who, both in nature and grace, speaks to us behind a veil, and teaches and rules us by His representatives. Conscience is the aboriginal Vicar of Christ.' Other commentators on Newman on conscience include: CDF, *Presentation of Cardinal Ratzinger on the Occasion of the First Centenary of the Death of Cardinal John Henry Newman*, Rome, 28 April 1990; E. D'Arcy, *Conscience and Its Right to Freedom* (New York: Sheed and Ward, 1961); J. Finnis, 'Conscience in the Letter to the Duke of Norfolk', in I. Ker and A. Hill (eds.), *Newman after a Hundred Years* (Oxford University Press, 1990), pp. 401–18; George Cardinal Pell, 'Conscience: "the aboriginal Vicar of Christ"', in *Be Not Afraid – Collected Writing*, ed. T. Livingstone (Sydney: Duffy and Snellgrove, 2004), pp. 283–300.
³ J. H. Newman, *An Essay in Aid of a Grammar of Assent* (1870; ed. I. Ker, Oxford University Press, 1985), pp. 40, 47 and 72–83, explains that 'we are accustomed to speaking of conscience as a voice' because it is so 'imperative and constraining, like no other dictate in the whole of our experience'; rather than relying upon itself, it 'vaguely reaches forward to something beyond self, and dimly discerns a sanction higher than self for its decisions'. Conscience is thus a bridge between the creature and the Creator.
⁴ John Paul II, *VS* 56, noted a similar kind of 'double truth' operative in attempts to legitimize supposedly 'pastoral' solutions to moral dilemmas contrary to objective moral truth and also in seeking personal exceptions in conscience from universally binding norms.

Over the centuries various theologies took people down just such a blind alley. The voluntarist followers of William of Ockham, for instance, thought morality was externally given.[5] On this account:

[T]he human will was a purely autonomous power, completely indeterminate and free. Its regulation came not from practical reason, or the intellect directing it from within, but from law, as an extrinsic principle obligating and constraining it. Here too, the idea of law was radically deformed. Whereas St Thomas Aquinas saw law as an 'ordinance of reason', that is, reason's own internal illumination and direction of the will, in Ockham's scheme law emerges as a gratuitous and arbitrary check upon the will. Obedience thus replaces prudence as the chief cardinal virtue. The virtues themselves, seen by Aquinas as 'excellences' or powers informing and educating the passions from within, are downgraded. They now exercise the negative function of repressing the passions and keeping them out of the will's way in its obedience to the law.[6]

Various schools of thought – 'laxists' and 'rigorists', 'probabilists', 'probabiliorists' and 'equi-probabilists' – gave different legal interpretations in diverse cases, but once the law applicable to the particular case was known it was thought that there was nothing more to do but conform. Thus, the Church's magisterium became the satellite navigator, and the role of conscience was to hear, interpret and obey this externally imposed law.

Many theologians and pastors today are heirs to this way of thinking. For some the solution to the contemporary crisis of moral authority is to return to submission to the magisterium as the inerrant satellite navigator. Moral tax-lawyers, on the other hand, equally concerned not to break the navigator's directions, try to find ways to 'sail as close to the wind as possible'. They ask: how far can you go? How much can you get away with before it becomes (seriously) sinful? Can you do a little bit of abortion (e.g. 'early induction' of anencephalic babies; use of the morning-after pill) or a little embryo experimentation (e.g. just on 'spare' embryos) or a little euthanasia (e.g. by withdrawing feeding from those thought better off dead) without 'really seriously' breaking the moral law? Can you reclassify some abortion or embryo experimentation or euthanasia as something else, so that these 'little bits' are not really exceptions at all? What both these approaches have in common with the late schoolmen

[5] T. Holopainen, *William Ockham's Theory of the Foundations of Ethics* (Helsinki: Luther-Agricola, 1991); T. Kennedy, *Doers of the Word*, vol. 1, *Tracing Humanity's Ascent to God* (London: St Paul's, 1996), ch. 5; B. Kent, *Virtues of the Will: The Transformation of Ethics in the Late Thirteenth Century* (Washington, DC: Catholic University of America Press, 1995); S. Pinckaers, *The Sources of Christian Ethics* (Washington, DC: Catholic University of America Press, 1995), chs. 10–14.
[6] D. Bohr, *In Christ, a New Creation: Catholic Moral Tradition*, rev. edn (Huntington, IN: Our Sunday Visitor, 1998), p. 174.

such as Ockham is a view of the magisterium as a voice external to the person and so set over against conscience, a voice that commands things to which the person and so conscience are not naturally disposed. If the person cannot find a way around such commands, he or she must simply acquiesce to the law-giver or disobey and take the consequences.

Freud's view of conscience as a psychic policeman, the inner remnant of childhood authority figures, and Nietzsche's view of conscience as a social policeman, the construct of a controlling community, both continued to posit a similar rivalry within conscience between an alien but now internalized legal voice and the freedom of the agent to disobey. Enlightenment liberalism and existentialism likewise enhanced the role of the free subject, not only over and against institutions such as church and state but also vis-à-vis God and nature. By 1875 Newman had already noticed that the idea of conscience was fast degenerating into 'an Englishman's prerogative to be his own master in all things'.[7] Revelation, tradition, community, even reason itself, were increasingly seen as adversaries of the free agent. Instead of being informed by right reason and purified by Church teaching, conscience was now about personal choice unfettered by such constraints. In modernity, autonomy would trump all and agents could pick and choose in the supermarket of values.

By the 1960s conscience had become something like strong feeling, intuition or sincere opinion – what Allan Bloom called 'the all-purpose ungrounded ground of moral determination, sufficient at its slightest rumbling to discredit all other obligations or loyalties'.[8] To appeal to conscience was to foreclose all further discussion and to claim an immunity to reasoned argument or the moral law. In Catholic circles 'a certain allergic aversion to law shifted the centre of gravity in moral theology away from law and toward personal freedom, the individual subject and conscience'.[9] 'Follow your conscience' came to be code for pursuing personal preferences or reasonings *over and against* the teachings of Christ and the Church in areas of sexuality, bioethics, remarriage and reception

---

[7] Newman, 'A Letter addressed'. In Discourse 5, 'Saintliness the standard of Christian principle', in *Discourses Addressed to Mixed Congregations* (1849; ed. J. Tolhurst, Leominster: Gracewing, 2002), p. 83, he observes: 'Left to itself, though it tells truly at first, [conscience] soon becomes wavering, ambiguous, and false; it needs good teachers and good examples to keep it up to the mark and the line of duty; and the misery is, that these external helps, teachers, and examples are in many instances wanting.'

[8] A. Bloom, *The Closing of the American Mind* (New York: Simon & Schuster, 1987), p. 326.

[9] S. Pinckaers, *Morality: The Catholic View* (South Bend, IN: St. Augustine's Press, 2001), pp. 56–7.

of the Eucharist.[10] 'Here one's conscience, anchored in genuine, authentic feeling, becomes the highest court of appeal' – it is infallible.[11] The language of *the primacy of conscience*, unknown to the tradition, more often implied contest with the Church rather than with the spirit of the age or the surrounding culture.[12] Sophisticated consciences yielded judgments in accord with the *New York Times* rather than *L'Osservatore Romano*.

By 1993 Pope John Paul II could sum up the 'blind alley' down which conscience had been taken in the West:

> The individual conscience is accorded the status of a supreme tribunal of moral judgment which hands down categorical and infallible decisions about good and evil. To the affirmation that one has a duty to follow one's conscience is unduly added the affirmation that one's moral judgment is true merely by the fact that it has its origin in the conscience. But in this way the inescapable claims of truth disappear, yielding their place to a criterion of sincerity, authenticity and 'being at peace with oneself', so much so that some have come to adopt a radically subjectivist conception of moral judgment. (*VS* 32)

This is not the Christian conception of conscience at all. As John Paul's collaborator and eventual successor, the then-Cardinal Ratzinger, observed, it is rather 'a cloak thrown over human subjectivity, allowing man to elude the clutches of reality and to hide from it' [79].[13]

A history of the conscience idea

The classical account of conscience begins by reflecting upon the universal experience of agency. I *can* choose and I *can* reflect upon past choices. In doing so I can judge present possibilities and past choices

---

[10] On these see: J. Finnis, 'Conscience, infallibility and contraception', *The Month* 239 (1978), 410–17, 'IVF and the Catholic tradition', *The Month* 246 (1984), 55–8, 'Faith and morals: a note', *The Month* 21(2) (1988), 563–7; G. Grisez, J. Finnis and W. E. May, 'Indissolubility, divorce and Holy Communion', *New Blackfriars* 75 (June 1994), 321–30.

[11] Bohr, *In Christ, a New Creation*, p. 170.

[12] See, for example, R. Gula, 'Conscience', in B. Hoose (ed.), *Christian Ethics* (London: Cassell, 1998), p. 114; L. Hogan, *Confronting the Truth: Conscience in the Catholic Tradition* (New York: Paulist, 2002); J. Keenan, *Commandments of Compassion* (Franklin, VT: Sheed and Ward, 1999), pp. 112 and 134; A. Patrick, *Liberating Conscience: Feminist Explorations in Catholic Theology* (New York: Continuum, 1996).

[13] Ratzinger continues: 'And this makes "conscience" the justification of a human subjectivity that refuses to let itself be called into question, as well as of social conformism that is meant to function as an average value between the various subjectivities and thereby enable human beings to live together. There is no longer any need to feel obliged to look for truth, nor may one doubt the average attitude and customary praxis. It suffices to be convinced of one's own correctness and to conform to others. Man is reduced to his superficial conviction and the less depth he has, the better off he is.'

rationally. I have a sense of responsibility, of accountability, of self-possession in my present and future decision-making and in reflection upon my past decisions and actions. This human capacity to know and choose the good and this human activity of thinking practically is 'conscience'.

The Old Testament has no word for 'conscience', but it does speak of the true *heart* (*lêb*) that interiorizes the divine law. God converts the hard of heart and creates the heart anew. Sometimes people experience God calling them to live his will or Law; at other times they sense him probing or judging their hearts (e.g. 1 Sam. 24:6; 2 Sam. 24:10; Jer. 11:20; 17:10; Prov. 21:2; Ps. 26:2; 95:7f.). The shame of sinful Adam and Eve and the repeated remorse of Israel are among many biblical examples of what was later called a retrospective judgment of conscience (Gen. ch. 3; Ps. 7:10; 26:2; Jer. 12:20; 17:10; 20:12). The Eden story also describes well the process of self-justification or blame-shifting that commonly occurs when people find their heart judging them sinful (Gen. 3:8–10). Jesus built on the idea of the right or pure or single heart that allows a man to judge justly and act authentically (e.g. Matt. 5:8; 6:19–23; 7:21–27; 15:10–20, etc.; cf. 1 John 3:19–21).

In the Septuagint and Vulgate translations, the Hebrew word 'heart' is sometimes translated with the Greek word συνειδησις or the Latin word *conscientia* (Job 27:6; Eccles. 7:22). In the Wisdom literature the guilty συνειδησις of the unrepentant man adds to his misfortunes (Wisd. 17:11). Such texts echoed the philosophical wisdom of the Graeco-Roman world where some, such as the Stoics, called συνειδησις the human faculty of right decision-making in harmony with the eternal world-plan or λογος. For these writers this *natural law* of the λογος would only be accurately discerned by the man with the virtuous habit of φρονησις (practical wisdom or prudence).

St Paul was heir to both these Hebrew-Christian and Graeco-Roman traditions. Some thirty times in his epistles and discourses he uses the term συνειδησις interchangeably with καρδια, which English-language bibles commonly translate respectively as *conscience* and *heart*. For Paul conscience is *not* some special faculty different from the rest of human thinking and choosing nor is it some secret wisdom given only to a few. Rather it is the human capacity to know and choose the good, the mind thinking morally and the will acting responsibly. Thus for Paul:

- συνειδησις is universal knowledge of God's law (e.g. 2 Cor. 4:2; Rom. chs. 1 and 2);

- συνείδησις is also experienced as an inner tribunal guiding, accusing or approving outer behaviour, in prospect or retrospect (e.g. Acts 24:16; 2 Cor. 1:12–14; Rom. 2:14–15; 9:1; 2 Tim. 1:3; Heb. 13:18);
- the judgments of συνείδησις, like other acts of the human mind, can be accurate but can also be mistaken, for the mind and will can be weak or corrupt (e.g. 1 Cor. ch. 8 and 10:23–30; 1 Tim. 1:5; Tit. 1:15; Heb. 10:22); conscience may falsely accuse us or remain silent when it ought to speak, so that we 'practise cunning and tamper with God's word'; it may even be so stifled as to be inoperative (2 Cor. 4:2; 1 Tim. 1:19; 4:2; cf. Matt. 6:22–23);
- the redeeming work of Christ and the action of the Holy Spirit heal, instruct and renew the human mind and will, including συνείδησις, so that we can 'put on the mind of Christ' (1 Cor. ch. 2; Rom. 9:1; 12:2; Heb. 9:14);
- συνείδησις must be honoured even if erring (e.g 1 Cor. 10:23–30; Rom. ch. 14).[14]

These themes, sketched only briefly by St Paul, were further developed by the Fathers.[15] In this period the term συνείδησις had been mis-transliterated into Latin as *synderesis*. St Augustine taught that God shares his saving truth with human beings through the illumination of their *synderesis*. However, ever since the Fall human beings have been inclined to errors of judgment, temptations, weakness of will and thus to sin They would not seek their genuine good without the tutelage of God's law, moderating habits, and the grace granted through Christ's saving death, all of which were, according to Augustine, only reliably communicated within the Church. Any tension between the individual's conscience and the Church was, for St Augustine, evidence of our fallen nature. Christians would always seek to 'put on the mind of Christ' by bringing *synderesis* into line with the Church's Scriptures and tradition.

In the scholastic and pre-modern eras, Peter Lombard, Stephen Langton, Philip the Chancellor, St Bonaventure, St Thomas Aquinas and

---

[14] See also Bohr, *In Christ, a New Creation*, p. 173; *VS* 62.

[15] See J. Aubert, 'Conscience et Loi', in B. Lauret and F. Refoulé (eds.), *Initiation à la pratique de la théologie* (Paris: Éditions du Cerf, 1984), vol. IV, pp. 204–8; D'Arcy, *Conscience*; G. R. Evans, *Augustine on Evil* (Cambridge University Press, 1982); D. Kreis, 'Origen, Plato and conscience in Jerome's Commentary on Ezekiel', *Traditio* 57 (2002), 67–83; Kennedy, *Tracing Humanity's Ascent*, ch. 5; Pinckaers, *Sources*, ch. 8; A. Schinkel, *Conscience and Conscientious Objections* (Amsterdam University Press, 2007), ch. 2. St Thomas Aquinas, *ST* Ia, 79, 13, notes the uses of the term *synderesis* in St Jerome (*Gloss. Ezech.* 1:6), St Basil the Great (*Hom. in princ. Proverb.*) and St John Damascene (*De Fide Orth.* iv. 22).

St Alphonsus Ligouri all wrote on *synderesis, conscientia* and *prudentia*.[16] Bonaventure followed St Augustine and Lombard in insisting that conscience was binding only because and to the extent that it heralds what God commands, having no authority of its own.[17] Aquinas added a good deal of Aristotle to the mix by providing: first, a theory of practical reason by which primary moral principles or 'natural laws' are known by reflecting upon human nature and choice (*synderesis*), secondary principles being derived and then applied in choice (*conscientia*); second, a moral psychology of virtues both natural and infused that integrate, moderate and direct character, especially that virtue most essential to right-reasoning in moral matters, prudence (*prudentia*); and finally, a theology of grace, revelation and beatitude that clarifies, motivates and enables agents to pursue rightly their final good. *Conscientia*, for Aquinas, was the immediate or proximate norm of morality – that last, best judgment by which a person of right reason seeks to apply objective moral truth in his own choices.[18]

While the concept of conscience played only a minor role in Aquinas' moral theory, in the early modern period it was 'hoisted to new heights' and a whole, lengthy tract was devoted to it in the manuals, while the roles of practical reason and prudence were diminished. Soon 'all roads, in the moral world, led to conscience'.[19] Newman insisted that while 'conscience is ever to be obeyed', it is not infallible. For believing Christians

---

[16] See: M. Baylor, *Action and Person: Conscience in Late Scholasticism and the Young Luther* (Leiden: Brill, 1977); D'Arcy, *Conscience*; J. Finnis, 'Natural law: the classical tradition', in J. Coleman and S. Shapiro (eds.), *The Oxford Handbook of Jurisprudence and Philosophy of Law* (Oxford University Press, 2002), pp. 1–60; D. Langston, *Conscience and Other Virtues from Bonaventure to MacIntyre* (University Park: Penn State University Press, 2001); R. McInerny, *Aquinas on Human Action: A Theory of Practice* (Washington, DC: Catholic University of America Press, 1992), pp. 92–5; Pinckaers, *Sources*, chs. 9 and 10; Schinkel, *Conscience and Conscientious Objections*, ch. 3; T. Potts, *Conscience in Medieval Philosophy* (Cambridge University Press, 1980), 'Conscience', in N. Kretzmann, A. Kenny and J. Pinborg (eds.), *The Cambridge History of Later Medieval Philosophy* (Cambridge University Press, 1982), E. Vallance and H. Braun (eds.), *Conscience and the Early Modern World 1500–1800* (New York: Palgrave Macmillan, 2003); D. Westberg, 'Good and evil in human acts: 1a 11ae 18–21', in S. Pope (ed.), *The Ethics of Aquinas* (Washington, DC: Georgetown University Press, 2002), pp. 90–102; R. Zachman, *The Assurance of Faith. Conscience in the Theology of Martin Luther and John Calvin* (Minneapolis: Augsburg Fortress, 1993).

[17] St Bonaventure, 11 *Sent.* 39, a 1, q 3, cited in *VS* 58.

[18] See Aquinas, *ST* 1a 79; 1a 11ae 19, 5; 11 *Sent.* 24, q 2, a 4; and *De Veritate* 17, a 4. On Aquinas' moral theory in general see the list of recent contributors to the Thomist revival in moral theology in note 29, Chapter 1; on Aquinas on conscience in particular see: D. Bradley, *Aquinas on the Twofold Human Good* (Washington, DC: Catholic University of America Press, 1997), chs. 5–7; J. Finnis, *Aquinas: Moral, Political, and Legal Theory* (Oxford University Press, 1998), pp. 123ff.; McInerney, *Aquinas on Human Action*, pp. 92–5; Westberg, 'Good and evil in human acts', pp. 97–8.

[19] Pinckaers, *Sources*, p. 272. cf. Vallance and Braun (eds.), *Conscience and the Early Modern World*.

the subjective authority of a conscience informed by merely natural arguments is replaced by the objective authority of a conscience informed by revelation.[20] Even for the non-believer true conscience is 'not a mere sentiment, not a mere opinion, or impression, or view of things' but rather the sense of a law higher than himself 'bidding him do certain things and avoid others' and over which he has no power himself, for 'he did not make it, he cannot destroy it. He may silence it in particular cases or directions, he may destroy its enunciations, but he cannot, or it is quite the exception if he can, emancipate himself from it. He can disobey it, he may refuse to use it; but it remains.'[21]

Conscience was to feature especially often in the documents of the Second Vatican Council – in fact the term conscience was used fifty-two times. In *Gaudium et Spes* the Council sought to make its focal point 'man himself, whole and entire, body and soul, heart and conscience, mind and will' (*GS* 3; cf. 61). Among the aspects of 'heart and conscience' identified by the Council are that:

- human dignity consists in being creatures who by nature have the God-like ability to reason and choose; thus all are bound to seek, embrace and live the truth faithfully (*DH* 1 and 2; *GS* 16 and 41);
- every human agent has the capacity and fundamental principles of conscience; conscience is experienced as an inner 'sanctuary' or 'tribunal' yet one which mediates a universal moral law which is objectively given rather than personally invented (*DH* 3; *GS* 16; cf. *EV* 29 and 40);
- thus conscience summons us to inscribe the divine law in every aspect of life by seeking good and avoiding evil, loving God and neighbour, keeping the commandments and universal norms of morality (*GS* 16, 43, 74 and 79; *LG* 36; *AA* 5; *DH* 3; *CCC* 1777);
- to follow a well-formed conscience is not merely a right but a duty; persons are judged according to how they form and follow particular judgments of conscience (*GS* 16; *DH* 1 and 11; *CCC* 1778);

---

[20] J. H. Newman, *An Essay on the Development of Christian Doctrine* (1845; ed. J. M. Cameron, Harmondsworth: Penguin Books, 1974), pp. 173–4: 'so the distinction between natural religion and revealed lies in this, that the one has a subjective authority, and the other an objective … The supremacy of conscience is the essence of natural religion; the supremacy of Apostle, or Pope, or Church, or Bishop, is the essence of the revealed; and when such external authority is taken away, the mind falls back again of necessity upon that inward guide which it possessed even before Revelation was vouchsafed. Thus, what conscience is in the system of nature, such is the voice of Scripture, or of the Church, or of the Holy See, as we may determine it, in the system of Revelation.'

[21] J. H. Newman, 'Dispositions of faith', in *Sermons Preached on Various Occasions* (London: Longman, Green and Co., 1908), pp. 64–5.

- whether because of their own fault or not, agents may err in matters of conscience (*GS* 8, 16, 43, 47 and 50); Catholics should therefore seek to form their consciences so that they are 'dutifully conformed to the divine law itself and submissive toward the Church's teaching office, which authentically interprets that law in the light of the Gospel' (*DH* 8 and 14; *GE* 1; *AA* 20; *IM* 9 and 21; *GS* 31, 50 and 87);
- claims of personal freedom or of obedience to civil laws or superiors do not excuse a failure to abide by the universal principles of conscience (*DH* 8; *GS* 79);
- freedom of thought, conscience and religion should be respected by civil authorities and people should not be coerced in matters of religion (*DH* 3; *GS* 79; *GE* 1, 6 and 8).

Three acts of conscience

In its summary of the teaching of the Second Vatican Council on conscience, the *Catechism of the Catholic Church* (1777–1802) distinguishes three acts or dimensions of conscience, which I will call Conscience-1, Conscience-2 and Conscience-3, respectively:

- Conscience-1: *synderesis* or the perception of the principles of morality;
- Conscience-2: their application in the given circumstances by practical discernment of reasons and goods;
- Conscience-3: judgment about concrete acts yet to be performed or already performed.

These dimensions of conscience require a little unpacking. I have already noted texts from St Paul, the Fathers, Aquinas, Newman and Vatican II that presume a very high – some might say even romanticized – doctrine of Conscience-1 as a voice, vicar or sanctuary of God.[22] These authors presume a long tradition of reflection on what we call today 'the first principles of the natural law', which are those norms of practical reason accessible to all people of good will and right reason.

The highest norm of human life is the divine law – eternal, objective and universal – whereby God orders, directs and governs the entire universe and all the ways of the human community by a plan conceived in wisdom and love. Man

---

[22] Though these authors most often refer to the principles of morality (Conscience-1) as a voice, vicar or sanctuary of God, to the extent that those principles are rightly applied in given circumstances (Conscience-2) and so yield an authentic judgment about what is to be (or should have been) done, the voice or whatever might also be said to be heard in Conscience-3.

has been made by God to participate in this law, with the result that, under the gentle disposition of divine Providence, he can come to perceive ever more fully the truth that is unchanging. Wherefore every man has the duty, and therefore the right, to seek the truth in matters religious in order that he may with prudence form for himself right and true judgments of conscience, under use of all suitable means. (*DH* 3)[23]

Because of their 'givenness' the principles of Conscience-1 provide us with bases both for self-criticism and for social criticism, so that when our passions or self-interest or social pressures incline us in one direction, these principles may suggest another. Conscience-1 is an antidote to the subjectivism of those who call 'doing my own thing' conscience or the relativism of those who think it means 'doing what the group does'. What Conscience-1 is not, however, is a satellite navigator, for it lacks the 'global positioning' that identifies the agent's whereabouts and goals. All it can give are general guidelines such as: 'wherever you are and wherever you want to go, you should keep to the road, not drive off the side of any bridges or into any lakes'. Conscience-1 cannot give directions about specified situations or how to navigate particular routes.

Conscience-2 involves further practical reasoning towards more particular moral principles and their application to given circumstances. It therefore requires certain habits of mind, especially *prudence in deliberation*. Some readers of the tradition, including some readers of St Thomas Aquinas, have suggested that this is the primary or only meaning of the word 'conscience'. These interpretations equate conscience with prudence.[24] Others have suggested, I think persuasively, that the habitually prudent operation of the mind when applying principles to circumstances is only one of the complex of acts of conscience and as a *habitus* of mind should be distinguished from the *acts* of the mind in practical reasoning.[25] Prudence is a quality of the virtuous mind and especially of virtuous doing, while conscience is the mind thinking practically and especially (as I will amplify below) practical reasoning toward good action.

---

[23] See also Benedict XVI, *Address to International Conference on Natural Law*, Lateran University, 12 February 2007.

[24] J. Pieper, *The Four Cardinal Virtues* (Notre Dame University Press, 1966), pp. 10–11, claims that 'conscience and prudence mean, in a certain sense, the same thing … Situational "conscience" is … intimately related to and well-nigh interchangeable with the word "prudence".' He acknowledges that what is commonly called conscience is a unity of *synderesis* ('innate or natural conscience') and prudence ('situational conscience').

[25] R. McInerney, *Ethica Thomistica*, 2nd edn (Washington, DC: Catholic University of America Press, 1997), pp. 104–8; John Paul II, *VS* 64.

In Conscience-2's process of *deliberatio* the mind often faces temptations, dilemmas and confusion. It is here that conflicts of conscience occur and, as I will argue later in this chapter, it is here that any tension between the teachings of the magisterium and other parts of one's moral reasoning process arises. To reason well at this level requires qualities such as foresight, sensitivity, seriousness, commitment, self-criticism, humility and discernment. So conscience must not only be *well informed* but also *well formed*.

Morality is not just a mind game. Its purpose, the ancients insisted, is action: the choice of some real action by a real person in real circumstances. Thus Conscience-3 is our best judgment 'about concrete acts yet to be performed or already performed'. When theologians such as Aquinas used the word *conscientia* it was usually in this sense. This explains why, unlike the manualists and to the surprise of some modern readers, Aquinas did not bother to provide a treatise specifically on conscience in the *Summa Theologiae*: the tracts on natural law, practical reasoning and the virtue of prudence sufficed for his purposes.

Conscience-3 is only worthy of respect when it can bite, i.e. when it can tell us to do what we might otherwise be disinclined to do or vice versa or when it can give us cause for remorse about something we have already done or failed to do or tell us that remorse is out of place. Once again, there is plenty of ground for error here. Thus while insisting that we must follow our last, best judgment of conscience as the proximate norm of action, Aquinas wrote a great deal about how we might ensure that such a judgment is a reliable application of moral truth. He would, I think, have been bewildered by contemporary talk of 'the primacy of conscience' or the primacy of any intellective operation. Just as the value of memory is in remembering accurately, so the value of conscience, for Aquinas, is in yielding the right choice. Truth always had primacy for him. Following Aquinas, Pope John Paul II wrote of conscience:

The dignity of this rational forum and the authority of its voice and judgments derive from the *truth* about moral good and evil, which it is called to listen to and to express. This truth is indicated by the *divine law, the universal and objective norm of morality*. The judgment of conscience does not establish the law; rather it bears witness to the authority of the natural law and of the practical reason with reference to the supreme good, whose attractiveness the human person perceives and whose commandments he accepts. Conscience is not an independent and exclusive capacity to decide what is good and what is evil. Rather there is profoundly imprinted upon it a principle of obedience vis-à-vis the objective norm which establishes and conditions the correspondence of its decisions with the commands and prohibitions which are at the basis of human behaviour. (*VS* 60)

The Catholic view of conscience presumes optimism about the human capacity to discern the good and ultimately, I would suggest, a theological position on the way man discerns God's will even after the Fall. The reasons for this optimism are: that God is the creator of the human mind and the origin of the 'natural law' of human beings; that God purifies and confirms that natural reasoning through revelation; and that God redeems the human mind through his healing grace. If we lack confidence in the human mind or in the objectivity and accessibility of the moral law, conscience is easily reduced to subjective sincerity. When this happens it is hard to see why we would take people's consciences so seriously or how we could have any real moral conversation – let alone consensus – with people different from us. Too often in recent years those desperate for moral education or advice have been fobbed off with 'follow your conscience' or indulged with 'do what you think is best'. Too often in international forums human rights documents have become weapons *against* the rights of some people and apparently innocent words used as a code cloaking sinister meanings. Without shared objective principles, appeal to conscientious belief degenerates into window-dressing for the raw expression of preference or power. We then have no way of knowing whether our conscience is well formed or not, well functioning or not, accurate or disastrously off course.

The authority of conscience

After the Second Vatican Council, some people, claiming to speak for the 'spirit of the Council' attributed to it, or to the tradition which fed it, the notion of the 'infallibility' or 'primacy' of conscience. But this phrase was unknown to the Council and the pre-Conciliar tradition. Though the Council celebrated the dignity of conscience, it habitually qualified the word with adjectives such as 'right', 'upright', 'correct', 'well-formed' or 'Christian' – allowing, by implication, that not a few consciences are confused, deformed, secularized or otherwise misleading and that there is some other standard by which to judge that has 'primacy' (e.g. *AA* 5 and 20; *IM* 9 and 21; *LG* 36; *UR* 4; *GE* 1; *GS* 16, 26, 43, 50, 52, 76 and 87). The Council pointed out that conscience often goes wrong, sometimes 'invincibly' (i.e. by no fault of the agent) and so without losing its dignity, but at other times 'voluntarily' (i.e. because of negligence or vice), in which case conscience is degraded.

In fidelity to conscience, Christians are joined with the rest of men in the search for truth, and for the genuine solution to the numerous problems which arise in the life of individuals from social relationships. Hence the more right conscience holds sway, the more persons and groups turn aside from blind choice and strive to be guided by the objective norms of morality. Conscience frequently errs from invincible ignorance without losing its dignity. The same cannot be said for a man who cares but little for truth and goodness, or for a conscience which by degrees grows practically sightless as a result of habitual sin. (*GS* 16)

Two thousand years before, St Paul had made the same point in rather more colourful language: 'To the pure all things are pure, but to the corrupt and unbelieving nothing is pure. Their very mind and conscience [συνείδησις] are corrupted. They profess to know God, but they deny him by their actions. They are detestable, disobedient, good for nothing' (Tit. 1:15–16). In the tradition that followed St Paul conscience, like any intellectual ability, could err because the human mind can be more or less mature, healthy, imaginative, prudent, integrated with passion. As a result conscience can be more or less sensitive, realistic, impartial, wise (cf. *EV* 4, 11, 24, 58 and 70). Even 'self-evident' goods and principles can be difficult to specify uncontroversially; the derivation of secondary principles and their subsequent application can be even more complex. People's thinking in these matters can be clouded or corrupted. Conscience is only *right conscience* when it *accurately* mediates and applies that universal natural law which participates in the divine law. It is erroneous when it does not. Thus, as I have suggested above, it may be more helpful to think of conscience as an activity, describing the human mind thinking practically towards good or godly choices, rather than thinking of it as a faculty or voice with divine qualities.[26]

Despite the fallibility of conscience, the Church maintains its high view of its dignity. From this it follows that we should:

- do our best to *cultivate a well-formed and well-informed conscience* in ourselves and those we influence;
- *take responsibility for our actions* and thus always seek seriously to discern what is the right choice to make;
- *seek to resolve doubt* rather than act upon it;
- *follow the last and best judgment of our conscience* even if, unbeknown to us, it is objectively in error;
- *remain humbly aware that our choice may be wrong* and so be ready, if we later realize it is, to repent and start afresh;

[26] *ST* 1a 79, 13.

- *avoid coercing people's consciences*: people should, if possible, be per-suaded rather than forced to live well and so be given a certain lati-tude for moral choice; we should expect and tolerate some differences of moral opinion.[27]

Such respect for persons and so for their 'heart and conscience' is perfectly consistent with denying that conscience is infallible or has 'primacy' over truth or faith or the teachings of Christ and his Church. As we will see, the role of the magisterium is to assist conscience to achieve a more reli-able mediation and application of moral truth.

THE VOICE OF THE MAGISTERIUM

What is the 'magisterium'?

The 'magisterium' refers to the teaching office of the Church, restating or unfolding authoritatively Christ's teaching and its implications.

The task of authentically interpreting the word of God, whether written or handed on, has been entrusted exclusively to the living magisterium of the Church, whose authority is exercised in the name of Jesus Christ. This magis-terium is not above the word of God, but serves it, teaching only what has been handed on, listening to it devoutly, guarding it scrupulously and explaining it faithfully in accord with a divine commission and with the help of the Holy Spirit, it draws from this one deposit of faith everything which it presents for belief as divinely revealed. (*DV* 10)

The Christian notion of magisterium begins with certain claims about the reliability of what the Church proposes: as Paul put it, the Church is 'the pillar and bulwark of truth' (1 Tim. 3:15). These claims are based upon Jesus' own promises to be with his Church always:

Now the eleven disciples went to Galilee, to the mountain to which Jesus had directed them. When they saw him, they worshiped him; but some doubted. And Jesus came and said to them, 'All authority in heaven and on earth has been given to me. Go therefore and make disciples of all nations, baptizing them in the name of the Father and of the Son and of the Holy Spirit, and teaching them to obey everything that I have commanded you. And remember, I am with you always, to the end of the age.' (Matt. 28:16–20; cf. Matt. 16:18–19; 18:18; John 21:15–19; Acts 1:8, etc.)

---

[27] On recent attempts to coerce the consciences of health professionals, see articles by M. Kramlich, N. Nikas, E. Furton, M. Latkovic and P. Cataldo in *NCBQ* 4(1) (Spring 2004).

Interestingly, Jesus' departing charge is not to teach the nations doctrines but rather his commandments. His promise to be 'with you always' and to send the Holy Spirit is a promise to sustain his Church in truth:

I will pray the Father, and he will send you another Counsellor, to be with you for ever, even the Spirit of Truth … When the Counsellor comes, whom I shall send you from the Father, the very Spirit of Truth, he will bear witness to me … When the Spirit of Truth comes, he will guide you into all truth. (John 14:16f.; 15:26; 16:13, etc.)

Thus in their various writings the apostolic generation set the trend of Church leaders offering a great deal of advice not merely on matters of 'faith' but also on the living out of that faith in daily life, sometimes offering only their own opinions but, at others claiming to teach with the authority of Christ or the Holy Spirit (cf. Acts 15:28; 1 Thess. 1:5; 4:8; 1 Cor. 7:10–16; Rom. 9:1; 1 Tim. 6:3, etc.). Thereafter Christians continued to rely upon certain authoritative guardians and interpreters of the Gospel. I need not examine the long and fascinating evolution of this reliance here.[28] On Francis Sullivan's view, Christians came to see that genuine Christian faith entails trust in the reliability of the Church as the mediator of that faith. This in turn entails the notion that the propositions in which the Church's normative faith is expressed are true:

I do not see how one can hold that the Church is really 'maintained in the truth' by the Holy Spirit, and at the same time hold that the Church could oblige its members to confess their faith in propositions which would actually be not merely human, partial, limited, capable of more adequate expression, culturally conditioned, etc., but downright false. In other words the indefectibility of the Church in the truth requires that its normative confession of faith be expressed in propositions which, for all their inevitable limitations, are still true.[29]

Consequently by the time of Vatican II, the Church could assert that Christ's faithful ought to give the unconditional obedience of faith (*obsequium fidei*) to all that it proposes as certainly true.

In the formation of their consciences, the Christian faithful ought carefully to attend to the sacred and certain doctrine of the Church. For the Church is, by the will of Christ, the teacher of the truth. It is her duty to give utterance to, and authoritatively to teach, that truth which is Christ Himself, and also to declare

---

[28] For example, J. Boyle, *Church Teaching Authority: Historical and Theological Studies* (Notre Dame University Press, 1995); A. Dulles, 'The magisterium in history: a theological perspective', *Theol Ed* 19(2) (1983), 7–26; L. Welch, 'The infallibility of the ordinary universal magisterium: a critique of some recent observations', *Heythrop Journal* 39(1) (1998), 18–36.

[29] F. Sullivan, *Magisterium: Teaching Authority in the Catholic Church* (Dublin: Gill and Macmillan, 1983), p. 16; cf. J. Haas (ed.), *Crisis of Conscience* (New York: Crossroad, 1996).

and confirm by her authority those principles of the moral order which have
their origins in human nature itself ... The disciple is bound by a grave obligation toward Christ, his Master, ever more fully to understand the truth received
from Him, faithfully to proclaim it, and vigorously to defend it, never – be it
understood – having recourse to means that are incompatible with the spirit of
the Gospel. At the same time, the charity of Christ urges him to love and have
prudence and patience in his dealings with those who are in error or in ignorance with regard to the faith. (*DH* 14; cf. *DV* 10)

How does this magisterium work in practice? In *Lumen Gentium* (12
and 25) Vatican II identified five modes of *infallible* teaching:

- The People of God, united with their bishops, are infallible when they
  manifest universal agreement on some matter of faith and morals.
- The bishops gathered together in an ecumenical council exercise their
  'extraordinary magisterium' when they teach that something is to be
  held definitively and absolutely.
- The bishops exercise their 'ordinary magisterium' when, though distributed around the world, they teach something in common to be held
  definitively and absolutely.
- The pope exercises his 'extraordinary magisterium' when he proclaims
  some doctrine in an absolute decision.
- The pope exercises his 'ordinary magisterium' when his definitions are
  in conformity with revelation transmitted integrally through the tradition or held by him in common with the bishops.

Of course to say that the Church is infallible in these situations is not
to say she is omniscient or inerrant in everything she says and does. In
addition to infallible magisterial teaching there are the many more everyday pronouncements of popes and bishops, of various curial departments
and Church bodies which are proposed with a lesser degree of authority or more tentatively. Such teachings must be taken seriously by believers out of respect for the Church as an inspired teacher, but they do not
command the unconditional 'obedience of faith' but at most some degree
of 'religious assent'. What degree of assent depends upon who teaches
and when and how. Sometimes these same leaders and departments will
venture opinions on various matters which are not themselves part of or
consequences of Catholic faith or morals, but only their private opinion
or prudential advice: in such cases no assent is required.

Unlike the unconditional obedience of faith, religious assent is provisional: while prima facie true, there is the possibility that what is proposed might need considerable qualification and development. Thus when

a person's own reasons against a particular non-infallible teaching are so convincing to him that he cannot give an honest interior assent to the teaching, he nonetheless remains a Catholic.[30] On the other hand, it must also be recognized that some teachings not yet infallibly defined may in fact belong to the core of Catholic tradition and might in the future be infallibly determined.[31] If unsure of their own conclusions believers will accordingly be inclined to follow even a non-definitive teaching until such time as they can clarify their own best judgment of what faith and reason require of them.

Examples of moral magisterium

What are some examples of magisterial teaching on moral matters of such high authority that they are infallible? St Paul, as usual, pulls no punches: 'Do not be deceived! Fornicators, idolaters, adulterers, catamites, sodomites, thieves, the greedy, drunkards, revilers, robbers: none of these will inherit the kingdom of God' (1 Cor. 6:9–10). In the Synoptic Gospels we hear Jesus repeatedly confirm the authority of the Decalogue:

> As he was setting out on a journey, a man ran up and knelt before him, and asked him, 'Good Master, what must I do to inherit eternal life?' Jesus said to him … 'You know the commandments: You shall not murder; You shall not commit adultery; You shall not steal; You shall not bear false witness; You shall not defraud; Honour your father and mother.' He said to him, 'Teacher, I have kept all these since my youth.' Jesus looked at him and loved him. (Mark 10:17–21)

The continuing authority of the Decalogue was confirmed by many of the Fathers, popes and councils of the Church.

There are many such passages in the Scriptures, as in the sacred tradition. An example of the latter is the Council of Trent's teaching in favour of monogamy and its anathema against polygamy.[32] More recently the Second Vatican Council condemned in no uncertain terms attacks on human life and dignity, the failure to share with the needy and the use of weapons of mass destruction against population centres (*GS* 26, 69 and 80; cf. *EV* 3). Rather than defining new moral dogmas in *Veritatis*

---

[30] Sullivan, *Magisterium*, p. 557; cf. Germain Grisez, *The Way of Our Lord Jesus*, vol. 1, *Christian Moral Principles* (Chicago: Franciscan Herald, 1983), ch. 35.

[31] L. Orsy, *The Church Learning and Teaching: Magisterium, Assent, Dissent, Academic Freedom* (Wilmington: Glazier, 1987).

[32] Council of Trent, *On Marriage*, can. 2: 'If anyone says that it is licit for Christians to have several spouses at the same time and that this is not prohibited by any divine law: let that person be anathema.'

Splendor (1993), Pope John Paul II recalled examples of moral matters already long taught definitively by the magisterium, e.g. 'Persons must do good and avoid evil, be concerned for the transmission and preservation of life, refine and develop the riches of the material world, cultivate social life, seek truth, practise good and contemplate beauty … It is right and just, always and for everyone, to serve God, to render him due worship, and to honour one's parents as they deserve' (*VS* 51–2).

Having laid this groundwork, John Paul then explicated three moral 'dogmas' subsequently in *Evangelium Vitae* (1995). Here he was careful to cite the texts from Vatican II regarding the papal and episcopal magisterium in moral matters and to use the language of Petrine authority. The clearest exercise of the highest level of papal magisterium was with respect to the *grave immorality of the direct and voluntary killing of the innocent* (*EV* 57). John Paul then applied this teaching to two pressing bioethical concerns. The Church's teaching that *direct abortion always constitutes a grave moral disorder* was, he argued, 'based upon the natural law and upon the written Word of God', 'taught by the ordinary and universal magisterium', confirmed by 'the doctrinal and disciplinary tradition of the Church', asserted 'with the unanimous agreement of the bishops' and now defined with 'the authority which Christ conferred upon Peter and his successors' (62). Likewise the Church's teaching that *euthanasia is a grave violation of the law of God* was, he said, 'based upon the natural law and upon the written word of God', 'transmitted by the Church's Tradition and taught by the ordinary and universal magisterium', and now 'confirmed' by him in his Petrine office of confirming the brethren and in his office as a bishop 'in communion with the Bishops of the Catholic Church' (65).[33]

This list of examples of definitive teaching in morals is by no means exhaustive, but it gives some sense of the range of matters to which Christ and his Church have turned their mind and voice.

Conscience versus the magisterium after Vatican II

Around the time of Vatican II, the influential Jesuit theologian Karl Rahner wrote an essay on 'The Catholic conscience' in which he explained that conscience is the proximate source of moral obligation and so must be

---

[33] Benedict XVI has been equally clear about the evils of abortion and euthanasia in his speeches since being elected pope and in his earlier writings; see for example *Christianity and the Crisis of Cultures* (San Francisco: Ignatius, 2006), part 2.

followed even when it is in fact mistaken; but that we must form our conscience rightly and avoid confusing it with mere subjective inclination or
personal preference. Moral maturity for a Christian requires keeping the
commandments given by God and proclaimed by the Church through
her ordinary or extraordinary magisterium, never appealing to conscience
to make an exception for oneself. If we realized that as Christians under
the cross we may well meet situations in which we must either sacrifice
everything or lose our soul, then we would not look for private exceptions
and our confessors would not use evasions like 'follow your conscience'
when there is some hard if sensitive teaching needed. Rahner concluded
by observing that if in our sinful world God's law seems unrealistic, the
trouble is not with God's law but with the world! [34]

Rahner wrote on the verge of a new age in which Christian ethics
faced challenges from many quarters, not least from within the Church.
Vatican II sought to restate and update Catholic moral teaching. Though
aware of the growing threat of individualism and relativism, the Council
fathers were optimistic to the point of *naïveté* about how their words
would be received. Many took up the Council's views on the dignity and
liberty of conscience with greater enthusiasm than they did its teaching
on the duty to inform conscience and the moral absolutes known to a
rightly reasoning conscience and proclaimed by the magisterium.

The Council had barely closed when Paul VI's encyclical on birth control, *Humanae Vitae* (1968), met a hostile reception even among many
clergy and theologians. A group of American theologians, led by Father
Charles Curran, asserted that Catholics might properly 'dissent' from
Church teaching on contraception and 'follow their conscience instead'.
Curran soon taught that Catholics could legitimately dissent from many
moral teachings of the Church.[35] Philip Keane suggested that pretty well
anything goes in the area of sexuality as long as it accords with personal
conscience: contraception, fornication, homosexual relations, extra-marital sex and so forth.[36] Hans Küng dismissed all of Vatican II's statements

[34] K. Rahner, 'An appeal to conscience', in *Nature and Grace: Dilemmas in the Modern Church*
(London: Sheed and Ward, 1963), pp. 49–69 at 50: 'Man has a duty to do everything he can to
conform his conscience to the objective moral law, to inform himself and let himself be taught,
and to be prepared to accept (how difficult this often is!) instruction from the word of God,
the magisterium of the Church, and every just authority in its own sphere.' This essay is more
fully analysed in Grisez, *Christian Moral Principles*, and W. E. May, *An Introduction to Moral
Theology*, rev. edn (Huntington, IN: Our Sunday Visitor, 1994).

[35] C. Curran, 'Ten years later', *Commonweal* 105 (7 July 1978), 429; cf. his *Transition and Tradition
in Moral Theology* (Notre Dame University Press, 1979) and *Critical Concerns in Moral Theology*
(Notre Dame University Press, 1984).

[36] P. Keane, *Sexual Morality: A Catholic Perspective* (New York: Paulist, 1977).

about the magisterium as having theological 'feet of clay'.[37] Even Rahner seemed to 'cross the floor' on the matter of the Church's ordinary authority in morals and the supposed conflict with the liberty or primacy of conscience.[38] Thus, the stage was set for the polarization of moral theology for the following quarter-century, as contending schools reacted to 'the crisis of 68', a crisis at least in part over conscience and authority, both in the Church and in civil society.

In the 1970s a number of theologians proceeded to deny that the Scriptures, the tradition and the hierarchy have any 'strong' magisterium in moral matters. As we saw in Chapter 1, the 'situationists' echoed the contemporary exaltation of human freedom and rejection of appeals to nature, reason, authority or any objective standards: what matters, in the end, is whether the person's 'heart is in the right place'. The 'proportionalists' asserted that the role of conscience was to identify and balance the upsides and downsides of options and that the Church could propose some 'rules of thumb' for this balancing act but no moral absolutes. Timothy O'Connell, in his popular textbook *Principles for a Catholic Morality*, suggested that conscience is infallible in its sense of moral responsibility and its fundamental moral principles. Once we move to specifics, however, people can disagree or make mistakes and so the Church can be helpful as a counsellor. Conscience, however, always has primacy over the magisterium. While Catholics believe the Holy Spirit guides the Church 'to some extent', the Church, he explained, is more the 'whore of Babylon' than 'the unblemished bride of Christ'. Though the Church might in theory be able to teach infallibly in morals, it has never done so. It has only ever taught in moral matters with its ordinary teaching authority and any ordinary teaching of the Church is 'susceptible to error and therefore fallible'.[39]

Similarly, Francis Sullivan in his book *Magisterium* asserted that even if very general principles of morality *could* be solemnly defined – and he was unsure that they could be – they would be so general as to be largely uninformative. More concrete moral norms such as, presumably, those against contraception, abortion, euthanasia and homosexual acts, are 'not among the truths which God has revealed to us for the sake of our salvation, nor can they be strictly deduced from any such truths'. Indeed such

[37] H. Küng, *Infallible? An Inquiry* (New York: Harper, 1971), p. 86.
[38] On Küng and Rahner, see Grisez, *Christian Moral Principles*, pp. 857–9.
[39] T. O'Connell, *Principles for a Catholic Morality* (New York: Seabury, 1978), pp. 89–95 (a second edition appeared in 1990); likewise R. Gascoigne, *Freedom and Purpose: An Introduction to Christian Ethics* (New York: Paulist, 2004), pp. 241–3.

matters 'do not admit of irreversible determination' and 'are not proper matter for irreformable teaching'. Sullivan's reasoning 'rules out not only the possibility of the infallible definition of such a norm, but also the claim that such a norm has ever been, or could be, infallibly taught by the ordinary universal magisterium'.[40]

CONSCIENCE IN POST-MODERNITY

Rome responds

In 1993 John Paul II celebrated the twenty-fifth anniversary of *Humanae Vitae* by publishing his great encyclical *Veritatis Splendor*. He reasserted the teaching of Vatican II that Christ and his Church can and do teach definitively in moral matters and that a well-formed Christian conscience will be informed by such authoritative teaching (60–4). In questions of morality, one ought to proceed with personal obedience of faith, submitting one's experience, insights and wishes to the judgment of the Gospel, prepared to reform oneself according to the mind of Christ authentically transmitted by the Church. Conscience is indeed the proximate norm of personal morality but its dignity and authority 'derive from the *truth* about moral good and evil, which it is called to listen to and to express'. Conscience is not infallible, and sincerity cannot establish the moral truth of a judgment of conscience, freedom of conscience never being freedom *from* the truth but always and only freedom *in* the truth. The magisterium does not bring to the conscience truths that are extraneous to it but serves the Christian conscience by highlighting and clarifying those truths that a well-formed conscience ought already to possess. A well-formed Christian conscience will seek to be both more objective about morality and truer to the Christian tradition than any morality based on sincerity or the balancing of good or evil consequences.

In previous documents the Congregation for the Doctrine of the Faith had taught that the magisterium has the task of 'discerning, by means of judgments normative for the consciences of believers, those acts which in themselves conform to the demands of faith and foster their expression in life and those acts which, on the contrary, are incompatible with such demands because intrinsically evil'.[41] In *Veritatis Splendor* John Paul II

---

[40] Sullivan, *Magisterium*, pp. 148–52.
[41] CDF, *On the Assent Due to Magisterial Teaching* (1990) 16, and *Profession of Faith and Oath of Fidelity* (1998).

explored further the vocation of the theologian and the limits to dissent (109–13). In *Ad Tuendam Fidem* (1998) he identified three categories of doctrine to be believed by the faithful.[42] The first are those doctrines of faith and morals 'contained in the Word of God, written or handed down, and defined with a solemn judgment as divinely revealed truths by the Roman Pontiff when he speaks *ex cathedra* or by the College of Bishops gathered in council, or infallibly proposed for belief by the ordinary and universal Magisterium'. The CDF pointed out that such doctrines 'require the assent of theological faith by all the faithful' and 'whoever obstinately places them in doubt or denies them falls under the censure of heresy'. The Congregation gave as an example of such a teaching in the moral sphere the first matter defined in *Evangelium Vitae* – 'the doctrine on the grave immorality of direct and voluntary killing of an innocent human being'.[43]

The second category of doctrines identified in *Ad Tuendam Fidem* is everything else 'definitively proposed by the Church regarding faith and morals' including 'all those teachings belonging to the dogmatic or moral area, which are necessary for faithfully keeping and expounding the deposit of faith, even if they have not been proposed by the Magisterium of the Church as formally revealed'. All the faithful are required to give 'firm and definitive assent to these truths' and 'whoever denies them would be rejecting a truth of Catholic doctrine and would therefore no longer be in full communion with the Catholic Church'. In this class the CDF included Church teaching on the illicitness of euthanasia, prostitution and fornication; the teaching on abortion presumably falls under this category as well, if not under the first category.

The third class of doctrines are those teachings on faith and morals presented as true or sure but not (yet) solemnly defined or definitively proposed by the magisterium, to which 'religious submission of will and intellect' are required. A proposition contrary to those teachings might be categorized as contrary, rash or dangerous.

Continuing division over moral conscience and authority

Cardinal Ratzinger opened his 1991 lecture on 'Conscience and truth' by observing that conscience has become the core issue in contemporary Catholic moral theology. As the bulwark of freedom, it supposedly

---

[42] John Paul II, *Ad Tuendam Fidem: Motu proprio to Defend the Faith* (1998).
[43] CDF, *Explanatory Note introducing Ad Tuendam Fidem* (1998).

confers on the agent a kind of private infallibility vis-à-vis any other authority. To say conscience is infallible is, he points out, contradictory, since any two persons' consciences may differ on a particular point. The 'traumatic aversion' some have to what they take to be 'preconciliar' Catholicism's faith-as-encumbrance affects their whole understanding of conscience and the magisterium. For them conscience is an escape hatch from a demanding religion, a religion they are loath to preach or counsel [75–8].

When a fellow academic posited that even the Nazis were saints because they 'followed their conscience', Ratzinger reports that he was 'absolutely certain that there is something wrong with the theory of the justifying power of the subjective conscience'. His exploration of ancient Scripture and modern psychology, Socrates and Newman, confirmed his intuition that the notion needed to be thoroughly purified. Why does the Psalmist beg pardon for hidden or unknown faults? Because 'the loss of the ability to see one's guilt, the falling silent of conscience in so many areas, is a more dangerous illness of the soul than guilt that is recognized'. The Pharisee's good works are undoubtedly good. The problem is that 'he knows not his guilt'. He has a completely clear conscience when he should not, and 'this silence of his conscience makes it impossible for God and men to penetrate his carapace – whereas the cry of conscience that torments the tax collector opens him to receive truth and love' [80–2; cf. Luke 18:9–14].

Thus Ratzinger argued that it is wrong 'to identify man's conscience with the self-awareness of the ego, with his subjective certainty about himself and his moral conduct'. Such a reduction does not liberate but enslaves, making us totally dependent on personal taste or prevailing opinions.

> To identify conscience with a superficial state of conviction is to equate it with a certainty that merely seems rational, a certainty woven from self-righteousness, conformism and intellectual laziness. Conscience is degraded to a mechanism that produces excuses for one's conduct, although in reality conscience is meant to make the subject transparent to the divine ... The reduction of conscience to a subjective certainty means the removal of truth ... [It] lulls man in false security and ultimately abandons him to solitude in a pathless wasteland. [82–4]

While a person's last, best judgment binds him at the moment of acting, this must not mean 'a canonization of subjectivity'. While it is never wrong to follow such a judgment, 'guilt may very well consist in arriving at such perverse convictions' [97].

As we saw in Chapter 1, polarization over freedom and authority is commonplace in modern society and religion and has certainly infected the Catholic understandings of conscience. At one end, there are those who think that if only people would attend more carefully and receptively to the magisterium instead of the *Zeitgeist*, all would be well. The faithful should be willing to obey, their leaders to lead and both should reject the me-generation obsession with 'doing it my way'. For them, as I have noted above, real *conscience* requires the Catholic driver to obey the ecclesial satellite navigator, which gives directions to the only destination that matters. At the opposite pole, are those who argue that conscience must have 'primacy'. On this account, Vatican II opened up a new space for Catholics to follow their personal satellite navigators, rather than relying too heavily on their pastors. The Church there demonstrated a renewed appreciation of personal experience and interpretation, of individual goals and of the freedom to pursue such goals without interference. Persons of *conscience* should listen respectfully to the magisterium but they must be willing to overrule it and make decisions for themselves.

It is interesting just how much these 'opposite' poles actually have in common. Both are convinced the other has betrayed Vatican II and endangers the Church's future. Both view the magisterium as an authority external to, indeed often a rival of and substitute for, personal conscience – as did the Ockhamists, the manualists and the Enlightenment liberals. Let us examine now whether the best of 'post-modern' ethics offers any ways forward.

A communitarian rapprochement between conscience and magisterium

The first suggestion comes from a major move in contemporary ethical theory explored in Chapter 1: communitarianism.[44] The very word *conscientia* might well point us in this direction: *scire* means 'to know' and *con* means 'with', so we could read the word itself to point to the importance of thinking *with* some moral community or tradition of fellow seekers after truth. Ratzinger noted in 1991 that conscience should appear 'as a window that makes it possible for man to see the truth that is *common* to us all, the truth that is our basis and sustains us … that makes possible a *shared* knowledge that could generate a *shared* will and a *shared*

---

[44] See the list of recent contributors to the recovery of community, tradition and culture in ethics in the notes to Chapter 1.

responsibility' [79]. Communitarians such as Alasdair MacIntyre and Charles Taylor complain that the autonomous ethics of modernity often fail to take seriously the extent to which community, tradition and shared narratives shape people's identity and values. Even our most private goals and life-plans are inevitably interrelated with those of others. More fundamentally, our sense of who we are and what matters to us is largely tied to family, workplace, party, nation, culture and, of course, church. Some of these ties are chosen, others simply 'received'. Pre-existing role-models (such as Christ and the saints) and social practices (such as how we worship God and respect and care for others) are relied upon in our moral thinking or emulated in our acting, and a great deal depends on what kinds of moral communities we belong to.

While the modern emphasis on autonomy has helpfully encouraged individuality, initiative and respect for other agents, it has also had very real costs in terms of emotional distress, normative ambivalence and political paralysis. Relationships are fractured, the young disoriented and for all their freedom many people feel powerless and resentful. In such situations communities like the Church can call people back into traditions of practice that help to knit them together and give them a sense of identity, direction and destiny. The common good requires a shared vision and lifestyle, handed down within the community and protected by certain authoritative figures or mechanisms.

Does this emphasis on communal values reduce Catholic morality to one among many value systems, all of which are culturally relative? In the next section I suggest that there are in fact some objective standards, but we must also allow that *some* Catholic beliefs and practices result from the Church's being in certain places at certain times. Communities, like individuals, face a range of moral options. Some will be excluded by sound moral reasoning and especially by revelation and the constitutive traditions of the group: intentional killing, mutilation, unjust discrimination, vengefulness, disrespect for conscience and so on. Others will be preferred on the basis of the particular history and culture of the group. Thus from among the range of reasonable options even self-consciously 'pluralistic' communities do not choose randomly or value-neutrally. They do stand for and against certain things and they do this by their prayer, worship, scriptures and creeds, by their public laws, policies and institutions and, of course, by their moral codes and common projects.

Thus even Sullivan observes that the faith of the Church is normative for the individual who wishes to belong to it because Christianity is not a buffet of beliefs and practices.

As the act of faith is free, so is the choice to belong to the community of Christian faith. No one can be forced to be a Christian against his or her will. But, on the other hand, once the free choice to be a member of the Church has been made, one is not free to choose one's own confession of faith, or to choose which articles of the Christian faith one will accept, which one will reject. The Christian Church has never understood itself as a collection of individualistic believers, each free to pick and choose among the various items offered for belief.[45]

While one might want to nuance Sullivan's claim that people are free to come and go with respect to faith and Church membership, he is surely right to say that once a person has chosen (and been chosen) to belong, certain practices 'come with the package', so to speak. If you are pro-abortion, pro-euthanasia and pro-cloning, the Catholic Church is not for you; or – better – since the Catholic Church *is* for you, you should convert to being anti-abortion, anti-euthanasia, anti-cloning and pro-life and love, pro- the sick and disabled, and pro- the body and its theology. Documents such as the *Catechism* thus function as an authoritative articulation of 'the Catholic story'. To be part of the Church is not only to believe certain things but also to live in certain ways.

A practical reason rapprochement between conscience and magisterium

The communitarian movement might be thought to reduce magisterium to culture and conscience to a social construct. Recent approaches to natural law and practical reason, also identified in the previous chapter, are therefore a useful complement.[46] The very word '*conscientia*' again provides a hint: for it means to reason (morally) *with knowledge* and not merely on the basis of opinions, feelings or fashions. We saw how certain basic or intrinsic goods are the ends of human nature, provide the reasons for all human actions and should be respected in every life and choice. The fundamental moral maxim that 'the good is to be sought and done and the evil avoided' can be specified as a series of underived basic principles such as those given by John Paul II in *Veritatis Splendor* : 'be concerned for the transmission and preservation of life, refine and develop the riches of the material world, cultivate social life, seek truth, practise good, contemplate beauty ... serve God, honour parents' (51–2). It is from such first principles that the positive and negative norms of 'common morality' are derived. This is the *natural* law written, as St Paul put it, even on the

[45] Sullivan, *Magisterium*, 12.
[46] See the list of recent contributors to the new natural law theory in the notes to Chapter 1.

hearts of pagans, and Christian faith recalls, clarifies and confirms it.[47] Because revelation affects the whole way we understand God, each other, the world and ourselves it inevitably colours the application of such 'natural' principles and brings some new norms. The Church serves in such a context as teacher-counsellor, helping us to grow in practical wisdom and understanding because conscience needs such assistance if it is to reach maturity (*VS* 64; *CCC* 1783).[48]

Morality, then, is no imposition of some external authority such as the Church but an internal pattern of life that challenges us to be more reasonable and mature and so to flourish. The magisterium, on this account, is *not* some external source of moral thinking with which private conscience must grapple. Rather, it *informs* conscience, much like a soul informs a body, giving it shape and direction from within. Any apparent conflict between conscience and magisterium is therefore either a conflict between what I am convinced is right and some other view, in which case I must favour the first or, more likely, it is a conflict *within* my conscience between some received magisterial norm and some other part(s) of my moral reasoning (including other received norms). If what is at stake is some moral truth taught with a high degree of authority and certainty, I, as a believer in that authority, will either follow it or be confused. When I do not know for sure whether what is taught is a matter of faith, I properly give that proposition my conditional or religious assent because it very well *might* be.[49]

Of course, when the Church ventures to teach non-definitively, this *may* represent a first stage in the development, articulation or application of its faith and morals or it may represent a false start. Here believers must assent to the Church's non-infallible pronouncements as to all else they know and do their best to reason and discern. Their goal will not be to argue a way out of following some Church-given norm or to 'limit the moral tax' payable to God but rather to embrace the moral vision

---

[47] Ratzinger suggests that 'It is only in this context that we can rightly understand papal primacy and its connection to the Christian conscience. The *true meaning of the teaching authority of the pope* is that he is the *advocate of Christian memory*. He does not impose something from the outside but develops and defends Christian memory. This is why [Newman's] toast must quite rightly begin with conscience and then mention the pope, for *without conscience* there would be no papacy at all. All the power of the papacy is the power of conscience at the service of memory' [95].

[48] See also Benedict XVI, *Address to International Conference on Natural Law*.

[49] Grisez, *Christian Moral Principles*, ch. 3; cf. Robert Smith, *Conscience and Catholicism: The Nature and Function of Conscience in Contemporary Roman Catholic Moral Theology* (Lanham, MD: University Press of America, 1998).

proposed by Christ and his Church and to seek to resolve any uncertainties before making an important decision.

This is quite different from situations of disagreement with the Church not as teacher but as *governor*. Church leaders may make executive decisions with which some members disagree. Sometimes there will be penalties for disobedience, as in any community. In this case the disagreement, if any, is between the moral agent and those with *governing* authority in the ecclesial community, not a conflict of *conscience*, which always occurs *within* the agent between different goods or precepts or sources. Of course conflicts with the Church, state or other governing authorities *can* also raise questions of conscience. Often people will obey decisions they disagree with, for the sake of the common good. At other times, as a matter of conscience, they cannot.

<h2 style="text-align:center">WHERE TO FROM HERE?</h2>

As early as 1969 the then-Father Joseph Ratzinger was expressing concern that false interpretations of *Gaudium et Spes* 16 on conscience were leading to a separation of freedom from truth and that this might lead to all sorts of aberrations in the name of 'creative conscience'.[50] The warning was prophetic. His great friend Pope John Paul was to devote much of his magisterium to recovering a true sense of conscience as a bridge between freedom and truth and, as pope, Benedict XVI is doing the same.

In this chapter I have sketched some traditional and recent views of conscience, its role in ethics and its relationship to sources of moral authority such as Scripture, tradition and Church hierarchy.[51] I have questioned the common claim that the Church cannot or does not teach definitively in moral matters. I have suggested that most cases of

[50] See H. Vorgrimler (ed.), *Commentary on the Documents of Vatican II* (New York: Herder, 1969), vol. v, pp. 134–6.

[51] Other recent authors on conscience include: D. Beauregard, 'What is conscience anyway?', in E. Furton (ed.), *Ethical Principle in Catholic Health Care* (Boston: NCBC, 1999), pp. 23–6; C. Caffarra, 'The autonomy of conscience and subjection to truth', in Hass (ed.), *Crisis of Conscience*, pp. 149–68; W. Giertych, 'Conscience and the *Liberum Arbitrium*', in Hass (ed.), *Crisis of Conscience*, pp. 51–78; S. Pinckaers, 'Conscience, truth and prudence', in Hass, *Crisis of Conscience*, pp. 79–93; R. Smith, *Conscience and Catholicism: The Nature and Function of Conscience in Contemporary Roman Catholic Moral Theology* (Lanham, MD: University Press of America, 1998); M. Rhonheimer, 'Natural moral law, moral knowledge and conscience', in J. Vial Correa and E. Sgreccia (eds.), *The Nature and Dignity of the Human Person as the Foundation of the Right to Life* (Libreria Editrice Vaticana, 2003), pp. 123–59; Schinkel, *Conscience and Conscientious Objections*; T. Williams, *Knowing Right from Wrong: A Christian Guide to Conscience* (Brentwood, TN: FaithWords, 2008).

supposed conflict between conscience and magisterium represent a confusion about the nature of conscience or of authority or both. In the face of continuing polarization I have outlined two complementary ways forward in ethical reflection: one sees magisterium as the moral authority of a person's community that shapes his identity and conscience; the other sees moral magisterium as authoritative teachings properly internalized in the conscience of the believer as someone engaged in practical reasoning. On neither of these accounts can conscience be seen as independent of or a rival of magisterium in some battle for 'primacy'. Both of these accounts are more easily reconciled with Christian tradition than views of conscience as autonomous or as an exercise in compliance. Ironically both these understandings of conscience see it functioning as a kind of satellite navigator. The autonomous conscience understands conscience as an internal voice distinct from moral reasoning and the compliant conscience sees magisterium as external to the believer's personal conscience.

The post-*Veritatis Splendor* Church is still struggling to recover a Catholic sense of conscience and authority. The task is essentially an evangelical and catechetical one (*VS* 106–8), one especially urgent in the Western world, where misconceptions about conscience have been commonplace, leading to many disastrous personal decisions and to the death or injury of millions. That there could still be Catholic institutions in some places performing or collaborating in abortion, euthanasia, IVF, sterilization and the distribution of condoms (even to children) beggars belief. That some Catholic theologians and pastors still support these or similar practices means that there is still much to do to recover a sense of the true ecclesial vocations of the theologian and the pastor (*VS* 109–17). That there are still Catholic politicians and voters willing to cooperate in those evils means that they have a faulty sense of the connections between conscience, truth and authority, whether ecclesial or civil – a matter to which I return in Chapter 11. Mistaken views of conscience have also been pastorally ruinous, resulting in diffidence about evangelization and catechesis, a decline in the practice of Confession and the abuse of Holy Communion.[52]

Unless properly understood, conscience will never be reliably at the service of the culture of life and love or of the growth of individuals in holiness (cf. *EV* 24). Even when we have a correct understanding of conscience, there will still be much to do in properly forming and informing

---

[52] George Cardinal Pell, 'The inconvenient conscience', *First Things* 153 (May 2005), 22–6.

our consciences and in drawing conclusions in the face of the complex contemporary dilemmas in bioethics and elsewhere. Further, thorough-going philosophical and theological analysis is required on particular ethical questions such as those to which the subsequent chapters are addressed.

CHAPTER 3

Cooperation: should we ever collaborate
with wrongdoing?

TRADITIONAL EXAMPLES

The complicity of intellectuals

In *Complicities: The Intellectual and Apartheid* Mark Sanders examines the role of thinkers during the apartheid era. He begins with the South African Truth and Reconciliation Commission, which attributed culpability not only to specific persons but also to groups including churches, healthcare organizations and the wider community. It challenged South Africans to recognize 'the little perpetrator' in each of them and to accept their responsibility both for the evil that happened and for ensuring it is never repeated. Nonetheless, Sanders says, 'until recently, there has been no full-scale philosophical exposition of complicity on which to draw'.[1] He turns therefore to Émile Zola, Karl Jaspers and Jacques Derrida for an explanation of how even those who do not formally support a particular evil can live symbiotically with it and have some responsibility for it. Some acquaintance with how sin (original, personal and structural) and cooperation in evil have been treated by Christian theology might have enriched Sanders' book. Even so, his work challenges intellectuals – pastors, ethicists, hospital chaplains, healthcare leaders – regarding their complicity with evils, including evils that the Church very publicly opposes.

In a world ablaze with headlines about cloning, over-the-counter abortifacients, resource shortages in hospitals, withdrawal of feeding from the unconscious and any number of other problems, the subject of *cooperation in evil* might appear obscure, even self-indulgent. Yet it is precisely in this area that so many moral dilemmas arise for people.[2] As Henry

---

[1] M. Sanders, *Complicities: The Intellectual and Apartheid* (London: Duke University Press, 2002), p. x.

[2] G. Grisez, *The Way of Our Lord Jesus*, vol. III, *Difficult Moral Questions* (Quincy, IL: Franciscan Press, 1997), including his extended essay on cooperation (pp. 871–98), demonstrates how common this is.

69

Davis remarked half a century ago, there is no more difficult question in moral theology.[3] Perhaps this explains why so little has been written on it compared with the headline issues.[4]

Traditional distinctions

We must all confront the issue of cooperation in evil because, especially for those who live 'in the world', it is inevitable that they will engage in such cooperation from time to time – indeed sometimes it is their duty to do so. Even Christ's little band paid taxes, some of which were no doubt used for wicked purposes. Despite his entreaties, when Jesus cured the sick some of them went on to sin some more, and after repeatedly evading persecutors, he eventually allowed himself to be arrested, tried and executed. All sorts of wickedness goes on in our society and we finance it through our taxes, elect leaders who perpetrate or allow it and fail to do much to change

[3] Cited in J. Keenan, 'Prophylactics, toleration and cooperation: contemporary problems and traditional principles', *International Philosophical Quarterly* 29(2) (1989), 205–20.

[4] Recent authors on cooperation in evil include: Archdiocese of Philadelphia, 'The Philadelphia protocol for collaborative relationships', in E. Furton (ed.), *Ethical Principle in Catholic Health Care* (Boston: NCBC, 1999), pp. 151–4; B. Ashley, J. deBlois and K. O'Rourke, *Health Care Ethics: A Catholic Theological Analysis*, 5th edn (Washington, DC: Georgetown University Press, 2006), pp. 55–7; G. Atkinson and A. Moraczewski, *A Moral Evaluation of Contraception and Sterilization* (Braintree, MA: Pope John Center, 1979); D. Bohr, *In Christ, a New Creation: Catholic Moral Tradition*, rev. edn (Huntington, IN: Our Sunday Visitor, 1999), pp. 226–34; J. Boyle, 'Toward understanding the principle of double effect', *Ethics* 90 (1980), 527–38, and 'Moral reasoning and moral judgment', *Proc Am Phil Assoc* 58 (1984), 37–49; P. Cataldo, 'A cooperation analysis of embryonic stem cell research', *NCBQ* 2(1) (2002), 35–41; Catholic Health Australia, *Code of Ethical Standards for Catholic Health and Aged Care Services in Australia* (Canberra: CHA, 2001); J. DeBlois, 'Catholic hospitals and abortion physicians', in Furton (ed.), *Ethical Principle*, pp. 129–32; M. Delaney, 'General medical practice: the problem of cooperation in evil', *CMQ* 56(2) (May 2006), 6–13; A. Fisher, 'Co-operation in evil', *CMQ* 44(3) (1994), 15–22; O. Griese, 'The principle of cooperation', in *Catholic Identity in Health Care: Principles and Practice* (Braintree, MA: Pope John Center, 1987), ch. 10; Grisez, *Difficult Moral Questions*, pp. 871–98; B. Häring CSSR, *Free and Faithful in Christ*, 3 vols. (Sydney: St Paul, 1978); C. Kaveny, 'Appropriation of evil: cooperation's mirror image', *Theological Studies* 61 (2000), 280–313; A. R. Luño, 'Ethical reflections on vaccines using cells from aborted fetuses', *NCBQ* 6(3) (2006), 253–60; A. Moraczewski, 'May one benefit from the evil deeds of others?', *NCBQ* 2(1) (2002), 43–7; National Catholic Bioethics Center, 'Avoiding formal cooperation in health care alliances' and 'Five principles for collaborative arrangements', in Furton (ed.), *Ethical Principle*, pp. 139–46 and 155–8; K. Peschke, *Christian Ethics: Moral Theology in the Light of Vatican II*, rev. edn (Alcester: Goodliffe Neale, 1997); A. Pruss, 'Complicity, fetal tissue and vaccines', *NCBQ* 6(3) (2006), 261–70; R. Smith, 'The principles of cooperation in Catholic thought', in P. Cataldo and A. Moraczewski (eds.), *The Fetal Tissue Issue: Medical and Ethical Aspects* (Braintree, MA: Pope John Center, 1994), pp. 81–92, 'Immediate material cooperation', *Ethics & Medics* 23(1) (1998), 1–2, 'Individual and corporate cooperation', in Furton (ed.), *Ethical Principle*, pp. 133–8; L. W. Sumner and J. Boyle (eds.), *Philosophical Perspectives on Bioethics* (Toronto University Press, 1996); H. Watt, 'Cooperation problems in care of suicidal patients', *CMQ* 55(2) (2005), 11–15, 'Cooperation problems in general practice', *CMQ* 8(3) (2008), 26–34.

things. More immediately, almost anything we do can be an occasion, opportunity or means for someone else to do something wrong. To avoid all active cooperation in evil would require that we abandon almost all arenas of human activity and this could well constitute a sin of omission.[5]

Reflection upon cooperation in evil begins, therefore, with some commonplace human experiences:

- We are all involved in webs of relationships that enable people to achieve both their good and bad ends whether by good or bad means.
- Sometimes we choose to involve ourselves in other people's bad ends or means, by seduction or conspiracy or deliberate cooperation in that evil, making at least part of their bad willing our own.
- At other times we make no such choice, but the otherwise good things that we do foreseeably assist others to achieve their bad purposes.
- This is an example of an act with a double effect – one good and intended; the other bad, unintended but foreseen.
- Accepting the bad side-effects of cooperation has implications for those who cooperate, those who are assisted by the cooperation in performing some evil act(s) and other parties who may be affected. It is sometimes unreasonable to engage in an act when we foresee such side-effects.
- People must decide whether to go ahead with a proposed action despite its connection with the morally objectionable action of another or whether to alter their plans, thereby possibly forgoing achieving whatever good they had contemplated.[6]

I need not rehearse the history, similarities and differences between different expositions of the principles of cooperation in the Catholic moral-theological tradition.[7] Suffice it to say that by cooperation in evil traditional

[5] Grisez, *Difficult Moral Questions*, p. 871: 'Some unreflective and/or unsophisticated people imagine problems regarding co-operation can (and perhaps should) be avoided by altogether avoiding co-operation. That, however, is virtually impossible and sometimes inconsistent with doing one's duty.'

[6] Kaveny, 'Appropriation of evil', makes a persuasive case for the category of 'appropriation of evil' as a mirror image of cooperation in evil. Her response to the present chapter can be found in 'Tax Lawyers, Prophets and Pilgrims', in H. Watt (ed.), *Complicity and Conscience* (London: Linacre, 2005), pp. 65–88.

[7] Traditional authors on cooperation in evil include: H. Davis, *Moral and Pastoral Theology*, 4th edn, 4 vols. (London: Sheed and Ward, 1945); B. Häring, *The Law of Christ*, 3 vols. (Cork: Mercier, 1961); E. Healy, *Moral Guidance: A Textbook in Principles of Conduct for Colleges and Universities* (Chicago: Loyola University Press, 1958); H. Jone, *Moral Theology* (Westminster, MD: Newman, 1945); J. McHugh and C. Callan, *Moral Theology: A Complete Course* (New York: Wagner, 1929); B. H. Merkelbach, *Summa theologiae moralis*, 3 vols. (Paris: Desclée, 1935); J. Noldin, *Summa theologiae moralis*, 2 vols. (Heildelberg: Kerle, 1944); D. Prümmer, *Handbook of Moral Theology* (New York: Kennedy, 1957).

authors meant performing an act that in some way assists the evil activity of another agent. Cooperation could be either *positive* or *negative*, depending upon whether the cooperator did something that helped the principal agent or failed to impede the principal agent when the cooperator could have done so. It could also be either *effective* or *occasional*, depending upon how much the cooperator's act actually contributed to the principal agent's act. It could be *necessitated* or *free*, depending upon how pressured or free the cooperator was. It could be *necessary* or *contingent*, depending upon how indispensable it was to the principal agent's wrongful action. It could also be *unjust* or merely *unlawful*, depending upon whether an innocent third party was injured and a duty of restitution or reparation thereby arose.

The most important distinction made by these writers, however, was that between *formal* cooperation, where the cooperator's act shared in the wrongfulness of the principal agent's act – his/her wrongful end or intention or will – and *material* cooperation, where the cooperator's action, though good or neutral in itself, had the foreseen effect of facilitating the principal agent's wrongdoing. Formal cooperation was subdivided by some authors into 'explicit' and 'implicit'. *Explicit* formal cooperation occurred where the cooperator clearly approved of the principal agent's evil action. *Implicit* formal cooperation, on the other hand, was said to occur when, though the cooperator denied intending the principal agent's object, no other explanation was sufficient to distinguish the cooperator's object from the principal's. The cooperator's action by its very nature or by the form it took in the concrete situation could have no other meaning.[8] Some used this same terminology to separate the cooperator who shared in the evil ends of the principal agent from the cooperator whose ends were different but who intentionally assisted the principal agent's act as a means to the cooperator's own ends.

According to some of these authors, the presumption should always be *against* cooperating, even materially, in evil unless there was a sufficiently grave reason to warrant proceeding. Others thought that if the cooperator's act were a good one the presumption should be *in favour of* the act unless the foreseen effects of cooperating were so grave that one should abstain from so acting. Either way, while formal cooperation was generally regarded as prohibited, material cooperation was seen as permissible, even required, if certain conditions were met.

[8] Catholic Health Australia, *Code of Ethical Standards*: '8.9: Care must be taken to ensure that arrangements which are claimed to distance a Catholic provider from the provision of prohibited services do not implicitly involve *formal* cooperation. Sometimes there is no reasonable explanation for one's cooperation other than that one endorses the others' wrongdoing.'

In specifying those conditions some authors distinguished *immediate* from *mediate* material cooperation on the basis of the degree to which the cooperator's act formed part of or physically overlapped with or was essential to the act of the principal agent, as opposed to being merely an occasion of or of assistance to it. Mediate material cooperation was then subdivided into *proximate* and *remote* on the basis of how closely the cooperator's action 'joined' or 'touched' upon the principal's action, geographically, temporally or causally.

Traditional examples

Elsewhere I have listed the sorts of examples that classical writers offered and that they thought were instances of formal cooperation or permissible and impermissible material cooperation in evil.[9] Here, a few chosen from the healthcare world must suffice. Examples of *formal* and therefore forbidden cooperation in evil included:

- a doctor or nurse assisting in an illicit procedure such as an abortion or sterilization, physically supporting every step of the principal surgeon, performing an essential part of the procedure and/or being ready to take over in case of necessity;
- a person volunteering his/her services to an abortion clinic, helping fill out forms in order to help women seeking abortions to get them;
- a hospital administrator deciding that the obstetrics department will offer sterilization and seeing to it that all patients about to be sterilized fulfil the usual consent requirements and that staff are effective when performing such surgery;
- a physician or counsellor referring someone for abortion;
- an agency (e.g. the army, a prison) distributing or disseminating contraceptives;
- a counsellor encouraging a person to engage in non-marital sexual activity or to take illicit drugs, in the hope that this will lead to the client's psychological growth, or to engage in contraception, sterilization or abortion because this is a 'lesser evil'.

Those traditional authors gave as examples of sometimes *permitted* material cooperation in evil:

---

[9] Fisher, 'Co-operation in evil'. More recent examples and distinctions are offered by the authors cited in note 4, above.

- a physician giving merely passive assistance at the preliminary instruction and preparation for an illicit operation, remaining aloof from every appearance of approval of the procedure;
- an anaesthetist, junior doctor or nurse in an operating room who merely performs his/her normal duties, such as the preparation of instruments, drugs and patients, but who finds in a particular case that this is assisting some immoral procedure;
- an engineer keeping utilities working in a hospital where abortions are done, not intending to facilitate abortion, only intending to make his living by supporting the good activities carried out there;
- a doctor or agency distributing medicine for healing a sexually transmitted disease, taking care that this is no inducement or invitation to engage in a sinful practice;
- a company manufacturing a drug or device that has good uses but which the company knows some people will abuse;
- a legislator who, having tried and failed to exclude abortion funding from a general appropriation bill, then votes for the bill only to bring about the good things it will fund.

Cases of *wrongful material cooperation in evil* included:

- a junior doctor or a nurse who is frequently asked to assist in immoral procedures doing so rather than protesting or looking for an alternative position;
- a pharmacist selling a substance such as a poison or a drug of addiction to someone he/she has reason to suspect will abuse it;
- a Catholic hospital permitting abortions or sterilizations on its premises.

Rather than multiply or analyse these textbook examples – some of which are certainly questionable – I look in the first half of this chapter at some more recent examples that have received comment from the magisterium of the Church, the response of some prominent theologians and the issues raised by both.

FIVE MODERN EXAMPLES

Sterilization in American Catholic hospitals

It was not until the 1970s that uniform *Ethical and Religious Directives for Catholic Hospitals* were adopted throughout the United States as a regulatory, educational and legal-defensive measure. In the face of continuing dispute about the appropriateness of various kinds of involvement by Catholic institutions in sterilization, the bishops submitted the matter to the Sacred Congregation for the Doctrine of the Faith (CDF). The CDF's 1975 response indicated that direct sterilizations, even those performed to avoid pathological medical conditions associated with pregnancy, were contraceptive in intent and so 'intrinsically evil'.[10] The official approval and, a fortiori, the regulation, management and execution of direct sterilizations by and in Catholic hospitals was 'absolutely forbidden' – apparently as constituting formal cooperation in evil. The document went on to explain that, with respect to other involvements:

> The traditional teaching on material cooperation, with its appropriate distinctions between necessitated and freely given cooperation, proximate and remote cooperation, remains valid, to be applied very prudently when the case demands it … Scandal and the danger of creating misunderstanding must be carefully avoided with the help of suitable explanation.

Thus even if permitting sterilizations was thought to be merely material and not formal cooperation by a Catholic agency, such cooperation was said to 'accord badly with the mission confided to such an institution and [to] be contrary to the essential proclamation and defence of the moral order'.

The US bishops issued a commentary on this document in 1977 and a fuller set of *Directives* in 1994.[11] While the main body of those *Directives* had been reviewed by the CDF before the bishops' vote, the Appendix on cooperation had not. It was soon subject to criticism for too readily allowing material cooperation in procedures such as abortion and sterilization on the grounds of pressure (called 'duress') from government, finance, patients or professionals.[12] Orville Griese and Germain Grisez,

---

[10] CDF, *On Sterilization in Catholic Hospitals* (1976), echoed in CDF, *On Uterine Isolation* (1993). 'Direct' sterilization was defined as 'actions which of themselves (i.e. of their own nature and condition) have a contraceptive purpose, the impeding of the natural effects of the deliberate sexual acts of the person sterilized.'

[11] National Conference of Catholic Bishops (USA), 'Commentary on the reply of the CDF on sterilizations in Catholic hospitals', *Origins* 7 (8 December 1977), 399–400, and 'NCCB statement on tubal ligation', *Origins* 10 (28 August 1980), 175; US Conference of Catholic Bishops, *Ethical and Religious Directives for Catholic Health Care Services*, 4th edn (Washington, DC: USCCB, 2001).

[12] The text read: 'Immediate material cooperation is wrong, except in some instances of duress. The matter of duress distinguishes immediate material cooperation from implicit formal cooperation. But immediate material cooperation – without duress – is equivalent to implicit formal cooperation and, therefore, is morally wrong.'

for instance, in their thorough treatments of cooperation, showed how hospital administrators, who commit themselves to ensuring that sterilizations are performed properly in their hospital, are *formally* cooperating in evil, however much they claim to disapprove of sterilization and however much they claim to be under financial or other pressure to provide it.[13] Grisez also criticized the slender list of indicia of unacceptable material cooperation in the Appendix and the minimal sense of the 'prophetic' responsibility of Catholic institutions to bear witness to moral truths.[14]

The CDF likewise criticized the way the 1994 Appendix was used to justify various activities such as sterilization in Catholic hospitals and pointed to the principles clearly enunciated in *Veritatis Splendor* 71–83 and *Evangelium Vitae* 74. The bishops responded by ordering an appendectomy of the cooperation section from the *Directives*. Two new directives (69 and 70) forbade Catholic providers engaging in 'immediate' material cooperation in immoral actions such as direct sterilization, abortion and euthanasia and cautioned against entering into arrangements with non-Catholic organizations who engage in such practices. At worst only 'mediate' material cooperation with such wrongdoing would ever be permissible.[15] The bishops also drew attention to the risk of scandal, counselled the use of more reliable theological advisers, directed Catholic agencies periodically to reassess whether their agreements with other parties are being implemented in a way that is consistent with Catholic teaching and insisted that the bishop has the final responsibility for addressing such issues.[16] No longer can a Catholic institution claim that financial, political or other pressure justifies cooperation in sterilization. What impact this has had on the large number of Catholic-managed care plans and healthcare providers who offer or contract out for sterilizations is unclear.[17]

---

[13] Griese, *Catholic Identity*, p. 388; Grisez, *Difficult Moral Questions*, pp. 391–402 and 892. See also G. Grisez, *Living a Christian Life* (Quincy, IL: Franciscan Press, 1993); M. McDonald, 'The limits of cooperation', *Catholic World Report* 10(11) (December 2000), 40.

[14] Grisez, *Difficult Moral Questions*, pp. 895–6.

[15] USCCB, *Ethical and Religious Directives*, 69 and 70. These are preserved in the fifth edition published in 2009.

[16] USCCB, *Ethical and Religious Directives*, 71 and 72. A footnote to Directive 71 cites *CCC* 2284 and 2287: 'Scandal is an attitude or behaviour which leads another to do evil … Anyone who uses the power at his disposal in such a way that it leads others to do wrong becomes guilty of scandal and responsible for the evil that he has directly or indirectly encouraged.'

[17] Catholic Health Australia, *Code of Ethical Standards*, ch. 8, on cooperation, avoids many of these pitfalls.

Condoms against HIV in the United States

In 1987 the Administrative Board of the US Catholic bishops published *The Many Faces of AIDS: A Gospel Response*.[18] Among other things the document proposed that 'if grounded in the broader moral vision' Church-sponsored educational programmes 'could include accurate information about prophylactic devices' and that 'if it is obvious that a person [with HIV] will not act without bringing harm to others' a health professional could reasonably advise, on a personal level, that the person use condoms to minimize the harm. Theologians such as Josef Fuchs SJ, Richard McCormick SJ, James Keenan SJ, Jon Fuller SJ, Enda McDonagh and Kevin Kelly were very supportive, suggesting that this was merely an example of 'the toleration of the lesser evil' whereby Christian leaders, right back to Augustine, did little or nothing to combat evils such as brothels because they thought any efforts likely to be ineffectual or counterproductive.[19] What these writers failed to explain, however, is how actively handing out information about condoms and even counselling in favour of their use could be compared with prudential silence.

Several American bishops and theologians, and eventually Cardinal Ratzinger, expressed concerns that suggesting use of condoms might be construed as approving or promoting extra-marital sexual activity, cause scandal and compromise witness, some also doubting the effectiveness of the condom strategy even from a purely pragmatic point of view.[20] Two years later the US bishops' pastoral on HIV/AIDS, *Called to Compassion and Responsibility*, made no mention of providing information and counselling about condoms. While urging compassion for people living with HIV, the bishops said chastity was the only 'morally correct and medically sure way' to prevent transmission of the disease. Accordingly, Catholic agencies should focus on educating people about chastity and its benefits and no one should be fooled by 'the "safe-sex" myth'.

---

[18] Administrative Board of the National Conference of Catholic Bishops, 'The many faces of AIDS', *Origins* 17 (24 December 1987), 481–9.

[19] See A. Fisher, 'HIV and condoms within marriage', *Communio* 36(2) (2009), 329–59. Most of these authors favour the distribution and more active promotion of condoms by Catholic agencies, not merely information-giving.

[20] For example, 'Reaction to AIDS statement', *Origins* 17 (24 December 1987), 489–93; 'Continued reaction to AIDS statement', *Origins* 17 (7 January 1988), 516–22; Joseph Cardinal Ratzinger, 'Letter to Archbishop Pio Laghi on "The many faces of AIDS", 29 May 1988', *Origins* 18 (17 July 1988), 117–18; Janet Smith, 'The many faces of AIDS and the toleration of the lesser evil', *International Review of Natural Family Planning* 12 (1988), 82–9.

The theological supporters of the earlier document were undeterred and even claimed a curial monsignor and the bishops of Brazil as supporters.[21] This was an improbable claim, given that the monsignor concerned had said 'using a condom to protect oneself against HIV amounts to playing Russian roulette'.[22] Not surprisingly, he said he had been mischievously misinterpreted, and the Brazilian bishops characterized the claims in *America* magazine as 'a flat lie'.[23] Since then, the Pope and curia, bishops' conferences and many individual bishops have publicly supported the position that condomized intercourse is neither safe nor moral and that cooperation in it is impermissible.[24]

Keenan nonetheless continued his campaign, claiming that almost all theologians and laity agreed with him and lambasting any critics of condom promotion, especially bishops, as fundamentally conservative rather than human. He said they lacked the clear distinctions and nuances of those who support condom promotion; that they radically misunderstood the Catholic moral tradition, which was always flexible and accommodationist; that they made that tradition look 'intolerant', 'inhuman' and 'useless'; and that this showed that they 'value their own teaching over the lives of those at risk'.[25] A side-effect of cooperation in evil not noted in the classical texts is the uncharitable *ad hominem* attacks it can draw from some theologians!

On his way to Cameroon in 2009 Pope Benedict XVI said again that he did not think the distribution of condoms was the solution to the HIV-AIDS crisis in Africa and may actually make it worse. Western commentators immediately reacted with feigned outrage. 'Impeach the Pope!' wrote a columnist in the *Washington Post*. 'Grievously wrong!' ruled the *New York Times*. 'This Pope is a disaster', said the *Telegraph* (London). 'Ignorance or ideological manipulation' declared *The Lancet*. 'Unacceptable' thundered the Belgian parliament. *Feigned* outrage all

[21] J. Fuller and J. Keenan, 'Tolerant signals: the Vatican's new insights on condoms for HIV prevention', *America* 183(8) (23 September 2000), 6–7, 'At the end of the first generation of HIV prevention', in J. Keenan (ed.), *Catholic Ethicists on HIV/AIDS Prevention* (New York: Continuum, 2000), pp. 21–40; cf. J. Suaudeau, 'Prophylactics or family values? Stopping the spread of HIV/AIDS', *L'Osservatore Romano*, 19 April 2000.
[22] J. Suaudeau, 'Il "sesso sicuro" e il profilattico a confronto con l'infezione da HIV', *Medicina e Morale* 4 (1997), 689–726.
[23] J. Suaudeau, 'Response to an erroneous interpretation of "Prophylactics or family values?"', *L'Osservatore Romano*, 27 September 2000; 'Condom claim "A flat lie," says bishop', *National Catholic Register*, 22–28 October 2000.
[24] See many sources in Fisher, 'HIV and condoms'.
[25] J. Keenan, *Practice What You Preach: The Need for Ethics in Church Leadership* (Milwaukee: Marquette University Press, 2000) and 'Prophylactics, toleration and cooperation', p. 219.

this, because the pundits knew this was the well-established position of the Catholic Church[26] – one shared by more than a few AIDS experts.[27]

Though largely unreported by the world's media, the Pope made his comment in the context of positive proposals: first, that attention, especially by Church agencies, be given to behavioural change through 'the humanization of sexuality', a conversion of heart and life; and second that 'true friendship' be offered to those with HIV-AIDS, including standing by them and investing ourselves in their care. Church workers and volunteers do in fact assist millions of people around the world in awareness-raising and education about HIV; they provide medical and other support to one in every four people living with the disease, regardless of race or creed.

In 2010 the Pope, speaking as a private theologian rather than as the voice of the magisterium, and seeking to clarify his remarks on the way to Cameroon, again insisted that fidelity within marriage and abstinence from sexual activity outside of marriage is the only morally permissible approach to chaste living and the only practicable solution to the HIV-AIDs epidemic. He called on the faithful to 'fight against the banalization of sexuality' which treats sex as a mere recreational drug, and to seek instead 'the humanization of sexuality' as the expression of marital love.[28]

However, pastors have long recognized that in cases such as homosexual intercourse, conception and marital acts are not at issue. Pope Benedict suggested that sometimes 'as perhaps when a male prostitute uses a condom' to protect his client from disease, this might be a sign of

[26] Pope Benedict had in fact already made similar points in several places: *Address to the Bishops of South Africa, Botswana, Swaziland, Namibia and Lesotho*, 10 June 2005; *Interview in Preparation for the Upcoming Journey to Bavaria*, 5 August 2006; *Address to the Ambassador of Namibia to the Holy See*, 13 December 2007; *Address to the Ambassador of Nigeria to the Holy See*, 29 May 2008.

[27] H. Epstein, *The Invisible Cure: Africa, the West and the Fight against AIDS* (New York: Farrar, Straus and Giroux, 2007); E. Green and A. Ruark, 'AIDS and the Churches: getting the story right', *First Things* 182 (April 2008), 22–6; E. Green *et al.*, 'A framework of sexual partnerships: risks and implications for HIV prevention in Africa', *Studies in Family Planning* 40(1) (2009), 63–70; M. Hanley, 'AIDS and "technical solutions"', *Ethics & Medics* 33(12) (December 2008), 1–3; M. Hanley and J. de Irala, *Affirming Life, Avoiding AIDS: What the West Can Learn from Africa* (Washington, DC: National Catholic Bioethics Center, 2009); N. Hearts and S. Chen, 'Condom promotion for AIDS prevention in the developing world: is it working?', *Studies in Family Planning* 35 (March 2004), 39–47; C. Iyizoba, 'Bleak stories behind failed condom campaigns', *MercatorNet*, 2 April 2009; G. Pollock, 'AIDS worker says Africans don't need condoms', *Zenit*, 25 March 2009; M. Potts *et al.*, 'Reassessing HIV prevention', *Science* 320 (5877) (9 May 2008), 749–50; J. Shelton, 'Ten myths and one truth about generalized HIV epidemics', *The Lancet*, 370 (9602) (1 December 2007), 1909–11. See also sources in Pontifical Council for the Family, *Family Values versus Safe Sex: A Reflection by Alfonso Cardinal López Trujillo* (2003).

[28] P. Seewald (ed.), *Light of the World* (San Francisco: Ignatius, 2010).

an awakening moral responsibility. But using condoms, the Pope restated, is still not 'a real or moral solution'. Even here the goal must be to move the individual to living a truly 'humane', that is a chaste and loving, sexual life. Cooperation by Church agencies in condom programmes would still seem to be ruled out.

Drug-injecting rooms in Australia

In June 1999 the Sisters of Charity Health Service (SCHS) in Sydney announced that it would conduct the first legal trial in Australia of a 'medically supervised' (or 'safe') injecting room for intravenous drug users. The author of the scheme, Dr Alex Wodak, explained that the proposal was 'a harm-reduction approach to illicit drugs' that would help reduce mortality and morbidity for drug users and the social nuisance of public injecting. The rationale was that since some people are going to take drugs no matter what we do, it is better that they do so in a sterile environment, where needles (and therefore diseases) are not shared and health professionals are on hand to assist after any overdose. Those interested in giving up drugs could also receive appropriate referral.[29]

No one doubted the sincerity of the Sisters of Charity and their employees, whose record in the care of the poor and marginalized has been outstanding. Catholic Health Australia and the Conference of Leaders of Religious Institutes, among others, made statements of spirited support. Critics complained that this reduced drug abuse to a *health* problem requiring public health 'containment' measures whereas it is in fact a psychological, moral and spiritual problem, as well as a medical (and social) one. All sorts of misgivings were expressed about whether a drug-injecting room would work, what would count as success and whether the means to that end were morally permissible or reasonable in the circumstances. Some even claimed that since drugs are immoral, that concluded the matter: you can't be involved with drugs, especially if you are nuns.

That last argument, of course, was too simplistic. We must first ask: did SCHS (owners, management, health professionals) share in the bad will of the drug pushers and abusers? Was drug abuse the proximate end of their project? As Grisez pointed out, in the case of hospital CEOs who say they deplore sterilization but then allow and manage it in their institutions, people *can* formally cooperate in things they do not like. Someone

---

[29] A. Wodak, 'Why trial a supervised injecting room?', *Bioethics Outlook* 10(3) (September 1999), 4–6.

who deplored drug abuse and who engaged in various projects to prevent or cure it, but who nonetheless provided some people with the where-withal for drug abuse *so that* they could/would sometimes engage in that wrongful activity, would be formally cooperating in evil. This is so even if this action were motivated by the hope of some other good effect, such as building a relationship of trust with drug abusers, eventual rehabilitation of some and so on.

Nonetheless, the vast majority of those involved in the SCHS proposal might well have said that it was no part of their goal that anyone take drugs; that their scheme was aimed at discouraging drug abuse or at least at keeping people alive and (relatively) healthy despite their bad choices; that they did not want to encourage even a single additional case of inject-ing; that if those who entered the injecting room chose not to inject them-selves with drugs, the scheme would not be thwarted but would rather be a success; and so on.

Even if SCHS were not formal cooperators in drug abuse, this was not the end of the matter. Since establishing and running an injecting room foreseeably facilitates drug abuse and has various predictable bad effects, it *is* at least material cooperation. The real debate becomes: is this mater-ial cooperation reasonable? Amid both public praise and public disquiet about the proposal the Archbishop of Sydney, Edward Cardinal Clancy, referred the matter to the CDF. With the referral came a submission from the Sisters of Charity in favour of the proposal. The Congregation, how-ever, found against the proposed injecting room. Cardinal Ratzinger's letter was never published in full.[30] It apparently gave the SCHS the benefit of the doubt in assuming that none of those involved would cooperate formally in drug taking. It nonetheless opposed the plan for reasons such as:

- the intrinsic immorality and extrinsic harmfulness of drug abuse, which impedes the ability of the human person to think, will and act responsibly; which destroys bodies, minds and lives; and which harms families and communities (*CCC* 2291);[31]
- the lack of a focus on freeing people from drug abuse and addiction because supervised injecting rooms, in order to attract clients, avoid

---

[30] Only excerpts of the document were published by the Archbishop of Sydney: see 'The debate on medically supervised injecting rooms: Cardinal explains Holy See's decision', *Catholic Weekly* (Sydney), 7 November 1999, 1.

[31] There are numerous speeches by Popes John Paul II and Benedict XVI on this. See also Pontifical Council for Health, *Charter for Healthworkers* (1994; English trans. 1995) 93–6.

any strong message about abstinence and rehabilitation and even imply
despair of such outcomes;

- the risk that the injecting room would actually encourage drug abuse
  by offering a secure venue for the practice;
- the danger that drug-trafficking might also be encouraged, by giving
  dealers and users a police-free location for their trade;
- the risk of (theological) 'scandal' in the sense of leading people into
  sin;
- serious doubts about the efficacy of such programmes;
- fear that state- and church-sponsored injecting rooms would represent
  a step towards decriminalization and 'normalization' of drug taking;
- the risk of compromising that clear Gospel witness which Catholic
  agencies should always give;
- the danger that an injecting room would undermine respect for law,
  further degrade social mores and mask inaction by government and the
  community to reduce drug abuse.

Addiction means that many drug abusers have very limited responsibility
for their actions. Because of their greater freedom, those who cooperate
with the evil of drug taking may be more morally culpable.

In a monograph that followed soon after, Keenan used the Vatican
intervention as his central case 'of a failure on the part of the Church to
practise what she preaches'.[32] Amid sinister talk of secret denunciations,
pre-emptive censorship, careerist bishops, old-boy networks, homopho-
bia, misogyny and deliberate falsification by Church leaders, he offered
his own version of the facts: Rome had responded in a knee-jerk way
to a well-meaning, openly discussed and thoroughly thought-through
proposal. At the time, however, even the SCHS's own ethical advisers
expressed surprise at how *little* consultation there had been with Church
leaders, moral theologians and the wider Church.[33]

Keenan claimed that the *real* object of this proposal was the good one
of rehabilitating drug addicts. 'The Sisters found a way of accompanying otherwise marginalized people precisely to bring them into rehabilitation and into a drug free lifestyle … to see if their presence and counsel
might successfully wean addicts off their addictions.'[34] Yet the published
case for the injecting room put weaning addicts rather low on the list

[32] Keenan, *Practice What You Preach.*
[33] For example, G. Gleeson, 'St Vincent's withdraws from supervised injecting room', *Bioethics Outlook* 10(4) (December 1999), 1–6.
[34] Keenan, *Practice What You Preach*, p. 6.

of goals. The public support of Dr Wodak, the scheme proponent, for a staged process – of reclassifying drug abuse as a *public health problem* and proposing, first, injecting rooms, then decriminalization of drugs, then prescription provision of heroin – provided little comfort for those advocating a rehabilitation and abstinence focus.[35] The proposed means also did not seem well suited to such a goal, nor had the 'harm reductionist' government partners in this project demonstrated much commitment to encouraging abstinence – given the long queues for 'detox' programmes in that state and inadequate follow-up for those trying to get off drugs. Cynics claimed that the political agenda was really to 'clean up the streets' before the 2000 Olympics and make it look like something was being done about drugs when in fact very little was on offer. Whether those charges were fair, to call a drug-injecting room a weaning or *rehabilitation* programme seems to me an act-description designed more to sell the project than to characterize it accurately.

Keenan next claimed that the CDF 'did not forbid the practice because of moral issues' at all, 'but rather practical ones'.[36] This distinction between moral and practical issues would mystify the great writers of the Western ethical tradition, almost all of whom have insisted that moral reasoning is *precisely* practical reasoning. That tradition has never reduced morality to compliance with a few negative moral absolutes and avoidance of formal cooperation – thereby relegating most decision-making, including all issues regarding material cooperation in evil and scandal, to the realm of the non-moral. If the CDF's conclusion was that this proposal involved such grave downsides and such dubious upsides as to amount, at the very least, to illicit material cooperation in wrongdoing, this was a *moral* judgment, based upon *moral* arguments. So, too, those who supported the injecting room proposal did so because they believed the good(s) in prospect considerable and the downsides relatively small. This grounded their *moral* judgment that it was permissible material cooperation. Whichever side one agrees with (if either), one is agreeing with the conclusion of a *moral* argument.

Counselling pregnant women in Germany

In June 1995 the German Bundestag legalized abortion in the first twelve weeks of pregnancy provided that the woman had a certificate that she

---

[35] For example, J. Santamaria, 'Heroin injecting rooms and Catholic health care services', *Bioethics Research Notes* 11(3) (September 1999), 25–6.

[36] Keenan, *Practice What You Preach*, p. 7; likewise at pp. 16 and 19.

had attended a *Schwangerschaftsberatungsstellen* – an approved counselling centre. In September of that year the German Bishops' Conference criticized the law but agreed to take part in Church–state abortion counselling boards. The bishops clearly believed that Church involvement would be at most material cooperation in the evil of abortion and that many women would be dissuaded from having an abortion by Church-sponsored counselling agencies.

Four years of discussions between the German bishops and the Vatican followed. The Pope cautioned against any cooperation in the legalization or practice of abortion. The bishops and several lay organizations declared their continuing support for Church involvement in the counselling services. The Pope responded by asking them to testify more clearly to the right to life and to ensure that no Church agency issued a certificate that could be used to procure an abortion.[37] The bishops countered by asking the Pope to support their existing programme.

In June 1999 John Paul II wrote again to the German bishops, and in September Cardinals Ratzinger and Sodano later reiterated, that Church agencies should issue no certificate that could be used to facilitate the death of an unborn child.[38] It was becoming increasingly clear that the certificates, despite being stamped 'Not for abortion', were being used precisely for that purpose by three out of four women seeking counselling – and also certificates – from Catholic agencies.[39] The bishops were increasingly divided. Bishop Johannes Dyba of Fulda, who had argued all along that counselling certificates amounted to 'licences to kill', had a growing number of allies.

On the other hand there were bishops who thought that if the Church withdrew from providing the counselling services it would be complicit in abortion. In October 1999 some wrote to the Pope asking if he would bear on his conscience that 'German children will be murdered because the Church can no longer counsel future mothers in conflict.' Cardinal Sodano responded by reaffirming the Pope's instructions. Even then some of the bishops hoped to change the Pope's mind during their *ad limina* visit to Rome. In November the Pope directed and the majority of the bishops voted to cease participation on the abortion boards. Only three

[37] John Paul II, 'Letter to the German bishops of 11 January 1998', *Acta Apostolicae Sedis* 90 (1998) 601–7.
[38] John Paul II, 'Letter to the German bishops of 3 June 1999', *L'Osservatore Romano*, 26–30 June 1999, 2.
[39] According to figures provided by Caritas in early 1999, only 5,000 of the 20,000 who had by then sought counselling from a Catholic agency had gone forward with their pregnancy. By late 2000 the figures would have been much higher.

said they would continue cooperating with the government programme in their dioceses.[40]

Some thought the promise of certificates amounted to formal cooperation in abortion-seeking (if not abortion itself), as the success of the programme depended upon 'tempting' women seeking abortion to come to the pro-life centre by promising them the certificate prerequisite for an abortion. Others denied that the German bishops and Catholic agencies were engaging in formal cooperation in abortion, but suggested that it was impermissible material cooperation because of (a) the gravity of what was at stake, i.e. innocent unborn human lives, (b) the witness that the German bishops were called to give to the sanctity of life and (c) concern about the corrupting effects on church-workers, pregnant women and the culture of even this much material cooperation in abortion.

Support for improving abortion laws

In Chapter 11 I explore at some length John Paul II's teaching in *Evangelium Vitae* 73, which was reiterated by the CDF in *The Participation of Catholics in Political Life*. Agreeing with the exegesis of Cardinal Bertone and John Finnis, I suggest that a legislator who, with a view to achieving or maintaining a permissive abortion regime, actively supports someone else's permissive law or bill or actively blocks someone else's restrictions to such a law or bill, engages in formal cooperation in the evil of the sponsor of the legislation. So too does one who supports such a bill or blocks such restrictions, in order to gain some other advantage, such as appeasing certain opponents, keeping his/her seat or trading support for some other (possibly noble) legislative objective. In such cases politicians can be guilty of formal cooperation in the evils of bad lawmaking and even of abortion itself, even if they disapprove of abortion and say so publicly. *Evangelium Vitae* says as much.

Evangelium Vitae also says that when it is not possible to defeat a pro-abortion law or bill, a politician could in certain circumstances licitly support a proposal aimed at 'limiting the harm done' by that bad law or bill. (There are big magisterial scare quotes around the phrase 'limiting the harm done'). That politician would not thereby be responsible for the far-from-perfect state of the law, despite the undesired support that such material cooperation might lend to offences against life.

[40] C. von Reisswitz, 'German bishops accept Pope's appeal', *Inside the Vatican*, January 2000, 25–7.

The Catholic tradition suggests that Christians should not remove themselves from political life but should rather play their full role as citizens.[41] They should be guided by a genuinely Christian conscience, seeking always the common good and being willing, like St Thomas More, to give witness to the faith in public life. The Church warns against cultural and moral relativism and against disingenuous appeals to tolerance or to the autonomy of lay involvement in political life that sanction 'the decadence of reason' and the disintegration of those 'non-negotiable ethical principles, which are the underpinning of life in society'. Thus Catholics have grave obligations to defend the right to life, marriage and the family, a drug-free society and so forth and never to vote for a programme or law so as to achieve some end that contradicts faith or morals.

The Church also recognizes 'the legitimate plurality of temporal options' that arise from 'the contingent nature of certain choices regarding the ordering of society, the variety of strategies available for accomplishing or guaranteeing the same fundamental value, the possibility of different interpretations of the basic principles of political theory, and the technical complexity of many political problems'. This explains why Catholics might belong to different political parties or come to different prudential judgments about how to protect human dignity and achieve the common good.

SOME FUNDAMENTAL ISSUES RAISED BY THESE EXAMPLES

These several examples, and the responses to them, suggest six fundamental issues worth further consideration: the human act, the intended end, duress, pluralism, reasons for and against material cooperation in evil and different moral worldviews.

The human act

How one views the human act is central to these issues. In *Evangelium Vitae* John Paul defined formal cooperation as 'an action, which either by its very nature or by the form it takes in a concrete situation, can be defined as a direct participation in an [evil] act ... or a sharing in the immoral intention of the person committing it'.[42] There is a great deal

---

[41] CDF, *On Participation of Catholics in Political Life* (2002).
[42] John Paul II, *EV* 74. The example the Pope uses of an intrinsically evil act here is of killing the innocent.

packed into the words 'by its very nature', 'direct participation' and 'sharing in the intention' – far more than I can explore in this chapter. *Veritatis Splendor* makes it clear that 'the object rationally chosen by the deliberate will' is what is at issue and that this way of characterizing human acts excludes the accounts of situationists, proportionalists and other subjectivists.[43]

These two encyclicals would seem to allow, however, at least two accounts of the human act: first, a *natural meanings* account whereby acts have a certain meaning by virtue of their intrinsic object or proximate end, whatever the private intentions or motives of the agent; and second, an *intended acts* account whereby acts can only be assessed 'from the perspective of the acting person' and the proximate ends deliberately willed.[44] This has been at the heart of debates between orthodox Catholic moralists about matters as diverse as sterilization, abortion and euthanasia, whether and what imperfect legislation one might support, ovulation-suppression after rape, vaccines grown on foetal cell-lines and craniotomy. I think it is also at the heart of why, in my earlier examples, some commentators thought the cooperators were principals, co-conspirators or at least formal cooperators, while others thought them material cooperators only and some thought them not to be cooperators at all.

Each of these writers might claim to find support in the encyclicals and elsewhere in the tradition for their understanding of the human act but some acts that, on the natural meanings account, are implicit formal cooperation in evil, whatever the agent claims to intend, are only material cooperation on the intended acts account. Likewise some acts that are only immediate material cooperation on the natural meanings account are formal cooperation on the intended acts account. To advocates of the natural meanings account, those who support an intended acts account

---

[43] John Paul II, *VS* 11.
[44] John Paul II, *VS* 78. CDF, *On Euthanasia* (1980) 1, 3, defined suicide as 'intentionally causing one's own death' and explained that pain relief is permitted as long as 'death is in no way intended or sought, even if the risk of it is reasonably taken; the intention is simply to relieve pain effectively, using for this purpose pain-killers available to medicine'. However, it defined euthanasia as 'an action or an omission which of itself or by intention causes death, in order that all suffering may in this way be eliminated. Euthanasia's terms of reference, therefore, are to be found in the intention of the will and in the methods used.' This definition of euthanasia seemed to suggest that an action could be euthanasia either *of itself* without any intention of causing death (a natural meanings account) or *by intention* (an intended acts account). But in *EV* 65 John Paul II amended 'or' to read 'and': 'Euthanasia in the strict sense is understood to be an action or omission which of itself and by intention causes death, with the purpose of eliminating all suffering.' In this definition and in distinguishing euthanasia from palliative care and from the withdrawal of burdensome treatments the Pope seemed to adopt an intended acts account.

look subjectivist and the encyclical's warnings against intentionalism seem very telling. To the second group, the first look physicalist and the encyclical's insistence on the perspective of the acting subject seems most revealing.

This in turn raises issues for the traditional casuistry of cooperation in evil. Is there, for instance, such a thing as an *implicit* intention, central to the idea of 'implicit formal cooperation' and possibly to the ideas of both immediacy and proximity in material cooperation? If so, what precisely does each mean? What is the difference between implicit formal cooperation and immediate material cooperation, which are categories used almost interchangeably by some casuists[45] but unknown to contemporary philosophy and ones which, for reasons I have explored previously, are of uncertain value?[46]

The intended end

Even if we resolve what precisely we mean by end and/or intention and what its importance is in the human act, *identifying what precisely is intended* in any particular act or proposal may itself be far from easy. Some will adopt a sanguine description of the object of a sterilization operation or an agreement between a Catholic provider and a non-Catholic partner for the latter to perform sterilizations for the former's clients as 'institutional survival under duress'. Some will call the object of condom information 'satisfying people's right to know' or 'protecting the common good'. Some will say that the object of drug-injecting rooms is 'to promote a drug-free lifestyle'. Such act-descriptions incline the agent to a very different judgment about the admissibility of those acts compared with the judgments of the magisterium noted above. Sometimes one suspects that predisposition colours description but, as Elizabeth Anscombe pointed

---

[45] Thus Keenan, 'Prophylactics, toleration and cooperation', p. 216, suggests that 'cooperation is immediate when the object of the cooperator is the same as the object of the illicit activity' – as when a surgical nurse actually performs the abortion herself. That is surely not immediate *material* cooperation but formal cooperation or, indeed, acting as the principal agent of the evil-doing. Keenan also uses as examples of immediate *material* cooperation a servant who, instead of assisting his master to engage in illicit sexual acts by bringing the ladder to the target's window actually performs the illicit sexual acts himself; and a wife who, instead of pressing a less dangerous weapon upon her violent husband, takes part in the beating herself. These are examples not merely of material cooperation, nor even merely of formal cooperation, but of being the principal agent of an evil.

[46] I think 'immediate' material cooperation commonly reduces to formal cooperation or relies upon a misconception of the human act: see Fisher, 'Co-operation in evil'.

out in her classic work on *Intention*, we cannot reasonably redescribe our acts to suit our own convenience.[47]

Even without self-serving pre-judgments, identifying intentions can be very difficult. As Anscombe herself observes, this will be all the more difficult when intentions come in chains of multiple means and ends or in complex configurations of intentions, further intentions, motives and wishes or with multiple agents (such as institutional owners, managers and clinicians) with diverse powers, responsibilities and ends.

Duress

A third matter that we might consider is *the relevance, if any, of pressure* of a financial or other kind. It was noted above that following the CDF's 1977 prohibition on Catholic hospitals performing direct sterilizations the US bishops' 1994 *Directives* originally included an Appendix on cooperation that allowed material cooperation in procedures such as abortion and sterilization on the grounds of pressure from government, finance, patients or professionals. The *duress* exception was at best muddled thinking. James Keenan and Thomas Kopfensteiner cited Henry Davis and others as arguing that a man may, under threat of death, destroy another man's property.[48] They thought that this shows that immediate material cooperation is sometimes permissible and that the tradition is 'flexible' enough to accommodate this. Yet it is far from clear that such destruction of property would be an objective evil at all, since property rights are not absolute. Of course, persons and groups under great pressure sometimes choose wrongly, even sharing in the evil willing of those who pressure them or else inappropriately choosing to cooperate materially with them. On the other hand, those who under great pressure panic, erupt, are paralysed or behave irrationally may have little or no moral responsibility for what they do, though they may be responsible for being in the situation or for being unprepared for it.[49] While external pressure may affect the benefits and burdens properly taken into account in assessing

---

[47] G. E. M. Anscombe, *Intention* (Ithaca, NY: Cornell University Press, 1957).

[48] Keenan, 'Prophylactics, toleration and cooperation', p. 216; Thomas Kopfensteiner, 'The meaning and role of duress in the cooperation in wrongdoing', *LQ* 70(2) (May 2003), 150–8. Likewise B. Lewis, 'Cooperation revisited', *Australasian Catholic Record* 77(2) (2000), 158–62, at 159 n. 1.

[49] See Grisez, *Difficult Moral Questions*, p. 896. In any case, most of the authors who used the immediate–mediate distinction did so not to be 'flexible' in the way that Keenan admires, but precisely to *exclude* cases of immediate material cooperation. None that I have found thought financial pressure would excuse such cooperation.

the permissibility of particular acts of material cooperation, neither philosophy nor theological tradition supports any special *duress* exception
to the prohibition on formal cooperation in evil. Thus the US bishops
directed the removal of the Appendix on cooperation and the inclusion of
the two new directives.

Ronald Hamel has observed that these new US directives resolve what
must now be the practice of Catholic healthcare institutions. They may
not enter into any arrangement that involves immediate material cooperation in the intrinsically evil actions of others. This would include 'such
things as ownership, governance, or management of the entity that offers
prohibited procedures; financial benefit derived from the provision of the
procedures; supplying elements essential to the provision of the services
such as medical or support staff or supplies; or performing or having an
essential role in the procedure'.[50] The footnotes attached to the directives
make it clear that the 'prohibited procedures' with which Catholic institutions may not cooperate include abortion, sterilization and euthanasia.

Despite the appendectomy of the cooperation section of the 1994 US
Directives Keenan and Kopfensteiner continued to assert that duress gives
hospitals leeway to decide whether to cooperate in sterilization and other
wrongful activities.[51] Given that Catholic hospitals experience pressure at
every point where their ethics differ from that of contemporary culture
or the powers that be, the *duress* exception would, if admitted, invite the
abandonment of anything distinctively Catholic in the identity and ethos
of Catholic healthcare institutions.

Pluralism

Australian theologian Brian Lewis has proposed another avenue for
'wriggle room' for Catholic hospitals. He argues that because theologians
such as Bernard Häring would allow sterilization in certain cases, this
is a theologically *probable* opinion and doctors must be given 'some dis-
cretion' in this area no matter what the magisterium has taught on the
question.[52] Häring had earlier taken a very different view:

[50] R. Hamel, 'Part Six of The Directives', *Health Progress* 83(6) (November–December 2002), 37–9
and 59.
[51] J. Keenan, 'Collaboration and cooperation in Catholic health care', *Australasian Catholic Record*
77 (2000), 163–74 at 171: 'Immediate material cooperation is always wrong, except in very rare
occasions of duress ... To capitulate or not is a question that the CEO, the bishop and others
must consider. The principle gives them some lee-way to decide.' Similarly Kopfensteiner, 'The
meaning and role of duress'.
[52] Lewis, 'Cooperation revisited', p. 162.

Any pharmacist, druggist, or clerk in a drugstore who ... is quite aware of the immoral objects [contraceptives] he is selling ... is, in my opinion, guilty of formal cooperation in every instance of sale. He cannot be excused from guilt merely on the score of having no choice. The excuse that he does merely what he is told is vapid. Excuses of this kind have been alleged in defence of the most unheard of crimes. A conscience attuned to the divine law steers clear of such an evasion and of the evil deed. This is not to deny that the manager or owner of the store in question obviously must be charged with far greater guilt than a mere clerk.[53]

Häring, of course, changed his mind on such matters but whichever of Häring's positions was right (if either), Lewis' proposal would seem to allow Catholic institutions or professionals to cooperate in almost any evil, despite clear magisterial teaching to the contrary. This is because today it is hard to think of any mainstream secular activity not advocated by some theologian. This *pluralism* exception, like the duress exception, is a version of what I have called 'tax-lawyer' morality, according to which the role of the moral adviser is to help people find a way *around* the law, avoiding as much tax as possible without getting caught in serious breach. This particular exception is analogous to shopping around for a legal opinion that supports your tax-avoidance scheme. The rationale is that despite what the Church says, a contrary view from a prominent theologian or two will give you *probable* or *more probable* or *equally probable* opinion and so you sidestep the issue of cooperation in evil. As early as the 1975 *Declaration* the CDF saw this coming and made the point that widespread theological dissent from the Church's teaching on a matter such as contraception or sterilization has no doctrinal significance in itself. Theologians do not offer 'a theological source which the faithful might invoke, forsaking the authentic magisterium for the private opinions of theologians who dissent from it'.[54]

Reasons to cooperate and not to cooperate materially

There are lots of good reasons to cooperate materially in any particular evil. There is the good aimed at in the cooperator's own chosen purpose. There are the spin-offs in terms of keeping one's position in healthcare: the opportunity to do all the other good things that the job or position allows (e.g. saving, healing and caring for others); the income this brings,

[53] Häring, *The Law of Christ*, p. 503.
[54] CDF, *On Sterilization in Catholic Hospitals* 2. See also CDF, *On the Ecclesial Vocation of the Theologian* (1990).

thereby supporting a reasonable lifestyle for oneself and one's dependants; a reasonable margin for the institution to focus on its mission; the friendship with the others with whom one works; and so on. When considering whether to engage in an action that has the foreseeable effect of assisting someone else's wrongful purposes, we must ask ourselves: how important are the benefits expected from this action, how probable, lasting, extensive and for whom? What kind of loss or harm would result (and how serious and for whom) from forgoing this proposed action? People with dependants, for instance, have more to lose from refusing to take part in certain procedures than do people with no dependants. People who can readily get another good job will be freer to say no. Someone who cannot readily fulfil some important responsibility, except by agreeing to cooperate materially, will have more reason to do so than someone with a ready, morally acceptable alternative.

On the other hand, as we will see in the section that follows on 'Why it matters so much', there are strong reasons not to cooperate in many cases. There are risks to self and others both from material cooperation in evil and from declining to cooperate materially in someone else's evil acts. *What would count as relevant, sufficient and even decisive reasons* to take such risks or permit such foreseen side-effects? To cooperate materially in evil a more serious reason is required:

- the graver (more serious, more probable, more lasting, more extensive, less preventable) the evil of the principal agent's act in itself;
- the graver the harm (including moral and spiritual consequences) which may be caused to the principal agent;
- the graver the harm which may be caused to third parties by the principal agent;
- the graver any other harm caused to third parties, e.g. their being corrupted by being given the impression that, on the cooperator's view, the wrong done is trivial;
- the graver the harm which may be caused to the cooperator, e.g. by inclining him or her to do similar or worse acts in the future; by compromising the cooperator's ability to give witness to true values; by damaging his/her relationship with God, the Church and other people;
- the harder it is to protest the evil and/or to avoid or minimize (theological) scandal, i.e. leading others into sin;[55]

[55] See Griese, *Catholic Identity*, pp. 414–16 on 'Dissipating the appearances of evil in scandal situations'.

- the more easily the same good could be achieved by another course of action without similar or worse side-effects;
- the more difficult it would be for the principal agent to proceed without the cooperator's involvement.[56]

Some writers would add immediacy and proximity to this list of factors. However, for reasons I have explored previously, the most important factors in determining the reasonableness of a particular instance of material cooperation will only sometimes correlate with immediacy and proximity.[57]

All these matters are in fact difficult to assess and are usually incommensurable with each other and with the goods hoped for in the cooperator's act. After appropriate moral reasoning and discernment, two people of good will and right reason might come to different judgments. In this situation, instead of polemic and name-calling, respectful dialogue is required and possibly some judgment from a competent authority.

Different moral worldviews

Approaches to cooperation in evil can highlight differences in moral worldview. For some there are moral absolutes, such as that against formal cooperation, which may not be compromised in any weighing exercise; for those who take this view, even merely material cooperation in another's wrongdoing is usually seen as a serious matter requiring justification. Morality on this account is part of the vocation to human perfection or holiness under grace and the presumption is *against* cooperating materially, unless there is a sufficiently strong reason to warrant proceeding. Such an approach seems to underlie the various magisterial judgments outlined above in the section headed 'Five modern examples'.

There are, however, a good many tax-lawyer moralists who sometimes seem to regard the moral law as a series of constraints on human freedom and happiness, rather than the roadmap to both. Preference fulfilment and social acceptability rather than conversion and self-sacrifice are paramount. Using traditional casuist categories, 1960s situationism or 1970s

---

[56] Cf. Grisez, *Difficult Moral Problems*, p. 883.
[57] Fisher, 'Co-operation in evil'. As Grisez, *Difficult Moral Questions*, p. 890, points out, 'involvement in others' wrongdoing usually is more likely to impede a cooperator's witness, be an occasion of sin to him or her, have bad moral effects on the wrongdoer, and scandalize others if it is immediate material cooperation than if it is mediate, and, when mediate, if it is proximate than if it is remote. Still, closeness of involvement is morally insignificant unless correlated with some factor that affects the strength of a reason not to cooperate.'

proportionalism, or the new (and otherwise very attractive) talk of virtue and narrative, these writers end up reducing almost all cases of cooperation in evil to material, not formal cooperation and in almost all cases material cooperation becomes permissible cooperation. Duress, probable opinion, proportionate reason, the common good, prudence and *epikeia* – such very traditional-sounding labels are attached to novel schemes for paying less moral tax.

Of course, there are more than two moral worldviews, but these two polarities are particularly evident in the scant literature on cooperation and this might help to explain why two people can describe and judge the same example of cooperation so differently. Positions near the first pole offer a 'line of best fit' for the several recent Church documents considered above. Those theologians who gather around the second pole can offer no such account and so they tend to dissent on many issues. As a result of this polarization, debate over such issues often gets nowhere.

WHY IT MATTERS SO MUCH

Cooperation, the love of God and the Christification of the human person

I conclude this chapter by suggesting three reasons why the question of the permissibility of cooperation in evil matters so much and why we should be reluctant to engage in material cooperation in serious evil unless there are very persuasive reasons to do so. In Chapter 1 I noted the efforts of recent popes and theologians to recover a sense of the distinctively Catholic-Christian in morality. Yet so often, instead of offering a distinctively Christian form of witness to the life of God's Kingdom, even unto death, we can settle for more comfortable accommodation to and collaboration with the powers of this world. As St Paul puts it so graphically, rather than lifting up Christ and his Church to God we take them down into the bed of the prostitute (1 Cor. 6:15–17). In so doing we damage our relationship with God, making him a cooperator in evil, for it is only by God's power that we are supported in being and by God's permissive will that we are free to do whatever ill we do. We also compromise our ability to give witness to the true and the good and so undermine the progress of the Gospel. A keen sense of the privilege that it is to be apostles and prophets, saints and even martyrs as well as a deep commitment to the new evangelization, will give us a greater sensitivity to issues of cooperation in evil than any purely secular account that sees cooperation principles as, at best, useful action guides and, at worst, hindrances to human freedom and happiness.[58]

Cooperation, the love of neighbour and mission to others

Those who wholeheartedly love God will also love their neighbours (Matt. 22:39–40; Rom. 12:9–10; 1 John chs. 3 and 4; Jas. ch. 2). Prima facie love of neighbour will mean helping one another with various projects. Even if evil side-effects sometimes require support to be withdrawn, the presumption will be *in favour* of working together. On the other hand, love of neighbour might be said to ground a presumption *against* material cooperation in evil because we should help our neighbour be and do good. We would need a very serious reason indeed to do anything that foreseeably helps in some significant way our neighbour to do evil, given the potential moral and spiritual consequences for him or her. Our cooperation might encourage our neighbour in sin and obduracy. Love for innocent third parties (such as unborn children) will also make us particularly sensitive to any foreseeable harm to them. What we do will either educate or mislead others; it will encourage those who imitate us to acquire particular virtues or vices. The example that healthcare administrators and senior clinicians give to juniors can, for example, elevate or corrupt those juniors. As Grisez observes:

Third parties can be scandalized by someone's material cooperation. This can happen in various ways. Sometimes the fact that 'good' people are involved makes wrongdoing seem not so wrong and provides material for rationalization and self-deception by people tempted to undertake the same sort of wrong. Perhaps more often the material cooperation of 'good' people leads others to cooperate formally or wrongly, even if only materially. Thus, if medical residents, compelled to choose between giving up their careers and materially cooperating in morally unacceptable procedures, give in to the pressure, their example may lead other health care personnel, who could resist without great sacrifice, to cooperate materially when they should not. This bad effect might suffice to require the residents to forgo what otherwise would be morally acceptable material cooperation.[59]

Thus Eleazar declared that he would rather die painfully than lead the young to disobey God's holy law (2 Macc. 6:18–31), Our Lord inveighed against those who corrupt others (Matt. 18:7; cf. 18:16; 12:13–15; Luke

---

[58] Cf. Catholic Health Australia, *Code of Ethical Standards*, 8.17.
[59] Grisez, *Difficult Moral Problems*, p. 881.

17:1–2) and St Paul counselled caution lest we scandalize our brothers even at table (1 Cor. 8:10–13; 10:25–29; Rom. 14:1–3, 15, 20–21; cf. *CCC* 2284 and 2287).

All these concerns, it seems to me, depend for their bite upon two things. The first is a strong sense of moral solidarity with others: we are, contrary to Cain's self-serving contention, our brothers' and sisters' keepers. Our example does, as the Maccabean heroes saw, impact upon those around us. As Christ commanded we must always be lights to the world, trying to draw people into the life of God's kingdom and wary of ever being an obstacle to their entry; our actions, as Paul insisted, do affect the whole body of Christ. Sanders has likewise argued that a rich sense of human 'folded-together-ness' will yield a much broader sense of co-responsibility for evils than will an individualism that focuses only upon personal blame, especially for grave acts of commission.[60] For this very reason, concerns about material cooperation in evil are likely to be less keenly felt in cultures strongly affected by Dutch-Calvinist or Anglo-American individualism. But recent philosophical work on the role of community and tradition in the formation of moral character and theological work on original and social sin suggest that we ignore the social dimension of our personal choices at our peril.[61]

Second, these concerns depend for their piquancy upon a high estimation of the moral possibilities of one's neighbour. All too often 'harm minimization' programmes at least implicitly amount to despairing of the other party's being capable of anything better. Catholic healthcare agencies must always seek to offer our society a witness to the dignity of the human person as a free and responsible agent, made for greatness and therefore worthy of our high expectations and our best care.

Cooperation, the love of self and authenticity of life

Christ commands that we *love* our neighbours as *ourselves*. Appropriate self-love includes an abiding concern for the kinds of persons we become as a result of our choices. Much reflection upon the nature of the human act and upon implicitness, immediacy and proximity in cooperation reflects a sharp awareness of the reflexive effects of human choice and habit, and of how corrupting cooperation can be. As Cathleen Kaveny

---

[60] Sanders, *Complicities*.
[61] See writers on communitarianism listed in the notes to Chapter 1. On original and social-structural sin see John Paul II, *Reconciliatio et Poenitentia: Apostolic Exhortation on Reconciliation and Penance* (1984), esp. 16, and *Sollicitudo Rei Socialis: Encyclical on Social Concerns* (1987), 46.

has pointed out, the Catholic moral tradition – like the Socratic – is agent-centred.

According to this tradition, the most significant aspect of a human action is the way in which it shapes the character of the person who performs it. Thus, according to traditional Catholic doctrine, individuals who engage in deliberate evildoing harm themselves far more than they do those who suffer injustice at their hands ... Agents who engage in actions [foreseeably but unintentionally resulting in the death of a human being], particularly if they do so repeatedly, can accustom their minds and hearts to causing the death of another human being, albeit unintentionally ... The experience of causing the death of a fellow human being can be brutalizing, even if it is justified. While not sinful in itself, it can make sinning in the future far easier.[62]

This appreciation of the self-creative effects of choice and thus of the burden of personal responsibility and integrity helps explain Christ's apparently extreme exhortations to cut off from ourselves everything that might cause us to sin and enter heaven disabled rather than hell with all our limbs; to avoid sexual promiscuity, violence and acquisitiveness not just of action but even of the mind; and to be ever conscious of what emerges from the deepest recesses of the human heart (Matt. ch. 5; 12:33–35; 15:10–20; 18:8–9; 23:25–28; Luke 12:34). A keen sense of who we are and of our Christian identity and vocation is essential to moral discernment in all difficult cases. A healthy resistance to occasions of, temptations to and habits of sin is especially necessary when discerning whether to cooperate materially in evil.[63] Sometimes this will require sacrificing our personal preferences, our desire to get on well with others, our institutional commitments or even the great goods that our actions might otherwise achieve.

CONCLUSION

I opened this chapter with a reference to Sanders' book, *Complicities*, which suggests that many thinkers during the era of apartheid colluded with that system. This invited reflection on the extent to which Catholic intellectuals and professionals have also cooperated with wrongdoing in the bioethical area, including those areas to which the magisterium has turned its attention in recent years. I then suggested some reasons for this cooperation. Some go to the heart of action theory and so to the heart of

[62] Kaveny, 'Appropriation of evil', pp. 303–4, citing Vatican II, *GS* 27.
[63] See Grisez, *Difficult Moral Problems*, pp. 879–80, on the temptation to cooperate formally, which often comes with material cooperation.

fundamental morality. Some ways of reading the human act allow almost any cooperation in evil acts to which the moralist may be already inclined and empty the categories of cooperation of their usefulness. Some 'tax-lawyer' and secular-individualist approaches to morality present morality, tradition and community as enemies of human fulfilment. On these views the function of ethics is to help healthcare managers and professionals avoid being caught engaging in flagrant violations of 'Church law'; in order to maximize the range of their activities they sail as close to the wind as possible. Such a perspective will orient the decision-maker in a particular way to questions of cooperation. I have also presented a contrasting orientation to morality that sees life as the pursuit of perfection or, in Christian terms, the wholehearted commitment to the holy love of God, neighbour and self, which is a far from easy undertaking, even under grace, but one that will make the agent much more sensitive to issues associated with cooperating in evil.

PART II

Beginning of life

CHAPTER 4

Beginnings: when do people begin?

METHOD, THESIS AND IMPLICATIONS

An influential book

In 2008 Nancy Pelosi, then Speaker of the US House of Representatives, was asked on *Meet the Press* about the status of the human embryo. She declared:

I would say that, as an ardent, practicing Catholic, this is an issue that I have studied for a long time. And what I know is, over the centuries, the doctors of the Church have not been able to make that definition … Saint Augustine said at three months. We don't know. The point is, is that it shouldn't have an impact on a woman's right to choose … I don't think anybody can tell you when life begins, human life begins. As I say, the Catholic Church for centuries has been discussing this.[1]

Pelosi's stance drew immediate fire from several US bishops and ultimately the Pope.[2] But her belief that when life begins is unknown and probably unknowable, but that it likely begins well after conception, has been reflected in her own political life. Pelosi has voted in favour of human cloning, human embryo research, US funding of abortion abroad and against every attempt to restrict abortion, even the bill to ban partial-birth abortions.[3] Where might this 'ardent' Catholic have found support for her thought that life begins well after conception?

In 1988 the philosopher-priest Father Norman Ford SDB published *When Did I Begin? Conception of the Human Individual in History,*

---

[1] K. Parker, 'Pelosi is wrong on "abortion rights"', *Chicago Tribune*, 27 August 2008.
[2] Many US bishops responded. Regarding Pope Benedict's words to Pelosi: *Comunicato della Sala Stampa della Santa Sede*, 18 February 2009; D. Gilgoff, 'Nancy Pelosi at the Vatican: the Speaker and the Pope at cross purposes', *US News*, 18 February 2009.
[3] www.ontheissues.org/CA/Nancy_Pelosi_Abortion.htm (accessed 1 January 2011).

Philosophy and Science.[4] In this book he aimed to resolve the debate on 'how far we can trace back our own personal identity as the same continuing individual living body, being or entity'. He concluded that there is no human individual or soul present until two to three weeks after fertilization. The book proved triply significant. First, it was and remains the most fully argued case for delayed 'animation' or 'hominization' – the view that the early human embryo is not a human being.

Second, Ford's book had implications for moral dilemmas around the manufacture of, experimentation upon and destruction of embryos and the use of abortifacient drugs and devices. Though Ford rejected such practices his book quickly became the favourite text of their proponents. It proved far more influential in politics and society than in the academy. As many already appreciated in 1988, if an early embryo is not a human being, it will have no rights and may perhaps be used as scientists and others desire. This is how the fourteen-day rule, which allows scientists in many countries to experiment upon human embryos up to that stage but not later, received its fullest intellectual justification. Even if few people today remember why this cut-off point was agreed or why identical twinning and the primitive streak are supposed to be important, it is widely assumed that something significant must happen around the fourteen-day mark.

Third, while at first glance Ford's book had little bearing on the morality of most abortions (which occur well after his fortnight marker), it in fact created much uncertainty around abortion by calling into question the minor premise of the Catholic and other 'pro-life' case against abortion, which is:

1 It is always wrong directly to kill an innocent human being.
2 From fertilization/conception the human organism is an innocent human being.
3 Therefore it is wrong to kill by abortion a human embryo or foetus.

---

[4] Norman M. Ford, *When Did I Begin? Conception of the Human Individual in History, Philosophy and Science* (Cambridge University Press, 1988); in the present chapter references in [square brackets] are to page numbers in this work. Ford's other contributions include: 'Moral issues that arise in experimentation on human embryos', *Australasian Catholic Record* 63 (1986), 3–20, 'Reply to Michael Coughlan', *Bioethics* 3 (1989), 342–6, 'When did I begin? A reply to Nicholas Tonti-Filippini', *LQ* 57 (1990), 59–66, 'Ethics, science and embryos: weighing the evidence', *The Tablet* 46 (1990), 141–2, 353 and 584, *The Prenatal Person: Ethics from Conception to Birth* (Oxford: Blackwell, 2002), *Stem Cells: Science, Medicine, Law and Ethics*, with M. Herbert (Sydney: St Paul's, 2003), 'The moral significance of the human foetus', in R. Ashcroft, H. Draper, A. Dawson and J. McMillan (eds.), *Principles of Health Care Ethics*, 2nd edn (Chichester: Wiley, 2007), pp. 387–92.

By casting doubt upon premise (2) Ford's book effectively undermined the case for any absolute prohibition on abortion and thus proved politically and culturally important for the liberalization not only of embryo experimentation and early abortion but for all later abortions also.

At the time of publication Ford predicted that the full implications of his work would not be felt for many years, when there had been considered responses to it.[5] By then Ford himself had repudiated his earlier position. But his first book was the one destined to have an enduring influence, and so it is to this that I here offer a response; there have been some others.[6] After summarizing Ford's methodology and thesis, I examine the science and metaphysics underpinning them. I then consider the criteria upon which to judge when a human being – a human individual – is present.

Ford's case

Ford's book began with a history of theories of reproduction and the beginnings of the human being. This is instructive, though one might contest some claims, e.g. that Aristotelian views on embryogenesis were commonly held for 2,000 years [xiv, 19, 39][7] and that the Church simply followed prevailing opinion regarding the unborn [xiv, 19, 39].[8] Ford then examines the concept of human *individuality* and brings this to bear on the biological data concerning conception and early human development.

---

[5] Supporters of Ford's position have included: Berit Brogaard, Peter Drum, J. T. Ebert, Vincent Genovesi, Kevin Kelly, Richard McCormick, Jeff McMahan, Jean Porter, Thomas Shannon, Barry Smith, James Walter and Mary Warnock.

[6] Critics of Ford's position have included: Benedict Ashley, Michael Coughlan, Tom Daly, Gregor Damschen, Jan Deckers, Willem Eijk, Anselm Etokakpan, John Finnis, Paul Flaman, Robert George, Alfonso Gómez-Lobo, Germain Grisez, Diane Irving, David Jones, C. Ward Kischer, Rose Koch-Hershenov, William E. May, Albert Moraczewski, Thomas Nelson, Laura Palazzani, Antonio Puca, Dieter Schönecker, Agneta Sutton, Nicholas Tonti-Filippini, J. R. Velez and Anthony Zimmerman. Several authors deal with these matters in Juan Vial Correa and Elio Sgreccia (eds.), *Identity and Status of the Human Embryo* (Libreria Editrice Vaticana, 1998).

[7] In fact scientific opinion fluctuated, and several of the Fathers disallowed the supposed distinction between formed and unformed foetuses: J. Connery, *Abortion: The Development of the Roman Catholic Perspective* (Chicago: Loyola University Press, 1977); D. Jones, 'The human embryo in the Christian tradition: a reconsideration', *J Med Ethics* 31 (2005), 710–14, and *The Soul of the Embryo* (London: Continuum, 2004).

[8] In fact the Church often critiqued prevailing views, as in Harvey's time, and has consistently refused to allow these matters to be reduced to contemporary scientific opinion and has increasingly held as 'probable' that human ensoulment occurs at conception. Here the Church has relied on contemporary biology and metaphysics but also the scriptural witness to the preciousness of unborn life, the unbroken Catholic tradition of opposition to abortion at any stage and the developing doctrines on the Incarnation, the Immaculate Conception, birth control and so forth. See: J. H. Channer (ed.), *Abortion and the Sanctity of Human Life* (Exeter: Paternoster, 1985); M. Gorman, *Abortion and the Early Church: Christian, Jewish and Pagan Attitudes in the Greco-Roman World* (New York: Paulist, 1982); J. R. Schmidt (ed.), *To the Unborn with Love* (Adelaide: Lutheran, 1990).

There is only a human being, he insists, when there is 'a living individual with the inherent active potential to develop towards human adulthood without ceasing to be the same ontological individual' [85]. The scientific data, especially that concerning monozygotic (identical) twinning, suggest to Ford that there is insufficient unity or coherence in the early embryo to ascribe individuality to it.

From the accumulation of such biological data and philosophical arguments, Ford comes to a strong conclusion: science and philosophy *prove* that the human being *could not* begin at conception. Rather, for its first two to three weeks, the embryo is merely a cluster of cells, each a distinct, ontologically individual organism, in simple contact with other individual organisms, each of which lives only a matter of hours before dying in the process of dividing. Only 'at the primitive streak stage and not prior to it, but most certainly by the stage of gastrulation'[9] do these few thousand organisms combine so that 'a human individual, our youngest neighbour and member of the human community, begins' [xviii, 139, 170]. The term *embryo*, as used before two to three weeks, is thus for Ford a collective noun. Only after the post-implantation 'transformation' does the term refer to a single entity that can properly be called a substance, being or ontological *individual*. Only then is there a *human soul* present.

Delayed hominization is not a new thesis, many having argued it before Ford, if none so fully. Its modern revival was led by the 'Transcendental Thomist' Joseph Donceel, whose influence is clear throughout Ford's works. Ford contributed more sophisticated biological evidence, as it existed in the late 1980s, to bolster those who challenged 'the commonly held view' that human individuals begin at fertilization.

A CLOSER LOOK AT THE SCIENCE

'The facts'

One of the clearest virtues of *When Did I Begin?* is its rich collection of biological information about early human development. Despite continuing controversy among embryologists, as among philosophers, Ford asserted that 'there is broad agreement amongst embryologists concerning

---

[9] The 'primitive streak' is a furrow that appears in the midline of the embryonic disk around fourteen days after conception, which forms the visible longitudinal axis around which embryonic structures will organize. During the third week after conception gastrulation occurs, which positions the three embryonic germ layers of endoderm, ectoderm and mesoderm which later develop into certain bodily systems.

these facts' [102; cf. 108]. However, even were there a scientific consensus, the Baconian account of science as providing 'the facts' for metaphysics to interpret is now widely questioned. As Ford admits: 'it will be difficult to draw the fine line between where the strictly scientific evidence ends and philosophical interpretation starts' [16; cf. 181].

Among the important critics of the assumptions operative in the sciences have been Michael Polanyi, Thomas Kuhn, Imre Lakatos, N. R. Hanson and Paul Feyerabend. They have exposed some of the assumptions behind naïve inductivism and the positivist distinctions between *fact* and *interpretation*, neutral *objective* science and committed *subjective* metaphysics and religion. They have demonstrated persuasively the 'theory-dependence of observation' and that the presumed objectivity of the scientific observer actually reflects considerable personal involvement, commitment and, accordingly, interpretation. Alasdair MacIntyre writes:

'Fact' is in modern culture a folk-concept with an aristocratic ancestry. When Lord Chancellor Bacon as part of the propaganda for his astonishing and idiosyncratic amalgam of past Platonism and future empiricism enjoined his followers to abjure speculation and collect facts, he was immediately understood by such as John Aubrey to have identified facts as collectors' items, to be gathered in with the same kind of enthusiasm that at other times has informed the collection of Spode china or the numbers of railway engines. The other early members of the Royal Society recognized very clearly that, whatever Aubrey was doing, it was not natural science as the rest of them understood it; but they did not recognize that on the whole it was he rather than they who was being faithful to the letter of Bacon's inductivism. Aubrey's error was of course not only to suppose that the natural scientist is a kind of magpie; it was also to suppose that the observer can confront a fact face-to-face without any theoretical interpretation interposing itself. That this was an error, although a pertinacious and long-lived one, is now largely agreed upon by philosophers of science.[10]

Just as modern science is learning to make much humbler claims, Ford seems to attribute to science an objectivity and certainty characteristic of the heady days of Bacon and Aubrey.

Ford generously thanks two leading embryologists, Alan Trounson and Roger Short, for the 'expert tuition, advice and constant encouragement' he needed for his work [xviii]. That these advisers were themselves very involved in human embryo experimentation might have given cause to pause before wholesale adoption of their account of *the facts* of early human development, not because those scientists' integrity is to be doubted but for the very reason that it is to be presumed. An honest

---

[10] A. MacIntyre, *After Virtue*, 2nd edn (London: Duckworth, 1984), p. 76.

embryo experimenter is likely to have formed the 'metaphysical' view that
the embryo is not a human person and his perception of the facts will be
accordingly value-laden.

Thus when Ford asserts that '*embryo* technically refers to the stage from
the third to eighth week of development' and advocates the use of the
term 'pro-embryo' or 'pre-embryo' for the first two weeks [210–12], he is
adopting the tendentious terminology of the experimentation lobby, terminology that in fact failed to catch on.[11] Ford's sources and defenders
such as Short and Trounson have themselves testified that they regard
these terms as quite arbitrary.[12] However arbitrary the definition of terms
such as 'embryo', 'human being' and 'person' may be, their sociological
and political import is undoubted: whoever gets these tags gains certain
protections. And if we are to turn to scientists for *the facts*, then we must
surely take seriously their almost unanimous conclusion, notwithstanding
Short and Trounson, that 'fertilization in mammals normally represents
the beginning of life for a new individual'.[13]

Syngamy

A few examples of the naïve distinction between fact and interpretation
must here suffice. In his description of *the facts* about which embryologists
broadly agree, Ford asserts that 'fertilization is not a momentary event but
a process that may last up to 20–24 hours' by which time syngamy (the
joining of the pronuclei derived from the gametes) has occurred. Indeed

---

11 Even when Ford was writing, J. Maddox, the editor of *Nature*, called the use of this term 'a
cosmetic trick' and IVF pioneer Robert Edwards also objected to its use: CIBA Foundation,
Human Embryo Research: Yes or No? (London: Tavistock, 1986); cf. A. Glenister, 'The first days
of life', *The Tablet*, 2 December 1989, 1398–400; D. Irving, 'Testimony before the NIH Human
Embryo Research Panel', *LQ* 61(4) (1994), 82–9, 'New Age embryology text books: implications
for fetal research', *LQ* 61 (1994), 42–62; M. Jarmulowicz, 'Ethics, science and embryos', *The
Tablet*, 10 February 1990, 181. Despite efforts by some in the embryo industry and the theological academy to promote this term, it never really caught on: see Jennifer Brinker, 'Bioethicist
debunks term "pre-embryo"', *St. Louis Review*, 22 September 2006; R. O'Rahilly and F. Müller,
Human Embryology and Teratology, 3rd edn (New York: John Wiley, 2001); J. Shea, 'The "pre-
embryo" question', *Catholic Insight*, January 2005, 18–21.
12 In his evidence to the Australian Senate Select Committee on the Human Embryo
Experimentation Bill 1985, Short said that 'really, any benchmarks that we care to put on this
are purely arbitrary and of our own making', and Trounson said that 'it is an arbitrary situation. I do not see that there is a magical change between day 13 and day 14. It just happens to
be an arbitrary time. It is like a slippery slope. I am prepared to come back and argue ... for
28 day embryos.' *Official Hansard Report of Submissions and Evidence* (Canberra: AGPS, 1986),
pp. 108–9 and 2159.
13 This is the opening sentence of R. Yanagimachi, 'Mammalian fertilization', in E. Knobil *et al.*
(eds.), *The Physiology of Reproduction* (New York: Raven, 1988), p. 135.

he includes this as part of the very definitions of fertilization and syngamy [102–8, 119, 211–12].

If this interpretation was already controversial in 1988, it is even less tenable today. Rather than being a long-drawn-out process, as Ford believed, fertilization is now known to be very speedy. The fusion of sperm and ovum is a more or less 'momentary' event. The sperm immediately ceases to exist and the ovum, too, changes radically. The new entity has all the organization – the biological self-directness – of an organism. The subsequent lining up of the DNA from each gamete is merely one of the series of changes within the organism that follows *because it is already a distinct organism*. Surveying the latest embryology, Maureen Condic explains:

Following the binding of sperm and egg to each other, the membranes of these two cells fuse, creating in this instant a single hybrid cell: the zygote or one-cell embryo. Cell fusion is a well studied and very rapid event, occurring in less than a second … Subsequent to sperm–egg fusion, events rapidly occur in the zygote that do not normally occur in either sperm or egg. The contents of what was previously the sperm, including its nucleus, enter the cytoplasm of the newly formed zygote. Within minutes of membrane fusion, the zygote initiates changes in its ionic composition that will, over the next 30 minutes, result in chemical modifications of the zona pellucida, an acellular structure surrounding the zygote. These modifications block sperm binding to the cell surface and prevent further intrusion of additional spermatozoa on the unfolding process of development. Thus, the zygote acts immediately and specifically to antagonize the function of the gametes from which it is derived; while the 'goal' of both sperm and egg is to find each other and to fuse, the first act of the zygote is immediately to prevent any further binding of sperm to the cell surface. Clearly, then, the prior trajectories of sperm and egg have been abandoned, and a new developmental trajectory – that of the zygote – has taken their place.[14]

Condic details the rapid development of this zygote as the maternally derived nucleus completes its final round of meiotic division within thirty minutes of sperm–egg fusion and the maternally and paternally derived nuclei undergo rapid structural and chemical changes. The DNA of both pronuclei is demethylated, the nuclei replicate their DNA in anticipation of the first round of cell division, transcription begins in both halves of the genome and the two pronuclei move towards the centre of the cell, in preparation for the first cell division (i.e. mitosis) of the zygote. Syngamy, she explains, is a rather minor moment in this drama, as the nuclear membranes that separate the two pronuclei break down and the maternally

[14] M. Condic, *When Does Human Life Begin? A Scientific Perspective* (Thornwood, NY: Westchester Institute, 2008).

and paternally derived chromosomes are co-located in the same general region of the cytoplasm. She concludes that:

Based on this factual description of the events following sperm–egg binding, we can confidently conclude that a new cell, the zygote, comes into existence at the 'moment' of sperm–egg fusion, an event that occurs in less than a second. At the point of fusion, sperm and egg are physically united – i.e., they cease to exist as gametes, and they form a new entity that is materially distinct from either sperm or egg. The behavior of this new cell also differs radically from that of either sperm or egg: the developmental pathway entered into by the zygote is distinct from both gametes. Thus, sperm–egg fusion is indeed a scientifically well defined 'instant' in which the zygote (a new cell with unique genetic composition, molecular composition, and behavior) is formed.[15]

Extra-embryonic tissues or embryonic organs?

Another of Ford's doubtful *facts* is that the zona pellucida and the placental tissues are 'extra-embryonic' membranes, rather than being parts of the 'embryo proper'. He asserts that 'one could scarcely argue' that the chorion biopsies, undertaken to test for genetic diseases, involve taking a part of the foetus [117–18, 124, 146, 153, 156–7, 171, 213] – but if it were not a part of the foetus what use would testing such samples be?

Ford's arguments for these tissues not being part of the 'embryo proper' are several:

- they have no nerves and are insentient – but this is true of several body parts;
- they are used only for the period of gestation and then discarded – but many body parts, such as milk teeth, hair and cells, are discarded at one time or another;
- they can be shared by two foetuses – but this is true of almost all organs, as evidenced by the various kinds of conjoined ('Siamese') twins;
- in chimaeras (where cell-lines from two or more genetically distinct organisms are incorporated into one) they can be from a source genetically distinct from the rest of the embryo – but again this is true of many organs of a chimaera at every stage in development and also true of adults who receive a transplanted organ from another adult [118, 133, 143–5, 157, 173].

---

[15] Condic, *When Does Human Life Begin?*

Ford fails to distinguish convincingly these tissues from other human organs. The biological evidence is that they are formed by and with the embryo, (usually) with its genetic constitution, for its use and sole benefit and they are indeed its organs. They are clearly not the mother's organs, nor a tumour, nor some alien third organism living symbiotically with mother and embryo.

It has long been established that the zona pellucida is an essential organ of the zygote, normally functioning to maintain the embryo's unity and unicity, preserving its characteristic cleavage pattern, protecting it during its 'journey to the womb' and preventing fusions with other zygotes. Thus biologists such as Moore (upon whom Ford normally relies) are convinced that the zona and the placenta are organs of the developing organism.[16] Ford, however, must deny that these are organs because that would suggest an organism and, as he himself observes: 'it would be a sufficient, but probably not a necessary, condition for an individual human being to exist that it be a living body with the primordium of at least one organ formed for the benefit of the whole organism'. Ford excludes the abundant evidence of an organ–organism relationship between the parts and the whole of the embryo by tagging all such evidence as mere 'confusion' [170].

Monozygotic twinning

Another example of *factual* information central to Ford's thesis that is actually quite controversial is his material on monozygotic twinning. While embryologists in 1988 admitted knowing very little about the identical twinning process,[17] Ford was definitive. First, he is sure when identical twinning occurs: 'the first human individual ceases when it divides and two human individuals begin' asserting that the alternative view, that the original human individual continues when a newly formed twin begins, is false [xii, xvi, 119–20, 123]. Were the second view correct, he says, it would be impossible to distinguish the original 'parent' zygote from the new 'offspring' zygote and such 'identical indiscernibles' cannot exist [122].[18] If we take the dividing amoeba as a model of what happens

---

[16] See the standard embryology books listed in the notes to Chapter 5.

[17] For example, T. Hilgers, 'Human reproduction: three issues for the moral theologian', *Theol Studies* 38 (1977), 136–52 at 149; J. M. McLean, 'The embryo debate', *The Tablet*, 7 April 1990, 449–50.

[18] Identical twins are, of course, no more *indiscernible* (i.e. indistinguishable) if they occur by the one-produces-another model than if they occur by the one-splits-into-two model; their differences in matter, in spatio-temporal origin and current location and continuity with different

in twinning, either *interpretation* of the process is equally valid because we have no empirical reason to choose one over the other.

Second, Ford asserts that the trigger of monozygotic twinning is probably environmental not genetic [119 and 135]. This claim is aimed at laying to rest any thought that there might be two *individuals* present from conception. The weight of evidence today, however, is that monozygotic twinning is indeed a genetic predisposition or is otherwise structurally determined (or at least a predisposition) from the time of fertilization for particular embryos.[19]

Finally, Ford claims that twinning 'could be triggered any time after the first mitotic cleavage during the following 10–12 days' but no later than the formation of the primitive streak [136, 172–3]. Some biologists, however, believe that certain foetal abnormalities that involve twinning occur *after* the implantation and primitive streak stage that Ford regards as decisive. Such abnormalities as 'Siamese' or conjoined twinning (where identical twins are joined, or fail fully to separate, in utero) and 'foetus-in-foetu' (an even graver abnormality, where one foetus is enveloped inside its twin and sometimes develops later) can occur either in the following days or even some weeks later.[20] Others suggest that twinning occurs much earlier and that the veterinary evidence upon which Ford relies is not applicable to human embryos.[21]

---

adults clearly distinguish them; and despite the tag 'identical', there are even genetic differences: C. Bruder *et al.*, 'Phenotypically concordant and discordant monozygotic twins display different DNA copy-number-variation profiles', *Am J Human Genetics* 82(3) (2008), 763–71; S. Gilbert, 'Non-identical monozygotic twins', in *DevBio: A Companion to Developmental Biology*, 8th edn (Sunderland, MA: Sinauer, 2006). M. J. Loux, *Substance and Attribute: A Study in Ontology* (Dordrecht: Reidel, 1978), pp. 117ff., noted that 'most metaphysicians (at least nowadays) would deny that the Identity of Indiscernibles is a matter of necessary truth'; he holds that there can be numerically different yet qualitatively indiscernible material bodies or persons.

[19] O. Bomsel-Helmreich and W. Al Mufti, 'The mechanism of monozygosity and double ovulation', in L. G. Keith, E. Papiernik-Berkhauer, D. M. Keith and B. Luke (eds.), *Multiple Pregnancy: Epidemiology, Gestation and Perinatal Outcome* (New York: Parthenon, 1995), 'Non-identical monozygotic twins'; J. Hall, 'Twins and twinning', *Am J Med Genetics* 61 (1996), 202–4; McLean, 'The embryo debate'. Ford himself recognizes that there is evidence of some propensity to monozygotic twinning inherited through the maternal line and of genetic characteristics that facilitate rather than trigger twinning [119 and 135].

[20] C. Austin, *Human Embryos: The Debate on Assisted Reproduction* (Oxford University Press, 1989), pp. 14–20 and 28; K. Dawson, 'Segmentation and moral status in vivo and in vitro: a scientific perspective', *Bioethics* 2 (1988), 1–14; M. H. Kaufman, 'The embryology of conjoined twins', *Child's Nervous System* 20(8–9) (2004), 508–24; R. Koch, 'Conjoined twins and the biological account of personal identity', *The Monist* 89(3) (2006), 351–70. Ford is apparently aware of the difficulty that this 'late' twinning poses for his thesis [171].

[21] McLean, 'The embryo debate'; R. Spencer, 'Theoretical and analytical embryology of conjoined twins', *Clinical Anatomy* 13 (2000), 36–53 and 97–120, and 'Conjoined twins: theoretical embryologic basis', *Teratology* 45(6) (1992), 591–602.

Contact between cells

Ford asserts, again as a matter of fact, that despite their 'close contact' and 'the appearance of a single organism or unity', the several cells of an early embryo are really ontologically distinct organisms. The membranes of these cells 'merely touch' and in the early stages are held 'loosely together' in 'simple contact' by desmosomes (glue-like junctions) and the 'cage' of the zona pellucida. 'This view seems to fit the facts better' [125, 137, 139 and 146]. Once more, little evidence is offered for this interpretation, which runs quite contrary to the understanding of most biologists or of any ordinary viewer of photographs of a multi-cellular embryo with the cells firmly pressed against each other, restricting each other's shape and position.[22] The only argument Ford offers is that 'each cell takes its own nutrients, thereby showing autonomy in a vitally significant way' [137, 170]. Until the organism has developed to the stage where it can have specialist organs for nutrition this is obviously necessary and we are offered no explanation of the 'vital significance' of this matter for cell autonomy. A more recent review of the literature has concluded that the cells of the human embryo act together in a united way so that the organism develops as, and only as, an individual of that species.[23]

An ambiguous conclusion

Ford concludes that:

With [i] the appearance of the primitive streak after [ii] the completion of implantation and about 14 days after fertilization [iii] identical twinning can no longer occur. This is when [iv] the human body is first formed with [v] a definite body plan and [vi] definite axis of symmetry ... [vii] most certainly by the stage of gastrulation when the embryo's primitive cardiovascular system is already functioning and blood is circulating. [xviii; cf. 168–77]

As my parenthetical inclusion of [numbers] suggests, Ford offers not one but seven different marker events, events that do not in fact coincide chronologically, though he dates them all at 'about 14 days after fertilization'. Why these should mark the advent of a human organism is

[22] When considering identical twinning, Ford suggests that *weak* desmosomes might be a genetic factor predisposing some embryos to fission [135]. He thereby implies that in normal embryos these are *strong* binding factors. H. Pearson, 'Developmental biology: your destiny, from day one', *Nature* 418 (4 July 2002), 14–15, reports on the many ways that the cells of an embryo interact with, restrict and direct each other's development in various ways.
[23] Pearson, 'Developmental biology'.

never successfully argued. Overall Ford's biological data do *not* support his denial of the organic individuality of the early embryo. We can now turn to the philosophical justification for his position.

Classical and contemporary metaphysics

When Did I Begin? outlines the classical biology upon which Aristotle and Aquinas based their metaphysical reflections [25–9, 33, 37–40]. Embryos, they thought, were spontaneously generated, following the action of the semen on the menstrual blood, both of which were residues of food and not alive; the semen acted like rennet coagulating the menstrual 'milk' into a vegetable seed and the womb was the soil in which this seed was planted. Thereafter followed a succession of souls as the embryo developed into a human being at forty days for males and ninety days for females. Classical biology inferred this series of generations and corruptions from misread observations of animal reproduction, miscarriages and putrefying corpses.

Almost all contemporary Thomists agree that had Aquinas known of the existence and functions of sperm and ovum and that their union brings about the epigenetic primordium of a single, whole-bodied human person, with all the already specified if still undeveloped genetic and other biological capacities, he would have favoured immediate animation, as indeed he allowed in Christ's case.[24] As explanatory entities ought not to be multiplied unnecessarily, where one soul suffices to explain the embryo, the concept of a succession of souls should be rejected.

Radically different biological data, such as we now have, might be expected to yield (or be met by) some new developments in ontology. Yet Ford insists that 'while modern science has corrected Aristotle's biological errors, his philosophical principles remain valid when applied to the relevant facts of modern embryology' and that Aristotelian principles 'are perfectly adequate to explain everything and solve the problems that arise' [xv–xvi, 21 and 129]. This means that Ford rarely, if ever, engages the contemporary philosophical literature on mereology (identity, multiplicity,

---

[24] Aristotelians and Thomists who argue for immediate animation include: Benedict Ashley, John Finnis, Robert George, Germain Grisez, John Haldane, Stephen Heaney, Pascal Ide, Mark Johnson, David Jones, Robert Joyce, C. Ward Kischer, Patrick Lee, Albert Moraczewski, Kevin O'Rourke, John Ozolins, Mario Pangallo, Augustine Reagan, Christopher Tollefsen and J. R. Velez.

counting, parts and wholes),[25] on natural kinds (and substances, essences, sortals and individuation criteria),[26] on organismic or systems biology[27] or on species and taxonomy,[28] even though these have immediate bearing upon the matters he raises. Instead Ford pours the new wine of Trounson and Short's embryology into the old wineskins of seminary Thomism (cf. Luke 5:33–39).

Aristotle's principles, while of perennial value, are by no means uncontroversial today. Jorge Gracia identifies at least six key problematic issues in medieval and contemporary thought regarding individuality: its *intension* (connection with such notions as indivisibility, distinction and identity); its *extension* (which entities are individuals, if any); its *ontological status* (the metaphysics of individuality and nature); the *principle of individuation* (the principle or cause of individuality and whether it is the same in all entities); the epistemological issue of its *discernibility*; and the linguistic issue of the *function* of proper names and indexicals. Ford's treatment

[25] The debate goes back to Locke, Leibniz, Schelling, Frege, Brentano, Husserl, Leśniewski, Deleuze, Bergson and Carnap. Contemporary contributors include: L. R. Baker, D. L. Baxter, Baruch Brody, Roberto Casati, Roderick Chisholm, Peter Geach, Brian Garrett, Henry Harris, Saul Kripke, D. K. Lewis, E. J. Lowe, Geoffrey Madell, F. Moltmann, H. Noonan, Eric Olson, Derek Parfit, Hilary Putnam, Michael Ruse, Sydney Shoemaker, Elliott Sober, T. L. Sprigge, Peter Strawson, Richard Swinburne, A. C. Varzi and John Wallace. Though he does not deal with this major strand of philosophy, Ford does review some Anglo-Saxon empiricists [68–72].

[26] This was, of course, one of the principal debates of the Middle Ages and continued through to Locke, Mill, Quine and others. Important recent contributors include: M. R. Ayers, J. A. Bernardete, Baruch Brody, Ronna Burger, Quassim Cassam, Nino Cocchiarella, John Dupré, C. L. Elder, B. Ellis, Evan Fales, Fred Feldman, Graeme Forbes, Max Freund, Laura Garcia, H. Granger, I. Hacking, D. L. Hull, Mark Johnston, J. LaPorte, N. von Lobkowicz, M. J. Loux, E. J. Lowe, Penelope Mackie, Stephen Makin, D. H. Mellor, S. Mumford, Stephen Napier, H. Noonan, Dan Passell, W. V. O. Quine, Michael Ruse, S. P. Schwartz, W. Schwartz, Gabriel Segal, S. Shoemaker, Peter Strawson, W. L. Uzgalis, David Wiggins, T. E. Wilkerson, M. B. Williams and Dean Zimmerman.

[27] The fathers of the organismic biology school were Ludwig von Bertalanffy and E. S. Russell, who were followed by W. E. Agar, J. H. Woodger, R. C. Lewontin and their disciples. Ford seems to be aware of this discussion in his ch. 3, but the most recent work he cites is from the 1940s. Important recent contributors include: C. Allen, A. Ariew, Nicanor Austriaco, George Bartholomew, M. Bekoff, F. Booger, Richard Boyd, Leo Buss, Scott Camazine, Maureen and Samuel Condic, R. Cummins, Walter Elsasser, Michael Ghiselin, Hiroaki Kitano, M. D. Mesarović, G. Lauder, Tim Lewens, S. M. Liao, R. G. Millikan, Ernest Nagel, Eric Olson, M. Perlman, Pietro Ramellini, U. Sauer, J. L. Snoep, R. Wehner, David Wilson and Jack Wilson.

[28] Aristotle taught that science seeks to classify substances according to sameness and difference (what today would be called a sortal and an indexical or deictic element). A real as opposed to a nominal definition identifies the essential properties as opposed to the accidents. This is far from uncontroversial today. Recent contributors include: Arthur Caplan, R. Boyd, R. N. Brandon, Ingo Brigandt, M. Claridge, J. Crane, H. Dawah, John Dupré, Marc Ereshefsky, M. T. Ghiselin, D. L. Hull, P. Kitcher, D. B. and D. J. Kitts, Richard Mayden, E. Mayr, R. G. Millikan, B. D. Mishler, C. Patterson, Thomas Reydon, Alexander Rosenberg, Michael Ruse, Elliott Sober, M. B. Williams and Robert Wilson.

makes no such distinctions. Instead he asserts that 'we all know' that a crowd, herd or hive are a class and that their members are individuals of that group and that a crystal is a natural kind [87]. In contemporary philosophy these claims are highly tendentious.

Ford's use of hylomorphism

Hylomorphism is the theory that living organisms are material organized by a particular form or *soul*, which gives them their nature and life. Hylomorphism was much used by Aquinas, though not uncritically. Because hylomorphism holds that each soul must inform distinct matter it is challenged today to explain a range of phenomena such as: the slime-mould which, depending upon environment and maturity, can be either an aggregate of organisms living loosely together or a single multi-cellular organism; transplants, where organs maintain considerable organizational integrity and can be moved from body to body; and conjoined twins. The contemporary debates noted above offer valuable insights that could revitalize without undermining a classical metaphysic such as Ford's, but this requires new work such as that indicated by R. J. Connell's *Substance and Modern Science*, of which Ford seems unaware.

Ford's use of an unmodified Aristotelian-Thomistic ontology, of the type long taught in seminaries, has several problems. First, it is entirely inconsistent with the Enlightenment view of the soul as 'mind stuff', a view into which Ford lapses from time to time [e.g. 78–9, 130].[29] At no stage does Ford explain what it is that informs the embryo (or each distinct cell of the 'cluster of cells') *before hominization* during the two to three weeks after fertilization. This is an extraordinary gap for one so attached to a classical metaphysic. The Aristotelian-Thomist theory of delayed hominization presumed a single organism informed by a succession of single souls, as Ford himself outlines [28–36]: the embryo is first formed with a single vegetable (nutritive) soul (or by a succession of increasingly sophisticated, single vegetable souls); in due course being replaced (from the inside) by a single animal (sensitive) soul (or by a succession of increasingly sophisticated, single animal souls); to be finally replaced (from the outside) by a single human (rational) soul. This theory did not allow for one human soul to unite and replace several vegetative or animal souls (each formerly informing a distinct, single-celled body) or to inform matter previously uninformed by any soul(s) at all, as Ford's

---

[29] Likewise Ford, 'Reply to Michael Coughlan', p. 344.

account suggests; rather, in the traditional theory, *one* higher soul replaced *one* lower soul in *one* organism.

This suggests a further difficulty in Ford's hylomorphism. For Aquinas the development of the embryo towards that stage at which it could fittingly receive a rational soul was directed by a series of *single* non-rational souls, with one present from conception and each replaced by another single soul. By denying that there is any such principle of unity Ford is at a loss to explain the coordinated development of the embryo. Instead he claims that 'a determinate, actual human individual gradually emerges and develops from what is potentially human and indeterminate in relation to its ultimate fate' [162]. Ford never gives a metaphysical (as opposed to a biological) account of why this occurs. In classical hylomorphism there can be no gradual emergence of unity (with things part-unity and part-multiplicity), or of humanity (with things part-human, part-animal). Either a substance is a unity or not, a human being or not. The soul is the *cause* of the organization of the being, not the after-effect as Ford's account suggests [130].[30] The reader is left with the impression that for Ford the *soul* is a spiritual component peculiar to human beings and infused *subsequent* to the production of a coherent human body. This is a thoroughly Cartesian view, quite alien to the Aristotelian-Thomistic account he claims to follow. While the appeal to Aristotle and Aquinas may attract some traditionalist readers while mystifying others, Ford's position is ultimately irreconcilable not only with the scientific data but also with the classical metaphysic that he claims to follow.

Problems with 'philosophical induction'

Despite the accumulation of merely indicative biological data and the justly tentative nature of his argument, generally couched in terms of 'seems' and 'suggests', Ford comes to a strong conclusion: the human individual clearly begins after implantation, and persuasive philosophical arguments, based on scientific evidence, show that there could not be an individual before that stage; indeed to speak of an individual would be 'extremely difficult to maintain', 'pointless', 'quite unreal' and 'impossible to say with any plausibility' [xvi–xviii, 3, 52, 122, 128, 130–5, 156, 159, 161, 168, 171–3]. The problem with this is that a multiplication of 'ifs' can never

---

[30] Likewise Ford, 'Ethics, science and embryos', p. 46: 'once the human individual is formed a human person is constituted by the creative power of God with a rational nature'.

produce such a strong and confident 'must'. The certainty with which Ford presents his conclusion is not supported by his argument.

Notwithstanding Ford's stated opposition to lethal or otherwise disrespectful procedures involving the early embryo and his support for Catholic teaching in this area [xii, 62, 97–9], his 'certain' conclusion directly contradicts the magisterial teaching that the presence of the human soul in the embryo is sufficiently credible and probable for prudence to require that it be treated as a person.[31] An opinion cannot be probable and impossible at the same time. Realizing that he was implicitly accusing the Church of incoherence, Ford later retracted his 'certainty' about this matter.[32] But by then the book had already been much cited by the embryo industry and politicians throughout the English-speaking world in lobbying for permissive laws and grants and the echoes continue in comments such as Nancy Pelosi's.

Common sense?

Ford has repeated recourse to 'what children know', 'common-sense realism', 'ordinary experience', 'universal agreement' and what we 'spontaneously recognize' to resolve philosophical problems [e.g. 19, 65–6, 72–3, 76–7, 82, 122–3]. This part-empirical, part-intuitive source seems to form the bridge between science and metaphysics in his theory.

We can readily identify a child and a dog. Our attitudes towards them differ because we recognize that the child is a personal being that is superior to the dog in nature and dignity ... Children know ... that both an arm and a leg

---

[31] Because Ford and his followers have cast doubt on the magisterial teaching that there is probably, credibly or even certainly a rational (human) being present from conception, I have extracted examples of those teachings in Chapter 5. In addition to these texts there are very many speeches by John Paul II and Benedict XVI and documents from various Bishops' Conferences and individual bishops about the unconditional respect owed to the human embryo from the moment of conception. Since the publication of Ford's book John Paul II's *Evangelium Vitae* (1995) and CDF, *On Certain Bioethical Questions* (2008) have suggested increasing certainty on the part of the Catholic Church that a human soul, individual or person is present from fertilization. The Pontifical Academy for Life, *On the Production and Use of Human Embryonic Stem Cells* (2000), held that it is immoral to produce and/or use living human embryos for the preparation of ES cells because: '1. On the basis of a complete biological analysis, the living human embryo is "from the moment of the union of the gametes" a human subject with a well-defined identity, which from that point begins its own coordinated, continuous and gradual development, such that at no later stage can it be considered as a simple mass of cells. 2. From this it follows that as a "human individual" it has the right to its own life; and therefore every intervention which is not in favour of the embryo is an act which violates that right ... 3. Therefore, the ablation of the inner cell mass (ICM) of the blastocyst, which critically and irremediably damages the human embryo, curtailing its development, is a gravely immoral act.'

[32] Ford, 'Reply to Michael Coughlan', p. 342, and 'Ethics, science and embryos', pp. 353 and 584.

are equally parts of the one developing individual being ... People all over the world, young and old, are able to refer successfully to human individuals ... Humans can easily be distinguished from horses, dogs and other animals ... The average citizen, no less than the philosopher, can recognize and identify a live human individual, a human person. Any acceptable philosophical definition of a human person must accord with the common-sense understanding of ordinary people. [3, 19, 66]

I sympathize with Ford's Strawsonian goal of using language and reasoning intelligible to non-philosophers but 'common sense' and 'common usage' have their limits. At the edges of our understanding, at the beginning and the end of life, these authorities are at their most strained and ambiguous.

It is simply not the case that every ordinary person can identify a human individual, as it were, from fifty paces. History is replete with controversies over how we should regard indigenous, black, Jewish and gypsy people and other supposed *Untermenschen* (subhumans). Much of the stuff of modern ethics is about how to regard embryos, the unborn, the severely disabled, the persistently comatose, some animals and even sophisticated artificial intelligences. The 'common sense of ordinary people' has yielded all sorts of regrettable conclusions in the past and may do so in the future. That is, in part, why we bother with philosophical clarification of concepts and terms. 'Common usage' is also unreliable in such matters. Despite the legal, political and socio-educational significance of titles such as 'embryo', 'human being' and 'person', linguistics alone cannot clarify these issues for us and we may need to revise our language. We might agree with Ford that Peter Singer's refusal to admit some human beings to the category of *persons* is wrong, but pleading that this does not accord with ordinary linguistic usage or wishfully declaring that 'nobody' holds this position is not a sufficient reply.[33]

A few more examples of Ford's characteristic but inconclusive 'common-sense' approach must here suffice:

[33] In response to those who require self-conscious rational acts for personhood, Ford says that this 'does not accord with the common understanding of person employed in ordinary linguistic usage' and that we spontaneously recognize that it is false [72, 76–7]. 'The sound judgment of people the world over recognizes that new-born babies are human persons', 'we almost unanimously recognize an infant and a foetus several months prior to birth as human beings', 'there is universal agreement that a human child is an actual human individual', 'nobody questions the humanity of a Down's syndrome foetus or child' or one with spina bifida or anencephaly and 'nobody doubts the personal and moral status of the adult' [77, 82, 122–3]. This consensus is wishful thinking on Ford's part.

- Ford asks which organism after twinning is the original (parent) zygote and which the new (offspring) zygote and answers with the assertion that 'logic and common sense' favour saying two new human individuals begin and that there is no continuing *parent* organism. Were one twin the *offspring* of the other 'these would be the grandchildren of their unsuspecting mother and father!' – apart from the exclamation mark, presumably indicating how surprising this result is, no real argument is offered against it.[34]
- Ford then judges the two-from-one view of twinning as 'paradoxical', 'unappealing', 'implausible' and 'unrealistic' – his only argument would seem to be that there is no dying observable with regard to the original organism and no corpse is left behind.
- Ford supports his claim that a human individual cannot be divided to form another one with the observation that 'our constant experience shows that cutting a human individual in two simply kills that individual' – but our 'experience' of asexual reproduction may simply be limited.
- Ford asserts that the placenta 'has always been regarded as extraembryonic tissue' and never offered respect, grief or funeral – but we do not hold funerals for a child's lost tooth and this does not mean we do not regard the child as a person. Parts of human beings are not normally given the respect due to the whole.
- Ford suggests that 'the persons most concerned in human reproduction', pregnant women, offer valuable support for delayed ensoulment because they first miss a menstrual period and so have the first hint of pregnancy about two weeks after fertilization – but too much reliance on this would mean that the embryos of women with irregular periods would be hominized earlier or later than other women's embryos [xvi, 120, 136, 157, 173, 176–7].

From the anomalies that emerge from these few examples, we can see the basic flaw in Ford's use of this methodology. We rely upon philosophy to resolve paradoxes, challenge prejudices, clarify our concepts and help interpret experience rather than merely confirm common misconceptions. Common sense and common usage fail to provide the much-needed bridge between Ford's biological data and his metaphysics.

[34] G. Grisez, 'When do people begin?', *Proc Am Phil Assoc* 63 (1989), 27–47, observes: 'It does offend common sense to say that a couple's identical twins are really their grandchildren. But common sense simply cannot be trusted when the subject matter is unfamiliar. Moreover, the twins are not grandchildren in the familiar sense, but descendents mediated in an unfamiliar way.'

INDIVIDUALITY CRITERIA

When Did I Begin? sets out 'to establish the necessary and sufficient criteria for determining when a human person or human individual begins' [12]. It is, as we have noticed, really a study of how we know when/if there is one, rather than several, beings present in a cluster of human embryonic cells. The constant refrain is 'ontological individuality'. Though we are assured that there is universal agreement about them [122] Ford never clearly specifies the criteria upon which this ontological individuality is to be assessed and why they are appropriate. Instead various yardsticks are used, implicitly or explicitly, in different parts of the book. These include untwinnability, unchimaerability, species membership and genetic uniqueness, spatial oneness, spatio-temporal continuity, differentiation of parts and organization and direction. If instead of these seven individuality criteria we adopted others we would get very different answers. If, for example, we were to use 'ability to reproduce itself' as an individuality criterion, as many theorists do,[35] the capacity of a twinning embryo to reproduce itself would make it more clearly an individual than a new-born infant. Ford's criteria are treated here at some length because I believe they are the crux of the argument.

Untwinnability

The ability of the early embryo to split into identical twins – twinnability – is the most crucial evidence Ford brings forward for its non-individuality. He asserts, first, that in twinning one zygote ceases to be and gives rise to two new ones; second, that this can occur at any stage in the first two weeks but no later; and third, that all embryos have this potential. From these assertions he concludes that the embryo *cannot be an individual.*

The same zygote would also have the natural active potential to develop into two human individuals by the same criteria. We could legitimately ask whether the zygote itself would be one or two human individuals. It would seem absurd to suggest that at the same time it could both be one and more than one human individual, granted that each must be a distinct ontological individual ... It would have to be both one, and more than one, human individual at the same time. [120–2; cf. xvi, 122–5, 135–6.]

---

[35] For example, R. J. Connell, *Substance and Modern Science* (Houston: Center for Thomistic Studies, 1988), ch. 13.

Ford's central argument fails on several grounds. He is right to say that 'it would seem absurd' to say that a thing is both one and more than one individual *at the same time* (and in the same respect) – but no one actually says this. Those who claim that the embryo is an individual argue that it is one individual until twinning, after which there are two individuals: at no stage, on this account, is there 'both one and more than one human individual' at the same time. To Ford's question 'how could a zygote be one distinct human individual whilst it still had the capacity to become more than one distinct individual?' we might answer: 'like any asexually reproducing creature, the twinnable embryo is one individual with a potential to *become* two'. Such asexual reproduction can be described as the original organism ceasing to exist and leaving no corpse or continuing to exist and giving rise to an identical offspring. Ford finds (this type of) asexual reproduction 'paradoxical', 'implausible' and 'unappealing', but it is no less real for that.

What is more, the very meaning of 'a capacity for one thing to become two' is that there is just one thing before the division and two afterwards. A piece of string has the capacity to become two but until cut it is really one piece of string. If things were otherwise, counting 'one' or 'two' would be impossible. Many organisms reproduce asexually, some reproducing both sexually and asexually.[36] If untwinnability is not a criterion of individuality for other objects or other living species, why should it be for human beings?

If cloning of human adults is achieved, will anyone claim that any adult with the potential to be cloned is not an individual? Ford ultimately demands of the embryo a standard of individuality than no adult human could satisfy. Wennberg suggests a useful thought experiment:

Imagine that we lived in a world in which a certain small percentage of teenagers replicated themselves by some mysterious natural means, splitting in two upon reaching their sixteenth birthday. We would not in the least be inclined to conclude that no human being could therefore be considered a person prior to

---

[36] Many plants, for instance, replicate both by fertilization (seeds or spoors) and by cloning (e.g. bulbs from daffodils, cuttings from roses, laboratory cloning of orchids). Likewise among the animals: many single-celled organisms (such as the amoebae, flatworm-like comb jellies, sea anemones, corals, jellyfish and box jellies) reproduce in both ways. Among the social insects, including wasps, bees, termites and ants and some parasites, up to 3,000 asexually produced twins may develop from a single sexually produced embryo. Sexually conceived nine-banded or long-nosed armadillo embryos normally split asexually to form four identical twins. While human embryos are obviously very different from these plant and animal species, these examples do demonstrate that the same species can reproduce sexually and asexually.

becoming sixteen years of age; nor would we conclude that life could be taken with greater impunity prior to replication than afterward.[37]

When the twinning argument was first raised in the late 1960s and early 1970s, Humber argued that while it may well be true that we cannot know how many lives are present at conception, we do have good reason for believing that *at least one* human life has begun.[38] Four decades later, and despite Ford's handling of complex new embryological evidence, we must draw the same conclusion.

Unchimaerability

Ford suggests another criterion for individuality: unchimaerability. He argues that 'experiments with mice show how single cells taken from three separate early mouse embryos can be aggregated to form a single viable chimaeric mouse embryo. In this case the resultant individual mouse certainly did not begin at the zygote stage' [xvii; cf. 139–46, 159–63]. The developmental potential of fertilized eutherian mammalian eggs is 'far too indeterminate and unrestricted' for ontological individuality [145].

As we have seen above, such a criterion could deny individuality to any organism that receives cells from another organism by way of transplant or transfusion. Embryos and foetuses would be disqualified well after the two- to three-week mark because the most common form of chimaera in humans is the 'blood chimaera' where blood cells from one foetal twin colonize another.[39] In the next chapter we will notice the thousands of current trials and proposals for deliberately manufacturing chimaeras by introducing genetically foreign stem cells into patients. No one seems to think that the capacity to receive such cells is proof that the patient is not an individual.

We have seen that in twinning it is unclear whether one *parent* embryo spawns a single *offspring* embryo or one embryo ceases to exist in creating two *offspring* embryos. Similarly in chimaeras it is sometimes unclear whether one embryo remains as the surviving 'recipient' of material from the donor(s), which may themselves cease to exist in the process, or

[37] R. N. Wennberg, *Life in the Balance: Exploring the Abortion Controversy* (Grand Rapids, MI: Eerdmans, 1985), p. 71. Another thought experiment, proposed by Nicholas Tonti-Filippini, 'A critical note', *LQ* 56 (1989), 36–50 at 43, is that of creating an exact replica of every cell in a human body by means of a super-computer that is able to scan every cell and then to replicate that body from raw materials.
[38] J. M. Humber, 'The case against abortion', *The Thomist* 39 (1975), 65–84 at 69.
[39] F. P. Filice, 'Twinning and recombination: a review of the data', *LQ* 48(6) (February 1981), 40–51.

whether all contributing embryos cease to exist in the creation of a new embryo. Once again, there may be no empirical way of deciding; however, neither case is inconsistent with the ontological individuality of the donor(s), the recipient(s) or any newly conceived hybrid embryos.

Species membership and genetic uniqueness

Ford admits that he formerly taught that it was sufficient evidence of ontological individuality that the zygote's 'genetic individuality and uniqueness remain unchanged during normal development' [xi]. Now he argues that this is not the case, because some human beings are not genetically unique (monozygotic twins) and some genetically human organisms are not human beings, such as live human organs separated from their host bodies, gametes, tumours and hydatid moles (a gestational trophoblastic disease that produces an anomalous growth in the uterus that apes a pregnancy).

Having established that biological humanity is too weak a requirement to confirm that an entity is a human person and that genetic uniqueness is too strong a requirement, one might be tempted to join Singer, who holds that personhood has no necessary connection to membership of the species *homo sapiens*. But Ford continues to maintain that personhood does require such human genetic membership [122]. Furthermore, the genome mediates much of the internal organization that ensures that the embryo normally develops towards human adulthood, unless untoward events occur. This characteristic is not found in the gametes, which, if left to themselves, inevitably die. Within the genome there is, as it were, 'a frozen memory, a clearly defined design-project, with the essential and permanent *information* for the gradual and autonomous realization of such a project'.[40] This is not to deny that the other constituents of the embryo apart from the genome are also important for the direction of its development as a human being and as *this particular human being*.

Ford himself resorts to a genetic definition of individuality when he argues that the possibility of animal embryos combining to form chimaeras, with parts derived from more than one genetic source, disproves the individuality of the early embryo [144–5, 159–63]. He says any attempt to argue otherwise 'lacks a sense of realism and appears to be a desperate

---

[40] Centre for Bioethics of the Catholic University of the Sacred Heart, Milan and Rome, 'Identity and status of the human embryo', 22 June 1989, www.priestsforlife.org/magisterium/centrodibioetica.htm (accessed 1 January 2011).

attempt to prop up the assumption that the zygote is already an on-going ontological individual of the species concerned'. However, many people, we now know, have cells or tissues derived from a genetic source other than their own. Chimaeras are no more problematical than transplants and transfusions (where organs or blood derived from a genetically different source are incorporated into an organism) or nutrition (where the whole or part of even a living organism is taken into the substance and reinformed by 'the soul' of the recipient). To require unchimaerability and genetic uniqueness for ontological individuality would exclude many people whose humanity is undisputed.

Spatial oneness

One significant 'common-sense' criterion for individuality is spatial oneness (unicity and unity). This requires that the being be spatially distinct from other things and not itself split into several parts separated by other things or by space: 'undivided in itself and distinct from others', 'one whole being … spread out in space', 'discrete quantities of matter' [87–8, 122, 125, 161]. This standard is in fact somewhat problematic: micro-investigations reveal large spaces between cells, molecules and atoms within organisms; and organisms can maintain their coherence despite including alien organic or inorganic matter, which acts as a partial dividing wall within the organism. Nonetheless, a nuanced version of this criterion can be helpful as one of a cluster of individuality criteria.[41]

The embryo is in fact a (relatively) continuous unity at all stages of its development. The cells touch and adhere to each other; until 'hatching', the zona pellucida surrounds and helps to hold the cells together. Apart from twinning they do not behave independently in the sense of wandering off, grouping and regrouping. Thus embryologists regard the embryo as a single multi-cellular organism, not a colony of unicellular organisms. Ford, however, judges this spatial unity as insufficient: human adults can live in close proximity without being regarded as one individual and these embryos can in fact split into twins or perhaps amalgamate to form chimaeras. If, however, spatio-temporal contiguity is not a test, how can we distinguish two embryonic twins, as Ford does? We can count them only

---

[41] P. Simons, *Parts: A Study in Ontology* (Oxford University Press, 1987), p. 326, suggests that there are *degrees* of integrity or wholeness. Thus New Zealand is one even though composed of several discontinuous land masses, and the one chess game might be interrupted at several intervals and so forth. For this reason Aristotle said that a rigid body is more truly one than a jointed body (*Metaphysics*, D6).

because they are each spatially continuous in themselves and spatially discontiguous as between themselves.

Hylomorphism explains this in terms of distinct souls informing different matter. To quote Ford himself: 'one twin is really distinct from the other: the matter of one is not that of the other'; 'they would be separate existent individuals even if in all other respects they were identical' [74 and 90]. This also answers Ford's concern about 'identical indiscernibles' [122]: the two twins are composed of different matter and spatially distinct; they might be hard to tell apart but they are *not* truly identical in a philosophical sense: a thing is only identical with itself. (As it turns out, they are not truly identical in a genetic sense, either.) Spatial unity points to individuality from conception.

Spatio-temporal continuity

Ford argues that 'the evidence does not seem to support the required continuity of ontological identity from zygote to early embryo, and much less from zygote to foetus, infant, child and adult' and that there can be no human individual until there is 'an on-going distinct embryonic body' [xvii]. By 'continuity' and 'on-going' Ford would seem to mean *spatio-temporal continuity with an adult*, since he regards as decisive two supposed spatio-temporal discontinuities: first, that many of the embryonic cells never form part of the 'embryo proper' and, second, that in twinning one body becomes two so that neither body can trace its existence back prior to twinning [121–5].

The failure of the placenta (and thus those embryonic cells destined to be part of it) to be part of the infant once born does not preclude their spatio-temporal continuity with the infant up to that point: like milk teeth, they are simply discarded when they are of no further use. In fact all our cells and the molecules that make them up may be replaced during our lifetime without affecting our spatio-temporal identity.[42]

The supposed discontinuity in twinning provides no argument against the individuality of the overwhelming majority of embryos, which do not twin. The vast majority of people *can* trace their spatio-temporal chain of being back to conception: only before conception are there two other individual entities (the gametes). What account do we give for the few

---

[42] Cf. D. Passell, 'Individuation', *Phil Research Arch* 14 (1989), 395–404; P. Strawson, *Individuals: An Essay in Descriptive Metaphysics* (London: Methuen, 1989). Ford himself allows for this in observing that one's identity remains unchanged despite weight fluctuations, loss of limbs, transplants and so on [93].

monozygotic twins? On the assumption that in twinning *one parent embryo gives rise to one child*, half of these identical twins would (like all non-identical twins) still trace their spatio-temporal being back to fertilization; however, every second identical twin would trace spatio-temporal being back only to the point of twinning, just as any future human beings manufactured by cloning will trace their origins to the point of parthenogenesis or renucleation. On the assumption that in twinning *one parent embryo gives rise to two offspring* and itself ceases to exist, all these twins would trace their spatio-temporal identity back to the moment of twinning, the parent embryo, after its short life as a distinct individual human being, ceasing to exist in the process of twinning and so not being spatio-temporally continuous with a foetus or adult. In this regard, it is like any early embryo that dies. As I have suggested above, there seems to be no way of deciding which of these two accounts is to be preferred but neither of them denies the spatio-temporal continuity and thus the individuality of the embryo at every point.

Ford's suggestion that there is some sort of genetic 'clock' mechanism that is 'set from the time of fertilization' and which controls the number of cell divisions is further evidence of spatio-temporal continuity, for if the embryo is only 'a cluster of a few thousand cells' of various ages, none of which has survived cleavage, then there is nothing that has existed since fertilization to carry this 'clock'. As Italy's premier bioethics institute notes:

From the formation of the zygote onwards, there is a succession of molecular and cellular activity, which is guided by the information contained in the genome and which is controlled by signals which come from interactions which continuously multiply at every level, in the embryo itself and between it and its environment. The rigorously coordinated expression of thousands of structural genes, which involves and which gives the organism developing in time and space its close unity, comes from this guide and from this control.[43]

Differentiation of parts

Ford includes among his criteria of human individuality that the organism be 'multicellular ... differentiated and determinate in relation to the organization and integrated articulation of its essential parts' [122]. The stipulation that an individual be multi-cellular excludes the single-celled

---

[43] Centre for Bioethics of the Catholic University of the Sacred Heart, 'Identity and status'; cf. T. Iglesias, 'In vitro fertilization: the major issues', *J Med Ethics* 1 (1984), 32–7.

zygote but only by an ad hoc definition. In support of his contention that
the later embryo is still not an individual, Ford argues that 'the developing cells have not yet differentiated sufficiently to determine which cells
will form the extraembryonic membranes (e.g. placenta) and those which
will form the inner cell mass, from which will develop the embryo proper
and foetus' [xvii; cf. 123–4, 148–9, 156, 161–3 and 172–4]. Until it is determined definitively which cells will develop and grow into 'the definitive
embryo proper' and the foetus and adult, there can be no individual present. The problem with this argument, however, is that it is built on the
false biological assumption that the extra-embryonic membranes are not
organs of the organism. Furthermore, it is well known that no foetal cells
survive through to adulthood, as all cells divide or are replaced over time.
If there can be no individual present until it is determined which cells
will constitute 'the definitive adult proper', then there can be no individual until there is an adult.

In fact the regularities of the shapes, the relationships between various
constituents of the cells and between the cells, and the stages of development indicate that in the embryo we have *from the beginning* a high
degree of differentiation and coordination of parts.[44] The *totipotency* of
early cells – their ability to divide and produce all the differentiated cells
in an organism, including the 'embryo proper' and its 'extraembryonic'
membranes – only indicates a weak potentiality because it cannot be fulfilled unless something unusual happens to the cell. As Tom Daly argued,
in 99.5 per cent of cases the cells develop normally, each limited by and
coordinated with the others, in the 'very specialized and urgent task: to
synthesize enough DNA and membrane material to cater for some thousands of cells, and to keep on being subdivided until the much smaller
size of an ordinary somatic cell is reached'.[45] Furthermore, well before
Ford's two to three week mark, the cells have differentiated into inner
and outer cell masses and lost their totipotency.

Organization and direction

Another criterion of individuality that we find in *When Did I Begin?* is
that the candidate must be 'determinate in relation to the organization
and integrated articulation of its essential parts, all of whose activities

[44] Pearson, 'Developmental biology'.
[45] T. Daly, 'When do people begin?', in K. Andrews and M. Stainsby (eds.), *Collaborating in Health Care: Proceedings of the 1989 Annual Conference on Bioethics* (Melbourne: St Vincent's Bioethics Centre, 1990), 4.1.

and functions are directed from within for the benefit, well-being, self-development and self-maintenance of the whole individual being'. At one point Ford defines an individual as follows:

An ontological individual is a distinct being that is not an aggregate of smaller things nor merely a part of a greater whole … There is only one human individual that really exists in the primary sense of actual existence, though there are many cells that share in the existence of that single living ontological individual. [xv–xvi; cf. 72 and 212]

A leading embryo experimenter persuaded Ford that in the IVF embryo 'each cell behaves as if it is significantly independent of the other cells' and that at most the cells are only 'loosely organized' [xi–xii, 13, 73, 93, 122–3; cf. 72, 93–4, 125, 148–9 and 175]. The question is: how loose is *loose* and how *independent* is 'significantly independent'?[46]

Everything in the material order is 'an aggregate of smaller things' (of organs, cells, molecules, atoms, sub-atomic particles and so on) and everything is also 'part of a greater whole' (of the body, family, nation, human race, cosmos and so on). At issue is how we judge whether there 'is only *one* human individual that really exists in the primary sense' despite being in other senses an aggregate of smaller parts and part of a greater whole? Ford does offer a test: once we can establish 'the primordium of at least one organ formed for the benefit of the whole organism' we have a sufficient condition for the existence of a human individual [88 and 170]. However, as we have seen, the embryo does have organs, unless we use an unusual definition of organ that excludes the zona and placenta.

Some light can be cast on these questions by 'organismic', 'organization' or 'systems' analysis of life.[47] According to this approach, a living organism is not just an accidental aggregate of cooperating parts but a self-directing, self-constructing, self-maintaining, self-repairing and self-reproducing entity with a real internal unity of organization; it is interdependently related to its environment in fulfilling these capacities.[48] The

---

[46] Simons, *Parts*, pp. 326–31, also suggests that there can be varieties of organizational integrity or wholeness, so that a system can be more loosely structured in some respects than in others.

[47] In his classic *Chance and Necessity* (New York: Harcourt, Brace & World, 1961) Jacques Monod identified teleonomy, autonomous morphogenesis and reproductive invariance as three characteristics of a living being.

[48] Thus when Ford requires of an ontological human individual that it have 'the natural active potential' or 'active capacity' to develop towards adulthood, and that all its parts, structures, organization and activities be 'purposive, goal-directed or teleological' and 'subordinated to serve its common interests and goals of life, directed by its species-specific instructions encoded in its programme of life' [81–96, 119–20, 125–6], he could be said to be describing the tendency or teleology or inbuilt plan, programme or memory of that particular 'living system'. While I am attracted by this approach, it is not without difficulties: for instance, all organisms to varying

zygote, blastocyst and embryo all qualify according to these criteria, as Ford occasionally admits. 'There are signs of finalism or purpose and directedness apparent in the way intercellular communications influence the specific morphogenesis of each species in the same typical way. Developmental activities are goal-directed' [149; cf. 103, 108, 123 and 157]. It is precisely this self-direction that persuades most embryologists and philosophers that the embryo is a single organism, yet Ford persists in claiming that each cell of the embryo 'goes it alone' as it were, developing for its own benefit (self-maintenance and so forth) and not as part of an organized whole.

Decades earlier, Paul Ramsey had pointed out that cells are from the beginning, in some sense 'doing their own thing' but they are doing it *together*.[49] Each cell does *not* set about building its own placenta. The 'group' of cells acts throughout in the interests of the group not the individual cell, with each cell interacting and 'communicating' in various ways with the others. The whole embryo dynamically balances its parts, being programmed by what Ford calls a 'genetic clock', set in its DNA from the time of fertilization,[50] so as to develop synchronically and grow in a coordinated way. Internal and external disturbances – even as drastic as cell removal in biopsy – do not break this chain of development. The embryo regenerates and perdures despite a constantly changing structure and environment. These 'purposive, goal-directed or teleological' characteristics of the embryo suggest organizational integrity sufficient for an individual life according to an organization–teleology criterion.

The organizational integrity that we find in the embryo accords well with the view that there is a single human *soul* present from conception. As Fienus, the seventeenth-century Aristotelian who led the movement in biology away from delayed hominization, argued: 'the soul is the principle which organizes the body from within, arranging an organ for each of its faculties and preparing its own residence, not merely consenting to be breathed into a physical being which has already organized itself' [47]. A more recent Aristotelian argued as follows:

---

degrees require 'inputs' and relate interdependently with their environments, so that their *self*-direction and *self*-maintenance need contextualizing.

[49] P. Ramsey, *Life or Death: Ethics and Options* (Seattle: Washington University Press, 1968), p. 196.

[50] Ford claims that their clock mechanisms are not synchronized until the primitive streak stage [175], but he never explains how they 'become synchronized and triggered' given that they are for him distinct organisms.

If we understand [the human soul] as that element of the human being which establishes it in its being as human, differentiating us from the lower forms of life, account must also be taken of it in our becoming. The development of the human being, from conception to full maturity, is a purposive one, which cannot be ultimately explained as a series of biochemical processes, any more than the fully formed human being ... In any purposeful development towards an end, the end is somehow present in the beginning, shaping the development towards the end.[51]

This approach seems to be in the background of the Church's declarations on abortion and artificial reproduction and its increasing insistence on respecting the embryo as a human person from fertilization. Ford's argument (against Singer and others) about the organizational tendency of the infant applies equally well to the embryo:

The growth and development of an infant is the growth and development of a human being to maturity, not growth and development into a human being. The developing infant gradually realizes its natural potential to express more fully what it already is. It does not grow into something else ... No animal has a human nature nor is any endowed with a human being's specific natural capacities. [77–8]

Ford accuses some of his opponents of 'surreptitiously, albeit unwittingly' advancing dualism – the idea that body and soul are really two different substances united in some (uneasy) way [130]. On the basis of what has been argued in this chapter it would seem that Ford's notion of human souls indiscernibly popping into existing animal colonies to unite and hominize them is far more dualistic than the view that the human soul is the principle of the continuous development of the human organism from fertilization towards human adulthood.[52]

---

[51] W. Daniel, 'Towards a theology of procreation: an examination of the Vatican instruction *Donum vitae*', *Pacifica* 3 (1990), 61–86. Likewise Tonti-Filippini, 'A critical note', p. 47: 'The embryo is so organized as to be developing toward human adulthood and must therefore have whatever it is in the way of form to have that organization, dynamism and integration within the first cell such that a human adult can result without any further addition of anything other than the nourishment which it assimilates into itself.'

[52] Daly, 'When do people begin?', and Tonti-Filippini, 'A critical note', characterized as 'magic' the 'transformation' that Ford claims occurs at this point. Good analyses of the dualism implicit in delayed hominization theories are: R. George and C. Tollefsen, 'Dualism and persons', in *Embryo: A Defense of Human Life* (New York: Doubleday, 2008), pp. 57–82; L. Kass, 'Thinking about the body', in *Toward a More Natural Science: Biology and Human Affairs* (New York: Free Press, 1985), pp. 276–98; P. Lee and R. George, *Body–Self Dualism in Contemporary Ethics and Politics* (Cambridge University Press, 2007); Gilbert Meilaender, *Body, Soul, and Bioethics* (Notre Dame University Press, 1995); P. O'Mahony, *A Question of Life: Its Beginning and Transmission* (London: Sheed and Ward, 1990), pp. 22–33; E. Olson, *The Human Animal: Personal Identity without Psychology* (Oxford University Press, 1997).

CONCLUSION

Ford charges that the traditional view 'uncritically assumes that the human person is present from fertilization' and 'ignores or selects the facts to suit a preferred philosophical theory' [130]. He, on the other hand, follows *the facts* wherever they lead him, offering the fullest and most influential argument to date for the claim that there is no human individual present until two or three weeks after fertilization. In defence of this thesis, Ford raises some important questions and collects together some important biological and historical data – even if his data need careful scrutiny and updating.

Ford's analysis clearly demonstrates that any surviving mythology of the *homunculus* – a very small but fully formed human being 'inside' the embryo – should be purged. He also convincingly refutes some common assertions in this debate, such as the restriction of personhood to the viable, those with sufficient brain matter or those who are actively reflective and also the inference from the 'natural wastage' of embryos to arguments about the status of the embryo. This chapter has shown, however, that he fails to prove his central thesis. Of course other arguments against human personhood from conception have been or might be adduced.[53] Nonetheless, after a close examination of all the history, philosophy and embryology that Ford offers, 'the commonly held view' that the human individual begins at fertilization stands unshaken.

[53] Excellent treatments of these issues include: E. Furton (ed.), *What Is Man, O Lord? Proceedings of the 18th Bishops' Workshop* (Boston: NCBC, 2002); George and Tollefsen, *Embryo*.

CHAPTER 5

Stem cells: what's all the fuss about?

SCIENTIFIC POTENTIAL AND CONCERNS ABOUT STEM CELLS

Whose stem cells?

Removing restrictions on federal funding of embryonic stem cell research was a priority for the Obama administration. This was a major policy shift, hailed as evidence of the President's commitment to science and progress. Why the fuss about these tiny human cells? Because stem cells are said to be the 'holy grail' of regenerative medicine. Ordinary cells are of specific types, such as nerves, skin, heart muscle or other kinds, and can make only more of the same ('unipotency'). Stem cells, by contrast, are relatively undifferentiated, having the prolonged capacity to multiply and, depending upon circumstances, to differentiate into various cell-types as needed ('pluripotency'). Thus stem cells can regenerate damaged tissues: their therapeutic potential is enormous.

There are six potential sources for these stem cells currently 'on the table':[1] human tissues where stem cells naturally occur; the placenta; other cells which can be reprogrammed to behave as stem cells; pseudo-human organisms; animal–human hybrids; and, finally, human embryos. I consider each in turn. The first is the natural source, used by the body itself since time began and by medicine for the past few decades. These are

---

In the scientific references in this chapter I have named only the first researcher in the team: *et al.* should generally be presumed.

[1] President's Council on Bioethics, *Alternative Sources of Human Pluripotent Stem Cells* (Washington, DC, May 2005). Likewise: D. L. Clarke, 'Generalized potential of adult neural stem cells', *Science* 288 (2000), 1660–3; J. C. Howell, 'Pluripotent stem cells identified in multiple murine tissues', *Ann New York Acad Sci* 996 (2003), 158–73; S. L. Preston, 'The new stem cell biology: something for everyone', *Mol Pathol* 56 (2003), 86–96; Southern Cross Bioethics Institute, *Briefing Note on Stem Cells* (Adelaide: SCBI, 2005); S. P. Westphal, 'Ultimate stem cell discovered', *New Scientist*, 23 January 2002. There are also many sources in the articles in *Cell Proliferation* 41 (Suppl. 1) (2008), 85–93.

131

called somatic or adult stem cells, though they can in fact be taken from people of all ages, not merely adults. Stem cells have been found in almost every body tissue, such as skin, muscle, fat, bone marrow, blood, major organs, brain, nerves, ear, nose and mouth. Sometimes these cells can be derived from the intended recipient, avoiding any immune-rejection difficulties. At other times they are taken from donors. In each case these stem cells are derived without harming anyone and are, in the view of the Catholic Church and many others, far preferable ethically to other routes proposed for deriving stem cells.[2]

Bone marrow stem cells have been shown to differentiate into brain neurones, heart muscle, pancreatic and other body tissues. More than 45,000 people now receive adult stem cell transplants each year.[3] They have proved especially effective in treating blood cancers. Adult stem cells have already been shown to be effective in tissue repair after stroke, Parkinson's and other neurological disorders, spinal cord injury, heart damage, other major organ damage or deficiencies, myeloma, lymphoma and other cancers, autoimmune diseases, anaemia and other blood diseases, eye diseases, bone damage and other conditions.[4] Some argue that adult stem cells have almost all the advantages of embryonic stem

[2] Thus the Pontifical Academy for Life: 'The possibility, now confirmed, of using *adult stem cells* to attain the same goals as would be sought with embryonic stem cells – even if many further steps in both areas are necessary before clear and conclusive results are obtained – indicates that adult stem cells represent a more reasonable and human method for making correct and sound progress in this new field of research and in the therapeutic applications which it promises. These applications are undoubtedly a source of great hope for a significant number of suffering people' (*On the Production and Use of Human Embryonic Stem Cells* (2000)). Likewise Pope Benedict XVI: 'Somatic stem-cell research also deserves approval and encouragement when it felicitously combines scientific knowledge, the most advanced technology in the biological field and ethics that postulate respect for the human being at every stage of his or her existence. The prospects opened by this new chapter in research are fascinating in themselves, for they give a glimpse of the possible cure of degenerative tissue diseases that subsequently threaten those affected with disability and death … I would like in particular to urge scientific structures that draw their inspiration and organization from the Catholic Church to increase this type of research and to establish the closest possible contact with one another and with those who seek to relieve human suffering in the proper ways.' *Address to Symposium of the Pontifical Academy for Life on Stem Cells*, 16 September 2006.
[3] K. Syrjala, 'Late effects of hematopoietic cell transplantation among 10-year adult survivors compared with case-matched controls', *J Clinical Oncology* 23 (2005), 6596–606.
[4] Numerous current clinical applications and current clinical trials of adult stem cells are listed by: Richard Burt, 'Clinical applications of blood-derived and marrow-derived stem cells for non-malignant diseases', *JAMA* 299 (2008), 925–36; Gonzalo Miranda (ed.), *The Stem Cell Dilemma: For the Good of All Human Beings?* (Boncourt: Foundation Guilé, 2002); David Prentice, 'Adult stem cell success stories: January–June 2008', *Insight*, 12 January 2009, and his previous research reports at www.frc.org/life – bioethics#stem_cells; Southern Cross Bioethics Institute, *Briefing Note on Stem Cells* (Adelaide: SCBI, 2005); www.i-sis.org.uk/HUASC.php; www.stemcellresearch.org; www.clinicaltrials.gov (all accessed 1 January 2011).

cells but are 'better behaved' and less inclined to chaotic development as tumours. These cells certainly have the best therapeutic record and greatest therapeutic potential, at least in the short and medium term, of all currently available sources of stem cells.

A second source for stem cells is placenta and umbilical cord blood, which are rich in stem cells. In some countries mothers now bank blood and tissue from the afterbirth which could then be used later for transplants. Once again, these cells would be derived non-destructively – from abandoned tissue – and be a perfect immunological-genetic match for the recipient.

Third, some ordinary body cells can be 'reprogrammed' to revert to pluripotency and behave as stem cells do. In November 2007 two teams of researchers – one in Japan, the other in Wisconsin, USA – demonstrated that regular adult skin cells can be reprogrammed in this way.[5] As with adult stem cells, these induced pluripotent stem cells (or 'iPS cells') are obtained non-destructively and can even be taken from the patient, thereby avoiding immune-rejection difficulties. As one commentator recently observed:

Since [2007] several crucial advances have made the technique more efficient, more effective, and safer, and the cells produced by this technique … have so far continued to display all the characteristics attributed to human embryonic stem cells. These techniques not only avoid any ethical concerns … but they offer a far cheaper and easier method of producing genetically matched or selected pluripotent stem cells, which makes them appealing to researchers. As a result this technique has begun to overtake the use of embryos in many stem cell labs. At last count (in the fall of 2008), there were approximately eight hundred laboratories using iPS cells in their work, which has cut sharply into the number of those using human embryos or cells derived from embryos.[6]

[5] B. Carey, 'Reprogramming of murine and human somatic cells using a single polycistronic vector', *Proc Nat Acad Sci* 106 (2008), 157–62; J. T. Henderson, 'Lazarus' gate: challenges and potential of epigenetic reprogramming of somatic cells', *Clinical Pharm Therapeutics* 83 (2008), 889–93; M. Nakagawa, 'Generation of induced pluripotent stem cells without Myc from mouse and human fibroblasts', *Nature Biotechnology* 26 (2008), 101–6; S. Nishikawa, 'The promise of human induced pluripotent stem cells for research and therapy', *Nature Reviews Molecular Cell Biology* 9 (2008), 725–9; K. Okita, 'Generation of germline-competent induced pluripotent stem cells', *Nature* 448(7151) (2007), 313–17; I.-H. Park, 'Reprogramming of human somatic cells to pluripotency with defined factors', *Nature* 451(7175) (2008), 141–6; K. Takahashi, 'Induction of pluripotent stem cells from adult human fibroblasts by defined factors', *Cell* 131 (2007), 1–12, and 'Induction of pluripotent stem cells from mouse embryonic and adult fibroblast cultures by defined factors', *Cell* 126 (2006), 663–76; M. Wernig, 'In vitro reprogramming of fibroblasts into a pluripotent ES-cell-like state', *Nature* 448 (2007), 318–24; S. Yamanaka, 'Induction of pluripotent stem cells from mouse fibroblasts by four transcription factors', *Cell Proliferation* 41 (Suppl. 1) (2008), 51–6, and 'Strategies and new developments in the generation of patient-specific pluripotent stem cells', *Cell Stem Cell* 1 (2007), 39–49.
[6] Y. Levin, 'Biotech: what to expect', *First Things* 191 (March 2009), 17–20.

A fourth, still hypothetical, way of obtaining pluripotent stem cells is to take them from pseudo-human organisms such as parthenotes (eggs that have been induced to divide as if they were embryos) and 'embryoid bodies' produced by altered nuclear transfer from human gametes or other cells with some process of gene deletion that ensures they are not and could not develop into a human embryo ('ANT cells').[7] Though there is considerable dispute about the practicalities and ethics of making such organisms, the advantage of such cells would be that they could be obtained without manufacturing or destroying human embryos.[8]

A fifth possibility is to manufacture human–animal hybrid embryos in order to derive stem cells that are as human as possible ('cybrid stem cells'). Driven largely by the shortage of human oocytes (a cell that develops into a female reproductive cell or ovum), various laboratories have already had some success in the production of such hybrids. This proposal raises new issues regarding the morality of such radical genetic and transgenic manipulation, a matter to which I return. A less controversial suggestion is the genetic modification of animal adult or embryonic cells to make them suitable for xenotransplantation, the process of transplanting organs from one species to another, especially from animals to humans. Apart from the practical problems associated with embryonic stem cells, both possibilities involve the additional risk that transgenic diseases might cross the species barrier between animals and humans.

The sixth and perhaps best-known source for pluripotent stem cells is the human embryo manufactured either by IVF or cloning, hence the name embryonic stem cells ('ES cells').[9] Moral controversy arises from the fact that deriving these cells kills the embryos themselves, a matter to which I also return. The enthusiasm of some laboratories, corporations

[7] H. Aarkes, 'Production of pluripotent stem cells by oocyte-assisted reprogramming: *Joint Statement* with signatories', *NCBQ* 5 (2005), 579–83; M. Condic, 'Alternative sources of pluripotent stem cells: altered nuclear transfer', *Cell Proliferation* 41 (Suppl. 1) (2008), 7–19; W. B. Hurlbut, 'Altered nuclear transfer as a morally acceptable means for the procurement of human embryonic stem cells', in President's Council on Bioethics, *Alternative Sources* and *NCBQ* 5 (2005), 145–51; Subgroup of the President's Council on Bioethics, 'The moral retrieval of ES cells', *Ethics & Medics* 30(7) (2005), 1–2. Parthenogenically derived 'embryoid bodies' have also been proposed: T. A. Breveni and F. Gandolfi, 'Parthenotes as a source of embryonic stem cells', *Cell Proliferation* 41 (Suppl. 1) (2008), 20–30.

[8] See, for example, the several positions outlined by Nicanor Austriaco, E. Christian Brugger, W. M. Byrnes, Robert Colombo, Maureen Condic, Edward Furton, José Granados, Paul Hoehner, William Hurlbut, Daniel McConchie, Lawrence Masek, J. Thomas Petri, David Schindler, Stuart Swetland, Adrian Walker and others in *Communio* and *NCBQ* from 2004 to 2006.

[9] J. A. Thompson, 'Embryonic stem cell lines derived from human blastocysts', *Science* 282 (1998), 1145–7.

and governments for ES cell research is strange given that these cells have still not demonstrated any therapeutic benefit in clinical trials, that there are still no approved treatments using such cells and that there have been few if any successes in animal models. Likewise few people know that ES cells taken from human embryos and any tissues grown from them will probably suffer immune-rejection unless we go down the path of manufacturing designer embryos for each patient. Such embryos would be live cloned twins of the patient, and huge numbers of human oocytes and embryos would be required. It is also not widely known that a high proportion of IVF embryos and almost all cloned embryos have lethal genetic defects, which would be carried by their stem cells and that ES cells are very difficult to control and prone to tumour formation and/ or tissue destruction.[10] The embryonic stem cell panacea is really wishful thinking for some (patients, doctors), deliberate exaggeration for others (researchers, corporations and governments) and plain confusion for most (the media and the general public). So far, at least, it is the stuff of science fiction.[11]

Questions asked

Some researchers are wondering publicly why so much of the limited medical research budget is being pumped into embryonic stem cell research. Dr Peter Rathjen, then head of molecular biosciences at the University of Adelaide, Australia, whose department conducted stem cell research with BresaGen, said: 'It's bloody nonsense that stem cells

[10] R. B. Cervantes, 'Embryonic stem cells and somatic cells differ in mutation frequency and type', *Proc Nat Acad Sci* 99 (2002), 3586–90; M. Condic, 'What we know about embryonic stem cells', *First Things* 169 (January 2007), 25–9; A. Maitra, 'Genomic alterations in cultured human embryonic stem cells', *Nature Genetics* 37 (2005), 1099–103; N. Scolding, 'Stem-cell therapy: hope and hype', *The Lancet* 365 (2005), 9477; J. L. Sherley, 'Human embryonic stem cell research: no way around a scientific bottleneck', *J Biomed Biotech* 2 (2004), 71–2, and 'The importance of valid disclosures in the human embryonic stem cell research debate', *Cell Proliferation* 41 (Suppl. 1) (2008), 57–64.

[11] M. Condic, 'Getting stem cells right', *First Things* 180 (February 2008), 10–12; R. Doerflinger, 'The problem of deception in embryonic stem cell research', *Cell Proliferation* 41 (Suppl. 1) (2008), 65–70; B. Healy, 'Why embryonic stem cells are obsolete', *US News & World Report*, 4 March 2009. Alan Lewis, President of Celgene Corp, observed that 'Many of the technologies we hyped to the general public haven't worked yet … Venture capitalists are very cautious about investing in embryonic stem cell companies because of uncertainty over the field's future.' P. Elias, 'Stem cell conference opens amid hope and trouble', Associated Press, 22 June 2005. When reversing his predecessor's ban on federal funding for embryonic stem cell research, President Obama said 'At this moment, the full promise of stem cell research remains unknown and it should not be overstated … Ultimately, I cannot guarantee that we will find the treatments and cures we seek' (www.nytimes.com/2009/03/09/us/politics/09text-obama.html (accessed 1 January 2011)).

might be able to cure Alzheimer's. We don't even know what causes it.' Neuroscientist Dr Colin Masters of the University of Melbourne agreed that stem cells might eventually have a role in replacing dead cells after traumas such as strokes or spinal injuries, 'but in diseases like Alzheimer's or Parkinson's, it's beyond our imagination'.[12] Johns Hopkins Alzheimer's expert Peter Rabins likewise told the US Senate: 'do not expect embryonic stem cells to play a role in Alzheimer's treatment'.[13] Ian Wilmut, the creator of Dolly the cloned sheep, recently announced that he was giving up on human cloning and ES cell derivation. He explained that he and others had tried this line of research but it had not worked, that he thought human cloning should be banned and that reprogramming adult cells was the way to go.[14] However, others remain hopeful that the ES cell route will be a shortcut to some major advance and the promises of miracle cures continue. The story is yet to be written on why so many researchers, funders, reporters and politicians were so smitten with the embryo industry and how adult stem cell researchers were so effectively silenced while their projects were cash-starved and the glamour money went to the embryo industry and their bioethics PR people.

Even with fabulous grants the embryo industry has its problems. There are too many IVF 'providers' and the market is saturated. Multiple IVF cycles can be administered to infertile couples and even to some sub-fertile and fertile couples; artificial reproductive technologies can be extended to surrogates, singles, same-sex couples, widows, the 'psychologically infertile' and the 'socially infertile', designing 'saviour siblings' with matched tissue to help an existing child, or designing children with hearing, growth or other disabilities which their parents want them to share with the rest of the family. But none of this will raise demand nearly enough to satisfy the industry.

Another problem is the reluctance of women to donate their oocytes (eggs) for assisted reproduction and experimentation programmes – after all, oocyte collection is a considerable burden and a not inconsiderable

---

[12] *Weekend Australian*, 29 June 2002.

[13] US Senate testimony, 11 May 2004. Michael Shelanski, co-director of the Taub Institute for Research on Alzheimer's Disease and the Aging Brain at the Columbia University Medical Center, New York, said: 'I think the chance of doing repairs to Alzheimer's brains by putting in stem cells is small.' Rick Weiss, 'Stem cells an unlikely therapy for Alzheimer's', *Washington Post*, 10 June 2004, A3.

[14] Roger Highfield, 'Dolly creator Prof Ian Wilmut shuns cloning', *Telegraph*, 10 November 2008; 'Dolly scientist abandons cloning', *BBC News*, 17 November 2007. Cf. Condic, 'Getting stem cells right'.

risk.[15] In addition, couples are often disinclined to hand over their 'surplus' embryos. If that situation is to change, a new social obligation must be invented: the duty to give up one's eggs and embryos for others.

A third problem for the embryo industry has been its practice of excessive oocyte collection, zygote production and embryo banking. There are now millions of human embryos in labs around the world, about which there is considerable unease. What are we to do with the 'frozen generation' left in freezers and denied parents or any life beyond the freezer? If it is to keep the embryo market expanding, the industry needs to find new rationales for the manufacture, exploitation and destruction of such embryos, and find them fast.

One recent ploy has been to encourage people to think of human embryos not as human lives but as human leftovers. 'Turn them into therapies', the industry whispers seductively, 'then you needn't feel so bad about the frozen generation.' However, for the reasons I have already suggested, embryonic stem cells are unlikely candidates for transfer to anyone as therapies.

If all this isn't going to yield therapies, what's the real agenda? In the first place, I think it is an example of the so-called salami technique. People are unwilling to concede all of A to Z, but if you slice thinly enough, A, then B, then C, one at a time, eventually you will have the whole salami. Sell people on using just a few *excess* embryos from IVF programmes that would be disposed of anyway, while promising them miracle cures for high-profile individuals. Then it will be much easier down the track to sell them on allowing you to manufacture new, better *designer* embryos to use for cells, tissues and other things you want. Take cloning off the agenda for a while, then introduce it under the title of 'therapeutic cloning' while pretending to be appalled by any suggestion that cloned children would be allowed. Then find a sad case of someone whose only chance of having a genetically related healthy child is by embryo cloning and before you know it, cloning will be fine too. Next introduce animal–human hybrids, again promising responsible limits and endless cures. All along there is really nothing you presently want to do that is excluded or unfunded, but you can make it look as if you are reluctantly submitting to severe constraints … and so it goes.

The really big markets for embryos may well not be in therapies but in gaining research grants, kudos and rewards for embryologists and their

[15] Editorial, 'Proceed with caution', *Nature Biotechnology* 23 (2005), 763–4; F. Shenfield, 'Semantics and ethics of human embryonic stem-cell research', *The Lancet* 365 (2005), 9477.

associates. Large stocks of embryos may also have been used for techni-
cian training, drug testing, toxicology and research on new contrages-
tives and abortifacients. This was expected to yield sufficient new markets
for the near future. But the general public remained queasy, and so was
repeatedly fed scientifically implausible promises of cures for Ronald
Reagan, Christopher Reeve, Michael J. Fox or their successors.[16]

ETHICAL CONCERNS ABOUT EMBRYONIC STEM CELLS

What is a human embryo? Science and philosophy

Were embryonic stem cells the panacea some people say they are, would
there still be a problem with exploiting them? I have already suggested
that there would be because the only way of getting these cells is by killing embryos at the blastocyst stage (around day five). Some people will
say that these embryos are too young or too tiny or too powerless to be
human beings. They *are* very small, having only developed to the stage of
120 cells or so since their manufacture by IVF or, perhaps in the future, by
cloning. They *are* still very young, approximately five to six days old, and
growing in a Petri dish culture, or a few years old if held in 'suspended
animation' in a freezer since their manufacture. Certainly they have not
had a long life: for all their promise at the time they were made in the IVF
laboratory, they have never been given a chance to develop. Nonetheless,
like us, they are human and they are alive – unless we remove some vital
part or otherwise intervene lethally.

Attempts to exclude the early embryo from the community of human
beings – such as those examined in the previous chapter – fail on philosophical grounds, even if they have proved very successful in influencing
public opinion and regulation. What does science say?[17]

---

[16] See J. W. Smith, 'Of stem cells and fairy tales', *Daily Standard*, 10 June 2004; A. Torda, 'Stem-
cell hard sell gets ahead of itself', *Sydney Morning Herald*, 15 October 2004. Defending the
hype, Ronald McKay, a stem cell researcher at the National Institute of Neurological Disorders
and Stroke, Bethesda, MD, said, 'To start with, people need a fairy tale. Maybe that's unfair,
but they need a story line that's relatively simple to understand.' Weiss, 'Stem cells an unlikely
therapy'.

[17] Bruce Alberts *et al.*, *Molecular Biology of the Cell*, 5th edn (New York: Garland, 2008);
D. M. Anderson (ed.), *Mosby's Medical Dictionary*, 8th edn (St. Louis: Mosby, 2009); L. B.
Arey, *Developmental Anatomy*, 7th edn (Philadelphia: Saunders, 1974); M. Brookes and A.
Zietman, *Clinical Embryology* (Florida: CRC, 1998); Bruce Carlson, *Human Embryology and
Developmental Biology*, 2nd edn (St. Louis: Mosby, 1999); R. Colombo, 'The process of fertil-
ization and its stages: from parental gametes to a developing one-cell embryo', in E. Sgreccia
and J. Lafitte (eds.), *The Human Embryo before Implantation* (Libreria Editrice Vaticana, 2007),
pp. 37–127; M. Condic, *When Does Human Life Begin? A Scientific Perspective* (Thornwood, NY:

An egg is programmed to form a new individual organism when activated by a sperm. (Alberts)

Conception: 1. The beginning of pregnancy, usually taken to be the instant that a spermatozoon enters an ovum and forms a viable zygote. 2. The act or process of fertilization. (Anderson)

The formation, maturation and meeting of a male and female sex cell are all preliminary to their actual union into a combined cell, or zygote, which definitely marks the beginning of a new individual. (Arey)

Individual life begins with conception by the union of gametes or sex cells ... Growth and development continue thereafter. (Brookes and Zietman)

We can confidently conclude that a new cell, the zygote, comes into existence at the *moment* of sperm–egg fusion, an event that occurs in less than a second. (Condic)

The beginning of the development of a new individual is the fusion of ... sperm and ovum ... The result of this fusion is the formation of the first cell of the new individual, the zygote. (Hamilton and Mossman)

Almost all higher animals start their lives from a single cell, the fertilized ovum ... The time of fertilization represents the starting point in the life history, or ontogeny, of the individual. (Patten and Carlson)

The precise moment of conception is that at which the male element, or spermatozoon, and the female element, or ovum, fuse together. (Thomson)

Sound philosophy and common sense agree with the biologists here: unlike any other kind of organism, human embryos have the inherent nature, organization, 'soul' as some call it, which means they grow up as human beings do, indeed as embryologists do, and never as kangaroos

Westchester Institute, 2008); W. J. Hamilton and H. W. Mossman, *Human Embryology*, 4th edn (Cambridge: W. Heffer, 1972); Dianne Irving, 'The impact of scientific misinformation on other fields: philosophy, theology, biomedical ethics, public policy', *Accountability in Research* 2(4) (1993), 243–72; K. and D. Irving, *The Human Development Hoax: Time to Tell The Truth!*, 2nd edn (Clinton, MI: Gold Leaf, 1997); C. W. Kischer, 'When does human life begin? The final answer', *LQ* 70(4) (2003), 326–39; W. Larsen *et al.*, *Essentials of Human Embryology* (New York: Churchill Livingstone, 1998); W. Larsen *et al.*, *Human Embryology*, 3rd edn (New York: Churchill Livingstone, 2001), pp. 1–3; K. Moore and T. V. Persaud, *The Developing Human: Clinically Oriented Embryology*, 8th edn (Philadelphia: Saunders/Elsevier, 2008), and *Before We Are Born: Essentials of Embryology and Birth Defects*, 7th edn (Philadelphia: Saunders/Elsevier, 2008); R. O'Rahilly and F. Müller, *Human Embryology and Teratology*, 3rd edn (New York: John Wiley, 2001), p. 20; B. M. Patten and B. M. Carlson, *Foundations of Embryology*, 6th edn (New York: McGraw-Hill, 2002); H. Pearson, 'Developmental biology: your destiny, from day one', *Nature* 418 (4 July 2002), 14–15; A. Serra and R. Colombo, 'Identity and status of the human embryo: the contribution of biology', in Juan Vial Correa and Elio Sgreccia (eds.), *Identity and Status of the Human Embryo* (Libreria Editrice Vaticana, 1998), pp. 128–77; G. Sica, 'The development of the pre-implantation embryo' and 'The embryo-maternal dialogue and preparation for implantation', in Sgreccia and Lafitte (eds.), *Human Embryo before Implantation*, pp. 128–37 and 138–45; L. Sweeney, *Basic Concepts in Embryology* (New York: McGraw-Hill, 1998); R. Yanagimachi, 'Mammalian fertilization', in E. Knobil *et al.* (eds.), *The Physiology of Reproduction* (New York: Raven, 1988).

do or roses do. They are beings continuous with human foetuses, babies, children, adults, senior citizens. They are the opening pages of someone's biography. The only thing that is different about these human beings is that they have been produced in unusual circumstances: some were manufactured for infertile couples in IVF programmes but are no longer wanted; others were produced with dismembering and death in mind from the beginning. If they *are* human beings, then the fact that they are tiny or young or unwanted or have experimental uses is no more relevant to their moral status than that they are black or white, Eastern or Western, male or female, at the beginning of life or soon to die.

Catholic teaching on the embryo

What does the Catholic Church teach on these matters? One thing that should be clear is that the Christianity is not anti-science, as some of the Church's detractors in the embryo industry suggest. In fact hospitals, universities, 'the scientific method' and modern genetic science all arose within the Church. Still today the Catholic Church is the largest provider of healthcare and tertiary education in the world, and this includes many medical research institutes. The Church is pro-science, as it is pro all knowledge and all technologies that genuinely serve human welfare.[18]

One might have thought that Catholic teaching on the status of and respect due the human embryo was well known, but continuing obfuscation in some quarters makes it worth recording the official teaching here. Citing numerous texts from Scripture and tradition, including the teaching of their predecessors, the popes have consistently taught that from conception embryonic human life must be given unconditional respect. Pope John XXIII said that 'Human life is sacred: from its very inception it reveals the creating hand of God.'[19] For this reason, Paul VI explained, 'the direct interruption of the generative process already begun and, above all, directly willed and procured abortion, even if for therapeutic reasons, are to be absolutely excluded' (*HV* 13–14).

It is worth quoting at length the most authoritative treatment of this issue to hail from the Catholic Church to date, that of John Paul II in his encyclical *Evangelium Vitae*, as this articulates something of the range of

---

[18] See Benedict XVI, *Address to Symposium of the Pontifical Academy for Life on Stem Cells*, 16 September 2006.

[19] John XXIII, *Mater et Magistra: Encyclical Letter on the Church* (1961).

argumentation used by the Church. First, an argument from biological evidence and metaphysical implications:

Some people try to justify abortion by claiming that the result of conception, at least up to a certain number of days, cannot yet be considered a personal human life. But in fact, from the time that the ovum is fertilized, a life is begun which is neither that of the father nor the mother; it is rather the life of a new human being with his own growth. It would never be made human if it were not human already. This has always been clear, and modern genetic science offers clear confirmation. It has demonstrated that from the first instant there is established the programme of what this living being will be: a person, this individual person with his characteristic aspects already well determined. Right from fertilization the adventure of a human life begins, and each of its capacities requires time – a rather lengthy time – to find its place and to be in a position to act.

Then an argument from probabilities:

Furthermore, what is at stake is so important that, from the standpoint of moral obligation, the mere probability that a human person is involved would suffice to justify an absolutely clear prohibition of any intervention aimed at killing a human embryo. Precisely for this reason ... the Church has always taught and continues to teach that the result of human procreation, from the first moment of its existence, must be guaranteed that unconditional respect which is morally due to the human being in his or her totality and unity as body and spirit: 'The human being is to be respected and treated as a person from the moment of conception; and therefore from that same moment his rights as a person must be recognized, among which in the first place is the inviolable right of every innocent human being to life.'

Also argumentation based on revelation:

In the texts of Sacred Scripture ... human life is sacred and inviolable at every moment of existence, including the initial phase which precedes birth. All human beings, from their mother's womb, belong to God, who searches them and knows them, who forms them and knits them together with his own hands, who gazes on them when they are tiny shapeless embryos and already sees in them the adults of tomorrow ... they are the personal objects of God's loving and fatherly providence.

Christian Tradition ... is clear and unanimous, from the beginning up to our own day, in describing abortion as a particularly grave moral disorder ... The Second Vatican Council, as mentioned earlier, sternly condemned abortion: 'From the moment of its conception life must be guarded with the greatest care, while abortion and infanticide are unspeakable crimes.'

Next the extension from the traditional consideration of abortion to other interventions involving the human embryo:

This evaluation of the morality of abortion is to be applied also to the recent forms of intervention on human embryos which, although carried out for purposes legitimate in themselves, inevitably involve the killing of those embryos. This is the case with experimentation on embryos, which is becoming increasingly widespread in the field of biomedical research and is legally permitted in some countries ... The use of human embryos or fetuses as an object of experimentation constitutes a crime against their dignity as human beings who have a right to the same respect owed to a child once born, just as to every person.

This moral condemnation also regards procedures that exploit living human embryos and foetuses – sometimes specifically 'produced' for this purpose by in vitro fertilization – either to be used as 'biological material' or as providers of organs or tissue for transplants in the treatment of certain diseases. The killing of innocent human creatures, even if carried out to help others, constitutes an absolutely unacceptable act. (*EV* 60–3)

The *Catechism of the Catholic Church* is equally emphatic.[20] In several addresses Pope Benedict XVI has followed and amplified his predecessors' teaching. Benedict uses some similar biological and philosophical argumentation:

Cultural trends exist that seek to anaesthetize consciences with spurious arguments. With regard to the embryo in the mother's womb, science itself highlights its autonomy, its capacity for interaction with the mother, the coordination of biological processes, the continuity of development, the growing complexity of the organism. It is not an accumulation of biological material but rather a new living being, dynamic and marvellously ordered, a new individual of the human species. This is what Jesus was in Mary's womb; this is what we all were in our mother's womb. We may say with Tertullian, an ancient Christian writer: 'the one who will be a man is one already' (*Apologeticum* IX, 8), there is no reason not to consider him a person from conception.[21]

But his style of argument is often more theological than philosophical:

In Psalm 139 ... God turns his loving gaze upon the human being, whose full and complete beginning is reflected upon. He is still an 'unformed substance' in his mother's womb: the Hebrew term used has been understood by several biblical experts as referring to an 'embryo', described in that term as a small, oval, curled-up reality, but on which God has already turned his benevolent and loving eyes ... The idea in our Psalm that God already sees the entire future of that embryo, still an 'unformed substance', is extremely powerful. The days which that creature will live and fill with deeds throughout his earthly existence are already written in the Lord's book of life ... the greatness of this little unborn human creature, formed by God's hands and surrounded by his love,

---

[20] *CCC* 2270–5.
[21] Benedict XVI, *Homily for Vigil for Unborn Life*, 27 November 2010.

also appears: a biblical tribute to the human being from the first moment of his existence.[22]

God's love does not differentiate between the newly conceived infant still in his or her mother's womb and the child or young person, or the adult and the elderly person. God does not distinguish between them because he sees an impression of his own image and likeness (Gen. 1: 26) in each one ... The Magisterium of the Church has constantly proclaimed the sacred and inviolable character of every human life from its conception until its natural end. This moral judgment also applies to the origins of the life of an embryo even before it is implanted in the mother's womb, which will protect and nourish it for nine months until the moment of birth: Human life is sacred and inviolable at every moment of existence, including the initial phase which precedes birth.[23]

Much Catholic teaching on these matters has been elaborated more fully by the Congregation for the Doctrine of the Faith.[24] In its most recent treatment of these issues the Congregation observed:

The reality of the human being for the entire span of life, both before and after birth, does not allow us to posit either a change in nature or a gradation in moral value, since it possesses *full anthropological and ethical status*. The human embryo has, therefore, from the very beginning, the dignity proper to a person ... This value belongs to all without distinction. By virtue of the simple fact of existing, every human being must be fully respected. The introduction of discrimination with regard to human dignity based on biological, psychological, or educational development, or based on health-related criteria, must be excluded. At every stage of his existence, man, created in the image and likeness of God, reflects the face of his Only-begotten Son.[25]

Why not kill a human embryo or two?

Of course human embryos are very young and therefore very vulnerable. The *International Convention on the Rights of the Child* provides that 'the child, by reason of his or her physical and mental immaturity, needs

---

[22] Benedict XVI, *General Audience*, 28 December 2005.

[23] Benedict XVI, *Address to the 12th General Assembly of the Pontifical Academy for Life*, 27 February 2006.

[24] Especially in CDF, *On Abortion* (1976), and *On Respect for Human Life and Procreation* (1987).

[25] CDF, *On Certain Bioethical Questions* (2008) 5 and 8. The Pontifical Academy for Life's *On the Production and Use of Human Embryonic Stem Cells* likewise held that it is immoral to produce and/or use living human embryos for the preparation of ES cells, because *biologically* there is from fertilization 'a human subject with a well-defined identity, which from that point begins its own coordinated, continuous and gradual development'; *philosophically* there is a 'human individual' with a right to life; *ethically* ES cell derivation 'which critically and irremediably damages the human embryo' is gravely immoral and cannot be justified by any therapeutic goal; and *theologically* this position 'is explicitly confirmed by the Magisterium of the Church'.

special safeguards and care, including appropriate legal protection, before as well as after birth'. However much we redescribe it, the derivation of embryonic stem cells is not life-saving and it is not therapy: for those human beings from whom these cells are taken, it means death.

People also ask: if human embryos already exist, are 'surplus' to requirements in an IVF programme and marked for destruction, *if they are going to die soon anyway, shouldn't we use them for something?* We might respond: elderly people, prisoners on death row, people with terminal illnesses and many unconscious patients are 'going to die soon anyway'. Indeed one might say that everyone is 'going to die soon anyway'. We hold back from killing or using people lethally because we are convinced human beings deserve better. History is already sufficiently littered with stories of people declared 'unworthy of respect', 'lacking the requisite capacities', 'useless eaters'. There are too many sorry tales of 'unwanted', 'spare' or 'leftover' people who others thought could be used up and disposed of. We must resist the temptation to do more of this. We must resist the notions of 'sub-human people', of people with a 'use-by date' and 'lab-rat humans'.[26]

Sometimes, of course, doctors must let people die. With the so-called 'excess' IVF embryos this may be the only morally and practically available course. There are limits to what we can and should do to save life. That is very different from deliberately aiming at death, whether by act or omission. We only dare entrust ourselves to health professionals when we are at our most vulnerable because we trust them not to kill. Not all doctors and nurses merit that trust.[27] However, the first principle of the Hippocratic tradition of medicine and medical research has always been 'primum non nocere' (first do no harm). In its *Declaration of Nuremberg* (1948) and *Declaration of Helsinki* (2000) the World Medical Association declared that 'in medical research on human subjects, considerations related to the well-being of the human subject should take precedence over the interests of science and society'. In its modern version of the Hippocratic oath the same body called upon doctors to vow: 'I will maintain the utmost respect for human life from the moment of conception.'

---

[26] M. Grompe, 'Alternative energy for embryonic stem cell research', *Nature Reports Stem Cells*, 11 October 2007, argues that the ethical concerns regarding the destruction of human life outweigh the potential benefits of producing new embryo-derived cell lines.

[27] As we are reminded by the shocking cases of Harold Shipman, a British doctor who killed several hundred patients between 1975 and 2000, and a Dutch nurse, Lucy de Berk, who may have killed dozens of hers in the late 1990s.

Speaking for the Christian but also the Hippocratic tradition, the popes have repeatedly called medicine back to this founding principle. In *Evangelium Vitae* (57) Pope John Paul II said:

The deliberate decision to deprive an innocent human being of his life is always morally evil and can never be licit either as an end in itself or as a means to a good end. It is in fact a grave act of disobedience to the moral law, and indeed to God himself, the author and guarantor of that law; it contradicts the fundamental virtues of justice and charity. Nothing and no one can in any way authorise the killing of an innocent human being … even an embryo … Nor can any authority legitimately recommend or permit such an action.

Before he was elected pope, Cardinal Ratzinger observed that:

For modern man, the idea of placing limits on research sounds like blasphemy. However, an intrinsic limit exists, and this is human dignity. Progress obtained at the price of the violation of human dignity is unacceptable. If research attacks man, it is a deviation of science. Even if we protest that this or that research will open possibilities for the future, we must say no when man is at stake. The comparison is a bit strong, but I would like to recall that already once before someone has carried out medical experiments on persons who were held to be inferior. Where will the logic that consists in treating a foetus or an embryo as a thing lead?[28]

Likewise, as pope, he observed:

Despite unjust accusations of hostility to science addressed to the Church, I remind you of her constant support for research dedicated to the cure of diseases and to the good of humanity throughout her 2,000-year-old history. If there has been resistance – and if there still is – it is to those forms of research that provide for the planned suppression of human beings who already exist, even if they have not yet been born. Research, in such cases, irrespective of efficacious therapeutic results, is not truly at the service of humanity … History itself has condemned such a science in the past and will condemn it in the future, not only because it lacks the light of God but also because it lacks humanity.[29]

What about stem cells derived from other sources?

I noted above that apart from human embryos, there are at least four other potential sources for pluripotent stem cells with therapeutic application.

[28] Interview with Joseph Cardinal Ratzinger, in Jean Sévillia, 'The abolition of man', *Le Figaro*, December 2001; Joseph Ratzinger, *God and the World* (San Francisco: Ignatius, 2002).
[29] Benedict XVI, *Address to Symposium of the Pontifical Academy for Life on Stem Cells*. See also: Benedict XVI, *Address to the Participants in the Plenary Session of the CDF*, 31 January 2008; US Conference of Catholic Bishops, *On Embryonic Stem Cell Research* (Washington, DC: USCCB, 2008); US Conference of Catholic Bishops Secretariat of Pro-Life Activities, *Stem Cell Research and Human Cloning: Questions and Answers* (Washington, DC: USCCB, 2008).

Adult stem cells, as we have seen, are already widely used and have enormous, as yet untapped potential for healing damaged tissues. Efforts to reprogramme other cells so that they behave as stem cells are also very promising. Other techniques for producing cells that are very much like embryonic stem cells are also being explored. These avenues offer all the therapeutic potential of embryonic stem cells – and perhaps more – but without the moral downside of destroying early human beings. They deserve our support.

I must sound a few notes of caution, however. Proposals to manufacture 'embryoid bodies' that are sufficiently like human embryos to be able to be or produce stem cells, but which lack something essential to be human embryos, are controversial partly because we are not sure what these organisms are. Are they non-human, like a hydatidiform mole (see Chapter 4) or are they seriously disabled human beings, like an anencephalic child? If, for instance, they have a gene disorder (deliberately introduced) that prevents their development beyond the first week or so, they might still be human beings, if genetically very disabled ones. Were a gene therapy introduced to correct the defect, would we regard this as the conception of a human being or as the correction of a defect in an already existing human being? Any direct manufacture or destruction of a quasi-human organism requires prior moral certainty that that organism is not a human being – and there may be other objections also. In the previous chapter I argued that 'a human being' means a uni- or multi-cellular biological entity, however formed, with the intrinsic orientation to develop in an integrated way as a human embryo and foetus does, given a suitable environment.[30]

Another possibility, noted above, is to make human–animal hybrids. One method of doing this is by enucleating an animal egg and replacing its nucleus with the nucleus of a human cell and sparking embryonic division. Such an embryo would still have some genetic and other material from the animal egg, even if it were '99 per cent human'. Other proposed

---

[30] Likewise: CDF, *On Certain Bioethical Questions*, 30: 'The ethical objections raised in many quarters to therapeutic cloning and to the use of human embryos formed *in vitro* have led some researchers to propose new techniques which are presented as capable of producing stem cells of an embryonic type without implying the destruction of true human embryos. These proposals have been met with questions of both a scientific and an ethical nature regarding above all the ontological status of the "product" obtained in this way. Until these doubts have been clarified, the statement of the Encyclical *Evangelium Vitae* needs to be kept in mind: "what is at stake is so important that, from the standpoint of moral obligation, the mere probability that a human person is involved would suffice to justify an absolutely clear prohibition of any intervention aimed at killing a human embryo."'

modes of hybridization and genetic engineering would allow greater and lesser amounts of human material to contribute to the production of the organism. Yet as the Catholic Bishops' Conference of England and Wales points out:

To seek to produce a creature who is a mixture of human and non-human is not compatible with respect for the human nature that God creates and redeems. Also it fails to respect the harmony of creation as a whole or to recognise that human beings are part of creation, formed out of the earth, and dependent on the rest of creation for our continued existence. Bishop Elio Sgreccia, President of the Pontifical Academy for Life, has described the proposal to create hybrids as 'a monstrous act against human dignity'.[31]

Even if we can be certain that embryoid bodies and/or animal–human hybrids are not human beings – and that therefore their destruction involves no offence against human dignity – their manufacture might do so. Using human eggs or sperm to manufacture these organisms or otherwise substituting human material for animal gametes involves deploying human reproductive potential for purposes other than those proper to the marital act.

In 'The wisdom of repugnance' the Jewish ethicist Leon Kass wisely wrote that 'revulsion is not an argument; and some of yesterday's repugnances are today calmly accepted though, one must add, not always for the better. In crucial cases, however, repugnance is the emotional expression of deep wisdom, beyond reason's power fully to articulate.' Popular repugnance at the idea of human–animal hybrids would seem to be an example of this. As with cloning, incest, bestiality, cannibalism and the desecration of corpses, we are repelled 'because we intuit and feel, immediately and without argument, the violation of things that we rightfully hold dear. Repugnance, here as elsewhere, revolts against the excesses of human wilfulness, warning us not to transgress what is unspeakably profound'. Because something is *beyond* reason or words does not mean it is

---

[31] Catholic Bishops' Conference of England and Wales, *Parish Resource Pack to Raise Awareness about the Human Fertilisation and Embryology Bill, Including Possible Changes to the Law on Abortion* (London: CBCEW, 2007). Likewise CDF, *On Certain Bioethical Questions* 33: 'Recently animal oocytes have been used for reprogramming the nuclei of human somatic cells – this is generally called hybrid cloning – in order to extract embryonic stem cells from the resulting embryos without having to use human oocytes. From the ethical standpoint, such procedures represent an offense against the dignity of human beings on account of the admixture of human and animal genetic elements capable of disrupting the specific identity of man. The possible use of the stem cells, taken from these embryos, may also involve additional health risks, as yet unknown, due to the presence of animal genetic material in their cytoplasm. To consciously expose a human being to such risks is morally and ethically unacceptable.'

contrary to reason. The modern dogma that strongly felt awe and deep-seated taboos are merely the worthless remnants of primitive belief systems fails to do justice to the sacred, sublime, unthinkable and ineffable. Certain things very naturally and properly cause us to pause, indeed bewilder and sicken us. As Kass rightly concludes, 'shallow are the souls that have forgotten how to shudder'.[32]

SOCIAL CONCERNS ABOUT EMBRYONIC STEM CELLS

Incautious drivers

What is driving the embryonic stem cell push? Is it a proper desire to save and cure that has been infected by a 'results are all that count' mentality, common sense degraded to expediency? Is it a techno-imperative by which the technology dictates the terms to humanity rather than vice versa and where there is only a pretence of moderation? Is it the logic of the free market, with its demand not just for commercial but also for moral laissez-faire, coupled with seductive promises of freedom from suffering – for a fee? Or is it an embryos as commodities ideology that treats some human beings as leftovers, lab-rats, the ultimate biological resource? The readiness of journals as prestigious as *Science* to credit and publish Hwang Woo-Suk's fraudulent human cloning research,[33] which was also illegal, highly exploitative of women and involved embezzlement, demonstrates how powerful these forces are today and where they can lead even top scientists.[34]

We are being asked to consent to the designation of a laboratory underclass: there are now the *wanted* embryos, who will be protected for what they already are and respected for what they will become; and then there are the *second-class* embryos, useable and disposable, whether leftovers from IVF programmes that have passed their use-by date or human lives deliberately manufactured for the purpose by IVF or cloning.[35] Should we

---

[32] L. Kass, 'The wisdom of repugnance', *New Republic* 216 (1997), 17–26 at 20.

[33] W. S. Hwang, 'Evidence of a pluripotent human embryonic stem cell line derived from a cloned blastocyst', *Science* 303 (2004), 1669–74, and 'Patient-specific embryonic stem cells derived from human SCNT blastocysts', *Science* 308 (2005), 1777–83.

[34] B. Walsh, 'A cloning cover-up', *Time*, 5 December 2007, 7; Center for Bioethics and Human Dignity, Trinity International University (Deerfield, IL), 'The real lesson of the Korean cloning scandal', www.cbhd.org/resources/cloning/ (accessed 1 January 2011).

[35] John Paul II, *EV* 14: 'These so-called "spare embryos" are used for research which, under the pretext of scientific or medical progress, in fact reduces human life to the level of simple "biological material" to be freely disposed of.'

venture into this territory? In 1997 the Pontifical Academy for Life suggested that we should not:

The human cloning project represents the terrible aberration to which value-free science is driven and is a sign of the profound malaise of our civilization, which looks to science, technology and the 'quality of life' as surrogates for the meaning of life and its salvation. The proclamation of the 'death of God', in the vain hope of a 'superman', produces an unmistakable result: the 'death of man'. It cannot be forgotten that the denial of man's creaturely status, far from exalting human freedom, in fact creates new forms of slavery, discrimination and profound suffering. Cloning risks being the tragic parody of God's omnipotence.[36]

Killing anyone harms not only the victim but the perpetrator, the profession and the society complicit in the killing. Admittedly we have been desensitized to this in recent years. Though it is untrue to say that we could not care less, it is true to say that we care less than we should. Church leaders and lay professionals have nonetheless insisted throughout that no hoped-for therapeutic good is sufficient to justify the immorality of killing our very young.

Once parliaments, medibusiness or individual laboratories take us down the slippery slope of killing some for the benefit of others, we are well down a path towards other developments tomorrow that public opinion today would not countenance.[37] What is not clear is how we will be able to resist such incremental pressure in the future, having in these past few years so hastily agreed to allow embryo destruction for research, so-called therapeutic cloning and human–animal hybrids. This, if anywhere, is an area of urgent need where sound philosophy and clear magisterial teaching can guide the broader community.

Better drivers

In 1997 the European Community promulgated the *European Convention on Human Rights and Biomedicine*, article 18 of which specifically forbids the manufacture of embryos for use in research. In 2002 the US President's Council on Bioethics recommended a moratorium on all

---

[36] Pontifical Academy for Life, *On Cloning* (1997).

[37] On the question of 'opening the floodgates' or 'slippery slopes', the leader of the Australian stem cell industry, Alan Trounson, said in relation to the Human Embryo Experimentation Bill 1985, 'I don't care if it is a floodgate. If it opens an opportunity to treat really serious diseases and disabilities it is all right with me.' Cited by Senator Gary Humphries, 'Second Reading Speech on the Prohibition of Human Cloning for Reproduction and the Regulation of Human Embryo Research Amendment Bill 2006', Parliament of Australia, *Senate Procedural Text*, 6 November 2006.

cloning,[38] and President Bush and the Congress put at least some brakes on the embryo industry. Bush's successor, President Obama, has sought to remove these brakes. In March 2005, the United Nations endorsed the universal *Declaration on Human Cloning*, which calls on all member states to 'prohibit all forms of human cloning inasmuch as they are incompatible with human dignity and the protection of human life'. The General Assembly made this declaration:

Guided by the purposes and principles of the Charter of the United Nations,

Recalling the Universal Declaration on the Human Genome and Human Rights ...

Aware of the ethical concerns that certain applications of rapidly developing life sciences may raise with regard to human dignity, human rights and the fundamental freedoms of individuals,

Reaffirming that the application of life sciences should seek to offer relief from suffering and improve the health of individuals and humankind as a whole,

Emphasizing that the promotion of scientific and technical progress in life sciences should be sought in a manner that safeguards respect for human rights and the benefit of all,

Mindful of the serious medical, physical, psychological and social dangers that human cloning may imply for the individuals involved, and also conscious of the need to prevent the exploitation of women, [and]

Convinced of the urgency of preventing the potential dangers of human cloning to human dignity.

Sadly, not all scientists and governments are guided by such principles. The Church, however, shares these concerns. Pope Benedict XVI has observed that:

The use society hopes to make of biomedical science must constantly be measured against robust and firm ethical standards. Foremost among these is the dignity of human life, for under no circumstances may a human being be manipulated or treated as a mere instrument for experimentation. The destruction of human embryos, whether to acquire stem cells or for any other purpose, contradicts the purported intent of researchers, legislators and public health officials to promote human welfare. The Church does not hesitate to approve and encourage somatic stem-cell research – not only because of the favourable results obtained through these alternative methods, but more importantly because they harmonize with the aforementioned intent by respecting the life of the human being at every stage of his or her existence.[39]

[38] President's Council on Bioethics, *Human Cloning and Human Dignity: An Ethical Inquiry* (Washington, DC: PCB, 2002).
[39] Benedict XVI, *Address to the Ambassador of the Republic of Korea to the Holy See*, 11 October 2007. Likewise Benedict XVI, *Address to Symposium of the Pontifical Academy for Life on Stem Cells*; CDF, *On Certain Bioethical Questions* 28–33; Pontifical Academy for Life, *On the Production and Use of Human Embryonic Stem Cells*.

As I said in the Introduction, the Church today operates in a pluralist environment and no one expects that all her teachings will be adopted by law-makers, professions or the community as a whole at any time soon. Nonetheless the Church must continue her dialogue with the world on such matters, mindful of her prophetic duty to engage in a vigorous defence of the life and dignity of every human being. Of course the Church gives expression to this not just in public pronouncements but also through the very substantial contribution her members make to healthcare, bioethics, education and research. Catholics all over the world join others in hoping for new developments in biotechnology and medicine that will improve the health and wellbeing of all, including the poor. We are convinced that there are ways of achieving such results without compromising research ethics or further polarizing our communities.

If such ways forward are to be found, we must pause before going any further into a brave new world of cloning, embryo farming, cybrids and lethal harvesting of early human lives for stem cells or other parts. We need a pause long enough, at least, to ensure that ordinary people and their leaders understand the language, the science, the issues, the promises and the moral, social and financial costs. We should give ourselves enough time to ask some serious questions: in what kinds of science do we want our brightest and best to engage? In what kinds of projects do we want our limited resources invested? In what kinds of manipulation of human life do we want to be complicit? What kind of society are we building in the process?[40]

---

[40] Other recent bioethical writing on stem cells, cloning and so forth includes: B. Ashley, J. deBlois and K. O'Rourke, *Health Care Ethics: A Catholic Theological Analysis*, 5th edn (Washington, DC: Georgetown University Press, 2006), pp. 119–22; C. Colson and N. Cameron (eds.), *Human Dignity in the Biotech Century* (Downers Grove, IL: InterVarsity, 2004); K. Fitzgerald, 'Proposals for human cloning: a review and ethical evaluation', in J. Monagle and D. Thomasma (eds.), *Health Care Ethics: Critical Issues for the 21st Century* (Gaithersburg, MD: Aspen, 1998), pp. 3–7; J. Leies *et al.*, *Handbook on Critical Life Issues*, 3rd edn (Boston: NCBC, 2004), ch. 10; S. McConnaha, 'Blessed are the pluripotent: New Testament guidance for the embryonic stem cell debate', *NCBQ* 5(4) (2005), 707–18; W. E. May, *Catholic Bioethics and the Gift of Human Life*, 2nd edn (Huntington, IN: Our Sunday Visitor, 2008), pp. 229–36; T. Pacholczyk, 'Stem cell research and cloning', in E. Furton (ed.), *Live the Truth: The Moral Legacy of John Paul II in Catholic Health Care* (Philadelphia: NCBC, 2006), pp. 95–112; G. Pence (ed.), *Flesh of My Flesh: The Ethics of Cloning Humans* (Lanham, MD: Rowman and Littlefield, 1998); President's Council on Bioethics, *Alternative Sources*; B. Tobin and G. Gleeson, 'The embryo stem cell debate', *CMQ* 54(2) (May 2003), 8–11.

CHAPTER 6

Abortion: the new eugenics?

THE PERENNIAL DEBATE ABOUT ABORTION

Christian theology: it's good to be alive

A recurrent theme in the Bible is that it is good to be alive. Of all living things, human beings are accorded the greatest dignity: they are said to be the pinnacle of creation (Gen. chs. 1 and 2; Zech. 12:1), made in God's image and likeness (Gen. 1:26–31; 5:1; 9:6; Wisd. 2:23; 1 Cor 11:7; Jas. 3:9), with his spirit or breath (Gen. 2:7; Isa. 42:5; 57:16; Job 27:3; 32:8; 33:4; 34:13–14; Acts 17:25) and, so, are little less than gods themselves (Ps. 8). The rest of creation is ordered to their good and only they are given dominion over it (Gen. 1:28–31; 9:1–7); they, in turn, are oriented to God, who alone is Lord of life (Hos. ch. 2; 2 Macc. 14:46). The Incarnation further dignifies human beings: the Son of God himself became human and died to redeem all people, to make them children of God and heirs of his Kingdom, and to renew them in his likeness (John 1:14; Acts 3:15; 1 Cor. 15:49; 2 Cor. 3:17–18; Rom. 8:29; Col. 3:10; Phil. 2:5–11; Eph. 4:22–24; ch. 5). According to this scriptural view, human dignity is based not on social acceptance, intellectual capacity, maturity, independence or wantedness but on membership of the human race, that one 'family' with whom God has this special relationship.

With this high estimation of the human person comes the basic principle that human beings must be reverenced for what they are in themselves and never reduced to mere instruments for the advantage of others. Included in this vision is that life is a trust given into our stewardship by God; that we are called to choose life and the ways of life, not death; that any killing demands justification and the taking of innocent human life is contrary to God's will; and that no one should usurp the rôle of God, who alone is the Lord of life and death.

You shall not murder. (Exod. 20:13; Deut. 5:17; Matt. 19:18)

God blessed Noah and his sons, saying to them, 'Be fruitful, multiply, and fill the earth ... I give you everything, with this exception: I will demand an account of every man's life from his fellow men. He who sheds human blood shall have his own blood shed, for man was made in the image of God.' (Gen. 9:1–6; cf. 4:8–11; 49:25; Exod. 20:13; 21:22–25; 23:7; 1 Sam. 2:6; 2 Kgs. 8:12; 15:16, etc.)

Behold, I am in your hands: do with me as seems good and right to you. But be sure of this: if you put me to death, you will be bringing innocent blood on yourselves, and upon this city and its citizens. (Jer. 26:14–15; cf. 7:30–32; 19:4; 26:14–15; Wisd. 16:13; Matt. 19:18; Rev. 2:10–11)

What does this 'pro-life' scriptural theme say to the abortion issue? Throughout the Bible children are presented as a great blessing and parenthood is highly esteemed:

Truly children are a gift from the Lord, a blessing, the fruit of the womb. (Ps. 127:3; cf. Gen. 4:1; 17:15–16; 18:11–14; 21:1–2; 28:3; 29:31–35; 30:22–23; 33:5; 49:25; 1 Sam. chs. 2, 9, 10; Ps. 103:13; 113; 127:3–5; 128; Jer. 31:15; Jonah 4:11; Isa. 29:22–23; 40:11; Hos. ch. 11; Mal. 4:6)

Jesus took a little child, set him in front of them, put his arms round him, and said to them: 'Anyone who welcomes one of these little children in my name, welcomes me ... Let the little children come to me; do not hinder them; for it is to such as these that the kingdom of God belongs.' (Mark 9:33–37; 10:13–16; cf. Matt. 18:10; 19:13–15, etc.)

In recent years some have questioned whether the scriptural reverence for children and for all innocent human life extends to life *before* birth. In the Old Testament the existence of the human being before birth is clearly recognized (e.g. Gen. 25:22; Ps. 51:5; Eccles. 11:5; Isa. 49:15; Jonah 3:3). Unborn children are already known and loved by God: Samson (Judg. 13:5–7; 16:17), David (Ps. 22:9–10), Solomon (Wisd. 7:1–6), Job (Job ch. 10), Isaiah (Isa. 49:1, 5, 15), Jeremiah (Jer. 1:4–5; Sir. 49:7), all the People of Israel (Isa. 44:1, 24; 46:3; Ps. 71:6 and 139). All these characters trace their personal identity from adult life back to the time of their conception or life in the womb.

Now the word of the Lord came to me, saying: 'Before I formed you in the womb I knew you, and before you came to birth I consecrated you.' (Jer. 1:4–5)

Your hands shaped me and made me: will you now turn and destroy me? Remember that you moulded me like clay: will you now turn me to dust again? Did you not pour me out like milk and curdle me like cheese, clothe me with skin and flesh, and knit me together with bones and sinews? You gave me life and showed me kindness and in your providence watched over my spirit. (Job 10:8–12)

O Lord, you examine me and know me,
　　you know when I sit and when I rise ….
You created my inmost self,
　　knit me together in my mother's womb.
For so many marvels I thank you:
　　a wonder am I, and all your works are wonders.
You knew me through and through,
　　my being held no secrets from you,
when I was being formed in secret,
　　textured in the depths of the earth.
Your eyes could see my embryo,
　　in your book all my days were inscribed.
　　　　　　　　　　　　　　　　　(Ps. 139:1, 13–16)

On the cusp between the Old and New Testaments John the Baptist heralds the embryonic Jesus while both are still in the womb: filled with the Holy Spirit the foetal John leapt for joy (Luke 1:13–15, 41–44). Christ himself was an embryo, foetus, infant, child, adolescent, adult. Paul, too, tells how he was chosen while still in his mother's womb (Gal. 1:15). All these passages suggest that personal identity for Jews and Christians is continuous from when God gives life at conception through maturity until death and consequently that the moral claims of the 'neighbour' upon us are present in our fellow human beings even from their conception.

Hence the killing of the unborn is deplored in the Old Testament (Exod. 21:22–25; 2 Kgs. 8:12; 15:16; Hos. 14:1; Amos 1:13–15), and the Jews stood out in the ancient world for their opposition to abortion and infanticide. Christians inherited this attitude. Dealers in poisons ('sorcerers' or 'pharmacists') are repeatedly anathematized in the New Testament (Gal. 5:20; Rev. 9:21; 21:8; 22:15) and other early Christian documents: according to Plutarch, these poison-dealers so deplored by Christians were abortionists (*Romulus* XXII). Just like the Jews, the early Christians were convinced that killing the unborn and the new-born was always wrong.[1]

---

[1] See also J. H. Channer (ed.), *Abortion and the Sanctity of Human Life* (Exeter: Paternoster, 1985); J. Connery, *Abortion: The Development of the Roman Catholic Perspective* (Chicago: Loyola University Press, 1977); Daughters of St. Paul (eds.), *Yes to Life: Source-Book of Catholic Teaching on the Sacredness of Human Life* (Boston: St. Paul, 1977); D. Di Mauro, *A Love for Life: Christianity's Consistent Protection of the Unborn* (Eugene, OR: Wipf and Stock, 2008); M. Gorman, *Abortion and the Early Church* (Eugene, OR: Wipf and Stock, 1998); Society for the Protection of Unborn Children, *Love Your Unborn Neighbour* (London: SPUC, 1994).

You shall not kill a child by abortion nor kill it after it is born. (*Didache* II, 2, *c.* AD 100)

Those on the way of darkness include … the murderers of children, aborting the work of God. (*Epistle of Barnabas* XX, 2, *c.* AD 135)

For us, since murder has been forbidden, it is also not permitted to dissolve what is conceived in the womb … nor does it make a difference whether one takes the life of one already born, or disturbs one in the process before birth: for the one who is becoming a human being is one already. (Tertullian, *Apology* IX, 8, *c.* AD 197)

The wicked Novatian … struck the womb of his wife with his heel and caused an abortion, thereby committing parricide. (St Cyprian of Carthage, *Epistle* 52 to Cornelius, *c.* AD 251)

He who deliberately destroys the foetus is guilty of murder. (St Basil the Great, *Epistle* 138, *c.* AD 375)

Some, when they realize that they have conceived outside of wedlock, take poisons for abortion, and frequently die themselves along with their child, and go to hell guilty of three crimes: murdering themselves, adultery against Christ, and murdering their unborn child. (St Jerome, *Epistle XXII*, 13, *c.* AD 380)

Some rich women, to avoid dividing the inheritance among many, kill their own foetus in the womb and with murderous poisons extinguish their children in the womb. (St Ambrose, *On the Hexaemeron* V, 18, *c.* AD 386)

To destroy the foetus is something worse than murder. The one who does this not only takes away life, but robs one of it who has not yet even had the chance of being born. (St John Chrysostom, *Homilies on Romans* 24, *c.* AD 391)

At times their lustful cruelty or cruel lust goes so far as to … destroy the foetus conceived within the womb, wishing their offspring … living in the womb to be killed before being born. (St Augustine, *De nuptiis et concupiscentia* I, 15, *c.* AD 419)

He who destroys what is conceived in the womb by abortion is a murderer. (Pope Stephen V, *Epistle to Archbishop of Mainz*, AD 887)

This attitude continued throughout the Middle Ages, even if (as we saw in Chapter 4) theologians and canonists continued to dispute over embryology, metaphysics and sanctions. Likewise beyond the Reformation: Luther and Calvin were every bit as opposed to abortion as their Catholic predecessors and contemporaries. It was not until the twentieth century that some Christian leaders started to favour abortion in certain situations. However, the Catholic Church remained unequivocal. In the words of the Second Vatican Council:

All offences against life itself, such as murder, genocide, abortion, euthanasia and wilful suicide … are criminal. They poison civilization and they debase the perpetrators even more than the victims … Life must be protected with the utmost care from the moment of conception: abortion and infanticide are abominable crimes. (*GS* 27 and 51)[2]

In the most important magisterial treatment of these issues, *Evangelium Vitae*, Pope John Paul II thought that among all the crimes committed against life abortion was especially deplorable:

The acceptance of abortion in the popular mind, in behaviour and even in law itself, is a telling sign of an extremely dangerous crisis of the moral sense ... Given such a grave situation, we need now more than ever to have the courage to look the truth in the eye and to *call things by their proper name* ... Procured abortion is *the deliberate and direct killing, by whatever means it is carried out, of a human being in the initial phase of his or her existence, extending from conception to birth.* The moral gravity of procured abortion is apparent in all its truth if we recognize that we are dealing with murder and, in particular, when we consider the specific elements involved. The one eliminated is a human being at the very beginning of life. No one more absolutely *innocent* could be imagined. (*EV* 58)

Aware of the philosophical disputes examined in the previous two chapters about the moral status of the unborn, John Paul nonetheless concluded that 'what is at stake is so important that, from the standpoint of moral obligation, the mere probability that a human person is involved would suffice to justify an absolutely clear prohibition of any intervention aimed at killing a human embryo' (*EV* 60). In addition to biological and philosophical arguments, the Pope then examined the Scriptures, the Catholic teaching and canonical tradition and the recent magisterium, and then formally taught:

By the authority which Christ conferred upon Peter and his Successors, in communion with the Bishops – who on various occasions have condemned abortion and who in the aforementioned consultation, albeit dispersed throughout the world, have shown unanimous agreement concerning this doctrine – *I declare that direct abortion, that is, abortion willed as an end or as a means, always constitutes a grave moral disorder,* since it is the deliberate killing of an innocent human being. This doctrine is based upon the natural law and upon the written Word of God, is transmitted by the Church's Tradition and taught by the ordinary and universal Magisterium. No circumstance, no purpose, no law whatsoever can ever make licit an act which is intrinsically illicit, since it is contrary to the Law of God which is written in every human heart, knowable by reason itself and proclaimed by the Church. (*EV* 62)

---

[2] Soon after this Paul VI taught: 'We must once again declare that the direct interruption of the generative process already begun and, above all, directly willed and procured abortion, even if for therapeutic reasons, are to be absolutely excluded' (*HV* 13–14.)

The Catechism of the Catholic Church (2270–3) and the documents *On Abortion* (1974), *On Respect for Human Life and Procreation* (1987) and *On Certain Bioethical Questions* (2008) of the Congregation for the Doctrine of the Faith have been equally definitive.[3]

Pope Benedict has continued this teaching tradition. Reflecting upon contemporary threats to peace he has observed:

> As far as *the right to life* is concerned, we must denounce its widespread violation in our society: alongside the victims of armed conflicts, terrorism and the different forms of violence, there are the silent deaths caused by hunger, abortion, experimentation on human embryos and euthanasia. How can we fail to see in all this an attack on peace? Abortion and embryonic experimentation constitute a direct denial of that attitude of acceptance of others which is indispensable for establishing lasting relationships of peace.[4]

Likewise, while praising the proper concern of many people for the natural environment, the Pope has suggested we must turn our attention also to the social environment, where the innate dignity of every human person is sometimes ignored, and various voiceless people put at risk, especially the unborn. 'How can it be that the most wondrous and sacred human space – the womb – has become a place of unutterable violence?'[5]

Common morality on the good of life and the evil of abortion

The classical case against abortion, though commonly argued by appeals to Scripture and tradition, is not based solely on revelation. In common with people of other religions and none, 'pro-lifers' (as they have come to be called) argue that all human beings matter, matter equally and matter very much. The source of this dignity is complex and can be couched in the language of theology, secular philosophy, human rights, poetry or song. Shakespeare's *Hamlet* (II.ii) put it thus: 'What a piece of work is a man, how noble in reason, how infinite in faculties; in form and moving, how express and admirable; in action, how like an angel; in apprehension, how like a god: the beauty of the world, the paragon of animals.'

As Shakespeare notes, human beings are organisms, part of the living world, members of the animal kingdom. Though like angels or 'gods' in intellect and will, we differ from such pure spirits in that bodily, organic life is a basic good for us, irreducible to mere pleasure, consciousness or social

---

[3] See also Pontifical Council for Health, *Charter for Healthworkers* (1994; English trans. 1995) 139 and 142.

[4] Benedict XVI, *Message for the Celebration of the World Day of Peace*, 1 January 2007, p. 5.

[5] Benedict XVI, *Address for Arrival for World Youth Day 2008*, Barangaroo, Sydney, 17 July 2008.

usefulness. Participation in bodily life makes much of what we do intelligible; it is an aspect of our individual flourishing and also of our common good. Many writers have offered a philosophical case for the view that human lives are of such intrinsic importance that no intentional choice to bring about an innocent person's death can be justified.[6] This sanctity of life principle is deeply embedded in the jurisprudence derived from the English common law tradition, international human rights documents and our common morality. It has also informed medical ethics back to Hippocrates, whose oath specifically repudiates the practice of abortion for health professionals.

As the reference to Hippocrates highlights, there is nothing new about abortion. It was known to the ancients and sometimes practised, if often hidden, even in ostensibly religious societies. Despite some deliberate overstatement of abortion rates before the 1960s and underreporting of increases thereafter,[7] it is now clear that numbers spiralled upwards as abortion became safer, legal, increasingly socially acceptable and available in many countries. In Chapter 1 I noted something of the social and cultural context for this phenomenon. Though reliable figures are unavailable for many countries, each year there are probably more than 10 million abortions in Asia (including over 6 million in China alone and 750,000 in India), possibly 4 million in Africa (850,000 in South Africa), 4 million in Latin America, 3 million in Eastern Europe (including over 2 million in Russia alone), 1.6 million in Western Europe (including 140,000 in France, 130,000 in Germany, 130,000 in Italy and 200,000 in the UK), a million in North America (850,000 in the USA and 100,000 in Canada) and over 100,000 in Oceania (mostly in Australia).[8]

---

[6] See the lists of recent contributors to the Thomist revival in moral theology and to the new natural law theory in the notes to Chapter 1.

[7] An example of such 'creative' accounting is the figure for Australia's abortion rate before 1970 given in National Health and Medical Research Council Expert Panel, *Information Paper on Termination of Pregnancy in Australia* (Canberra: AGPS, 1996), on which see A. Fisher, 'What we can learn from the Abortion Report', *Australasian Catholic Record* 75(3) (1998), 286–98. Similarly wild exaggerations occurred with American figures on abortion numbers and abortion-related deaths. Bernard Nathanson, former director of the National Association for the Repeal of Abortion Laws, admitted: 'How many deaths were we talking about when abortion was illegal? In NARAL we ... always [said] 5,000 to 10,000 deaths a year. I confess that I knew that the figures were totally false and I suppose that others did too if they stopped to think of it. But in the "morality" of our revolution, it was a useful figure.' Bernard N. Nathanson, *Aborting America* (New York: Doubleday, 1979). Cf. 'Abortion statistics and trends over the past thirty years: out of the long dark night', *National Right to Life News*, 1 January 2003; H.-J. Prill, 'Zur Aufhellung der sogenannten Dunkelziffer bei Abtreibungen', *Medizinische Klinik* 67(17) (1972), 619–22.

[8] Some of these figures are guesstimates at best, especially those for Asia, Africa and Latin America. The most reliable source I have found is Bob Johnston at www.johnstonsarchive.net/policy/abortion/index.html (accessed 1 January 2011). The World Health Organization and various family planning organizations overstate illegal abortion numbers in Third World countries. See also R. Whelan (ed.), *Legal Abortion Examined: 21 Years of Abortion Statistics* (London: SPUC, 1992).

The acceleration of the per capita abortion rate since the 1960s refutes the claim that there is a certain definite pool of women who will have abortions 'no matter what' and that abortion laws and availability do not affect demand. It is now clear that the more available, quick and simple abortion becomes, the more women will seek it, not merely because this ease is weighed in the balance against the burdens of going to term with a child, but more importantly because abortion availability is a major factor affecting sexual behaviour and thus pregnancy rates. We now have abortion on an unthinkable scale, more devastating in sheer number of fatalities than the two World Wars, yet so commonplace as to be regarded by many as trivial. In 1999 two Americans were convicted on the same day for killing: one, a Milwaukee man who had shot his cat because it hissed at him, was sentenced to 21 years in prison; the other, a New Yorker, who had illegally performed abortions on babies mature enough to survive outside the womb, was given five years' probation.[9] In many Western countries a quarter or third of women now have an abortion in their lifetime.[10] In places such as Russia abortion is even more common. The emotional, ideological and financial investment of many in the practice of abortion is therefore considerable. In the global 'South' abortion is far less common, but there is continual pressure upon such countries to embrace 'termination of pregnancy' as part of 'reproductive health' programmes. Yet whether they agree with the 'pro-life' view that the unborn are morally equal to older human beings or not, hardly anyone thinks this huge scale of abortion is a good thing.[11] It requires too much intellectual, emotional and cultural gymnastics to keep excluding unborn children from our species, family or community: they are, after all, *of us*; they are, fairly obviously, *like us*; they are *our* future. They cry out for justice, love, remembrance – and their deaths harm us as well as them.[12]

[9] G. Schuldt, 'Man gets 21-year prison sentence for killing cat', *Milwaukee Sentinel*, 31 August 1999; M. Gallagher, 'Letting abortion doctors get away with murder', *uexpress*, 30 August 1999, www.uexpress.com/maggiegallagher/index.html?uc_full_date=19990830 (accessed 1 January 2011).

[10] National Health and Medical Research Council (Australia), *Termination of Pregnancy in Australia: A Review of Healthcare Services* (Canberra: NHMRC, 1998), p. 44.

[11] J. I. Fleming, 'Analysis of new data on Australian attitudes to abortion', in Fleming and N. Tonti-Filippini (eds.), *Common Ground? Seeking an Australian Consensus on Abortion and Sex Education* (Sydney: St Paul's, 2007), ch. 2, found that most Australians (64%) think the abortion rate is too high, and by far most (87%) would like to see numbers reduced, especially if this can be done without restricting access; while most (70%) support legal abortion they are deeply conflicted about the morality of exercising that 'right' apart from 'hard cases' such as maternal health or foetal handicap. See also Selina Ewing, 'An evidence base for counselling, social policy and alternatives to abortion', in Fleming and Tonti-Filippini (eds.), *Common Ground?*, ch. 7.

[12] Other recent writing on abortion includes: B. Ashley, J. deBlois and K. O'Rourke, *Health Care Ethics: A Catholic Theological Analysis*, 5th edn (Washington, DC: Georgetown University Press, 2006), pp. 80–1, 101–2; F. Beckwith, *Defending Life: A Moral and Legal Case against Abortion*

PRE-NATAL TESTING: A SEARCH-AND-
DESTROY MISSION?

The new genetics

In Chapter 1 I identified some of the social and cultural factors that have
contributed to the rise in abortion numbers. I noted that technology itself
has been a strong driver. In the second half of the twentieth century suc-
tion aspiration machines, abortifacient drugs and antibiotics made abortion, both legal and illegal, much safer and more accessible. The biggest
recent technological development influencing the upward abortion spiral
has been the new genetics.[13]

We naturally rejoice in the extraordinary achievement of the human
genome project and other research, which has contributed so much to
our understanding of the genetics of the human condition and which
is so pregnant with therapeutic possibilities. Prudent therapeutic interventions aimed at correcting genetic diseases and preventing their
occurrence or onset are in principle good uses of genetic science and
healthcare. This is so even if there is cause for caution with respect to
experimentation, privacy, equity of access, 'germ line therapy' and 'genetic enhancement'. The big problem is that now and for the foreseeable future the principal use of this technology will not be therapeutic
at all. Alongside ultrasound and other procedures genetic technology
will be used for testing the unborn and, where diagnosed as carrying

Choice (Cambridge University Press, 2007); Di Mauro, *A Love for Life*; J. Finnis, 'Abortion
and healthcare ethics', in R. Gillon (ed.), *Principles of Health Care Ethics* (Chichester: Wiley,
1993), pp. 547–58; Anthony Fisher and Jane Buckingham, *Abortion in Australia: Answers and
Alternatives* (Sydney: Foundation for Human Development, 1991); I. Gentles (ed.), *A Time to
Choose Life: Women, Abortion and Human Rights* (Toronto: Stoddart, 1990); G. Grisez, *Abortion:
The Myths, the Realities and the Arguments* (New York: Corpus, 1970); S. Heaney (ed.), *Abortion:
A New Generation of Catholic Responses* (Braintree, MA: Pope John Center, 1992); P. Kreeft, *Three
Approaches to Abortion* (San Francisco: Ignatius, 2002); P. Lee, *Abortion and Unborn Human Life*
(Washington, DC: Catholic University of America Press, 1996); J. Leies *et al.*, *Handbook on
Critical Life Issues*, 3rd edn (Boston: NCBC, 2004), chs. 6–8; W. E. May, *Catholic Bioethics and
the Gift of Human Life*, 2nd edn (Huntington, IN: Our Sunday Visitor, 2008), ch. 5. An excellent
journal dealing with these matters is *Human Life Review*.
[13] For a fuller account of my own views: A. Fisher, 'Adult science and adolescent ethics', in
H. Regan, R. Horsfield and G. McMullen (eds.), *Beyond Mere Health: Theology and Health
Care in a Secular Society* (Melbourne: Australian Theological Forum, 1996), pp. 145–68, 'The
brave new world of genetic screening: ethical issues', in J. Flader (ed.), *Death or Disability?
Proceedings of a Seminar at the University of Tasmania* (Hobart: University of Tasmania, 1996),
pp. 16–34, and 'The human genome project: hopes and fears', *Philippiniana Sacra* 30(90)
(1995), 483–98.

some disease or other unwanted characteristic, the child will routinely be 'terminated'.[14]

In a moving article about his daughter Domenica, who has Down's syndrome, Dominic Lawson wrote about the complicity of genetic technology in a 'search-and-destroy mission' against babies like Domenica.[15] Down's syndrome, cystic fibrosis, spina bifida, diabetes, asthma: where will the list of conditions or 'defects' end? A 1993 American poll found that 11 per cent of couples would abort a foetus with a predisposition to obesity.[16] More recently, it has been suggested that autism could be detected prenatally and affected babies eliminated.[17] In India and China widespread antenatal testing followed by abortion for female babies, combined with infanticide for girls who make it to birth, has resulted in serious sex imbalances and millions of 'missing women' in those countries.[18] Thus the Chinese Academy of Social Sciences recently predicted that by 2020 more than 24 million Chinese men of marrying age will find themselves without spouses.[19] The range of conditions for which a prenatal genetic test is available is growing all the time and new DNA microarray technologies (the so-called 'gene chip') permit screening for thousands of genetic disorders or characteristics at once. Were the fears of parents and the prejudices of the surrounding culture not sufficient to tip people in this direction, 'non-directive' genetic counselling will almost certainly do so.

The unasked question is: who decides which genetic qualities warrant death, before or after birth, on what basis and in whose interests? Some years ago I was consulted about an ethical and pastoral conundrum

[14] A. Harmon, 'Genetic testing + abortion = ???', *New York Times*, 13 May 2007; W. Saletan, 'Prebirth defects: prenatal tests, genetics and abortion', *Slate*, 29 October 2008.

[15] D. Lawson, 'All you need is life', *Spectator*, 17 June 1995. On the 'meaning' of such disabled and sometimes short lives see A. Fisher, 'Thomas Walter Joseph Ryan: celebration of a life', *Bioethics Outlook* 8(2) (1997), 1–3; K. Gilges, *A Grace Given* (New York: Cider Press Publishing, 2008); Stanley Hauerwas, *God, Medicine and Suffering* (Grand Rapid, MI: Eerdmans, 1990); A. MacIntyre, *Dependent Rational Animals: Why Human Beings Need the Virtues* (Peru, IL: Open Court, 1999).

[16] J. Matthews, 'Here comes a confused new world of gene shopping', *International Herald Tribune*, 9 November 1994, 4.

[17] S. Boseley, 'New research brings autism screening closer to reality: call for ethics debate as tests in womb could allow termination of pregnancies', *Guardian*, 12 January 2009.

[18] 'India loses 10m female births', *BBC News*, 9 January 2006; G. Aravamudhan, *Disappearing Daughters: The Tragedy of Female Foeticide* (New York: Penguin, 2007); A. Coale and J. Banister, 'Five decades of missing females in China', *Demography* 31(3) (1994), 459–79; J. Gittings, 'Growing sex imbalance shocks China', *Guardian*, 13 May 2002; A. Sen, 'More than 100 million women are missing', *New York Review of Books*, 20 December 1990; S. Sheth, 'Missing female births in India', *The Lancet* 367(9506) (21 January 2006), 185–6.

[19] *BBC News*, 11 January 2010, http://news.bbc.co.uk/2/hi/8451289.stm (accessed 1 January 2011).

for some hospital staff. A couple suffering from achondroplasia (dwarfism) had presented requesting genetic screening of their already quite
advanced unborn child. On being told their child was of normal stat-
ure they declared that they wanted an abortion because they wanted
only a dwarf child. The clinical staff were stunned. Despite long experience of abortion on demand, they had never before faced a case where a
child was to be aborted specifically because she or he was (in common
parlance) 'normal'. This raised for them all sorts of questions about the
nature of health and disability, about who should decide which conditions warrant the death of a child and according to what criteria. Must
health professionals assist in every request for abortion, however perverse? Where is the new genetics leading us? Is this the re-emergence of
eugenics – that discredited nineteenth- and twentieth-century project to
improve the race, or at least particular families, by getting rid of those
with unwanted genes?

Until recently the targets of prenatal screening were those with severe
(or relatively severe) disabilities, especially those who could not long survive after birth. Now hardly a week passes without a report of another
genetic attribute or predisposition being identified. In the last few years
genes have been identified that are thought to cause or confer predis-
positions to syndromes such as Down's, Patau's, Edward's, Turner's
and fragile X; to cystic fibrosis, dwarfism, haemochromatosis, haemo-
philia, Huntington's chorea and muscular dystrophy, phenylketonuria,
sickle-cell anaemia, spina bifida and thalassaemia, as well as much more
common conditions such as cardiovascular disease, Alzheimer's, many
cancers, osteoporosis, epilepsy, asthma, diabetes, deafness and hyper-
tension. Genes are being identified that are associated not only with
physical diseases, but with various physical features such as height,
body shape, the colouring of skin, hair and eyes, sex, various immun-
ities, longevity and athletic and other physical potential. Of course no
test is 100 per cent accurate: there will be false negatives and false positives; people will have the genes but never present with the condition or
exhibit the characteristic; there may be a broad range of impairments
from trivial to severe, often without any means of accurate prediction.
The diagnostic tests tell us, at best, what very well *might* be on a somatic
or bodily level.[20]

---

[20] On the difficulties of interpreting genetic test data see: Rob Stein, 'Fresh hopes and concerns as
foetal DNA tests advance', *Washington Post*, 26 October 2008.

There are also psychological qualities to consider. In recent years scientists have confidently declared the following qualities among those entirely or largely genetically determined or at least predisposed to: intelligence of various kinds, insomnia, migraines, depression, substance dependency, schizophrenia and psychosis; shyness and aggressiveness, risk aversion and thrill-seeking, optimism, extroversion, alienation, leadership and career choice; aesthetic sensibility, sexuality, tastes, memory, creativity and docility; even political and religious ideals.[21] There is much debate about the degree of genetic influence on these attributes, and once again there is a broad range among those who demonstrate each such quality.

Many issues are raised by the new genetics: the revolution in human self-understanding; the enormous potential for treatments; the danger of reducing people to their genes; the pressure that the very availability of these tests puts upon parents and health professionals to use them; the genetic abortion treadmill, on which couples may find themselves after having antenatal screening; the power of the technological imperative to sweep people along and to become an overarching ideology for medicine; the informative natural revulsion of ordinary people towards eugenics and genetic engineering; the widespread uncertainty about what constitutes 'the perfect child' and whether we should be trying to achieve one. But now that we have this genetic knowledge, the big question is what to do with it?

What should we do with this knowledge?

Prenatal screening and testing are increasingly routine parts of the obstetric treadmill.[22] The most common reason prospective parents submit to prenatal tests is that the suppliers (doctors) tell the consumers (their trusting patients) that they need them. For most, whose babies test negative, this provides reassurance and perhaps an opportunity for closer bonding. For some, who receive a positive result for some condition, it allows time to treat both mother and child: a drug, hormone or vitamin supplement administered to the mother may vastly improve her child's prospects if the defect is identified early enough. There may even be direct therapeutic

---

[21] G. Colt, 'Were you born that way?', *Life*, 1 April 1998, 38–50; cf. J. Giles, 'Are political leanings all in the genes?', *New Scientist* 2641 (2 February 2008), 28–31, and J. Jost, 'The end of the end of ideology', *American Psychologist* 61 (2006), 651–70.

[22] House of Commons Science and Technology Committee, *Human Genetics: The Science and Its Consequences. Third Report* (London: HMSO, 1995), vol. 1, p. 87.

interventions upon the child in the womb: drugs, surgery, blood transfusions, shunts, laser treatment, radio therapy or gene therapy – these are possibilities in some cases.[23] There may also be benefit in preparing parents and others before the birth for the difficulties ahead. None of these benefits is, however, without its costs such as a risk of foetal loss or injury, maternal hazards and anxieties, disruption of bonding or false reassurance, and there is also the resource burden of widespread prenatal testing. If no therapeutic benefit to the child is in view, such risks would seem unwarranted.

Also problematical is the sharing of such information with others, such as relatives or employers, especially without the patients' permission. Increasingly health insurers want their prospective policyholders and their unborn children screened so that they can avoid taking on any high-risk clients. The implications for privacy and health are obviously enormous. Several countries have moved in recent years to make unauthorized release or use of information gleaned from prenatal tests a crime, as well as strengthening anti-discrimination laws.[24]

Overwhelmingly the most common use for this information is to give the parents the option of aborting a child with a disability. A positive result is commonly followed by gently steering the couple towards choosing abortion, even if this is called 'non-directive counselling'. Many doctors and genetic counsellors report that abortion has followed a positive result in almost every case of testing for a defect that they have dealt with. Sometimes these tests are inaccurate – so-called 'false positives' – and so some healthy babies are lost in the effort to screen out unhealthy ones. Usually they are accurate, and they are accurately used like heat-seeking missiles to ensure that those babies who have certain genetic disorders never see the light of day.

The moral arguments for and against abortion are well known. For those persuaded that abortion involves the wrongful killing of an innocent human being, genetic and other antenatal testing with a view to possible termination of pregnancy is also unethical: such tests involve unjust

[23] S. Adzick, 'Fetal lung lesions: management and outcome', *Am J Obstet Gyn* 179(4) (1998), 884–9; W. F. Anderson, 'Human gene therapy', *Science* 256 (1992), 808–13; D. James, 'Recent advances: fetal medicine', *Brit Med J* 316 (1998), 1580–3; S. Kumar and A. O'Brien, 'Clinical review: recent developments in fetal medicine', *Brit Med J* 328 (2004), 1002–6; D. Walsh *et al.*, 'Fetal surgical intervention', *Am J Perinatology* 17(6) (2000), 277–83; C. Willyard, 'Tinkering in the womb: the future of fetal surgery', *Nature Medicine* 14 (2008) 1176–7.
[24] I have considered the privacy issues more fully in A. Fisher, 'Old paradigms and new dilemmas in medical confidentiality', *Bioethics Outlook* 10(1) (1999), 1–12.

cooperation in direct killing of the innocent. Thus Pope John Paul II noted that:

Prenatal diagnosis, which presents no moral objections if carried out in order to identify the medical treatment which may be needed by the child in the womb, all too often becomes an opportunity for proposing and procuring an abortion. This is eugenic abortion, justified in public opinion on the basis of a mentality … which accepts life only under certain conditions and rejects it when it is affected by any limitation, handicap or illness. (*EV* 14)[25]

In Chapters 4 and 5 I argued that attempts to exclude human embryos from the class of human beings or human individuals fail. Some nonetheless seek to exclude some or all unborn human beings from the class of those who have 'personhood'. They claim that something additional to being a live human individual is required for us to *qualify* for the status of person with all its attendant rights and interests. The qualification varies but it commonly includes consciousness, memories and preferences, social relationships and/or independence. Such qualifications (and evidence required for each) conveniently exclude the unborn in general and the disabled unborn in particular. These standards are arbitrary and may well exclude other people, too. Human beings only ever manifest such élite capacities because they have human nature from the start, and without some shared and worthy conception of natures, notions such as disability and rights are ultimately incoherent.

Freedom to abort those with disabilities?

Many people believe that genetic testing and/or abortion are private decisions for the mother and whomever she chooses to consult, because she has the right to control her own body and everything that lives in her

---

[25] CDF, *On Respect for Human Life and Procreation* (1987) I.2, and *CCC* 2274: 'Is Prenatal Diagnosis Morally Licit? If prenatal diagnosis respects the life and integrity of the embryo and the human foetus and is directed towards its safeguarding or healing as an individual, then the answer is affirmative … But this diagnosis is gravely opposed to the moral law when it is done with the thought of possibly inducing an abortion depending upon the results: a diagnosis which shows the existence of a malformation or a hereditary illness must not be the equivalent of a death-sentence. Thus a woman would be committing a gravely illicit act if she were to request such a diagnosis with the deliberate intention of having an abortion should the results confirm the existence of a malformation or abnormality. The spouse or relatives or anyone else would similarly be acting in a manner contrary to the moral law if they were to counsel or impose such a diagnostic procedure on the expectant mother with the same intention of possibly proceeding to an abortion. So too the specialist would be guilty of illicit collaboration if, in conducting the diagnosis and in communicating its results, he were deliberately to contribute to establishing or favouring a link between prenatal diagnosis and abortion.'

body. Since she is left 'holding the baby' both literally and figuratively with respect to the pregnancy, birth and (usually) upbringing of the child, especially a child with a disability, her decisions in this matter must be paramount. Few today dare to question the primacy of autonomy. Even if non-pregnant women do not have an absolute right to do what they please with their bodies, we are loath to suggest anything less for pregnant women.

The obvious answer, of course, is that when any liberty is claimed, the same right must be conceded to others – in this case, to the child in the womb and to disabled people generally. What we really need to ask is whether the focus on *rights* and *autonomy* is helpful in this area in any case. Such talk often comes with individualistic notions of relationships and notions of bodies and persons as property. A more nuanced account of human relationships will resist any view of the unborn as the mother's tissue, property or even her rival. Motherhood is not about ownership or competition. A richer conception of freedom will also recognize that few pregnant women fit the bill of the idealized freely contracting agent in a perfect market, especially when notionally free decisions are made on the prenatal-screening–genetic-abortion treadmill. Even fewer will make 'free' or 'rational' decisions when suffering the natural disappointment, grief, shame or anger when told their unborn child carries a genetic disorder. Fear of social rejection, inexperience of what caring for a child with a disability might actually involve, information deficit or overload – all these significantly limit people's freedom in this situation, and counselling will help only to some degree. Freedom is further reduced by pressures from well-meaning doctors, who automatically make appointments or referrals for abortion, or from others who see 'termination' as the only option. When abortion has become the knee-jerk reaction to adverse genetic test results, supposedly *liberal* societies need to look seriously at what real options and support they offer to distressed women and their disabled children.[26]

In addition, much 'right to choose' talk fails to take account of the intrinsic morality of our choices and their self-constitutive effects: what these choices do to us, what they make us and what they say about us. Whatever we think of abortion itself, do we like what it makes us as individuals, professions and communities? Talk of abortion rights also fails to take into account the web of relationships in which any choice operates

---

[26] G. Naik, 'The toughest test', *Wall Street Journal*, 25 October 2008; M. Tankard-Reist, *Defiant Birth: Women Who Resist Medical Eugenics* (Melbourne: Spinifex, 2006).

and fails to consider the implications of our choices for other people's lives and for the common good. The choice to diagnose and then end the life of a child with a disability affects people beyond the mother and child. We might ask, for instance, what it communicates to surviving children of the same couple or to those people with disabilities in the wider community who have survived to birth or what effect it has on attitudes in the rest of the community towards those with disabilities.

Even if they are persons, aren't the disabled unborn better off dead?

Some people admit that the disabled unborn child is one of us but assert that such a child may be (like many new-born and older people) better off dead. It is probably incoherent to regard death as a better state than life (since there is no one to be 'better off' after death) or to presume to weigh up the good and bad things of one's life as on a scale. It is to pile presumption upon such incoherence to make that judgment *for someone else*, declaring that they would be better off if they had never existed or that their disabilities are so severe as to warrant oblivion. People with disabilities themselves seem to be at least as happy as anyone else to be alive!

Of course 'better off dead' talk can be well-meaning, rooted in compassion towards the child rather than insensitivity or selfishness on the part of onlookers. Here the debate over prenatal screening shades into the euthanasia debate, a topic to which I return in Part III. But if *compassion* for the disabled were our real concern, we would expect addressing the difficulties of people living with disabilities to be our first response. We would be doing our best to ensure that disabled children were given access to high-quality healthcare, special education and other assistance. We would ensure that their families also had access to appropriate support networks and respite. We would be looking for creative responses to disability rather than discrimination, abandonment or homicide. For as long as these positive tokens are so rarely in evidence, it is hardly credible that compassion is driving support for prenatal screening and genetic abortion.

Indeed prejudice is more in evidence than compassion here. Though genetics has shown us just how common and relative disability is, though sound philosophy has shown us that people with disabilities are our moral equals, though long history and recent experience have shown us how well people can accommodate to or even overcome their disabilities, especially if well supported, there are many who hold on stubbornly to the view that people with disabilities are better off dead, better off never born. When dead, they are certainly less burdensome to others; but then we should be honest with ourselves and with the disabled and admit that we are putting them out of *our* misery, not theirs.

The new eugenics

So we come to the real argument for prenatal diagnosis with a view to abortion: that *others* would be better off if the disabled were dead, indeed never born. Genetic abortion bridges the new genetics and the old eugenic mentality. As Evelyne Shuster, medical ethicist for the Philadelphia Veterans Affairs Medical Center observed, 'Prenatal genetic screening allows parents to take on the rôle of gene police, and to erect a roadblock at which they search and examine their children-to-be before birth.'[27] This changes the nature of parenthood, making all pregnancies provisional, conditional upon the unborn child passing the roadside examination. Couples are encouraged to adopt a 'try before you buy' attitude to their children, rather than opening their hearts to accept their children when they come and how they come, however imperfect both children and parents may be.

Meanwhile many in the medical profession and the wider community applaud: antenatal screening followed by eugenic abortion is thought to relieve many people of the unnecessary burden of caring for a person with a disability: parents, family and friends, the health, education and welfare systems and wider society. Most people in contemporary Western societies, even if uneasy with or opposed to abortion-on-demand, support abortion in the case of foetal disability.[28] All the while the list of those conditions or qualities for which abortion is thought warranted keeps growing, partly as a result of increased technical capacity to identify more and more of them, more and more accurately, and partly as a result of the shifting consensus on what is worthwhile existence.

The new eugenics by prenatal testing and abortion relies upon a humanly indefensible conception of our relationship to our children and a philosophically indefensible assertion that one person's life is more important than another's or else relies on the proposition that the welfare

---

[27] E. Shuster, 'Microarray genetic screening: a prenatal roadblock for life?', *The Lancet* 369(9560) (2007), 526–9.

[28] Fleming, 'Analysis of new data', found that support for abortion is strongest in the case of severe foetal disability (85%) or mild foetal disability (60%); but where the foetus is healthy and there is no abnormal risk to the mother, support for abortion drops dramatically.

of the group is more valuable than the life of the (disabled) individual. Dark Ages prejudices, more 'enlightened' benevolent feelings or perennial pragmatism may get the better of sound ethics, drawing us into thinking that killing someone, however heavy-heartedly, is best for all concerned. To base decisions upon such feelings or calculations comes at the cost of compromising fundamental values (such as respect for the dignity of every person) and contradicting the internal goal of medicine (which is saving and curing). Such compromise is lethal for the victims and coarsens the consciences of all who get used to it.[29]

THE NEW ABORTION DEBATE

Challenges to the pro-abortion consensus

In 2004 Australia's minister for health and ageing, Tony Abbott, described Australia's abortion epidemic as a 'national tragedy' and claimed that even those who think that abortion is a woman's right should be troubled by the huge numbers of unborn babies destroyed every year. The minister's candour on this matter was rare among leaders in recent decades, as was the support he received from the then governor-general and prime minister. Soon after this, Julia Black's controversial documentary *My Foetus* was screened worldwide. There were debates about abortion and values in the lead-up to elections, not just in the USA (where this is

---

[29] Other writing on the ethics of the new genetics and pre-natal diagnosis includes: D. Beeson and P. Jennings, 'Prenatal diagnosis of foetal disorders: ethical, legal and social issues', in J. Monagle and D. Thomasma (eds.), *Health Care Ethics: Critical Issues for the 21st Century* (Gaithersburg, MD: Aspen, 1998), pp. 29–44; E. Furton (ed.), *What Is Man, O Lord?* (Boston: NCBC, 2002), pp. 79–130; House of Commons Science and Technology Committee, *Human Genetics*; E. Juengst, 'Prenatal diagnosis and the ethics of uncertainty', in Monagle and Thomasma (eds.), *Health Care Ethics*, pp. 15–28; L. Kass, 'Perfect babies: prenatal diagnosis and the equal right to life', in *Toward a More Natural Science: Biology and Human Affairs* (New York: Free Press, 1985), ch. 3, and 'The age of genetic technology arrives', in *Life, Liberty, and the Defense of Dignity: The Challenge for Bioethics* (San Francisco: Encounter Books, 2002), ch. 4; T. Lee, *Gene Future* (New York: Plenum, 1994); May, *Catholic Bioethics and the Gift of Human Life*, pp. 229–58; N. Messer, 'The human genome project, health and the "tyranny of normality"', in C. Deane-Drummond (ed.), *Brave New World: Theology, Ethics and the Human Genome* (London: T&T Clarke, 2003), pp. 91–115; H. Monsour (ed.), *Ethics and the New Genetics* (Toronto University Press, 2007); A. Moraczewski, 'The human genome project and the Catholic Church', *Int J Bioethics* 2 (1991), 229–34; J. Nelson (ed.), *On the New Frontiers of Genetics and Religion* (Grand Rapids, MI: Eerdmans, 1994); President's Council on Bioethics, *Human Cloning and Human Dignity* (New York: Public Affairs, 2002), and *Beyond Therapy: Biotechnology and the Pursuit of Happiness* (New York: Regan Books, 2003); M. Sandel, *The Case against Perfection: Ethics in the Age of Genetic Engineering* (Harvard University Press, 2007); A. Sutton, *Prenatal Diagnosis: Confronting the Ethical Issues* (London: Linacre Centre, 1990).

customary) but in Australia, Britain, Spain and elsewhere. Various new forums, groups and publications appeared questioning what the media took to be the established consensus on abortion, and several pieces of new research appeared on attitudes to abortion. It was as if this was a debate societies (other than the USA) had long been avoiding but which they 'had to have'. Though abortion was something supposedly settled a generation ago, the unresolved issues occasioned by four decades of virtual abortion-on-demand in Western nations would not go away.

So what had changed? A new generation of women (and men) has emerged with a rather different agenda from that of the generation that fought for and against the abortion increase of the 1970s and 1980s, and they are finding their voice. New groups bring together large numbers of younger people, especially young women, who do not accept that abortion policy has been settled by their predecessors and that it is a no-go area for them.

Another new factor is the very same technological revolution that has been one of the drivers of the abortion revolution. The new genetics has meant that no one who has studied even rudimentary science believes that the early human organism is just a clump of the mother's tissue or vegetable matter waiting for a human soul. Ultrasound imaging and uterine photography allow people to see the unborn child for the human being he or she is and to bond emotionally with that child much earlier. The more we know about the life of the unborn, the greater the community ambivalence about abortion, especially about late-term abortion.

In several places in this book I have treated philosophical issues around the humanity, personhood and rights of the unborn. In popular culture some cut the deck between non-persons and persons at birth, others at conception and others at various stages in-between. In response to each attempt to justify abortion by defining the unborn out of the class of humanity or persons, people now ask: what is the unborn before it is human/personal? What makes the unborn become human/ personal? Ask any grieving mother of a stillborn child or who has had a miscarriage whether it was a child that has died. Try telling her it was 'a pre-personal organism of doubtful moral status'. Recent research shows that what feminist writer Naomi Wolf called 'the foetus-as-nothing paradigm' is no longer intellectually or emotionally tenable for most people.[30]

---

[30] *Weekend Australian*, 7 October 1995, 27.

Apart from generational change and developments in science and society, our religious climate has also developed. A lasting legacy of Pope John Paul II will undoubtedly be his having positioned Catholicism as a defender of the unborn and a builder of a civilization of life and love as an alternative to that of the 'culture of death'. Catholics are not alone in this struggle. Evangelicals, Muslims and other believers are increasingly vocal about their pro-life beliefs. The latest theological explorations of these topics – such as David Jones' excellent *The Soul of the Embryo* – suggest a new generation of theologians and moralists who are more pro-life than many of their predecessors.

Women's experience

Pro-lifers sometimes fall into the same trap as their opponents in over-generalizing: abortion can be presented by them as disastrous in every respect, just as pro-abortionists sometimes pretend there are no ill-effects of abortion. Both sides should recognize that the results of abortion are by no means homogeneous, nor is it universally experienced as all good or all bad. Many women – as well as men, families and societies – experience great relief from fear or threat after abortion,[31] even if they are often (or, as one suspects, almost always) ambivalent about it. Realizing this helps to underline what pro-lifers already know: that we should be very slow indeed to judge a woman who has had an abortion. We cannot know how free she really was, what options she had or thought she had, what pressures she was under, what fears or threats pregnancy and life as a mother presented or how well she understood what was involved. Most probably she was frightened and lonely, abandoned or pressured by the father, family, friends, peers and societal or financial considerations. Time and again women who have had an abortion report that they felt they would 'die' whatever they did; that abortion was for them just the 'least worst' option or the only real option they had. Some of this may be self-delusion or self-justification. But women do not have abortions as a conscious, perverse choice against life, humanity or morality; they do not do so out of hatred for children in general or for their particular child; they do not think their child's death is good in itself.

[31] S. Ewing, *Women and Abortion: An Evidence-Based Review* (Sydney: Women's Forum Australia, 2005), p. 30; NHMRC, *Termination of Pregnancy in Australia*, p. 33.

Nonetheless it is important to address the ill-effects of abortion, because
so often the abortion industry and its promoters in politics and the media
(e.g. in many women's magazines) present abortion as deceptively simple
and safe. A number of physical complications are associated with abortion, ranging from death, which fortunately is now rare, to the much less
serious but much more common side-effects such as uterine haemorrhage
associated with cervical trauma, uterine perforation, uterine atony (with
or without retained placental tissue), pelvic infection and enduring cervical incompetence. There is also growing evidence of increased infertility, breast cancer and other side-effects.[32]

The psychological complications from abortion are more significant
than the physical ones. At one end of the range are those women who
suffer severe psychiatric breakdowns consequent upon abortion: they are
rare, but if only 0.1 per cent of the 25 million women who have abortions each year suffer abortion-related breakdowns, that is 25,000 women.
At the other end of the range there are those women who report that
they experience nothing but relief following abortion. In-between there
are many more women who suffer various degrees of mild psychological
ill-effects such as unresolved guilt and regret, some anxiety and perhaps
sleeplessness, sometimes surfacing immediately after the abortion but for
others not until much later.[33] Whatever the professional literature and the
psychiatric associations might say about 'post-abortion syndrome', the
fact is that many psychologists, counsellors, priests and pastoral workers

[32] E. Bachiochi (ed.), *The Cost of Choice: Women Evaluate the Impact of Abortion* (San Francisco:
Encounter, 2004); Ewing, *Women and Abortion*; H. Morris and L. Williams, 'Physical complications of abortion', in I. Gentles (ed.), *A Time to Choose Life* (Toronto: Stoddart, 1990),
pp. 74–84; NHMRC, *Termination of Pregnancy in Australia*, pp. 24–6; M. Parthun, H. Morris
and L. Williams, *Abortion's Aftermath: The Psychological Effects of Induced Abortion and the
Physical Complications* (Toronto: Human Life Research Institute of Ottawa, 1985); E. Ring-
Cassidy and I. Gentles, *Women's Health after Abortion: The Medical and Psychological Evidence*,
2nd edn (Toronto: deVeber Institute, 2003); T. Strahan (ed.), *Detrimental Effects of Abortion: An
Annotated Bibliography with Commentary*, 3rd edn (Springfield, IL: Acorn, 2001).
[33] In addition to sources in the previous note see: N. Adler *et al.*, 'Psychological responses after abor-
tion', *Science* 248 (1990), 41–4; E. J. Angelo, 'Psychological sequelae of abortion', *LQ* 59(2) (1992),
69–80; C. Barnard, *The Long-Term Psychosocial Effects of Abortion* (Portsmouth, NH: Institute for
Pregnancy Loss, 1990); J. Brende, 'Post-trauma sequelae of abortion', *Journal of Interdisciplinary
Research in Values and Social Change* 7(1) (1994), 18–21; L. de Veber *et al.*, 'Post abortion grief',
Humane Medicine 7(3) (1991), 203–20, and 'Abortion and bereavement', in Gentles (ed.), *A Time
to Choose Life*, pp. 85–94; P. Ney *et al.*, 'Mental health and abortion', *Psychiatric Journal of the
University of Ottawa* 14(4) (1989), 506–16; J. Robotham, 'Abortion linked to mental problems',
Sydney Morning Herald, 3 January 2006; V. Rue, *Post-Abortion Trauma* (Lewisville, TX: Life
Dynamics, 1994); V. Rue and A. Speckhard, 'Post-abortion trauma: incidence and diagnostic
considerations', *Medicine and Mind* 6 (1991), 57–74; T. Selby, *The Mourning After: Help for Post-
Abortion Syndrome* (Grand Rapids, MI: Baker, 1990); A. Speckhard and V. Rue, 'Post-abortion
syndrome: an emerging public health concern', *J Soc Issues* 48(3) (1992), 95–120.

deal with the aftermath of abortion, and one suspects that many women who need such help never receive it.[34]

If physical and psychological consequences are rarely appreciated, the moral and spiritual ill-effects of abortion are even less well understood. Guilt, shame and remorse are not only, or even primarily, psychological problems; nor are they necessarily pathological. Many pastors and counsellors encounter women suffering emotionally and psychologically as a result of abortion, and this is a perfectly normal response to a grave evil perpetrated and suffered. Christians expect grave sins to have grave spiritual consequences, just as ancient and more modern secular philosophers recognize that such actions deeply affect the character of the agent. In *Evangelium Vitae* John Paul II noted the factors that drive many women to abortion and diminish their responsibility, possibly entirely: factors such as domestic violence, pressures from outsiders, dire personal difficulties, isolation and abandonment, fear and loneliness, the struggle to make ends meet, unbearable pain and suffering (*EV* 58–9). For these victims of abortion, as for all women who have been through the abortion mill, the Pope had only words of compassion, calling them back into the life of Christ and his Church (*EV* 99). This points to the very real challenge for the Church to provide good counselling and sacramental care for women considering abortion or who have had abortions, in addition to forming priests, pastoral assistants and counsellors for this work.

Despite abortion being the most common surgical procedure in the world, knowledge of its after-effects is surprisingly limited. The acquisition and distribution of such information is subverted by a lack of adequately resourced and independent research, a lack of receptiveness to findings, financial and professional vested interests, cultural collusion in the practice of abortion and the relative powerlessness of

[34] From very different perspectives: J. Angelo, 'Project Rachel: post-abortion ministry', in J. V. Correa and E. Sgreccia (eds.), *La Cultura della Vita: Supplemento* (Libreria Editrice Vaticana, 2002), pp. 32–8; B. and S. Banks, *Ministering to Abortion's Aftermath* (Kirkwood, MO: Impact Books, 1982); T. Burke *et al.*, *Rachel's Vineyard: A Psychological and Spiritual Journey of Post-Abortion Healing* (Staten Island, NY: Alba House, 1995); C. De Puy and D. Dovitch, *The Healing Choice: Your Guide to Emotional Recovery after an Abortion* (New York: Fireside, 1997); L. Freed and P. Salazar, *A Season to Heal* (Nashville, TN: Cumberland, 1993); K. Kluger-Bell, *Unspeakable Losses: Healing from Miscarriage, Abortion, and Other Pregnancy Loss* (New York: HarperCollins, 2000); S. Massé and J. Phillips, *Her Choice to Heal: Finding Spiritual and Emotional Peace after Abortion*, 2nd edn (Colorado Springs: David C. Cook, 2009); J. O'Neill, *You're Not Alone: Healing Through God's Grace after Abortion* (Deerfield Beach, FL: Health Communications, 2005); D. Powlison, *Healing after Abortion* (Greensboro, NC: New Growth, 2008); D. Reardon, *The Jericho Plan: Breaking Down the Walls Which Prevent Post-Abortion Healing* (Springfield, IL: Acorn, 1996); T. and P. Reisser, *A Solitary Sorrow: Finding Healing and Wholeness after Abortion* (Wheaton, IL: H. Shaw, 1999).

victims. The abortion industry and its promoters play down the ill-effects of abortion for commercial and ideological reasons. As long as being pro-abortion is the membership test for some segments of the women's movement or for a selection of women candidates in some political parties, the very people who should be demanding rigorous research and information-giving will be mute on this issue. It is a remarkable fact of women's health history that while feminist groups have exposed the dangers of caesarean sections, mastectomies, hysterectomies and some contraceptives, they have allowed the damage done to women by surgical and chemical (medical) abortion to continue largely unexamined and uncriticized. The lack of aftercare for women after abortion matches the disturbing lack of pre-abortion information and option-giving. Even so, the 'abortion is safe and easy' line does not wash with most people any longer, nor are women as willing to be as silent as they were in the past. Increasingly, stories and studies are emerging of the physical, psychological, emotional and spiritual toll of the abortion revolution.[35]

Abortion was supposed to win women freedom. Yet as feminist matriarch Germaine Greer has observed:

What women 'won' was the 'right' to undergo invasive procedures in order to terminate unwanted pregnancies, unwanted not just by them but by their parents, their sexual partners, the governments who would not support mothers, the employers who would not employ mothers, the landlords who would not accept tenants with children, the schools that would not accept students with children. Historically the only thing pro-abortion agitation achieved was to make an illiberal establishment look far more feminist than it was.[36]

Many young feminists today are convinced that a women-centred approach to abortion could and should mean less abortion not more.[37]

---

[35] T. Burke, *Forbidden Grief: The Unspoken Pain of Abortion* (Springfield, IL: Acorn, 2002); L. Clarke, *Can't Keep Silent: A Woman's 22-Year Journey of Post-Abortion Healing* (Mustang, OK: Tate Publishing, 2006); P. Ervin, *Women Exploited: The Other Victims of Abortion* (Huntington, IN: Our Sunday Visitor, 1985); B. Harak (ed.), *Real Abortion Stories: The Hurting and the Healing* (El Paso: Strive for the Best Publishing, 2007); D. Marshall and M. Crean, 'The human face of a woman's agony', in Gentles (ed.), *A Time to Choose Life*, pp. 134–46; D. Reardon, *Aborted Women: Silent No More* (Springfield, IL: Acorn, 2002); M. Tankard-Reist, *Giving Sorrow Words: Women's Stories of Grief after Abortion* (Sydney: Duffy and Snellgrove, 2000).

[36] G. Greer, *The Whole Woman* (New York: Doubleday, 1999), p. 86; cf. Bachiochi, *The Cost of Choice*.

[37] See, e.g., B. McKenna-Vout, 'Reframing the anti-abortion message: pro-life and/or pro-woman?', and M. Riordan, 'Moving beyond the polarised debate on abortion: the way of the future', in Fleming and Tonti-Filippini (eds.), *Common Ground?*, chs. 5 and 6.

Effects on others

Four decades' experience shows that large-scale abortion is like throwing a stone in a pond. There is an immediate and obvious splash: the death of an unborn child and relief for and often wounding of the mother. There are also waves that go out in all directions. Try as we may, such matters can never be entirely privatized. As John Donne put it: 'Any man's death diminishes me, because I am involved in mankind; and therefore never send to know for whom the bell tolls; it tolls for thee.'[38] What are some of these waves?

Just as many women experience relief after abortion, so too may their husbands, partners, existing children, parents and friends. As with the women, there can also be ambivalence for these 'abortion survivors'. Little is known about the effects of abortion grief upon the fathers and upon other surviving family members but there is plenty of anecdotal evidence of ill-effects.[39] Despite the predictions that abortion would produce a caring society in which every child would be a wanted child, the reported incidence of physical abuse of children doubled in each decade with the abortion revolution. Abortion also carries physical risks to future children of premature birth, low birthweight and physical and mental retardation. Whether some of these children also suffer 'survivor guilt' or other resentment is also unresearched.

The most obvious effect of abortion on health professionals is a sense of a job well done, a service provided, a person assisted, a problem out of the way. For some there is the satisfaction of taking part in an activity to which they are ideologically committed. For others there is a lucrative income: abortion is now a multimillion dollar industry and its profits are concentrated in the hands of a relatively small group of practitioners with a strong interest in promoting abortion. Still others take part less willingly: considerable pressure is brought to bear on medical students, doctors, nurses, pharmacists, genetic counsellors and social workers to

---

[38] John Donne, *No Man is an Island* (Meditation XVII from 'Devotions Upon Emergent Occasions', 1624).

[39] K. Burke, D. Wemhoff and M. Stockwell, *Redeeming a Father's Heart: Men Share Powerful Stories of Abortion Loss and Recovery* (Bloomington, IN: Author House, 2007); B. Mattes, 'The impact on men of losing a child by abortion', www.lifeissues.org/men/impact.html (accessed 1 January 2011); Philip Ney, 'Relationship between abortion and child abuse', *Can J Psychiatry* 24 (1979), 610–20; M. Simon, 'Male partners and the psychological sequelae of abortion: a psychodynamic-relational view', www.afterabortion.com/ mens_react.html (accessed 1 January 2011); E. Ring-Cassidy and Ian Gentles, 'Abortion: its effect on men', in *Women's Health after Abortion*, ch. 16; V. Rue, 'The effects of abortion on men', *Ethics & Medics* 21(4) (1996), 3–4; A. Shostak, G. McLouth and L. Seng, *Men and Abortion* (New York: Praeger, 1984).

become involved in abortion despite conscientious or emotional objections. In some places the legal and professional right of conscientious objection to performing, assisting in or referring for abortion is being gradually whittled away. To object can cost people their careers. This is despite the evidence of psychological ill-effects on the abortionists themselves, of high staff turnover rates, difficulty of finding abortionists in some places despite the financial rewards and reports of burnout and psychological disturbance.[40]

The rising abortion rate has also had a significant effect on professional ethics. The fundamental orientation of healthcare has traditionally been to save, cure and care. Increasingly health professionals are pressured to assume the values of the free market, to become 'service providers for a fee' or even 'hired guns'. There is a demand for abortion, so it should be supplied. Lack of medical indication for the procedure is irrelevant. Not all doctors and nurses have embraced this consumerist ethic, but there has been a discernible revolution in attitudes to early human life. Previously it was held that the pregnant woman and her child presented the doctor with two patients, and this was acknowledged in the official position of the health professional bodies and the practice of many of their members.

Another group that is radically affected by the escalating abortion rate are infertile couples. In addition to professional curiosity, the driving force behind in vitro fertilization and the other reproductive technologies has been the fact that at least one in ten couples in many Western nations is infertile. Many of these want to bring up children, but adoption has become very difficult because unwanted children, though still regularly conceived, are rarely born any more, though childless couples could have given them a loving home.

Another effect of the abortion revolution rarely considered is demographic. Western societies are ageing rapidly: by 2050 there could be a million centenarians in the USA alone. Meanwhile the birth-rate is below replacement in most of these countries. Demographers tell us that the low birth-rate, which has been well below replacement level for a long time, is more significant for the ageing of the population than increased longevity. Why the falling birth-rate? Contraception in Western nations has led to a 'copulation explosion' and rather than decreasing, the number of unplanned and unwanted pregnancies has often actually increased.

---

[40] See Nathanson, *Aborting America*. Thus NHMRC, *Termination of Pregnancy in Australia*, p. 39, recommends the provision of appropriate individual or group counselling for abortion practitioners and their staff.

Abortion then becomes the backstop in a babies-on-demand culture and is what brings down the birth-rate. Children still get conceived in large numbers; it's just that nowadays many are killed before they are born.[41]

Effects on the whole community

A last consequence of the abortion revolution is the effect it has had on our communities as a whole. What does the fact that our community sustains abortion at epidemic proportions say about us? What does this make us? Moral choices constitute persons and communities. Even discounting the unborn children killed and other individuals directly or remotely involved (the mother, the father, the abortionist, the counsellor, friends/family and so on), abortion is not victimless, because the society that tolerates, condones, finances or otherwise supports it is also significantly harmed in the process. A society that says by its actions that some people lack inherent worth or may be killed to benefit others has seriously undermined a first principle of justice and community: a willingness to treat every member of that society with equal concern and respect. The absence of that willingness is likely to be fateful for others. Logically and psychologically, medical homicide once accepted will eventually be extended to other individuals and groups.

Abortion treats the unborn child as radically unequal, profoundly subordinate, to adults who decide whether she will live or die. In the process the parties involved and the community buy into a dynamic of violence and domination, however well we rationalize it. We add a new weapon to the arsenal of discrimination and oppression: in the case of prenatal screening with a view to aborting those with disabilities, a weapon for lethal discrimination and for a new eugenics. We accept a patriarchal, individualistic way of relating: me against my baby, me against my community, my life and my body as my property, the freedom to do as I please as paramount. We buy into a selective blindness so that we can systematically ignore the consequences of abortion and the thousands wounded in the process, pregnant women as well as others. For all the talk about reproductive freedom, we do precious little about providing alternatives to abortion so that women can make real choices.

Growing appreciation of the complex personal and social effects of abortion has enriched the debate about its intrinsic morality. Many are

[41] L. Roberge, *The Cost of Abortion: An Analysis of the Social, Economic, and Demographic Effects of Abortion in the United States*, 2nd edn (Lagrange, GA: Four Winds, 1995).

now questioning the smug 1970s and 1980s consensus on abortion, that abortion is inevitably a commonplace and that the community should turn a deaf ear to the ethical arguments and a blind eye to the ill-effects.

Responding to the new abortion scene

Never has abortion been so widespread, so readily available and so institutionalized. The Obama administration in the USA is giving the industry a new lease of life, but the industry can no longer rely upon a consensus, even among the academic, journalistic and feminist cognoscenti, and certainly not among ordinary people. This presents new points of entry for pro-life discourse, new opportunities to convert the culture, new hope for building a civilization of life and love. What must we do?

First, Catholics and others will need to keep proclaiming the humanity of the embryo and foetus – that the unborn child from conception to birth is a human being, a member of the human family, our little brother or sister – and that killing the innocent, however expedient this may sometimes appear, is never morally right. Despite often seeming fruitless, four decades of pro-life work has had some effect here. For all the efforts of the much better resourced abortion industry and its friends, polls demonstrate that the community is still not convinced by the foetus-ain't-a-person rhetoric, let alone the foetus-as-nothing paradigm. Indeed the community is less and less convinced of the soundness of these positions.

Second, we must respond to the culture of choice. On the one hand, we must contest the assumption that all that matters in life is getting our own way. Having conquered the communist separation of the common good from freedom, Pope John Paul II's great project for the Western world was to challenge the consumerist separation of freedom from truth, a critique that Benedict XVI has continued and amplified (see Chapter 2). The idea that we can simply choose, as a matter of personal or communal taste, whom to include in the 'in-group' of persons and whom to cast beyond the pale and its protections, or that we can choose to kill some we recognize are indeed fellow human beings, must be challenged: freedom, we must insist, is the opportunity freely to do the good, not to do what is arbitrary, intrinsically evil or wantonly harmful. At the same time, even as they question the dogma of autonomy-trumping-all, pro-lifers can benefit from its ascendancy by honestly pressing for women's freedom to choose well, rather than being railroaded into abortion. Ironically, after forty years' rhetoric of 'the woman's right to choose', only the pro-life side are campaigning to give women *real* alternatives. Giving them a breathing space is a start. When the Adelaide Women and Children's Hospital introduced mandatory independent counselling before abortion, they saw a 25 per cent reduction in abortion numbers, prompting calls from the abortion industry to ban such independent counselling and calls from others to ensure that independent information, options-giving and counselling are made much more widely available.[42]

Sadly governments and insurers have for many years spent ten or more times as much on counselling for abortion by abortion providers as they have spent on abortion alternatives counselling offered by pro-life pregnancy counselling services. When women think that pregnancy is death to their planned life story, we need to help them, not only to revise their proposed biography, but also to be less afraid of the revised version. We also need to ensure that pregnancy and childbirth are not the end for women who seek an education, a career or any other reasonable goal. This raises big questions regarding maternity and paternity leave, educational and workplace practices, childcare, tax structures and other social policies, which need to be much more mother-friendly and family-friendly. Church and pro-life groups have long provided constructive alternatives for women with unplanned pregnancies. The challenge may be even greater in the future. We should not, however, lose sight of just how much has been achieved: a substantial network of people give generously of their time and energy, skills and care, in direct pregnancy, postnatal and post-abortion support, as well as in lobbying, writing and otherwise working for a more just and merciful community.

Third, we must question the widespread notion of abortion as a *necessary* evil, as something we have just got to accept however little we all like it. The harm minimizationalists sell us a low view of human possibilities (even under divine grace) and encourage us to think that women, their partners and their doctors cannot be expected to abstain from abortion. They tell us that whatever we say or do, abortion will continue, so it is best to provide safer circumstances for it. We must respond by demonstrating that ordinary people can indeed be noble, generous, even heroic, in the face of threats to their life-plans, comfort and security – especially if they are well formed and supported. We have to be ready, too, with

---

[42] *Adelaide Sunday Mail*, 25 July 2004. Fleming, 'Analysis of new data', found that 99% of respondents believe that women contemplating an abortion should have access to counselling and that 98% of those polled thought that women should be advised of any health risks involved in having an abortion before choosing an abortion.

answers to the old chestnuts about abortion to save the mother's life or to save the child from life, abortion to save the woman's health or to save her child from disability, even if we now know these situations are very rare. We can surely offer people a better account of the good life, one that appeals to the gifts and strengths of women (and men) and enables them to 'take control' of their lives, not by robbing anyone else of life but by a gift of themselves that is ultimately life-giving for them also.

Fourth, we need also to empower men to take their part in supporting pregnant women. Many feel impotent to contribute either to social debate or individual decisions in this area, even when they are the father. Many men evade commitment, responsibility or sacrifice: they are afraid of growing up.[43] We must help them recover healthy ideals of manhood, sex and fatherhood, which replace the recreationalization of sex and diminishment of women which came with the contraceptive revolution. In the face of the decades-long emasculation of men, we must re-image men as potential fathers rather than carriers of pregnancy, a terrible sexually transmitted disease. Men must not continue to be disconnected from spousal and familial responsibilities. By recovering a love of their bodies and their fathering potential and by regaining a sense of the place of sex within committed marital love, both men and women are liberated to say what they mean and mean what they say when using the sexual language of their bodies.

Fifth, we must challenge the natural assumption that the way to reduce abortion rates is more value-free sex education and greater access to contraception. After four decades of pursuing this very panacea in the West, abortion rates remain high and in some places continue to rise. There are already high levels of contraceptive knowledge and use among those who have abortions. Indeed, most abortions in Western countries occur among people who are already using contraception.[44]

Sixth, Christians and other pro-lifers need to get much smarter about their messaging: how we say what we say, when and where and in whose voice, is as important as the message itself if converting real people and real cultures is our goal. There can be a perverse pleasure in screaming

[43] An interesting recent treatment of this matter is G. Cross, *Men to Boys: The Making of Modern Immaturity* (New York: Columbia University Press, 2008).
[44] See, e.g., W. Abigail *et al.*, 'Changing patterns in women seeking terminations of pregnancy: a trend analysis of data from one service provider 1996–2006', *Aust NZ J Public Health* 32(3) (2008), 230–7; M. Aston, 'Sex education and contraception do not reduce abortion rates', *Guardian*, 5 March 2008; J. Richters *et al.*, 'Sex in Australia: contraceptive practices among a representative sample of women', *Aust NZ J Public Health* 27(2) (2003) 210–16.

into the storm, hitting our heads against the wall, proclaiming the same message we always have in a language we know few listen to. We can feel we are the ethical remnant, martyrs in a corrupt and doomed civilization. Instead, we need to do sound research into social attitudes, into what approaches and messages work with people and be willing to let go of well-worn strategies or rhetoric that do not work or that no longer work. This does not mean abandoning moral principles, selling out for quick popularity or sacrificing some to save others. It does mean reading the signs of the times and bringing our ancient principles and contemporary prudence to bear upon the real challenges and opportunities of these times.

Lastly, we must beware of casting ourselves as the permanently carping critic. Respect for human life, we know, requires more than just not killing people. We express our reverence for life by supporting the precept against killing but also by working to promote life and love. Motivated by justice and compassion, we must seek to build a world where violence is not seen as an answer; where the treatment of the weak and defenceless is the measure of our community's self-esteem; where pregnancy is no longer seen as a millstone around a woman's neck but an occasion for rejoicing; where those who have unplanned pregnancies are supported in every way possible through those nine months and for the years beyond. We await the advent of that Kingdom where the wolf shall dwell with the lamb, the leopard lie down with the kid and children will be free from danger; when men will beat their swords into ploughshares, their spears into pruning hooks; when nation shall not lift up sword against nation; when the peacemakers will be called children of God (Isa. ch. 11; Matt. 5:9). Such a positive vision is demonstrated when we promote the Christian pro-life vision in all its dimensions and act to ease the burdens of those driven to despair. In word and deed we live for the day when we can use again that ancient folk metaphor for security: 'as safe as a child in its mother's womb'.

PART III

Later life

CHAPTER 7

Transplants: bodies, relationships and ethics

LOVE BEYOND DEATH

The French-Canadian film *Jésus de Montréal* is a secular retelling of the life-sharing death of Jesus and his 'resurrection' in the lives of other people. When the Jesus figure in this young people's Passion play is killed, his bodily organs are harvested and so several people's lives are saved.[1] Pope John Paul II drew a similar parallel with respect to transplantation: 'The progress of medical science has made it possible for people to project even beyond death their vocation to love. Analogously to Christ's Paschal Mystery, in dying, death is somehow overcome and life restored.'[2]

Transplantation is one of the real success stories of modern medicine and is rightly celebrated for the lives it has saved or improved. Progress in this area has been very rapid, and an ever-growing variety of individual major organs (and even multiple major organs), blood, bone and other tissues, cell lines and stem cells are being successfully transferred from one party to another. So successful is transplantation that demand for tissues far outstrips supply. New sources for tissues are therefore constantly being sought, and there are regular campaigns to encourage people to donate renewable tissues, such as blood or bone marrow, and to consent in advance to the use of their tissues after death for transplantation. Some jurisdictions now presume such consent unless there is evidence to the contrary, which has become a source of continuing bioethical and biolegal debate. In other jurisdictions there is little or no regulation in practice and a thriving trade in organs. The principal 'donors' are, of course, the poor, and sometimes the unwilling, especially

---

[1] *Jésus de Montréal* (1989), directed by Denys Arcaud and starring Lothaire Bluteau. The film won the Ecumenical Jury Prize at the Cannes Film Festival in 1989 and the Genie Award for Best Canadian Film in 1989.
[2] John Paul II, *Address to the First International Congress of the Transplantation Society*, 20 June 1991, 4.

185

from Asia and the Near East; the tissue recipients are the wealthy of all nations. Meanwhile research continues apace, with 'xenotransplants' or 'heterografts' – the transfer of valves, skin and other parts from animals to human beings – already taking place and much more proposed for the future. As we saw in Chapter 5, others hope to extract stem cells or other tissues, even from embryos and foetuses, possibly cloned as perfect genetic matches for the recipient.

Whatever the degree and kind of tissue transfer, it must be viewed from two perspectives: every such tissue has to come *from* someone or somewhere before it goes *to* someone else – hence the 'trans' in trans-plantation. In what follows I consider some ethical issues relating to *obtaining* organs and other tissues, then ethical issues with respect to *receiving* such tissues. I first reflect on how different conceptions of the human body and the relationship between the various parties involved colours or preconditions our ethical reasoning about tissue transplantation.[3]

CONCEPTIONS OF THE BODY AND RELATIONSHIPS IN TISSUE TRANSPLANTATION

There are at least three competing, if also overlapping, conceptions of the human body and of the tissue transfer relationship operative in contemporary bioethics and transplantation practice: first, the body as 'property' of someone and tissue transfer as a kind of 'transaction'; second, the body as something received 'on trust' and tissue transfer as a 'gift'; and, third, the body as 'personal' (some*one* rather than some*thing*) and tissue transfer

---

[3] Other recent writing on the ethics of transplantation includes: B. Ashley, J. deBlois and K. O'Rourke, *Health Care Ethics: A Catholic Theological Analysis*, 5th edn (Washington, DC: Georgetown University Press, 2006), pp. 103–8, 123 and 169–77; A. Caplan, *If I Were a Rich Man Could I Buy a Pancreas?* (Bloomington: Indiana University Press, 1992), part IV; F. Delmonico, 'Why we should not pay for human organs', *NCBQ* 2(3) (2002), 381–9, and 'The evolving practice of tissue donation', in E. Furton (ed.), *Live the Truth: The Moral Legacy of John Paul II in Catholic Health Care* (Philadelphia: NCBC, 2006), pp. 269–78; J. DuBois, 'Organ transplantation: an ethical roadmap', *NCBQ* 2(3) (2002), 413–53; R. Fox and J. S. Dwazay, *Spare Parts: Organ Replacement in American Society* (Oxford University Press, 1992); E. Furton, 'Brain death, the soul and organic life', *NCBQ* 2(3) (2002), 455–70; E. R. Gold, *Body Parts: Property Rights and the Ownership of Human Biological Materials* (Washington, DC: Georgetown University Press, 1996); L. Kass, 'Organs for sale? Propriety, property and the price of progress', in *Life, Liberty, and the Defense of Dignity: The Challenge for Bioethics* (San Francisco: Encounter Books, 2002), ch. 6; D. Lamb, *Organ Transplants and Ethics* (Aldershot: Avebury, 1996); J. Leies *et al.*, *Handbook on Critical Life Issues*, 3rd edn (Boston: NCBC, 2004), chs. 11 and 15; W. E. May, *Catholic Bioethics and the Gift of Human Life*, 2nd edn (Huntington, IN: Our Sunday Visitor, 2008), ch. 8; W. Smith, 'Organ donors or organ farms?', *Culture of Death: The Assault on Medical Ethics in America* (San Francisco: Encounter, 2000), ch. 5; H. ten Have and J. Welier (eds.), *Ownership of the Human Body: Philosophical Considerations* (Dordrecht: Kluwer, 1998).

as a 'sharing of life'. I examine each of these briefly before exploring how they play out in one ethically contentious area: xenotransplantation, the transplantation of non-human tissues to human patients.

The body as property

The model of the *body as property* and *tissue transfer as transaction* is perhaps the most common today, especially among individualists and consequentialists, who dominate Western bioethical discourse. On this view, the body is a merely material reality, the subject of various uses by the 'self' or by others. If organs and other tissues are conceived as commodities belonging to the autonomous agent, people will be happy for them to be bought, sold, given or bequeathed, along the lines of the free market. If they are conceived as resources serving the common good, people will be happy for them also to be commandeered or redistributed, especially after death. Such a conception is often behind talk of tissue 'procurement' or 'harvesting', whereby the body is conceived as a series of parts belonging to someone that can be procured or harvested by someone else, such property then being conveyed to a third party for his or her use.

Such a view of the body is, I believe, indefensibly dualist and inclines people to instrumentalize their bodies and those of others.[4] It is a view by no means peculiar to the transplantation scene: it runs very deep in our culture today and plays out in many ways in healthcare, e.g. in gender reassignment surgery, attitudes to the embryo, sterilization, various forms of psychosomatic manipulation, denial of nutrition and hydration to the 'vegetative', some of which are considered in this volume. It is also very common outside healthcare, e.g. in the recreationalization and commercialization of sex and drugs, in pop culture's language of 'the real me' and the 'inner person' and so forth.[5]

The body as trust

The second model, that of *the body as trust* and *tissue transfer as gift*, is common in Christian writing and in some Catholic magisterial teaching in this area. Here bodily life is conceived of as a gift received

---

[4] See P. Lee and R. George, *Body–Self Dualism in Contemporary Ethics and Politics* (Cambridge University Press, 2007).
[5] D. Joralemon, 'Organ wars: the battle for body parts', *Med Anthrop Q* 9(3) (1995), 335–56; Lee and George, *Body–Self Dualism*; L. Sharp, 'Organ transplantation as a transformative experience: anthropological insights into the restructuring of the self', *Med Anthrop Q* 9(3) (1995), 357–89.

on trust by the person from God (and parents and ancestors). Rather than conceiving of the body and bodily life in terms of ownership, we should think of ourselves as trustees, guardians or stewards. Bodily life is not a resource with which to do as we please, individually or as a community; it is given into our stewardship so that we might live well according to God's laws and the principles of practical reason (cf. Matt. 25:14–30).

On this account, any other use of the body is an abuse. One good use we can make of the body, as trustees, is to give it to others: in the bodily love-making of marriage or – more unusually – in tissue donation to those in need. Here the donor freely gives, expecting no return, and the recipient gratefully receives, the self-gift of the body. The language of 'donation' and 'gift' appropriately reflects this understanding, rather than the language of 'procurement' and 'harvest'. Yet this model, too, can risk commodifying the body and objectifying organs and other tissues, so that while they cannot be sold or confiscated, they are still something distinct from the giver of the gift. A great deal of personalist philosophy is required – such as John Paul II offered in his *Theology of the Body* – to avoid a subtler dualism and instrumentalization.[6] Furthermore, it is hard to see how tissue donation can be described as the deceased person's *gift* unless the person actually volunteered before they died to make this

---

[6] Such language is used in several places by Pope John Paul II, e.g.: 'It is in this context, so humanly rich and filled with love, that *heroic actions* too are born. These are *the most solemn celebration of the Gospel of life*, for they proclaim it *by the total gift of self* ... A particularly praiseworthy example of such gestures is the donation of organs, performed in an ethically acceptable manner, with a view to offering a chance of health and even of life itself to the sick who sometimes have no other hope' (*EV* 86). 'With the advent of organ transplantation, which began with blood transfusions, man has found a way to give of himself, of his blood and of his body, so that others may continue to live ... we are challenged to love our neighbour in new ways; in evangelical terms, to love "to the end" ... the love which gives life to others. Thus the progress of the bio-medical sciences has made it possible for people to project beyond death their vocation to love ... Above all, this form of treatment is inseparable from a *human act of donation*. In effect, transplantation presupposes a prior, explicit, free and conscious decision on the part of the donor or of someone who legitimately represents the donor, generally the closest relatives. It is a decision to offer, without reward, a part of one's own body for the health and well-being of another person. In this sense, the medical action of transplantation makes possible the donor's act of self-giving, that sincere gift of self which expresses our constitutive calling to love and communion. Love, communion, solidarity and absolute respect for the dignity of the human person constitute the only legitimate context of organ transplantation ... The Death and Resurrection of the Lord constitute the supreme act of love which gives profound meaning to the donor's offering of an organ to save another person. For Christians, Jesus' offering of himself is the essential point of reference and inspiration of the love underlying the willingness to donate an organ, which is a manifestation of generous solidarity, all the more eloquent in a society which has become excessively utilitarian and less sensitive to unselfish giving' (John Paul II, *Address to the First International Congress of the Transplantation Society*, 20 June 1991, 2–4).

bequest. The consent of our next of kin makes the donation of our tissues really their gift, not ours.

The body as personal

This leads to the third and preferred model: *the body as personal* and *tissue transfer as sharing life*. On this account, the body is the enfleshment of the soul, embodying the human person, while the soul integrates and informs the body. Even if there is more to me than my material elements, my living body is *me*; it is not some*thing* I own or give, it is the some*one* that I am. In tissue sharing, therefore, I do not give something distinct from me, even if, once given, it is also that: I give *of* myself, I give my*self*. I share my life in what is therefore a kind of solidarity, friendship or communion with the one who receives my organ(s) or other tissues. If I have died my kin agree to this and they too become part of this communion, this sharing of life and hopes. This way of conceiving the body and the tissue transfer relationship is also found most commonly in the teachings of the Church.[7]

This third account highlights the need for care that no undue emotional, financial or other pressure is brought to bear upon potential donors or their kin, the need to attend to the needs of the grieving families and health professionals and the need for good aftercare for tissue recipients. It might also imply that there should be some kind of ongoing relationship between donor and recipient or between the family of a deceased donor and the recipient, which contrasts with the normally anonymous transaction and gift models. It also means that health professionals should see themselves not merely as intermediaries in a transaction or even as carriers of gifts but as mediators of a life-giving sacrifice of love.

---

[7] For example, Pope John Paul II: 'Transplants are a great step forward in science's service of man and not a few people today owe their lives to an organ transplant. Increasingly, the technique of transplants has proven to be a valid means of attaining the primary goal of all medicine – the service of human life ... Here precisely lies the nobility of the gesture [of tissue donation], a gesture which is a genuine act of love. It is not just a matter of giving away something that belongs to us but of giving something of ourselves, for by virtue of its substantial union with a spiritual soul, the human body cannot be considered as a mere complex of tissues, organs and functions; rather, it is a constitutive part of the person who manifests and expresses himself through it. Accordingly, any procedure which tends to commercialize human organs or to consider them as items of exchange or trade must be considered morally unacceptable, because to use the body as an 'object' is to violate the dignity of the human person' (*Address to the Eighteenth International Congress of the Transplantation Society*, 29 August 2000, 1 and 3; cf. Pontifical Council for Health, *Charter for Healthworkers* (1994; English trans. 1995) 85).

Our view of the body and of the relationship between donor and recipient has important implications for issues around xenotransplantation.[8]
For one thing, such a process *cannot* involve a relationship of solidarity
or communion between the animal from which the tissue is taken and
the person to whom it is transferred. As we will see later in this chapter,
some deontological critics of xenotransplantation believe it involves a lack
of reverence for animals and an improper relationship between animals
and human beings. Yet many people who are uncomfortable with xenotransplantation are happy to eat meat, which on the face of it is equally
catastrophic for the animal and arguably an even more demeaning use of
it. There are ontological and psychological differences, of course. Whereas
meat once eaten is broken down and incorporated fully into the substance
of the carnivore, an animal organ grafted onto a human being seems to
be both *human* (in the sense that it is united with and serves the rest of
the body and is informed by a human soul) and *animal* (in its origins,
design and DNA). Furthermore, we have barely begun to tease out the
psychological and social implications of grafting major animal organs
onto human beings.

Another way of looking at this question would be to ask ourselves if
and why we would oppose animal–human hybridization *at a genetic level*.
Obvious answers about the risks seem limp here: there is a deeper abhorrence at stake, one we might describe as *the indignity concern*. Somehow
it demeans the human being to include non-human animal bits in his or
her genetic structure, even if this might mean the person could run faster,
breathe better under water or fly through the air. Indeed we are not even
sure how to think of such a being! Here I will add a theological argument, though one that is very tentative. Christians believe Jesus Christ
is the Alpha and the Omega of the entire universe (Rev. 1:8), the image
of the invisible God, the first-born of all creation (Col. 1:15–29), like us
in all things except sin (Heb. 4:15), the norm or standard of the human
race. So the late Albert Moraczewski OP asked: is Jesus a norm only of
our relating and acting, our moral and spiritual lives, or is he also in some
way a norm of our psychosomatic lives?[9] Obviously he is not the latter
if we focus merely on his colour, sex, weight or shoe size. But the Book
of Genesis taught that bodily beings are the image and likeness of God
(Gen. 1:26–31; 5:1; 9:6; cf. Wisd. 2:23; 1 Cor. 11:7; Jas. 3:9). St Paul taught

---

[8] On this see also B. Cole, '*Prospects for Xenotransplantation*: a brief overview', *NCBQ* 2(3) (2002),
   291–7.
[9] A. Moraczewski, 'A Roman Catholic response', in J. R. Nelson (ed.), *On the New Frontiers of
   Genetics and Religion* (Grand Rapids, MI: Eerdmans, 1994), pp. 139–43.

that it was because he came in our flesh that Christ could redeem us and restore us to the divine likeness (Rom. 8:3–4; Phil. 2:6–10; Eph. 4:22–24) and that, without losing our individuality, our resurrected bodies will in some sense be fashioned after Jesus' glorified body (Phil. 3:21). By uniting himself to our human nature in the Incarnation, the Second Person of the Trinity consecrated and elevated our bodily natures to a dignity and destiny far in excess of that already granted in our creation. That may have implications for how far we ought dare to go in manipulating our bodily natures.

Moraczewski's suggestion is that if Christ is the perfect exemplar not just of our behaviour but also of our psychosomatic structure, we ought not to do anything that would evolve us into, or generate parallel to us, a distinct species. I have proposed some supporting reasons for this elsewhere.[10] Suffice it here to say that the basis of our salvation, our universal human respect and our sense of a common calling and destiny is, in large part, our shared nature, our being members of one family, one species, our sharing a particular kind of body. If this sounds a note of caution for animal–human hybridization at a genetic level, it might also have some force at the somatic level, especially with the most radical kinds of xenotransplantation. Major organ transplantation is not merely adding new clothes or new tools to a person's cupboard: it is much closer to the grafting of part of one animal onto another. What is at issue is human nature and personal identity.

FASHIONABLE BIOETHICAL APPROACHES TO TISSUE PROCUREMENT

Consent to tissue removal

Many more ethical issues arise in relation to tissue procurement than arise in relation to receiving transplanted tissue. For one thing, unlike tissue transplantation, tissue procurement is not strictly speaking *healthcare*: while procurement requires many of the same professional skills, it is *not* focused upon saving or healing the person concerned. In some ways, it is more like mutilation – the destruction of a healthy function of the body – something traditionally opposed by Hippocratic medicine and

---

[10] I have argued this in A. Fisher, 'Adult science and adolescent ethics', in H. Regan, R. Horsfield and G. McMullen (eds.), *Beyond Mere Health: Theology and Health Care in a Secular Society* (Melbourne: Australian Theological Forum, 1996), pp. 145–68.

Judeo-Christian ethics. So this immediately raises a cluster of questions: what approaches, principles, models of care and virtues should guide our decision-making in this rather unusual area? How are we to take appropriate account of the interests of 'donors', their relatives, carers and others affected by the donors' welfare, while being concerned to serve the health-care needs of the recipients and to respect the interests of their relatives, carers etc?

Another cluster of questions surrounds the issue of *consent*. Who should consent to tissue removal and how? Should the law require the (written) consent of a person or their next of kin before their tissues can be taken (an 'opting-in' system), as is presently the case in the USA, Britain and Australia? Or should the law presume consent unless otherwise indicated (an 'opting-out' system), as applies in France, Spain, Israel, Sweden and Singapore? Or should it constructively consent on behalf of all deceased and even some living persons (a 'no-option' system), as has been proposed by some philosophers? Should relatives, friends or executors be able to veto the express wishes of the deceased regarding tissue donation? Should tissue salvage always be unpaid – strictly speaking, this is the only genuine tissue 'donation' – or should people be able to put parts of themselves up for sale, just as labour, sex and blood have been sold for a long time now? Does it all depend on the source of organs or other tissues? The living sources of tissues include:

- freely consenting adults;
- non-consenting or semi-consenting adults;
- children and mentally incompetent adults;
- human foetuses and embryos;
- animals, animal–human hybrids and 'embryoid bodies'.

The potential cadaveric sources of tissues include:

- those who freely gave consent;
- those who specifically refused consent;
- those who died without expressing any intentions with respect to tissue donation or were incompetent to express such intentions.

Our answers to these questions, as to all questions in applied ethics, depend crucially upon our ethical perspective or methodology. All too often health professionals work on the basis that either there is only one such perspective – that of 'the profession' – or that all that matters is the private view of the particular health worker. Moreover, it is also presumed that the relevant perspective cannot be subjected to criticism. Sometimes health professionals are quite unaware of the personal perspective out of which they operate. Considering tissue procurement from the perspective of six current perspectives may help us not only to uncover our own assumptions but also to compare and assess the other perspectives.

Liberal-individualist approaches

Liberal, individualistic or *subjectivist* approaches give primacy to personal choice over all other values in ethical decision-making. Simply put this means getting my own way is what matters: as long as I am not harming anyone else, I should be allowed to follow my own life-plans and particular preferences in healthcare as elsewhere; governments, professions, churches and others should interfere as little as possible in people's choices. From different angles writers such as Tristram Engelhardt and Joseph Fletcher have supported what might be broadly described as a 'do your own thing' bioethics. So, too, to a significant extent, have Thomas Beauchamp and James Childress, the fathers of the 'Georgetown mantra': while for them *respect for autonomy* is supposedly one of several guiding principles in healthcare, in reality it is the one that usually trumps all others.[11] These approaches have proved especially agreeable to 'liberal' societies such as the United States and its cultural satellites, and they continue to dominate mainstream bioethics despite critiques from many quarters in recent years.[12]

Applied to the issue of tissue procurement, liberal-individualist ethicists leave it to individuals whether they consent to giving or selling any part of their bodies to others. For them the ethical debate more or less ends there. Of course there is a great deal packed into the term 'consent'. For

[11] T. Beauchamp and J. Childress, *Principles of Biomedical Ethics*, 6th edn (Oxford University Press, 2008); M. Charlesworth, *Bioethics in a Liberal Society* (Cambridge University Press, 1993); H. T. Engelhardt, *Bioethics and Secular Humanism: The Search for a Common Morality* (London: SCM, 1991), and *Foundations of Bioethics*, 2nd edn (Oxford University Press, 1996); J. Fletcher, *Situation Ethics: The New Morality* (Philadelphia: Westminster Press, 1966), and *The Ethics of Genetic Control: Ending Reproductive Roulette* (Buffalo, NY: Prometheus, 1988).

[12] For example, K. D. Clouser and B. Gert, 'Morality vs. principlism', in R. Gillon (ed.), *Principles of Health Care Ethics* (Chichester: Wiley, 1993), pp. 251–66; E. DuBose, Ronald Hamel and Laurence O'Connell (eds.), *A Matter of Principles? Ferment in U.S. Bioethics* (Valley Forge, PA: Trinity, 1994); J. Finnis and A. Fisher, 'Theology and the four principles: a Roman Catholic view', in Gillon (ed.), *Principles of Health Care Ethics*, pp. 31–44; D. Irving, 'The bioethics mess', *Crisis* 19(5) (May 2001), 16–21, and many other articles by her; A. Jonsen, *The Birth of Bioethics* (Oxford University Press, 1998), and *A Short History of Medical Ethics* (Oxford University Press, 2008); G. Meilaender, *Body, Soul, and Bioethics* (Notre Dame University Press, 1995). In the notes to Chapter 1 I noted several other critics of liberal–individualist approaches to ethics generally and to bioethics in particular.

each of the sources of tissues identified above there are particular issues surrounding the donor's competence and freedom to ask for or agree to a procedure and whether such consent is sufficiently informed. For the strict individualist, the only legitimate sources of organs or other tissues are persons who were competent, free and informed at the time of their consent or bequest. To remove tissues from non-consenting adults, children and the mentally incompetent, if this is not for their own benefit, is an affront to their dignity and an 'assault'; guardians may only consent if it is in their client's interests. Neither should family and friends override the express bequest of a deceased person: individualists oppose the veto commonly allowed to next of kin. So, too, opt-out approaches derogate from the donor's human rights and inhibit genuine altruism. As most liberal-individualist writers hold that human embryos, foetuses and live animals are not persons and have no rights, consent to removal of their tissues would only be required from their 'owners'.

A final problematic category for the individualist is what we might call the 'semi-consenting' adult: a person in medical need who agrees to supply tissue(s) in return for healthcare, one in financial need who supplies tissue in response to a monetary incentive, one who has only limited understanding of the implications of tissue removal or one who is institutionalized or otherwise vulnerable to coercion or undue pressure to 'volunteer' their tissue(s). Here the individualist is torn between the view that these matters should be left up to each person to decide individually and the view that some people's personal autonomy is so compromised that we should not accept their choices as determinative. Most individualists, however, lean in the direction of maximizing freedom, including the freedom of the poor to sell their tissues in order to feed their children or pay the mortgage. Prima facie individualists would also allow donors to specify who may (or may not) receive their tissues, e.g. 'no blacks or Jews'.

Part of the attraction of liberal-individualist approaches is that they ostensibly recognize the dignity and rights of each person as a free agent and no one's slave or pawn. They avoid grand moral theories that may not do justice to the complexity of individual situations and to pluralism of opinion. The downside of such approaches is that they can reduce conscience to a private internal voice or intuition beyond external criticism, with authority to decide what to do without much regard for objective reality, truth or tradition. Autonomy-based approaches to morality also offer little or no basis for scrutinizing personal prejudices and give puzzled individuals no help in making decisions. They allow people to compromise basic values such as reverence for life and compassion for the suffering, and can easily become anti-social or adversarial with respect to others. Thus Pope John Paul II in *Veritatis Splendor* criticized moral theories that separate freedom from truth and truth from authority and tradition [*VS* 31–53].

Communitarian or group-conscious approaches

Despite the globalization of Anglo-American individualism, many people and cultures remain more group-focused or other-focused. This includes members of 'traditional' extended family or kinship group cultures (especially in Asia and the Southern hemisphere), followers of the great Eastern philosophies, 'communitarian' critics of liberalism such as Alasdair MacIntyre and Charles Taylor, as well as Marxists, feminists and other radical social critics and proponents of culture-specific ethics. These approaches give primacy to our interconnectedness with others and value loyalty, sacrifice for the common good, compassion in relationships and respect for the group and its traditions over personal preference and fulfilment. Simply put: living well with others is what matters. Families, neighbourhoods, societies, cultures, governments, professions, churches and others have an important role here in knitting people together and promoting shared values and projects.

Communitarian approaches to tissue procurement emphasize the social responsibility to donate tissues, especially where this involves little or no burden on the donor. Bernard Teo, for instance, has argued that the 'distinctive feature of transplantation is that, in contrast to other forms of healthcare, its success depends upon full communal good will and participation'.[13] Many communitarians therefore support tissue procurement not only from freely consenting living adults, but also (in particular circumstances) from the dead who have not expressed any particular wish in the matter, and so they would favour the opt-out system. Children and the mentally incompetent might be expected to give up tissues for others, especially their own family members, as occurs when parents consent to bone marrow transfer between their children. Criminals, too, might give up surplus and renewable tissues as a way of making restitution to the community.

Though communitarians may seem more enthusiastic about tissue procurement than individualists, they can also be more sensitive to

---

[13] B. Teo, 'Is the adoption of more efficient strategies of tissue procurement the answer to persistent organ shortage in transplantation?', *Bioethics* 6 (1992), 113–29.

complexities such as the grief of the family and carers, the complex family and social pressures that shape tissue 'donation' decisions, the dangers of commercializing the tissue transfer process and of privatizing decision-making in this area and justice in the allocation of finite community resources.[14]

In the section dealing with 'Promising developments' in Chapter 1, I noted that communitarian approaches to ethics have the advantage of recognizing that, far from being independent atoms, human persons are all part of a web of relationships and form and express their values in company with others. Even recognition of individual rights requires a rich view of the common good and joint effort with others to promote the flourishing of all. But at least as important as rights are ties to family, community, tradition. Such approaches avoid the asocial individualism of the capital and technology-driven scientific age and encourage people to take responsibility not only for their own health but for that of others. The downside of such theories is that they can discourage personal initiative and promote the dream of some corporatist utopia. As the twentieth century demonstrated repeatedly, the vain attempt to achieve such dreams usually comes at a great cost to individual freedom and even life. Community or group-conscious approaches commonly fail to allow space for individual differences and can incline their followers to a blind obedience to the group that reduces to a cultural relativism. They can leave people with little or no basis for criticizing the customs and prejudices of those they live and work with in healthcare as elsewhere. As Pope Benedict XVI has argued repeatedly, cultural relativism can be every bit as tyrannical as private subjectivism.[15]

Deontological or duty-based approaches

The third perspective is that of *deontological* or duty-based approaches to ethics, which emphasize moral norms and responsibilities. Simply put this means doing your (moral) duty is what matters: there are moral authorities to obey (God, Church, family, profession and so forth) and moral rules to follow, whatever our particular circumstances, motives

---

[14] J. Dwyer and E. Vig, 'Rethinking transplantation between siblings', *Hastings Center Report* 25(5) (1995): 7–12; P. Grasser, 'Donation after cardiac death: major ethical issues', *NCBQ* 7(3) (2007), 527–43; P. Marshall, 'Introduction: organ transplantation – defining the boundaries of personhood, equity and community', *Theoretical Medicine* 17(1) (1996), 5–8.

[15] Joseph Cardinal Ratzinger, *Homily for Mass for the Election of the Roman Pontiff*, 18 April 2005, and *Christianity and the Crisis of Cultures* (San Francisco: Ignatius, 2006).

or preferred outcomes (the Ten Commandments, the Hippocratic oath, international or local medical association codes). Coalescing here are many faith or tradition-based moralities, as well as Kantian and other more secular deontological ethics. Here we might include the adherents of the great monotheistic religions and philosophers within the Kantian tradition such as Alan Donagan and Onora O'Neill. To some extent 'conservative' Jewish and Christian writers such as Paul Ramsey, Leon Kass, Benedict Ashley and Gilbert Meilaender might be included in this camp.[16]

From this perspective there are some things health professionals and others should always do and other things they should never do. *One may never use oneself or others as a mere means*; persons must always be treated as ends in themselves. The unease that many people feel about transplantation seems to be founded on this concern: that in the rush to save lives there is a temptation to treat potential donors as mere harvest grounds rather than people (or recently deceased people) also worthy of our respect. Even if they (or, after death, their families) consent to tissue retrieval, donors do not become mere resources to be plundered. Opt-out and no-option approaches to tissue procurement and the sale of tissues would almost always represent immoral instrumentalization of persons. On this basis children, the mentally incompetent, prisoners, the poor and the desperate should also not be used as donors.

The most extreme case of instrumentalization is killing another and most duty-based ethical systems would hold that killing contravenes a moral maxim. Some deontological ethicists and many ordinary members of the public have expressed concern that in 'cadaveric' tissue procurement definitions of death and clinical indicators may be conditioned by demand for tissues and that sometimes donors may be killed by the tissue retrieval process rather than their prior disease or trauma. Z. R. Wolf writes that 'the use of the terms brain-dead, dead-dead, living-dead, newly-dead and nearly-dead emphasise only a few of the grey areas that surround the definition of death'.[17] In this book I consider the ongoing debate about the definition and medical determination of death only in

---

[16] Ashley, deBlois and O'Rourke, *Health Care Ethics*; L. Kass, *Toward a More Natural Science: Biology and Human Affairs* (New York: Free Press, 1985), and *Life, Liberty, and the Defense of Dignity*; G. Meilaender, *Bioethics: A Primer for Christians* (Grand Rapids, MI: Eerdmans, 1996), and *Neither Beast nor God: The Dignity of the Human Person* (New York: Encounter Books, 2009); P. Ramsey, *The Patient as Person: Explorations in Medical Ethics* (Yale University Press, 1970), and *Ethics at the Edges of Life* (Yale University Press, 1978).
[17] Z. R. Wolf, 'Nurses' responses to tissue procurement from non-heart-beating cadaver donors', *AORN Journal* 60(6) (1994), 968–81 at 981.

passing (in Chapter 8). Suffice it to say that if so-called 'brain death' is in fact reversible, less than total or does not mark the irreversible disintegration of the human organism, it is deeply suspect. It is troubling that much of the work on brain death (ever since the 'Harvard criteria' were developed) has been by those directly concerned with tissue procurement. There is likewise a worrying trend to declare people dead who are only partially brain dead, such as anencephalic babies and persistently comatose people, thereby reducing persons to consciousness and allowing those who lack this to be exploited and killed.[18]

Another example of instrumentalization – prohibited by most deontological ethics – is *mutilation*.[19] When a Californian prisoner, who had already donated a kidney to his daughter, volunteered his remaining kidney also, doctors were understandably reluctant: the man would either die as a result or receive dialysis for the rest of his life (costing the state $40,000 a year). The UC–Stanford Bioethics Committee concluded that

[18] Pope John Paul II pointed out that: '*The death of the person* is a single event, consisting in the total disintegration of that unitary and integrated whole that is the personal self. It results from the separation of the life-principle (or soul) from the corporal reality of the person. The death of the person, understood in this primary sense, is an event which *no scientific technique or empirical method can identify directly*. Yet human experience shows that once death occurs *certain biological signs inevitably follow*, which medicine has learnt to recognize with increasing precision … [In addition to] the traditional cardio-respiratory signs … [there is now] the so-called "*neurological*" *criterion*. Specifically, this consists in establishing, according to clearly determined parameters commonly held by the international scientific community, the complete and irreversible cessation of all brain activity (in the cerebrum, cerebellum and brain stem). This is then considered the sign that the individual organism has lost its integrative capacity … [This criterion,] if rigorously applied, does not seem to conflict with the essential elements of a sound anthropology. Therefore a health-worker professionally responsible for ascertaining death can use these criteria in each individual case as the basis for arriving at that degree of assurance in ethical judgment which moral teaching describes as "moral certainty"' (*Address to the Eighteenth International Congress* 4–5).
   For useful explanations of (and cautions on) brain death see: G. Brown, 'Reading the signs of death: a theological analysis', *NCBQ* 7(3) (2007), 467–76; P. Byrne *et al.*, 'Life, life-support and death: principles, guidelines, policies and procedures for making decisions that respect life', *LQ* 64(4) (1997), 3–31; E. Diamond, 'John Paul II and brain death', *NCBQ* 7(3) (2007), 491–7; J. DuBois, 'Organ transplantation', and 'Avoiding common pitfalls in the determination of death', *NCBQ* 7(3) (2007), 545–59; J. Eberl, 'Dualist and animalist perspectives on death: a comparison with Aquinas', *NCBQ* 7(3) (2007), 477–90; L. Hostetter, 'Higher-brain death: a critique', *NCBQ* 7(3) (2007), 499–504; P. McCullagh, *Brain Dead, Brain Absent, Brain Donors: Human Subjects or Human Objects?* (Chichester: Wiley, 1993); J. Menikoff, 'Doubts about death: the silence of the Institute of Medicine', *J Law, Med & Ethics* 26(2) (1998), 157–65; J. Seifert, 'Is "brain death" actually death?', *The Monist* 76(2) (1993), 175–202; A. Shewmon, 'The brain and somatic integration: insights into the standard biological rationale for equating "brain death" with death', *J Med & Phil* 26(5) (2001), 457–78, and 'Definitions of death, the Persistent Vegetative State and Anencephaly', in D. Maher (ed.), *The Bishop and the Future of Catholic Health Care: Challenges and Opportunities* (Boston: Pope John XXIII Center, 1997), pp. 136–53.

[19] J. Haas, 'The totality and integrity of the body', in E. Furton (ed.), *Ethical Principle in Catholic Health Care* (Boston: NCBC, 1999), pp. 85–8.

such an operation might violate both donor and surgeon. Arthur Caplan of the University of Pennsylvania Bioethics Center was more direct: maiming someone and risking murdering them are both unethical, above all for health professionals.[20]

Unlike the individualist view, the deontological approach holds that killing and mutilation are unethical even if the 'victim' consents to them. This does not preclude tissue donation after death, as there is no harm to anyone; nor would a deontological approach exclude live tissue donation where the tissue (such as blood or bone marrow) is regenerative or where the removal of the organ (such as one kidney) does not present any serious risk to function. It would, however, exclude well-intentioned but ultimately unethical donations such as giving up one's only kidney.

Xenotransplantation, especially of whole organs, multiple organs and limbs, presents particular challenges for proponents of a deontological bioethic. Some of these theorists regard animals, or at least higher-order animals, as worthy of the same or similar respect as human beings. Tom Regan, for instance, objected to the Baby Fae case *not* because the child was subjected to a high-risk experiment but because a baboon was sacrificed for the purpose: he thought this represented a failure of respect for the particular animal and for animals generally.[21] One does not have to go all the way with the animal liberation lobby to have some unease with vivisection, especially of primates and other higher-order mammals. Hybrids of human beings and animals are the stuff of ancient mythology and nightmare, and the taboo against bestiality runs very deep in all cultures. Such revulsion may be informative: as we saw in Chapter 5, in the discussion of ethical concerns over embryonic stem cells, Jewish bioethicist Leon Kass begins his argument against animal–human hybridization on a genetic level by reflecting upon this repugnance which he thinks is 'the emotional expression of deep wisdom, beyond reason's power, fully to articulate'. So, too, the magisterium of the Catholic Church, while comfortable with corneal and valve xenotransplants, has consistently opposed gonad and brain xenotransplants from animals to humans and animal–human hybridization at a genetic level, and remains cautious about any

[20] A. Caplan (ed.), *The Ethics of Organ Transplants: The Current Debate* (New York: Prometheus, 1998); E. Nieves, 'Girl awaits father's second kidney and decision by medical ethicists', *New York Times*, 5 December 1998.
[21] T. Regan, 'The subject is Baby Fae', *Hastings Center Report* 15(1) (1985), 9. Cf. J. Nelson, 'Moral sensibilities and moral standing: Caplan on xenograft "donors"', *Bioethics* 7(4) (1993), 315–22. A much more favourable position on the use of animals for human benefit informs Pontifical Academy for Life, *Prospects for Xenotransplantation* (2001), 8 and 9.

major organ xenotransplantation that might compromise the identity of the tissue recipient.[22]

The attraction of deontological approaches to transplantation ethics and to bioethics more generally is that they offer a clear, principled approach to healthcare dilemmas, enable formation of conscience in duty and obedience and refuse to compromise basic human goods and norms of morality even for the best of goals. Unlike the liberal-individualist and communitarian/group-conscious approaches, these duty-based bioethics provide a basis for criticism of personal and social prejudices. Critics, however, contest the alleged self-evidence of the norms of duty-based approaches or of the authority upon which they are based. They suggest that such deontological ethics yield moral absolutes that are arbitrary, legalistic and inflexible, and that it is often unclear how to resolve conflicts between competing norms or duties. As even the *Catechism of the Catholic Church* insists, the commandments are not laws unto themselves or programmes for moral robots: rather, they are the most reliable ways to love God and neighbour, to live life to the full and to attain eternal, blessed life.

Consequentialist or results-focused approaches

The fourth and highly influential variety of modern ethics is *consequentialism*. Consequentialist approaches range from an unsystematic pragmatism to elegantly nuanced utilitarian theories, but they have in common the idea that *results* are what count, indeed are all that count. The intrinsic end of the act itself, the means used and the motives of those involved are not decisive here: rather, when deciding how to act, we should take into account all predictable good and bad consequences of all the options before us and choose the option that maximizes the net sum of good (over bad). Consequentialist approaches to bioethics have been popularized by utilitarians such as Peter Singer, John Harris and Julian Savelescu, Christian proportionalists such as Richard McCormick and John Mahoney and many results-driven practitioners in the field.

While the consequentialist concern that the risks and costs be weighed in any decision could tell against too ebullient an approach to tissue transfer, such downsides are likely to diminish with time and practice

---

[22] Pius XII, *Address to the Italian Association of Corneal Donors, Clinical Ophthalmologists and Legal Medicine*, 14 May 1956; John Paul II, *18th Transplantation Congress*, 7; Pontifical Council for Health, *Charter for Healthworkers* 89; Pontifical Academy for Life, *Prospects for Xenotransplantation* 10 and 11.

and must be weighed against the very great benefits of saving life and improving its quality. The contribution tissue transplantation makes to 'the greater good' means that not only consenting adult donors but those who wish to sell their tissues for profit would be potential tissue sources, as would children, the mentally handicapped, prisoners, the poor, the deceased, even those who refuse consent before they die or whose next of kin refuse consent. Consequentialists prefer an opting-out system over an opting-in one,[23] but they may go further, suggesting a 'no-option' approach at least for cadaveric donation. After all, they say, 'you don't need your organs anymore when you're dead'. So enthusiastic was John Harris for organ harvesting that he proposed in the prestigious journal *Philosophy* that all adult citizens should be enrolled in an 'organ lottery'.[24] As in jury service, people would be chosen at random from the electoral roll, but rather than giving up time and judgment they would be required to give up superfluous or renewable tissue (blood, bone marrow, skin, a kidney) to those who needed them. While this might involve some discomfort and inconvenience for the donors, it would be far outweighed by the lives that would be saved. The greatest good for the greatest number would be served by sharing the organs around.

Michael Green responded tongue-in-cheek with an even more radical scheme for organ redistribution.[25] Certain people would be chosen randomly to give up *all* their major organs and tissues: heart, both lungs, both kidneys, liver, pancreas, bone marrow, corneas, skin, blood. Of course this would be lethal for those donors, but it would save or help many people at the expense of only one and so the greatest good would clearly be served for the greatest number. Forced to admit that this was where his original logic could lead, Harris stopped advocating a compulsory organ lottery.

This example of the application of a 'results are all that count' ethic to transplantation may seem far-fetched, but it serves as a salutary warning about where enthusiasm to save or care can lead when unbounded by (other) moral norms. Many people are wary of tissue donation precisely because they fear that such pragmatism is driving definitions of death, the choice and application of clinical criteria, decisions to use or remove life-support and tissue procurement protocols. Yet consequentialist approaches remain very much in vogue because they appeal so directly

[23] For example, L. G. Hunsicker, 'Medical considerations of procurement', in D. Keyes (ed.), *New Harvest: Transplanting Body Parts and Reaping the Benefits* (Clifton, NJ: Humana, 1991), pp. 59–77.
[24] J. Harris, 'The survival lottery', *Philosophy* 50 (1975), 81–7.
[25] M. Green, 'Harris's modest proposal', *Philosophy* 54 (1979), 400–6.

to the benevolence and 'can-do' mentality of many in 'the helping professions'. Many healthworkers have little time for rules that constrain advances and prefer a scientific mindset focused on effectiveness and efficiency. Such approaches fit well with the modern scientific–commercial mindset, but they may 'get results' by inviting us to compromise justice, the sanctity of life, human rights, truth-telling and promise-keeping and enduring traditions such as those of Hippocratic medicine, when this serves 'the greater good', however defined. Applied to tissue procurement, these approaches meet the usual consequentialist difficulties: what is a good result? What counts as a benefit and a loss, how are we to predict, measure, aggregate and compare all the apples and oranges involved, how are we to make rational comparisons across individuals and communities? Does anything go, as long as the best result is achieved?[26] As Pope John Paul II pointed out in *Veritatis Splendor* and *Evangelium Vitae*, the moral calculus required by these approaches is philosophically incoherent, socially dangerous and contrary to the Christian precept that one can never do evil to achieve good (Rom. 3.8).[27] While benefit–burden analyses have their place in transplant decision-making, they are clearly not enough and may indeed be counterproductive, as when potential donors or their next of kin fear that tissue harvesting is driven by consequentialism and proves a disincentive to volunteering tissues.

BETTER BIOETHICAL APPROACHES TO TISSUE PROCUREMENT

Natural law or practical reason approaches

Each of the four rival stables of approaches to bioethics so far considered seems to capture some important aspects of moral reasoning about tissue procurement but to miss out on others. Most people operate more out of one than the others, and each has its persuasive power as well as its limitations. Much more satisfactory, I believe, are the natural law approaches outlined in previous chapters. Applied to our present question they ask whether a particular transplantation proposal aims at securing a genuine good for people and in a reasonable way. Prima facie tissue transfer seeks to enable someone's participation in the crucial human goods of life and

---

[26] See also D. Oderberg and J. Laing (eds.), *Human Lives: Critical Essays on Consequentialist Bioethics* (London: Macmillan, 1997).
[27] John Paul II, *VS* 71–83, and *EV* 15, 23 and 63–4.

health. Of course there may be other, less elevated drivers about which we must also be realistic: kudos or profit, the lure of technology, the illusory search for indefinite mortal life and many more.

The next questions for any natural law ethic are: even if the end is good, are the means of achieving it morally reasonable? Does it breach any moral absolutes? Tissue procurement can, and usually does, seem to satisfy fundamental moral precepts such as: show care and respect for the person; rescue the dying and heal the sick; act fairly towards all those affected; help the needy and distressed. Once again we must be careful here, for in our enthusiasm to *do good* we might forget that we must *first do no harm*. Killing and mutilating people is contrary to practical reason because it directly attacks a fundamental good (life or health) and contradicts a basic precept of common morality (against harming the innocent). Such actions harm not only the victim (whose life, health and physical integrity are always valued) but also the perpetrator (who makes himself a killer or maimer), the profession (whose reputation, ethic and relationship of trust with patients are put at risk) and the common good. They set a dangerous precedent, and they violate established religious, legal and professional codes. Tissue retrieval can in fact kill, maim or disrespect the donor or bystanders, even as tissue transfer seeks to save or heal or show care and respect for the recipient. Thus natural law approaches, while positively disposed to tissue transplantation in principle, eschew foetal tissue transplantation,[28] embryonic stem cell therapies,[29] organ trading[30]

---

[28] John Paul II: 'This moral condemnation [of abortion] also regards procedures that exploit living human embryos and foetuses – sometimes specifically "produced" for this purpose by *in vitro* fertilization – either to be used as "biological material" or as *providers of organs or tissue for transplants* in the treatment of certain diseases. The killing of innocent human creatures, even if carried out to help others, constitutes an absolutely unacceptable act' (*EV* 63). Likewise Benedict XVI: 'Transplant abuses and their trafficking, which often involve innocent people like babies, must find the scientific and medical community ready to unite in rejecting such unacceptable practices. Therefore they are to be decisively condemned as abominable. The same ethical principle is to be repeated when one wishes to touch upon creation and destroy the human embryo destined for a therapeutic purpose. The simple idea of considering the embryo as "therapeutic material" contradicts the cultural, civil and ethical foundations upon which the dignity of the person rests' (*Address to the International Congress on Tissue Donation of the Pontifical Academy for Life, the International Federation of Catholic Medical Associations and the Italian National Transplant Centre*, 7 November 2008). See also G. Grisez, *The Way of the Lord Jesus*, vol. III, *Difficult Moral Questions* (Quincy, IL: Franciscan Press, 1997), pp. 385–8; J. Keown, 'The Polkinghorne Report on Foetal Research: nice recommendations, shame about the reasoning', *J Med Ethics* 19(2) (1993), 114–20.

[29] See Chapter 5.

[30] John Paul II: 'The body cannot be treated as a merely physical or biological entity, nor can its organs and tissues ever be used as items for sale or exchange. Such a reductive materialist conception would lead to a merely instrumental use of the body and therefore of the person. In such a perspective, organ transplantation and the grafting of tissue would no longer correspond

or (unpaired) vital organ retrieval before death has been determined with moral certainty. [31] To avoid any real or perceived conflict of interests, the declaration of death and the decision to remove ventilation should be made only by those charged with the care of that patient, not by the tissue retrieval team and certainly not by the transplantation team. Even after death the tissue procurement team must demonstrate continuing respect for the deceased's body and reasonable wishes, and not merely plunder the body for parts. An operating theatre must never be an abattoir, and surgical staff must never be grave-robbers.

Natural law approaches also ask: who is affected and does the process do justice to all or injustice to any? Relatives and friends of any potential cadaveric donor must be respected. They should be kept fully informed, prepared for what is likely and given reasonable time, counselling and other support. In particular it is important for them to understand what is involved in life support, brain death, withdrawal of ventilation, tissue

to an act of donation but would amount to the dispossession or plundering of a body' (*First International Transplant Congress* 4). Benedict XVI: 'The body can never be considered a mere object; otherwise the logic of the market would gain the upper hand. The body of each person, together with the spirit that has been given to each one singly constitutes an inseparable unity in which the image of God himself is imprinted. Prescinding from this dimension leads to a perspective incapable of grasping the totality of the mystery present in each one. Therefore, it is necessary to put respect for the dignity of the person and the protection of his/her personal identity in the first place ... The possibility of organ sales, as well as the adoption of discriminatory and utilitarian criteria, would greatly clash with the underlying meaning of the gift that would place it out of consideration, qualifying it as a morally illicit act' (*Address to the International Congress on Tissue Donation*).

[31] John Paul II: 'Nor can we remain silent in the face of other more furtive, but no less serious and real, forms of euthanasia. These could occur for example when, in order to increase the availability of organs for transplants, organs are removed without respecting objective and adequate criteria which verify the death of the donor' (*EV* 15). Benedict XVI, *Address to the International Congress on Tissue Donation*: 'In these years science has accomplished further progress in certifying the death of the patient. It is good, therefore, that the results attained receive the consent of the entire scientific community in order to further research for solutions that give certainty to all. In an area such as this, in fact, there must not be the slightest suspicion of arbitrariness and where certainty has not been attained caution must prevail. This is why it is useful to promote research and interdisciplinary reflection ... Respect for the life of the donor must always prevail so that the extraction of organs be performed only in the case of his/her true death. The act of love which is expressed with the gift of one's vital organs remains a genuine testimony of charity that is able to look beyond death so that life always wins. The recipient of this gesture must be well aware of its value. He is the receiver of a gift that goes far beyond the therapeutic benefit. In fact, what he/she receives, before being an organ, is a witness of love that must raise an equally generous response, so as to increase the culture of gift and free giving.' Likewise the Pontifical Council for Health: 'Cadaveric tissue retrieval is legitimate as long as the corpse must always be respected as a human corpse ... [and] the certain death of the donor has been ascertained ... In order that a person be considered a corpse, it is enough that cerebral death of the donor be ascertained, which consists in the *irreversible cessation of all cerebral activity*. When total cerebral death is verified with certainty, that is, after the required tests, it is licit to remove organs' (*Charter for Healthworkers* 87).

retrieval and transplantation. If the family are not ready or say they do not wish tissue retrieval to go ahead, that should be respected. They are the ones who are grieving and must be helped to come to 'closure'. The gift is not only that of the deceased but theirs, too. If possible the family should be given the opportunity to view their loved one at rest, with the ventilator briefly switched off, before tissues are removed, so that they can see that their loved one really has died. Too often relatives of cadaveric donors are left suspicious, even guilty, because they are unsure (sometimes with good reason) about what death is and what actually killed their loved one. Chaplains can assist here, though they must be alert to real ethical dilemmas in this area. Some health professionals also experience anxiety and distress in tissue procurement, and they too must be helped to understand the issues and procedures and helped to come to resolution.[32] The challenge is to find ways of humanizing the practice of tissue retrieval, so that well-founded trust can exist on all sides.

Natural law ethics is not only concerned that people do what is right but that they do so from 'a good heart' or will. They must be strengthened in virtue rather than vice, so that doing the right thing comes more and more naturally or easily. Tissue retrieval can be a demonstration of virtues such as respectfulness and empathy, generosity and mercy, truthfulness and humility. Tissue transplantation can in turn enact virtues such as compassion and rescue, patience and practical wisdom, moderation and fairness. We must, however, look deep within our hearts to discover whether tissue retrieval and transplantation might also sometimes represent cowardice in the face of human mortality, an intemperate desire for everything that medicine can do (if needs be at someone else's expense) or a false mercy that fails to consider the genuine good of the person and the community.

Christian wisdom

I opened this chapter with the thought – both in a popular film and in an address of Pope John Paul II – that tissue donation can have a Christological dimension, as giving of one's own flesh can bring life to others. Likewise Francis Delmonico has written that 'tissue donation is a wonderful display of giving to others, of service to others, of love for another, given as one way Christ has taught us to be for others,

[32] K. L. Kawamoto, 'Tissue procurement in the operating room: implications for perioperative nurses', *AORN Journal* 55(6) (1992), 1541–6; Wolf, 'Nurses' responses to tissue procurement'.

"so that others might live"'.[33] Of course, in addition to any distinctively Christian insights into transplantation, Catholics will share aspects of the several ethical approaches outlined above, especially the natural law approach.

In his 1991 address Pope John Paul II noted that transplant surgery makes possible treatment for many illnesses that, up to a short time ago, could lead only to death or, at best, a painful and limited existence. He commended this development as an example of solidarity and charity on the part of the donors and a great service to life on the part of health professionals. It is a unique kind of charity and service, as it allows people 'to give part of themselves, of their blood and of their bodies, so that others may continue to live'. Whereas Pius XII had thought it permissible, if less admirable and more likely to produce conflicts, for blood and cornea donors to receive 'recompense', John Paul emphasized that giver and receiver of the tissue see this process as an example of a 'sincere gift of the self', a free 'donation'.[34] 'Projecting beyond death their vocation to love', persons who consent to cadaveric donation, or their kin who act on their behalf after death, engage in 'a great act of love, that love which gives life to others'. Here the health professional is a mediator of that most meaningful of gifts, the gift of life and love, the gift of the self. 'The difficulty of the intervention, the need to act promptly, and the need for maximum concentration on the task, should not lead to the doctor's losing sight of the mystery of love contained in what he is doing.'

Without detracting from his obvious enthusiasm for transplantation, John Paul insisted that there are 'certain limits which cannot be transgressed, limits placed by human nature itself'.[35] These boundaries include those outlined above: one cannot donate what would deprive the donor of life, seriously impair function or compromise personal identity.[36] While a certain reverence is appropriate to a corpse, it does not have the dignity of a living human subject. 'A corpse is no longer, in the proper sense of the term, a subject of rights, because it is deprived of personality, which alone can be the subject of rights.' Hence, as long as there is moral certainty

---

[33] F. Delmonico, 'Organ transplants', in Maher (ed.), *The Bishop and the Future*, pp. 59–62 at 61.
[34] John Paul II, *First International Transplant Congress*; cf. Pontifical Council for Health, *Charter for Healthworkers* 83–91.
[35] John Paul II, *First International Transplant Congress*.
[36] Thus Pontifical Council for Health, *Charter for Healthworkers* 86: 'Tissue retrieval from living donors is legitimate provided it is a question of organs of which the removal would not constitute a serious and irreparable impairment for the donor. One can donate only what he can deprive himself of without serious danger to his life or personal identity and for a just and proportionate reason.'

that death has occurred, transferring organs or other tissues may be 'morally blameless and even noble', as Pope Pius XII had taught.

In *Evangelium Vitae* (1995) John Paul II again praised tissue donation as a 'celebration of the Gospel of life' where donors 'by the gift of self' extend life and hope to the otherwise hopeless. He compared this gift with 'the highest degree of love, which is to give one's life for the person loved', indeed with the very mystery of the Cross (*EV* 86). The Pope also warned health professionals against being so carried away by enthusiasm for tissue retrieval that they fail to observe adequate objective criteria for verifying death, thereby engaging in 'furtive' homicide or reducing human embryos and foetuses to mere tissue banks for exploitation (*EV* 15 and 63).

In 2000 Pope John Paul II returned to this subject a third time in an address to the International Transplantation Society. Restating the Church's support for scientific research and medical practice in keeping with God's law and the integral good of the human person, he celebrated advances in life-saving and life-improving transplantation surgery and praised donors for their 'noble' gift. He warned, however, that the body must not be reduced to 'a mere complex of tissues, organs and functions' but rather be seen as 'a constitutive part of the person who manifests and expresses himself through it'.[37] Tissue donation, therefore, 'is not just a matter of giving away something that belongs to us but of giving something of ourselves'. He thus criticized 'any procedure which tends to commercialize human tissues or to consider them as items of exchange or trade' and any process that fails to ensure authentic informed consent on the part of the tissue donor, relatives or the recipient.

Repeating the Church's concern that lethal organ removal should never occur, the Pope clarified what would be required for moral certainty of death:

[*T*]*he death of the person* is a single event, consisting in the total disintegration of that unitary and integrated whole that is the personal self. It results from the separation of the life-principle (or soul) from the corporal reality of the person. The death of the person, understood in this primary sense, is an event which *no scientific technique or empirical method can identify directly*. Yet human experience shows that once death occurs *certain biological signs inevitably follow* ... the traditional cardio-respiratory signs ... [or] the complete and irreversible cessation of all brain activity.[38]

---

[37] John Paul II, *Eighteenth International Transplantation Congress* 3, quoting CDF, *On Respect for Human Life and Procreation* (1987) 3.

[38] John Paul II, *Eighteenth International Transplantation Congress* 4–5.

Another important question, considered for the first time by the Pope in this address, was the matter of the just allocation of organs. He taught that

- waiting-lists for transplants must be based on 'clear and properly reasoned criteria' that recognize the intrinsic value of each human person;
- criteria for assigning organs should be non-discriminatory, i.e. not based on age, sex, race, religion, social standing and so on;
- criteria for assigning organs should be non-utilitarian, i.e. not based on work capacity, social usefulness and so on;
- judgments should be made on the basis of clinical factors – presumably urgency of medical need and capacity to benefit.[39]

With respect to future directions in transplantation John Paul cautioned that xenotransplants must not compromise the psychological or genetic identity of the recipient and that stem cells and other tissues must not be obtained by manufacturing, by cloning or other means, and then destroying human embryos. He recommended pursuing adult stem cell research instead and called on philosophers and theologians to keep reflecting on these matters.[40]

Pope Benedict XVI addressed a conference on tissue donation in 2008. He praised tissue donation as 'a unique testimony of charity' in a time all too frequently marked by 'various forms of egotism' and recalled Christ's teaching that it is only by giving one's life that it can be saved (Luke 9:24).[41] He also celebrated tissue transplantation as 'a great conquest of medical science' and a 'sign of hope for those suffering serious, and often grave, illnesses'. He emphasized the gratitude due to donors and their families. 'The recipient should be aware of the value of this gesture that one receives, of a gift that goes beyond the therapeutic benefit. What they receive is a testament of love, and it should give rise to a response equally generous, and in this way grows the culture of gift and gratitude.'

Like his predecessor, Benedict is troubled by the tendency to treat the body as a mere object to be exploited according to the paradigm of the free market. He insists on a Christian anthropology: 'The body of each person, together with the spirit that is given to each one individually, constitutes an inseparable unity upon which is impressed the image of God himself.' Materialist perspectives 'are incapable of understanding the totality of the

[39] John Paul II, *Eighteenth International Transplantation Congress* 6.
[40] John Paul II, *Eighteenth International Transplantation Congress* 7–8.
[41] Benedict XVI, *Address to International Congress on Tissue Donation*.

mystery present in each person' and commonly fail to respect his or her dignity. The Pope condemns consequent 'abuses in transplants and organ trafficking, which frequently affect innocent persons, such as children' and the manufacture and destruction of human embryos as if they were mere 'therapeutic material'. He repeats, even strengthens, his predecessor's caution regarding brain death and cadaveric tissue retrieval, insisting that if serious doubt about death remains we must err on the side of protecting the donor's life.

In these several examples of Catholic contributions to the ethics of tissue transplantation we see both greater enthusiasm and greater caution than in some other approaches. The Christ-like charity of the gift or sharing of the self is admired and encouraged; even so, attention to the underlying anthropology highlights the dangers of anything that instrumentalizes the body, compromises the freedom of the gift (and its concomitant solidarity, friendship and communion), undermines the integrity of the donor or recipient or disrespects the human person.

ETHICAL ISSUES IN TISSUE RECEPTION

Great benefits, significant risks

The rationale for tissue removal is obviously its transfer to someone else. The rationale for tissue reception is the hope that it will help the recipient. The overall success rates for major organ transplants such as heart, liver, kidney and lung are now high and continue to improve, as do success rates for tissue transplants such as blood, bone marrow, skin and so on. When they work, transplants rescue people from death, cure existing illnesses, prevent further ones occurring and alleviate suffering and disability. This is clearly in keeping with the fundamental orientation of healthcare, at least as understood in the Hippocratic–Christian tradition, and is prima facie praiseworthy.

Of course, the usual norms of bioethics apply to transplantation. For instance, transplant recipients or their legal guardians have a right to reliable information about their prognosis with and without the transplant and to be told about the likely and possible side-effects, the benefits and the risks. Provided this requirement is satisfied and when the prognosis is very poor without transplantation, then considerable risk-taking is clearly permissible. Heart transplantation surgery, for instance, was originally highly experimental and predictably often fatal, but the goal was always saving the particular patient as well as improving the technique, and with each attempt more and more was learnt. Nowadays it is highly successful.

Technical judgments must, in fact, always be made about the best means to achieving the desired transfer of tissues, maximizing the chances of the graft taking and minimizing immune-rejection and other problems. Such assessments of warranted risks and tolerable side-effects have an ethical, not merely a mathematical dimension for the health professionals, recipients and guardians. When a baby, for instance, receives multiple organs and dies – as expected – within hours of the traumatic surgery, people are understandably concerned. Xenotransplantation also comes with its own peculiar range of attendant risks. Thus in 'Baby Fae: the "anything goes" school of human experimentation', George Annas rather dramatically likened a case of a baby who received a baboon heart but died soon afterwards to the Nazi experimentation forbidden in the Nuremberg Code.[42]

Since that famous case there have been several other attempts to transplant porcine and other animal hearts into human adult recipients, so far without success.[43] But improvements in immune suppressant drugs and experiments in genetically engineering animal organs which are human enough to fool the human immune system may reduce this objection to xenotransplantation in the near future.[44] More problematical is the danger of human contamination with diseases ordinarily found only in animals.[45] There is evidence that the terrible influenza epidemic that followed the First World War, the 'Hong Kong flu' of 1957 and 1968 and the 'Mexican flu' of 2008–9 were porcine in origin; HIV is thought to have originated in African chimpanzees; bovine spongiform encephalopathy ('mad cow disease') crossed the species barrier to human beings in Britain in the 1980s and 1990s; avian flu crossed to humans in Asia in 1997 and 1999; and other animal diseases periodically threaten populations with no evolved immunity. Though these diseases did not 'hop the species barrier' through tissue transfer, xenotransplantation does pose such a risk – one all the more serious in patients whose immune resistance may be significantly reduced.

[42] G. Annas, 'Baby Fae: the "anything goes" school of human experimentation', *Hastings Center Report* 15(1) (1985), 15–17.
[43] M. Micjejda, 'Transplants', in Maher (ed.), *The Bishop and the Future*, pp. 83–92 at 85.
[44] C. McCarthy, 'A new look at animal-to-human organ transplantation', *Kennedy Institute of Ethics Journal* 6(2) (1996), 183–8.
[45] Doctors and Lawyers for Responsible Medicine, 'Press release following media reports of Britain's first pig-to-human heart transplant', London, 12 May 1998.

Resource and identity issues

Costs are another concern. Some transplant surgery is very expensive; healthcare resources are finite; spending on such care competes with other health and welfare projects. As a result some US states and health insurers have taken transplants off the list of sponsored treatments. Health planners also fear an explosion of transplant procedures as new procedures are developed and as we seek to extend life indefinitely. On the other hand, kidney transplants are now more cost-effective than long-term haemodialysis. Costs can also come down as knowledge is gained and skills developed.

A related ethical concern, one that we saw raised by Pope John Paul II in 2000, is that organs be distributed fairly. I have treated these questions elsewhere.[46] Suffice it here to say that medical need and ability to benefit should be the principal criteria, not ability to pay, social contribution, quality of life or whether you have been far-sighted enough to volunteer as a donor yourself. Of course any consideration of justice in the distribution of tissues opens up bigger questions about whether countries should be pursuing high-tech and high-cost therapies while people in those same countries or in poorer ones lack even the most basic treatments.

In the section above on conceptions of the body, we considered some issues regarding donor consent. This is not only an issue for donors and 'brokers' or tissue bankers. In their 'lust' for an organ, would-be recipients are not always very particular about the circumstances in which the organ was obtained and the complexities of consent, especially when the tissue provider is poor or powerless. In China organs of prisoners awaiting execution are put on the market in advance and the prisoners killed at military hospitals at a convenient time for the recipient(s) of their organ(s). Meanwhile organs are sometimes stolen from people in other countries or obtained under circumstances little short of coercion. Tissue recipients have a duty to ensure that they are not cooperating in such unethical practices.

Among the more exotic proposals in tissue transplantation are that gonads might be transferred from person to person, that human or animal organs, tissues or genes might be transplanted for enhancement reasons (to create a super-human being), and that human brains (or parts of human brains) might be transplanted into the bodies of other human

---

[46] A. Fisher and L. Gormally (eds.), *Healthcare Allocation: An Ethical Framework for Public Policy* (London: Linacre Centre, 2001).

beings or even animals. While strongly supporting transplantation for therapy, the Church opposes these proposals on the grounds that they undermine personal and procreational identity, uniqueness and dignity.[47]

CONCLUSION

There is much to be cautiously optimistic about when it comes to transplantation of major organs, tissues, cells and products, but we must also be optimistically cautious if we are to avoid moral mischief. In this chapter I have suggested that much depends upon our perspective on the human body, relationships and morality generally. Of course this works both ways. Not only do these matters inform transplantation practice: the practice itself increasingly influences the way we think about ourselves, each other and healthcare in general. For this very reason we should not allow ourselves to be swept along by technological advances which presume or encourage a view of the human body and relationships we would find unacceptable or even repugnant had we considered in advance the path down which we were being impelled.

[47] Pontifical Council for Health, *Charter for Healthworkers* 88.

CHAPTER 8

Artificial nutrition: why do unresponsive patients matter?

CIVILIZATION AFTER SCHIAVO

Introduction to the contest

In 2005, following a series of interventions by family, doctors, lawyers, courts, politicians and the media, all nutrition and hydration were removed from Terri Schiavo. She had been diagnosed as being in a 'persistent vegetative state' (PVS) but with tube feeding looked like living for many more years. Without it she died, on 31 March 2005, aged 41.[1]

Schiavo's is one of a string of legal cases in the United States, Canada, Britain, Italy and Australia regarding assisted feeding and hydration.[2] Because modern Western cultures are so divided over issues of human nature, life and death, dignity and rights, relationships and social responsibilities, such cases are given a high profile. Certain fundamental differences that might once have been recognized as arguments in metaphysics, ethics and religion are now played out in hospitals, courts and the media. Underlying conflicts of values and beliefs are often left unidentified, with people talking at cross-purposes, each assuming the other is homicidal or vitalist, authoritarian or uncompassionate.

Why are some health authorities and providers, public guardians and ethicists so anxious to withdraw assisted nutrition and hydration from

---

[1] Surveying the medical evidence on Terri Schiavo and the debate about the diagnosis of PVS see: D. Henke, 'Consciousness, Terri Schiavo and the Persistent Vegetative State', *NCBQ* 8(1) (2008), 69–86; R. Marker, 'Terri Schiavo and the Catholic connection', *NCBQ* 4(3) (2004), 555–69.

[2] On the Schiavo decisions: http://news.findlaw.com/legalnews/lit/schiavo/ (accessed 1 January 2011). Important prior cases in the United States are: *Re Quinlan* 355 A2d 647 (NJ 1976); *Brophy v. New England Sinai Hospital* 398 Mass. 417 (Mass 1986) 497 NE2d 626; *Cruzan v. Missouri Department of Health* 497 US 261 (1990). In Canada: *Rodriguez v. Attorney General of Canada* [1994] 2 LRC 136. In Britain: *Airedale NHS Trust v. Bland* [1993] AC 789; *Re D, Medical Law Review* 5 (1997) 225. In Australia: *Northridge v. Central Sydney Area Health Service* [2000] NSWSC 1241; *Gardner; re BWV* [2003] VSC 173. In Italy the 2009 case of Eluana Englaro raised similar issues.

213

those at a very low ebb, if needs be by force of law? Diverse motives and rationales converge here. There are those who favour euthanasia: by the time people need long-term assistance with nutrition and hydration they are presumed to be better off dead. There may be economic and logistical imperatives, as people conclude that such patients do not merit health resources and human attention. There is also genuine concern for the dignity and freedom of patients, including their right (and that of their guardians) to say no to over-treatment or to being kept 'alive' indefinitely on life support.

In health and aged care there has been a shift in the last few decades from professional paternalism to patient autonomy. This reflects the individualism in contemporary Western cultures, whereby personal preferences usually rule and sometimes trump even reason and community. It often suits governments, health insurers, medibusiness, taxpayers and consumers to equate being human with having a sovereign will. As a result those least able to press their claims are most likely to have them dishonoured. If the test of a civilization is how it treats its weakest and most vulnerable members, cases such as Terri Schiavo's are emblematic of much more than just the care appropriate to one person suffering a severe cognitive impairment.

Autonomy talk

While a student in Oxford in the early 1990s I attended a seminar given by the American-born philosopher of law Ronald Dworkin. Week by week we went through the manuscript of a book he was writing, which later appeared as *Life's Dominion*.[3] The book was in large part an attempt to dissuade the US Supreme Court from pulling back on *Roe* v. *Wade* in its then-forthcoming judgment in *Casey*, as it was thought to have done in *Webster*.[4] In due course Dworkin hoped the court would legalize euthanasia as well. The class was set up as a gentlemanly debate between Dworkin (with evolving text) and another eminent Oxford philosopher, Bernard Williams, before an audience of adoring students. The class was swept along with Dworkin's high rhetoric about the dignity of the person and the sanctity of life and how respect for both sometimes required us

---

[3] R. Dworkin, *Life's Dominion: An Argument about Abortion, Euthanasia, and Individual Freedom* (New York: Knopf, 1993).

[4] *Roe* v. *Wade* 410 US 113 (1973); *Webster* v. *Reproductive Health Services* 491 US 397 (1989); *Planned Parenthood* v. *Casey* 505 US 833 (1992).

to kill unborn babies. There were hardly any expressions of dissent, with Dworkin's sparring partner really only helping with fine-tuning.

Finally Dworkin came to his draft chapter on euthanasia.[5] Until then autonomy was the trump card in all moral issues – the autonomy of adults anyway. 'But what about granny', he asked, 'sitting around all day watching cartoons on TV and eating peanut-butter and jelly sandwiches?' The class laughed. 'She thinks she is happy', he said. 'She wants her life to carry on. But we know better don't we? We know her life is now like the "white noise" on the TV after the station has stopped transmitting. We know she would be better off if the TV were switched off. And we know we should help that to happen.'

You could have heard a pin drop. A class full of autonomy-trumpets suddenly saw where it might be leading. 'This is not really about autonomy at all, but about quality of life', one till-now-wide-eyed student complained. 'No', responded Dworkin, 'it *is* about respecting dignity and autonomy. When autonomy is permanently compromised by old age or disease we are better off dead. We know that at that point we would want some help to die, so we should show a similar courtesy to others.' That gave me my opening, as a subversive among the students, to raise a few questions in and out of class! When the book appeared in due course, that chapter had been considerably toned down. Nonetheless its emphasis on *autonomy-personism* remains: the view that people who lack full autonomy are not fully persons. Sentimentality or nostalgia might distort our judgment here, but on this account the description of Terri Schiavo by her husband's lawyer as a 'houseplant'[6] was in some ways more accurate than her parents' reference to her as 'our daughter'.

Dworkin is one prominent champion and Peter Singer another of a bioethic descending from John Stuart Mill. Liberals advance at least two, not entirely compatible, reasons for not feeding those who cannot exercise rational autonomy. The first is the view (supposedly from Mill's *On Liberty*) that what really matters in life is 'doing it my way': being able to pick and revise my own values and life-plans, make my own choices, satisfy my own preferences. The second view (after Mill's *Utilitarianism*) is that what matters in life is maximizing good sensations or fulfilled preferences and minimizing bad or unfulfilled ones. Both views accommodate rationality to preference rather than vice versa. Both conclude

---

[5] This anecdote is based on class notes and my memories and those of others in the class, not an exact transcript: my apologies for any inaccuracy.

[6] Quoted in P. Johnston, 'Is it "murder" to pull Terri's feeding tube?', *Intellectual Conservative*, 22 March 2005.

that real respect for those who will never again be free choosers and for caring for them requires withdrawing any life-sustaining care and even actively accelerating their deaths. Both are powerful strands of contemporary culture. Their combined effect in both rhetoric and practice has been not only that autonomy trumps all other moral concerns, but that the kind of autonomy that has this power is quite different from autonomy as it was traditionally understood. No longer is autonomy conceived of as rational-critical endorsement and implementation of reasons (as in the tradition of Aristotle, Augustine, Aquinas and Kant) but as the freedom to act on immediate desires and sensations. The appeal to autonomy has slipped (without much resistance) from the appeal to reason to the appeal to wants.

In this chapter I use a broad definition of autonomy. I ask why people who cannot exercise rational autonomy in the senses I have outlined still matter, objectively speaking, and matter very much. I will also ask what the implications of this might be for how we treat them. I will take it, too, that rational autonomy, at least in the sense of being in control and acting for reasons we endorse, matters very much to us subjectively. Most of us take the possession and frequent exercise of rational autonomy for granted; we abhor the prospect of its future reduction; and we miss it deeply when it is compromised in ourselves or someone we care about. What is also perplexing, however, is the recent move from the claim that 'rational autonomy matters very much' to the claim that 'people only matter *because* of their rational autonomy' and therefore to the dual conclusions that 'people who can no longer exercise rational autonomy are better off dead' and that 'their deaths may therefore be hastened by direct action or by calculated omission of basic care'.

Catholicism as a sign of contradiction

Christianity, and especially Catholicism, is opposed to many of these shifts in attitudes to the human person and so has become a 'sign of contradiction' in this area. Why is that? One reason is the variety of philosophical anthropologies available today: the person as functional system, ghost, rat, computer, sentience, self-consciousness, language user, chooser ... Christianity holds to a realist account of the person as a being that is material, living, animal, rational, free, social, emotional and immortal, and so offers metaphysical and biological arguments for this personhood from the first moment of that being's existence to his or her last. This provides a clear and egalitarian ontology of persons that applies also to persons unable to respond appropriately to stimuli, to think clearly or to express themselves. Certain norms of appropriate conduct towards persons may follow.

Entering this contemporary fray, Pope John Paul II argued that autonomy is *not* the source of human value or values; the significance of freedom and conscience is in its pursuit and choice of objective truth; freedom is always freedom *in*, not *from*, the truth (e.g. *VS* 19, 31–5, 40–3, 60–4). He re-emphasized the moral absolute against killing known to natural reason and Christian faith (e.g. *VS* 51–3; *EV* ch. III) and warned of the effects of failure to respect such norms upon victims, professionals, institutions and communities (*EV* 4, 11–12, 69, 74, 89–90). John Paul noted the growing tendency to value life 'only to the extent that it brings pleasure and well-being', to view all suffering as 'an unbearable setback, something from which one must be freed at all costs' and to view 'the growing number of elderly and disabled people as intolerable and too burdensome' (*EV* 64). 'In this context', the Pope noted, 'the temptation grows to take control of death and bring it about before its time, "gently" ending another's life.' While seemingly logical and compassionate, it is in fact 'the height of arbitrariness and injustice' to take it upon ourselves to judge who should live and who should die (*EV* 66).

Thus John Paul clarified the motives of euthanasia (whether selfish or compassionate) and the intention of euthanasia (to relieve suffering by deliberately hastening death). This served to highlight the risks of a mentality that declares some people *sub-human*, some lives of *no benefit* and some deaths *no loss*. It also demonstrated that euthanasia can be committed by omission of due care, as readily as by action such as poisoning. Repeating Christ's injunctions to be neighbours to all and to feed those in need (Luke 10:29–37; Matt. 25:40) the Pope insisted that 'the service of charity must be profoundly consistent. It cannot tolerate bias and discrimination … it is an indivisible good. We need then to show care for all life and for the life of everyone' (*EV* 87). In his subsequent *Allocution on Feeding Those in a 'Persistent Vegetative State'* (2004) John Paul II made it clear that a refusal to feed unresponsive people in need of food is an example of this kind of 'intolerable discrimination' and can amount to euthanasia.[7] Under his successor Benedict XVI the CDF confirmed that teaching.[8] The Church's magisterium strongly contests the views that

---

[7] John Paul II, *Allocution to the International Congress on Life-Sustaining Treatments and the 'Vegetative State'*, 20 March 2004.
[8] CDF, *On Artificial Nutrition and Hydration* (2007).

persistently unresponsive patients are dead or as good as dead or would
want to be dead,[9] or that others would be better off were such patients
dead; likewise it opposes the view that such people do not warrant continued care such as tube-feeding and that it is permissible to bring about
death in these cases by calculated omission of such care.[10]

Pope John Paul was not alone in his critique of certain views of personhood, autonomy and the reverence due to both. The liberal cult of autonomy has been criticized by authors such as MacIntyre, Taylor, George
and others (see the section in Chapter 1 on 'Promising developments');
applied to bioethics, this questions the autonomy-as-trump ideology so
strong in contemporary healthcare. Having set something of the scene
of the recent debate over whether people who lack the exercise of rational
autonomy matter, I now make two cases, one philosophical, the other
theological. By both routes I argue that such people *do* matter, that they
matter *enough* to be worthy of feeding, that they *should normally* be fed
and hydrated and if needs be fed and hydrated artificially.

WHY THE UNRESPONSIVE STILL MATTER:
A PHILOSOPHICAL ACCOUNT

Dignity and personhood

One common response to liberal claims about those lacking the present
exercise of rational autonomy has been to play the *dignity* card. This often
functions more as rhetoric than elaborated ethical argument. In its popular form it suggests a simple progression from the proposition that 'all
human beings have dignity' to the position that 'human life is inviolable'
and then, for some, to the conclusion 'there is a duty to feed all human
beings, if needs be even artificially'. This progression is, however, simplistic. Human dignity, properly understood, is shorthand for quite complex
arguments in anthropology and ethics. The 'inviolability of life' is a tag

9   C. Burant and S. Younger, 'Death and organ procurement: public beliefs and attitudes', *Kennedy Institute of Ethics Journal* 14(3) (2004), 217–34, found that 34% of respondents identified someone in PVS as dead and 57% viewed someone in an irreversible coma as dead.
10 Cf. J. Boyle, 'The American debate about artificial nutrition and hydration', in L. Gormally (ed.), *The Dependent Elderly: Autonomy, Justice and Quality of Care* (Cambridge University Press, 1992), pp. 28–46; A. Fergusson, 'Should tube-feeding be withdrawn in PVS?', *J Christian Med Fellowship* April (1993), 4–8; G. Grisez, 'May a husband end all care of his permanently uncon-scious wife?', *LQ* 63(2) (May 1996), 41–6 at 45; K. McMahon, 'Catholic moral teaching, medic-ally assisted nutrition and hydration and the vegetative state', *NeuroRehabilitation* 19(4) (2004), 373–80; W. E. May, 'Criteria for withholding or withdrawing treatment', *LQ* 57(3) (August 1991), 81–90.

for multifaceted contentions and conclusions of ethics and law. 'The duty
to feed' is likewise shorthand for elaborate discussions in political and
social philosophy as well as in bioethics and healthcare practice.

Can human dignity function as an independent ethical concept carrying at least some of the weight of argumentation for a duty to feed?
It can, but it is vulnerable: people will not accept it as more than rhetoric unless they also accept some additions to classical anthropology,
such as those that Rousseau, the Kantians and personalists such as Karol
Wojtyła (John Paul II) proposed to fill out this concept. In this European
tradition, dignity is a special sort of value possessed by persons because
they are a form of existence able to actualize themselves and not just to
respond to external causality. On this view, one cannot understand persons merely in terms of what motivates them, cannot measure their value
in terms of usefulness or any other attribute, cannot reduce them to mere
means: therefore one must accord them an independent value 'beyond
price'. While *dignity* language has been used in such 'secular' arenas as
the United Nations, it is especially popular nowadays in Church circles,
where it has come to be closely associated with 'the sanctity of life'.

Thus for a theorist such as Wojtyła the dignity of the human person might be said to consist in his rational autonomy but that is only
so because that rational autonomy is the very nature or essence of the
person. On this account, from the first to the last moment of existence,
a human being has human dignity because it is *of the very nature* of the
human person to be the kind of being that has reason and free will – as
well as embodiment, sensations, emotions, mobility, fertility, sociability,
immortality. This is so *whether or not the individual can exercise those capacities* at any particular moment. Accordingly, even when illness renders
a person unlikely ever again (in this life) to exercise one or more of those
capacities, the person retains this human nature and so is of inestim-
able value or dignity. Many contemporary liberals regard the tradition
expressed by Kant, Wojtyła or the early documents of the United Nations
as obscurantist or 'metaphysical' at this point. They do not acknowledge
'human dignity' as grounding respectable argument, even if they still
use cognate terms such as 'human rights' from time to time. For this
reason, to argue today for equal care, respect and protection from the
concept of human dignity demands some attention to underlying ontology and deontology.

The contemporary liberal idea that someone unable to exercise one or
more of the normal adult capacities is thereby not a 'someone' any longer
is surely one of the more bizarre ideas in the recent history of philosophy.

It would have been regarded as plain dishonourable in almost every age and culture before our own, as almost all ages and cultures have honoured (or at least believed they should honour) the elderly, sick and dying. Anyone coming to this notion cold and unprejudiced would classify it with some of the least edifying propositions of ethics and politics, along with the view that some people are natural slaves, that no woman is citizen enough to vote, that interracial marriage is immoral, that those without property have no interest in who governs them or that people with disabilities are useless eaters.

Alasdair MacIntyre responds to what might be called the élitist account of human personhood by arguing persuasively that we are fundamentally *dependent* beings and that this dependence is not just chronologically but logically and ontologically prior to our independence or autonomy.[11] He also makes a strong case that our ethics must be grounded in our bodily, animal nature. Here he joins Aristotle, Aquinas, John Paul II and many contemporary authors who have argued that the body and bodily life are *not* merely instruments somehow distinct from and serving 'the real me', 'the self' or, as Richard Rorty calls it, my 'mind-stuff'.[12] These writers demonstrate that mind-stuff approaches presuppose an indefensibly dualist conception of the human person. Human beings are rational *animals*, living organisms, not angels or spirits connected or disconnected to an animal body. They are their bodies. Their life *is* bodily life. To end the bodily life of a human being is to kill someone.[13]

---

[11] A. MacIntyre, *Dependent Rational Animals: Why Human Beings Need the Virtues* (Peru, IL: Open Court, 1999).

[12] L. Kass, 'Thinking about the body', in *Toward a More Natural Science: Biology and Human Affairs* (New York: Free Press, 1985), ch. 11; M. Latkovic, 'The morality of tube-feeding PVS patients', *NCBQ* 5(3) (2005), 503–13; P. Lee and R. George, *Body–Self Dualism in Contemporary Ethics and Politics* (Cambridge University Press, 2007); G. Meilaender, *Body, Soul, and Bioethics* (Notre Dame University Press, 1995); P. O'Mahony, *A Question of Life: Its Beginning and Transmission* (London: Sheed and Ward, 1990), pp. 22–33; E. Olson, *The Human Animal: Personal Identity without Psychology* (Oxford University Press, 1997); P. Ryan, 'The value of life and its bearing on three issues of medical ethics', *Voices* 15(2) (Summer 2000), 503–13. Rorty discusses 'mind-stuff' in *Essays on Heidegger and Others* (Cambridge University Press, 1991).

[13] Several authors have made the point that any attempt to tie basic human rights to the possession of 'personhood' is a recipe for the arbitrariness characteristic of injustice. Almost all the personhood characteristics such as consciousness, self-determination and sociability come in degrees, uncorrelated to each other, and variously related to age, mental health or other supposedly objective indicators; this invites self-serving classifications and the gradual exclusion of more and more people from protection or provision in the interests of the majority or the powerful. If humanity per se is no longer sufficient, then not only consciousness and agency but other qualities (e.g. intelligence of a certain level, social relationships, productivity and so on) may come to be regarded as necessary for the receipt of healthcare or feeding. Liberalism at this point collapses into totalitarianism.

Inviolability

Belief in and arguments for the equal inviolability of human persons often come paired with belief in and arguments for the equal dignity of every human being. The denial of one often comes with a denial of the other, but not always. Some concede that those lacking rational autonomy are persons with human dignity (whatever that might mean) but assert they are not inviolable. Humanity is divided, then, not into 'persons' and 'non-persons' but into 'protected persons' and 'unprotected persons' or into 'persons who should live' and 'persons who should not'.[14]

Historically, this move has been made by many of the same thinkers and legislators who made the élitist distinction between human and subhuman (examined in the previous section) or by others in the same communities. The results have included slavery, totalitarianism, apartheid, segregation and genocide. Any suggestion that our society is of this sort would be met with howls of protest, which to some extent would be justified. However, before we get too smug, we should recall that no society before ours has killed a quarter of its new members (before birth) or killed on such a scale and so unashamedly. Asylum seekers and suspected terrorists are examples of other groups increasingly denied full human rights. Older people are progressively pressed to sign 'living wills' that vitiate their feeding rights if they become incompetent.[15] Now it is proposed that a new class of human beings – the persistently unresponsive – will be denied food and water, allowed to die of dehydration, by fiat of the medical profession and the law. Our culture may not be as morally superior as we imagine.

Those who argue for personhood but against equal protection and care for all persons commonly speak of non-treatment 'in the patient's best interests', 'avoiding unnecessary suffering' or 'letting nature take its course'.[16] The driver here is often not the interests of the cognitively impaired but those of the bystanders who are more autonomous, powerful and vocal. Sometimes it is asserted that the incompetent patient 'would not have wanted to go on in this way' and so would not have wanted to be

---

[14] John Paul II, *EV* 19, notes the contemporary tendency to exalt the concept of consciousness or subjectivity 'to an extreme' and to recognize 'as the subject of rights only the person who enjoys full or at least partial autonomy and who emerges from a state of total dependence on others'.

[15] Cf. N. Tonti-Filippini, J. Fleming and M. Walsh, 'Twenty propositions', *Human Life Review* 30(1) (Winter 2004), 83–109.

[16] John Paul II, *EV* 11, notes that 'the value of life can today undergo a kind of "eclipse" as is evident in the tendency to disguise certain crimes against life in its early or final stages by using innocuous medical terms which distract attention from the fact'.

fed artificially. Hypotheticals about what someone 'would have wanted' are dubious at the best of times, let alone when those constructing them are exhausted or disadvantaged by the person's ongoing life or care. Even had a person made their preferences known in advance – which was *not* the case in the Schiavo, Bland or BWV cases – we might question the validity of such 'directives' given when a person does not suffer the condition being addressed, does not really know all the options that will later be available and so could not really make an informed decision.

Moreover, encouraging people to consent in advance to being starved should they become incompetent will not simplify ethically complex situations. People, especially weak people, who respond to the invitation of authoritative others to renounce their inviolability, are not exercising true autonomy. Homicidal acts or omissions do not become right simply by becoming policies or by getting the victims to sign their own death warrants: in many ways these sops to conscience only aggravate the evil being perpetrated.[17]

Is the life of every human being *really* to be regarded as inviolable? Various cases have been made for this moral claim. One begins with the idea that *life* is a good basic to human choice and flourishing (e.g. *EV* 68). Life here signifies *organic* or bodily existence, its preservation, prolongation and transmission. Terms such as 'liveliness', 'vivacity', 'business life', 'social life' and 'the good life' depend for their sense upon the prior organic understanding of life. Of course, some deny that organic life, as such, is a dimension of human flourishing or a good rationally pursued in human choices: life, they say, is only 'worth living' because of the things it enables. People only want to go on living so as to be able to do their work, care for their children, enjoy playing tennis and so on. On this view it is *biography* not life per se that matters: what we consciously experience and choose, what we write with our lives, is what is important. On this account organic life is a very important, *instrumental* good; but when it no longer serves other goods through conscious experience, choices and actions, it is no longer valuable.

One might respond as follows: the instrumental uses of organic life do not exhaustively explain its value. Life is also enjoyed 'for its own sake'.

---

[17] *EV* 66: 'To concur with the intention of another person to commit suicide and to help in carrying it out through so-called assisted suicide means to cooperate in, and at times to be the actual perpetrator of, an injustice which can never be excused, even if it is requested. In a remarkably relevant passage St Augustine writes that "it is never licit to kill another: even if he should wish it, indeed if he request it because, hanging between life and death, he begs for help in freeing the soul struggling against the bonds of the body and longing to be released; nor is it licit even when a sick person is no longer able to live."'

That is why no one expects us to give reasons for promoting life, avoiding death and so on: we regard these objects as sufficient reasons in themselves; we value human life per se. Someone can say meaningfully 'it's good to be alive' without having to explain what they are doing with that life. This sense that life is *intrinsically* valuable is behind our talk of the right to and inviolability of human life. We express this same insight in many of our actions and institutions. We celebrate births and birthdays, and grieve over deaths and anniversaries of deaths. We delight in good health and recovery of health, and lament sickness, disability and pain. We send a congratulations card at a birth, a sympathy card at a death. We bring children into the world and nurture them. We protect life through life-savers, sea-rescue operations, road safety laws, anti-smoking campaigns. We punish attacks on life through our legal systems. We promote life through hunting and gathering, fishing and farming; through markets, food shops and pharmacies; through healthcare, welfare and education. In explaining what we are up to in this broad range of activities and commitments, 'life' is sufficient explanation. Directly to deprive an innocent person of life, therefore, is prima facie to deny that person a good that is properly enjoyed and always to do that person a harm.

Of course, we also value life for what it enables, what we can achieve in it. Even those who value life only for its instrumental uses may recognize the importance of defending the weak and vulnerable from medicalized homicide and protecting health professionals from the corrupting effects of taking part in direct killing. Without strict rules against killing in the healthcare environment, the category of the 'expendable' and the pressures to get rid of them are likely to keep growing, and the trust of patients in their health professionals will decline.

Qualifications

A few qualifications are in order here. To say that life is a basic human good is not to say that it is reasonable for everyone to prolong or transmit life at all times and in all circumstances, at whatever cost to themselves and others and by whatever means. Neither does it mean that life is the only value or the most important value or an absolute value. Rather it says that the pursuit of life makes some human choices, activities, claims and commitments intelligible, whether or not they are reasonable in the circumstances. Grisez and Finnis have argued convincingly that no one basic good properly overrides all others. There will often be good reasons to do things that protect or prolong life: the good of life itself, the other good things life enables, responsibilities to others, especially dependants, and so on. There may well be concurrent good reasons *not* to do so: burdens of various kinds for the person whose life would be prolonged or for those who would be engaged in their care, the risks involved and opportunity costs and so on. A reasonable decision will take these things into account.

Of course, no one wants to suffer persistent unresponsiveness or dementia, to be a subject only of the goods of (continuing) life, (diminished) health and (received) love, none experienced consciously. No one wants to see anyone else living like that. Nonetheless, even the severely cognitively impaired are living human beings: their life is their very reality as persons and as such remains a good, even if their life is not consciously enjoyed by them and however little it appeals to us. This is why we still care for persistently unresponsive people: such care ensures their continued participation in the goods of which they can still be subjects and maintains our bonds of interpersonal communion or solidarity with them. This also explains why we do not exploit or harm or bury alive such people or otherwise subject them to indignity.

The 'inviolability of human life' doctrine follows from notions such as that life is a basic human good, that good is always to be pursued and evil avoided and that evil may not be done even to achieve some great good (such as 'merciful release'). The natural law precepts to 'preserve life' and 'not to kill' follow so immediately from understanding that life is a basic good that they might be said to be self-evident. The negative norm – never to take innocent human life – is held by the Catholic tradition (among others) to be a moral absolute.[18] Of course, certain further principles, virtues and life-plans will be required if a basic good such as life is to be pursued reasonably and basic principles such as 'preserve life' and 'do not kill' are to be understood and applied appropriately to specific situations.

Feeding and caring

It is one thing to say that there is a positive norm requiring us to feed ourselves, those in our care and those within our reach; it is another to assert that a failure to feed is always wrong. No one can ever exhaust the

---

[18] *EV* 40–1, on the implications of the inviolability norm, and *EV* 57, which rehearses the philosophical and theological arguments and then defines the negative moral absolute as a matter of Catholic dogma.

demands of a positive norm such as 'feed the hungry', and we are not morally responsible for the death of every person we might conceivably have helped, as long as we are devoting our time and energies to morally reasonable purposes and fulfilling our responsibilities. Even in particular cases of persons in need of food who are within our reach, there may be good reasons for not satisfying the positive norm, e.g. because to feed is impossible, ineffective, overly burdensome to the patient or to others or because to feed conflicts with another (equally serious) duty to that person or to others.[19] None of these omissions to feed is unethical. On the other hand, sometimes people choose to withhold or withdraw necessary care precisely so as to hasten death, and this is homicide. The commonplace practice of denying infants with disabilities even fairly simple surgical interventions to correct blockages (tagged euphemistically 'benign neglect by physician') is an example. Though the agent may plead 'I didn't *do* anything', that is precisely the problem: he or she could have and should have done something but failed to do so because the agent thought that it would be better all round if the patient were dead. Whatever the legal situation, from the moral point of view it makes no difference whether one kills by action or calculated omission of reasonable care, if killing is the goal. In such cases, the failure to fulfil the positive norm to feed is also a failure to observe the negative norm against killing.

In really hard cases, such as those of people who are persistently unresponsive to external stimuli, sympathy tempts us to compromise such moral norms or to make an 'exception', while telling ourselves we can still hold the line 'as a general rule'. However, rational reflection and human experience show that the implications of such exceptions go far wider than the relief of particular hard cases. Here we bump up against the ultimate question for end-of-life ethics and indeed for all ethics: the mystery of evil. How are we to face ineradicable suffering or decline, when we have tried all we reasonably can to combat pain, disease and dying? The pervasive temptation in the modern consumer culture is to demand an immediate technological, market or government 'fix' and to rail like a petulant child until that happens; and when a fix is impossible, people in this same culture stand in gaping incomprehension, go into denial, withdraw support and/or marginalize those who cannot be fixed. We must realize that there are evils we cannot 'solve' in any simple, morally acceptable way. Such evils can, however, call forth much that is most noble in the human

---

[19] See P. Gummere, 'Assisted nutrition and hydration in advanced dementia of the Alzheimer's type', *NCBQ* 8(2) (2008), 291–306.

spirit: patient endurance, perseverance, fortitude, even heroism, on the part of patients, doctors, families and communities. Sometimes more *patience* will be asked of the bystanders than of the *patients* themselves; impatience (with a slow dying) can be at the heart of a decision to stop feeding. As Cardinal Ratzinger put it in his homily at the funeral mass of Pope John Paul II: 'The world is redeemed by the patience of God. It is destroyed by the impatience of man.'

If we do accept that those who lack rational autonomy are persons and should not be violated, is it clear that they should be fed and, if so, how and by whom? The Second Vatican Council, quoting Gratian and the Fathers, said 'Feed the man who is starving: for if you do not feed him you are killing him.'[20] Starving or dehydrating someone to death by preventing them from obtaining food and water or by failing to provide it when they depend on others to receive it, has always been considered not only killing but a particularly egregious form of killing. Why is that? I think it is because food and water are not only sources but symbols of life and community. To deny things that are so basic to someone is not only to deny them something they need but to deny all solidarity with them. When tyrants starve people such as St Maximillian Kolbe to death, they demonstrate contempt not only for the precept against killing but also for the humanity and dignity of the person so degradingly killed.[21]

Refusing food or water to someone is a powerful symbol of exclusion from the circle of the community or humanity: but to do this when someone is weak or dying is especially revealing. Our normal response is to shield the frail and the dying from the eyes of curious strangers, from lethal neglect of basic care and from all attacks, whether this is from television cameras, greedy relatives, hospital number-crunchers, organ harvesters or others. With the frail and dying, protecting what is left of their lives and ensuring that they have rudimentary care, such as nutrition, hydration, warmth, prayer and company, may be about all we *can* do for them. Such shielding care maintains our solidarity with them while this is still possible and declares to them, ourselves and society that these people still matter very much. On traditional understandings, to ask 'should we care for the frail and dying?' is only a question for the callous, the selfish and the morally colour-blind. It is the same as asking 'Should we care for those who most need our care?' Caring for the frail and dying is criterial

[20] Vatican II, *GS* 69; cf. Gratian, *Decretum*, c. 21, dist. LXXXVI (ed. Friedberg I, 302). According to Flannery this axiom is also found already in *PL* 54, 591A.
[21] Cf. S. Miles, 'Nourishment and the ethics of lament', *LQ* 56(1) (August 1989), 64–9.

for caring: it is part of how we understand, and how we show that we understand, what care *is*.

Assisted feeding and hydrating

Feeding and hydrating have traditionally been regarded as nursing care rather than medical treatment. Philosophers since Aristotle and Hippocrates noted that while certain foods and drinks, taken in appropriate circumstances, have medicinal properties, the primary purpose of food and liquid is not to address sickness but simply to nourish and hydrate the body so that the most fundamental processes underlying physical and mental health can occur. Thus doctors do not usually feed patients: nurses, family or the patients themselves do, and they do so whether they are sick or well. Not only are there different workforces involved but different goals: while doctors focus on *treatments*, which seek to prolong life at risk, cure disease, heal damage or halt degeneration, nurses (and others who do nursing) provide *care*, which sustains life in the meantime. Such nursing care continues to be appropriate even when medicine has achieved a cure or when there is no more that medicine can do. Of course there may be some overlap, and some of the same principles apply to deciding what should be provided to whom but there may also be some differences of ethos and ethic between 'treatment' and 'care'.[22]

If there is a duty to feed (and hydrate), then there is a duty to feed a person what is appropriate to their needs and by means that are effective. Just as the positive duty to feed has its limits, so will the duty to assist feeding with various techniques and devices. The harder it becomes to achieve effective nutrition and hydration, the less comfort such provision also offers, the more burdensome the mode of delivery is to the recipient

[22] There is, however, considerable dispute about how assisted feeding should be regarded. While inserting the tube, monitoring it and prescribing dietary supplements are usually performed by physicians, the actual feeding through the tube is usually performed by nurses, relatives or even patients themselves. The goal of the activity of all the carers here is a *non-medical* one: nutrition and hydration. Thus Pope John Paul II, *On Life-Sustaining Treatments* 4, joined others in resisting the designation of assisted feeding as medical treatment: 'the administration of water and food, even when provided by artificial means, always represents a natural means of preserving life, not a medical act. Its use should be considered, in principle, ordinary and proportionate, and as such morally obligatory, insofar as and until it is seen to have attained its proper end, which in the present case consists in providing nourishment to the patient and alleviation of his suffering.' On this address see: R. Doerflinger, 'Pope John Paul II on nutrition and hydration for the seriously ill and disabled', in E. Furton (ed.), *Live the Truth: The Moral Legacy of John Paul II in Catholic Health Care* (Philadelphia: NCBC, 2006), pp. 233–52, and W. E. May, 'Caring for persons in the Persistent Vegetative State and John Paul II's Address', *Medicina e Morale* 55(5) (2005), 533–55.

or to others, the closer the recipient is to death (and therefore to not needing nutrition), the less reason there will be to use such means. Thus the case for feeding the frail, disabled and dying, if needs be by tube, is based on two lines of argument: one which focuses on the inviolability of life and the unethical intention to kill that underlies many denials of assisted nutrition and hydration; and another which focuses upon the symbolic and social import of feeding and hydrating, something contradicted by a choice to allow someone to starve to death.

WHY THE UNRESPONSIVE STILL MATTER: A THEOLOGICAL ACCOUNT

From the imago Dei *to the duty to feed and vice versa*

In the previous section I noted the common progress in the pro-life dignity argument from the proposition that 'all human beings have dignity' to 'human life is inviolable' to the conclusion 'there is a duty to feed all human beings, if needs be artificially'. I proposed various elaborations and nuances that are necessary if this argument is to work. There is a theological parallel – what we might call the sanctity of life argument – which runs from the proposition that 'human beings are made in the image of God' to 'the lives of all human beings are sacred' to the same conclusion that 'there is a duty to feed all human beings, if needs be artificially'. Once again these propositions are conclusions and shorthand expressions for some profound concepts and complex arguments. To describe people as 'the image of God', for instance, is to quote an ancient and somewhat opaque scriptural text and to express a stance towards the questions of the divine–human relationship, human self-understanding, the limits and scope of human freedom, rationality and stewardship. To talk of 'the sanctity of life', at least in a theological context, is to identify human beings as created, redeemed and destined for greatness in this life and the next, to identify God as the Author and Redeemer of those lives, and to assert that only God may give or take such life (cf. *EV* 34–6, 53–5).

In theology, as indeed in philosophy, argument sometimes works in a reverse direction to what first appears, with premises and conclusions qualifying each other in complex ways. Sometimes we reason, whether consciously or not, from the 'conclusion' (perhaps given by revelation or the magisterium or common sense or intuition) that we should feed those in need, if necessary with some artifice, to the 'premise' that all human life is sacred, not just the lives of the fit and active. Having grasped this, we elaborate a theology of the human person as 'the image of God'. However, this conclusion itself becomes a premise for the argument that human life is so precious as to be worthy of the tags 'sacred', 'inviolable' and 'food-worthy' and that certain norms follow. I begin this theological exploration, therefore, with the precept to feed, even artificially.

'All I ask as I die is this: honesty, comfort and the
food I need' (Prov. 30:7–8): evolution of Catholic
teaching on tube feeding

Over the past two decades many individual bishops and bishops' conferences around the world have addressed the issue of assisted feeding and hydration for people suffering from persistent unresponsiveness and similar conditions. In 1992 the US Bishops' Committee for Pro-Life Activities issued the pastoral statement *On Nutrition and Hydration*, concluding that there must be a presumption in favour of tube feeding for persistently unconscious patients and that such measures should not be withdrawn unless they offer no reasonable hope of sustaining life or pose excessive risks or burdens.[23] A similar position was taken by several state bishops' conferences (e.g. Florida, New Jersey, Washington-Oregon and Pennsylvania) though not all (e.g. Texas). In 1994 the US bishops approved a new set of *Ethical Directives for Catholic Health Care* which upheld the position that tube feeding is not morally obligatory when it provides neither nutrition nor comfort, but insisted that 'there should be a presumption in favour of providing nutrition and hydration to all patients, including patients who require medically assisted nutrition and hydration, as long as this is of sufficient benefit to outweigh the burdens involved to the patient'.[24] In 2001 a similar position was adopted in the *Code of Ethical Standards for Catholic Health and Aged Care Services in Australia*.[25]

[23] US Bishops' Pro-Life Committee, 'Nutrition and hydration: moral and pastoral reflections', *Origins* 21(44) (9 April 1992), 705–12 at 707.

[24] US Conference of Catholic Bishops, *Ethical and Religious Directives for Catholic Health Care Services*, 4th edn (Washington, DC: USCCB, 2001), pp. 56–8.

[25] Catholic Health Australia, *Code of Ethical Standards for Catholic Health and Aged Care Services in Australia* (Canberra: CHA, 2001), 5.12: 'Continuing to care for a patient is a fundamental way of respecting and remaining in solidarity with that person. When treatments are withheld or withdrawn because they are therapeutically futile or overly-burdensome, other forms of care such as appropriate feeding, hydration and treatment of infection, comfort care and hygiene should be continued. Nutrition and hydration should always be provided to patients unless they cannot be assimilated by a person's body, they do not sustain life, or their only mode of delivery imposes grave burdens on the patient or others. Such burdens to others do not normally arise in developed countries such as Australia.'

The first Vatican document to address the matter of tube feeding specifically was the *Charter for Healthworkers* published by the Pontifical Council for Health in 1994. It restated the usual distinctions between homicidal withdrawals of care and those justified by imminence of death or burdensomeness. It then added a telling rider: 'The administration of food and liquids, even artificially, is part of the normal treatment always due patients when this is not burdensome for them: their undue suspension could amount to euthanasia in a proper sense.'[26] This teaching has since been reaffirmed by the CDF, the Pontifical Academy for Life and various bishops.[27] In 2009 the US bishops added to their healthcare directives that:

In principle, there is an obligation to provide patients with food and water, including medically assisted nutrition and hydration for those who cannot take food orally. This obligation extends to patients in chronic and presumably irreversible conditions (e.g., the 'persistent vegetative state') who can reasonably be expected to live indefinitely if given such care. Medically assisted nutrition and hydration become morally optional when they cannot reasonably be expected to prolong life or when they would be 'excessively burdensome for the patient or [would] cause significant physical discomfort, for example resulting from complications in the use of the means employed'. For instance, as a patient draws close to inevitable death from an underlying progressive and fatal condition, certain measures to provide nutrition and hydration may become excessively burdensome and therefore not obligatory in light of their very limited ability to prolong life or provide comfort.[28]

The papal magisterium on assisted feeding

In his great encyclical on bioethics, *Evangelium Vitae*, John Paul II condemned euthanasia as 'a grave violation of the law of God', symptomatic of the 'culture of death' in many Western countries and contrary both to natural law and revelation as clarified by the magisterium (*EV* 65). In elaborating his rich theological argument for this, the Pope drew on a long line of sources from the Old and New Testaments, through the Fathers and scholastics, to the writings of his predecessors (especially Pius

---

[26] Pontifical Council for Health, *Charter for Healthworkers* (1994; English trans. 1995) 120.

[27] For example, CDF, *On Artificial Nutrition and Hydration*; Australian Catholic Bishops and Catholic Health Australia, *Briefing Note on the Obligation to Provide Nutrition and Hydration*, 3 September 2004. Bishop (now Cardinal) Elio Sgreccia and several other bishops were outspoken in some of the court-ordered removal of feeding cases noted above.

[28] US Conference of Catholic Bishops, *Ethical and Religious Directives for Catholic Health Care Services*, 5th edn (Washington, DC: USCCB, 2009), 58

XII), the Second Vatican Council and the curia. He was careful to make the necessary distinctions between euthanasia ('an action or omission which of itself and by intention causes death, with the purpose of eliminating all suffering') and appropriate pain relief or non-treatment. Catholic teaching, he recognized, has never required the prolongation of life at all costs; 'heroic', 'extraordinary' or very burdensome treatments may properly be forgone, especially when death is clearly imminent and inevitable, 'so long as the normal care due to the sick person in similar cases is not interrupted'.

What might be included in such 'normal care' was not spelt out by the Pope until 1998 when he reminded the bishops of California, Nevada and Hawaii that:

[A] great teaching effort is needed to clarify the substantive moral difference between discontinuing medical procedures that may be burdensome, dangerous or disproportionate to the expected outcome – what the *Catechism of the Catholic Church* calls 'the refusal of "over-zealous" treatment' – and taking away the ordinary means of preserving life, such as feeding, hydration and normal medical care … The omission of nutrition and hydration intended to cause a patient's death must be rejected and, while giving careful consideration to all the factors involved, the presumption should be in favour of providing medically assisted nutrition and hydration to all patients who need them. To blur this distinction is to introduce a source of countless injustices and much additional anguish, affecting both those already suffering from ill health or the deterioration which comes with age, and their loved ones.[29]

Finally, in 2004, when himself suffering a degenerative disease which would eventually compromise his ability to swallow, the Pope clarified the matter even further. He insisted that people who are unresponsive to stimuli, demonstrate no awareness of self or environment and seem unable to interact with others, should never be tagged or treated as less than human. They are not 'vegetables'. 'Even our brothers and sisters who find themselves in the clinical condition of a *vegetative state* retain their human dignity in all its fullness. The loving gaze of God the Father continues to fall upon them, acknowledging them as His sons and daughters, especially in need of help.'[30]

The 'fundamental good' of life, the Pope reminded us, cannot be outweighed by quality of life or cost considerations. For others to make care decisions based on such factors amounts to attributing more or less dignity

[29] John Paul II, *Ad limina Address of the Holy Father to US Bishops of California, Nevada and Hawaii*, 2 October 1998, 4.
[30] John Paul II, *On Life-Sustaining Treatments* 3.

to that particular patient, thus introducing arbitrariness and unjust discrimination into social relations. Instead of such negativity, positive measures must be taken to support people with severe intellectual disabilities and their loved ones.[31] In *Evangelium Vitae* John Paul II had already written of the 'intolerable' neglect that some of the elderly, disabled and dying experience even in affluent nations. He exhorted us 'to preserve, or to re-establish where it has been lost, a sort of covenant between the generations', a relationship of acceptance and solidarity, closeness and service. His 2004 allocution might therefore be read as unpacking some of the implications of this covenant relationship by considering how we should regard and care for the persistently unconscious.

Thus instead of the 'Never Feed', 'Always Feed' and 'Seldom Feed' views proposed by some with respect to assisted feeding of people who are at a very low ebb, the magisterium has consistently proposed a 'Usually Feed' view and has repudiated both a 'vitalism' that would tube feed even when this no longer works or is gravely burdensome and a 'euthanasist' approach that would deny food because it is judged that it would be best all round if the persistently unresponsive patient were dead. Everyone is entitled at least to food and water, clothing, shelter, sanitation, company and prayer. So if they need help, even artifice, with nutrition or hydration (or clothing or sanitation and so on), and this can easily be given them, it should normally be given. Even persons suffering from persistent unresponsiveness or like conditions deserve such basic, natural, normal or minimal care as John Paul II called assisted nutrition and hydration in these cases. As the Pope pointed out, this kind of care is only 'in principle' obligatory, i.e. for as long as it achieves its 'proper goal' of nourishing or comforting.[32] Thus the Catholic tradition, like the Hippocratic one, has long held treatments and/or forms of care inappropriate where:

- the patient has died;
- death is imminent;
- where giving such treatment is ineffective care ('futile');
- where the mode of delivery places an unreasonable burden upon the patient or others.

This means that it will sometimes be appropriate to withhold, reduce or withdraw assisted nutrition and hydration. It also means that prima facie

---

[31] John Paul II, *On Life-Sustaining Treatments* 5.
[32] John Paul II, *On Life-Sustaining Treatments* 4.

assisted nutrition and hydration should be given to those suffering persistent unresponsiveness or like conditions. Despite frequent claims to the contrary, they are not dead, not dying, not burdened by assisted feeding. Tube feeding does work for them in the same way that it works for anyone else, sustaining their bodily life and thus their person. In the First World, at least, it can usually be provided relatively easily and inexpensively. The presumption in favour of feeding, including tube feeding when this is necessary to sustain life, is thus well supported in the recent magisterial tradition. Following our logic of working 'backwards' from conclusion through premises, let us now examine whether there is a basis for the 'prior' claim that there is a duty to provide feeding and hydration.

'When I was hungry did you feed me?' (Matt. 25:31–45)

All religion is bound up in some way with food and feeding, feasting and fasting. Faith traditions identify mystical, communitarian, symbolic and ethical dimensions of offering and eating food, as well as of moderation and gluttony. There may be food taboos and cycles of fasting and abstinence, but feeding those in need of food is required in every serious religion and appears antiphonally as a charge in the Jewish and Christian Scriptures.[33] Food and drink are God's good gifts to be shared in turn with others.[34] According to the prophets, only the knave and the fool 'lie about God or fail to feed the hungry or deprive the thirsty of drink' (Isa. 32:6–7). To stand by and do nothing while another person starves is the very antithesis of religion: believers succour others and offer food sacrifices to their god(s) precisely so that the spiritual and material advantages of food are made more fully available both to themselves and to the hungry. Withholding food so as to kill contravenes serious religion, just as it does natural reason.

But what was and is different about the Christian faith here? The Scriptures single out an aspect of Jesus' ministry that marks his attitude to food (and so that of the Christian religion) as potentially different. In the gospels we hear one of the more spiteful pieces of gossip about Jesus: he was nick-named 'a glutton and a drunkard' (Matt. 11:18–19; Luke 7:34; cf. Mark 2:18–27). It was not just that Jesus hungered and thirsted like

[33] For example, Deut. 10:18–19; 14:29; 24:17–22; Prov. 25:21; Sir. 4:1–6; Job 22:7; Isa. 58:6–9; Ezek. 18:7, 16; Tobit 1:16–17 and 4:16; Matt 10:42; 25:31–45; Mark 9:41; Luke ch. 10; Rom. 12:20; Jas. 2:15–17; 1 John 3:17.
[34] For example, Gen. 43:34; 1 Kgs. 17:4, 8; 21:7; Ps. 81:16; 107:9; 146:7; Eccles. 8:15; Sir. 31:23–31; Ezek. 34; Matt. 6:25–33; Luke 15:23.

any human being and so ate and drank (Matt. 4:2; Mark 2:23; 11:12; John 4:6–7; 19:28). The complaint seems to have been that Jesus and his followers were too worldly by half; that genuinely religious people (like John the Baptist) would abstain, especially if the end-times were coming; but Jesus and the lads were, in contemporary parlance, 'party animals'. Elsewhere I have suggested that this complaint, coming from the scribes and Pharisees, was especially sinister: it implied that Jesus was a sluggard, a wastrel, a useless eater, someone that the Old Testament predicted would come to nothing and so deserved death rather than food (Deut. 21:18–21; Prov. 21:17; 23:20–21; 28:7; Sir. 31:12–22; 37:27–31; Tit. 1:12).[35] In the context of our present discussions, this is especially poignant.

Jesus was of course often at wedding feasts, Pharisees' dining tables, eating with tax collectors and sinners, 'at home' with his friends or out hosting picnics in the hills. His preaching was full of talk of vineyards, grapes, wine and wineskins; of wheat, yeast and bread; of oil, mustard seeds, figs, mint, dill, cumin, eggs, salt, fish and a fattened calf; of table etiquette and feasts. Many of the turning points in his life were marked by eating and drinking. His first great sign is turning water into wine; his first preaching to a Gentile began with a request for a drink and ended with a promise of endless living water; his most-recorded miracle is the multiplication of loaves and fishes; his last wonder before his Ascension is the huge haul of fish. All these miracles were of end-time proportions, divine in their extravagance, a foretaste of the longed-for messianic banquet (Isa. 25:6–8; 1 Sam. 2:5; Luke 1:53). As his ministry came to its climax, he took his closest friends aside for a last meal, investing the Passover Seder with new significance: his own Pasch, memorialized and perpetuated in the Eucharist. Before returning to the Father he dined again with disoriented disciples in Emmaus, with confused apostles at the Sunday gathering and with his nearest and dearest at the lakeside breakfast in Galilee.

Elsewhere I have argued that attitudes to food and drink have implications that run deep for our theology of creation and eschatology, incarnation and redemption, sacramentality and spirituality, politics and ethics.[36] Here I want to suggest that our attitudes with respect to whom we feed and our practices[37] with respect to how we feed them say something powerful about both them and us. With respect to whom we feed, it tells something of who is the 'in-group' and who is on the outer described above.

---

[35] A. Fisher, 'The incarnation and the fully human life', *New Blackfriars* 73 (1992), 396–407.

[36] A. Fisher, *Jesus: 'Glutton and Drunkard'* (Manchester: Blackfriars Publications, 1995).

[37] In the sense of *practices* in A. MacIntyre, *After Virtue*, 2nd edn (Notre Dame University Press, 1984).

The theological parallel is *communion*. When we share food, especially the Eucharistic meal, we are 'in communion' and when we do not, it signifies some rupture. Accordingly, to refuse food or water to someone is not merely to fail in an ethical duty: it is to excommunicate that person, to place him or her outside the pale of human friendship and deserving, to deny that person the status of brother or sister and to record some defect in fellowship. This is why Christ made whether we feed the starving a test of communion and ultimately of salvation: to deny food and drink is to refuse fraternity and ultimately to refuse the God who made the needy and the 'little ones' our special responsibility (Matt. 25:31–46; cf. *EV* 43).

Power eating

Whom Jesus fed and with whom he dined were highly significant. Jesus' critics complained not just that he took food and drink too seriously – or, when it came to pre-dinner ablutions, not seriously enough – but also about the company he kept at table. He was, it seems, altogether too inclusive, bringing people into relationship with him rather than keeping them at a distance, regardless of whether they were ritually impure, morally dubious or socially outcast. Few of them were the bold and beautiful people. If none was persistently unresponsive, one at least was dead before he raised and fed her (Mark 5:35–43) and others were from outside the social pale.

Such inclusiveness was, of course, deliberately subversive. So were the role reversals: Mary's Magnificat tells of God's coming kingdom in which the poor are filled with good things and the rich sent empty away; a prodigal son feasts while his law-abiding brother excommunicates himself; the high and mighty are self-excluded from the wedding banquet while the tramps are brought in from the highways and byways; the rich man rots in hell while one who was formerly starving goes to Abraham's bosom (Luke 1:53; 12:37; 14:15–24; 15:25–27; 16:19–31; 22:27). Indeed hell is that unbridgeable chasm between the sated and the needy, such that Dives would not share with Lazarus even the scraps from his table, and Lazarus could not put even a drop of water on Dives' tongue. Jesus' feeding miracles also undermined the system of public patronage and were quickly read as political. Finally, in the Eucharistic texts we find the most striking of Christ's food texts: here he *is* the food. No more comprehensive overturning of what we might call 'power eating' can be imagined. Far from using the feast to exercise control, Jesus makes himself the waiter and the meal, washing bodies and feeding souls, emptying himself of all pretensions to power at the very moment when all authority will soon be given him in heaven and on earth. His moment of glory would be precisely when his body would be broken and his blood spilt for the world – and at that moment he would once more join all those in need as he cries out from the Cross 'I thirst' (John 19:28; cf. chs. 4, 12 and 16).

It is hardly surprising that Jesus' food practices posed difficulties for the early Christians. In the churches in which the gospels were written and in Galatia there were divisions over table fellowship between Jewish and Gentile Christians and between sinners and the righteous; at Corinth over who should be fed and over idol meat; in James' community over class distinctions within the Eucharistic assembly; and in the Third Letter of John over hospitality for itinerant prophets. Paul it was who first formulated the idea of unity-in-Christ in a way that prevented the power structures and ideologies of pagan antiquity from finding a foothold in the nascent churches. This unity-in-Christ was to be expressed in the sacred meal, so that the Eucharist would function as cement in the life of the community. However, Paul, Luke, James and John immediately recognized that there is something deeply artificial about Eucharistic egalitarianism while members of that very community are in need of food or otherwise neglected. How, then, are we to respond?

'Now give them something to eat yourselves!' Jesus commanded (Matt. 14:16). The Church must be the stomach with which Christ still feels. The Gospel writers use the graphic Greek word '*splangchnizomai*' for that stomach-churning/gut-wrenching compassion Christ felt for the hungry masses (Matt. 9:36; 14:14; 15:32; 18:27; 20:34; Mark 1:41; 6:34; 8:2; 9:22; Luke 7:13; 10:33; 15:20), which drove him to feed them what they needed (Matt. 14:16 *et par.*; 25:31–46; John 21:15–17; cf. Rom. 12:20). That was precisely what the early Christians did, taking up collections of food and money to distribute to the poor, even appointing specialists – the deacons – to ensure this happened (Acts 4:34–35; 6:1–6; Rom. 15:26–27; 1 Cor. 16:1–4; 2 Cor. 9:13). Social historian Rodney Stark has suggested that the catalyst for the spectacular take-off of Christianity in the Graeco-Roman world was this special concern it showed the poor and needy.[38] With surprising speed Christianity overturned popular morality and social expectations all around the Mediterranean world, challenging and converting cultures as well as individuals.

---

[38] R. Stark, *The Rise of Christianity: A Sociologist Reconsiders History* (Princeton University Press, 1996).

'See how these Christians love each other!' people said in astonishment.[39] The early Christians were notorious for their respect for every human person: they refused to engage in the commonplace practices of abortion, infanticide, suicide or euthanasia, even in hard cases; they looked after the poor, starving, widowed, crippled, sick, elderly and dying, even in difficult situations; they stayed around to care, even when there was a plague. Their simple, egalitarian approach had a tremendous kerygmatic effect. No longer did racial, ethnic, cultural, citizenship, social or gender differences mark the boundaries of moral concern and obligation. Now people of every class and background were to be loved and protected for themselves. The distribution of food and other alms to the poor preached as powerfully as the apostles' words a subversive inclusiveness of the nobodies in this new 'kingdom of God'.

In due course the Christian virtue of *hospitalitas* meant the erection of the first hospices, poor houses, soup kitchens and feeding stations, in local churches and monasteries; later it motivated great social institutions such as hospitals, orphanages, chivalric orders of hospitallers, St Vincent de Paul conferences, Caritas and the rest. We now take all this for granted as basic to what Christians do, but without chapter 25 of the Gospel of Matthew and a Bible full of admonitions to feed and water those in need it would never have happened. In the process this ethical imperative changed not only how the starving were treated but also how they were viewed: even the lives of the least were sacred.[40]

The biblical significance of food and drink, eating and drinking, suggests that even where feeding has to be assisted it should ideally be done in a way that is as close as possible to the experience of a communal meal. No one would pretend that PEG-feeding is as humanly satisfying as enjoying a several-course meal with friends. It is a poor substitute for taste, texture and company. (So, of course, are many modern 'meals'.) Though tube feeding ensures that some of the same values are achieved as ordinary feeding, it can also mark us off and separate us from others. There is a real challenge to humanize feeding in institutional environments, as indeed there is to humanize other aspects of the care of the

[39] Tertullian, *Apologia* 39; cf. John 13:35.
[40] In this chapter I have focused principally on the Gospel as a source of a theology of food and feeding. A more complete treatment would survey other important Christian sources, such as the Old Testament, the Epistles, the works of the Fathers and the scholastics, sacramental practice (especially the Rites of Care for the Sick, Dying and Recently Deceased), sacred art and music and so forth. Useful for some of these is Adam Cooper, *Life in the Flesh: An Anti-Gnostic Spiritual Philosophy* (Oxford University Press, 2008).

sick and dying, making it as familiar and close to 'normal' experience as possible.

The sanctity of life and the imago Dei

Talk of 'the sanctity of life' often functions as a kind of Christian version of the secular accolade 'the dignity of the person' and/or the philosophers' norm 'the inviolability of life'. Often 'sanctity of life' is contrasted with 'quality of life', as if believers want longer, low-grade lives and non-believers want better if shorter lives. Neither is true of course: most people, religious or not, want long, good lives for themselves and those they care about, though opinions vary on what counts for a high-quality life. Christ said he came not just that we might have life, but life *to the full* (John 10:10) and Thomas à Kempis wrote in *The Imitation of Christ*: 'It is vanity to wish for long life, if you care little for a good life' (bk 1, ch. 1). Where quality-of-life talk does mark a real difference is where some argue that those below a certain quality-of-life threshold do not command the same respect and care as those above it. Here sanctity-of-life talk functions, much like dignity talk, to insist that all human lives – *being sacred* – equally deserve care and respect. In addition, much like inviolability talk, it functions to insist that even low-quality lives should not be deliberately shortened. The problems with contemporary quality-of-life thinking are well known and I need not repeat the arguments.[41] I would note, however, that this kind of thinking is far from the monopoly of the non-religious. Christian versions of the quality-of-life threshold regularly appear, e.g. in the better-dead-than-not-having-spiritual-experiences line which I examine below.

One way of reading 'sacred' in 'the sanctity of life' is to say it means that Christians have a reverence for human beings in excess of that commanded by secular 'dignity' or that they take a more absolute line on the inviolability of human life than purely philosophical argument would warrant. I want to suggest that sanctity talk has most bite at the margins, where it is hardest to hold on to the principles of caring for and not killing the innocent. Take, for instance, the philosophers' chestnut of the man in the burning car who cannot be rescued and begs to be put out of his misery; or the rather more common example of a couple considering abortion because their child has anencephaly.[42]

---

[41] For example W. E. May, *Catholic Bioethics and the Gift of Human Life*, 2nd edn (Huntington, IN: Our Sunday Visitor, 2008), pp. 266–7, 273 and 280–1.

[42] I considered this particular human tragedy in A. Fisher, 'Thomas Walter Joseph Ryan: celebration of a life', *Bioethics Outlook* 8(2) (June 1997), 1–3.

Even those who hold to the inalienable dignity and inviolability of the human person are sometimes tempted to make exceptions in such cases. The contrary tug in such people or in others, against killing even in such awful circumstances, could be plain superstition, stubbornness or insensitivity. It might, however, be due to something else called 'sanctity of life'. If I am right, it is a quality in the valuer as much as in the person valued. As in the apostolic age it is often better demonstrated by exemplary lives than by words: Frederick Ozanam, Mary Aikenhead, Catherine McAuley, Frances Xavier Cabrini, Damian of Molokai, Mother Teresa of Calcutta, Jean Vanier and Cecily Saunders are all relatively recent examples.

There are many more ancient examples of saints who saw Christ present in the most desperate of people and stayed around to help. An example from my own Dominican tradition is St Catherine of Siena. Her first biographer, Raymond of Capua, wrote of Catherine's 'street ministry' caring for the most hopeless cases, offering her gentle touch to lepers, refusing to flee as others did in the face of bubonic plague. She was very aware of her impotence to do more than basic nursing, praying and loving. In 1375 a Sienese youth, Niccolò di Tuldo, was condemned to death for a political crime. Hearing of his bitterness and despair, Catherine threw herself into accompanying him on death row. She built up his courage and persuaded him to receive the Last Rites. At his request she went all the way to the scaffold with him and ultimately caught his severed head in her hands. Like Our Lady at the foot of the Cross, she knew there was no more she could do than stand by and pray. This standing-by is, however, precisely what I think is meant by reverence for 'the sanctity of life' – even when it is 'hopeless', even when there is 'nothing we can do', there *is* hope and there *is* something we can do: we can stand by, watching, praying, loving. These incidents in Catherine's life came to a head when, furious at the moral evil of people dying on the executioner's block and at the natural evil of others dying of plague, she remonstrated with the figure of Christ on the Cross. The *corpus* answered her back: 'Turn around, and see who it is I love enough to die for.' And turning around she saw the halt and the lame, as well as the privileged and powerful, the victims and their persecutors, all of them. Her task, she knew, was to expand the range of those she loved and to persevere in her care for them, no matter how repugnant she found their condition.[43]

---

[43] Raymond of Capua, *Life of St Catherine of Siena*, trans. George Lamb (New York: P. J. Kennedy, 1960).

That ability *to reverence those whose condition we find repugnant* and *to care for those for whom we feel we can do nothing* is, I think, where sanctity of life talk really bites. It is here that the notion of the *imago Dei* also becomes important. St Catherine, Mother Teresa and the others I have mentioned reported that, sometimes at least, they could see God in those they nursed. Catherine spoke of God being *pazzo d'amore* (insanely in love with us) and wanting us to catch that wild love. This madness cut in precisely as the condition of her lepers became hopeless, as their bodies and spirits disintegrated, as they faded out of consciousness or were dying, when all she could do was give them basic care and wait. It is in those very cases that I think the liberal account of why people matter and the Christian one most radically diverge. For Mill, Dworkin and Singer, human persons matter because of sentience and mobility, preferences, hopes and plans, reason and choices, language and social interaction – all the stuff of rational autonomy. For Christians, while all those things matter, what makes people so valuable is their creation in the very image of God, their creation as the kinds of beings who will ordinarily exercise not only rational autonomy but unitive love and other capacities. What matters is their restoration by Christ's redemptive sacrifice to God's likeness despite their brokenness; their sharing human nature with a God who became man so that they might become 'divine';[44] the graces they receive and enact in this life in good (not merely free) choices; and the destiny to which they are called in heaven. As MacIntyre and Hauerwas have both demonstrated, it is often the profoundly disabled who best draw our attention to what we really value – or should really value – in the human person: namely, their intrinsic, metaphysical nobility rather than their presently apparent, contingent abilities.[45]

What I am suggesting, then, is that the Christian notion of the sanctity of life is more than secular dignity and inviolability dressed up in religious poetry. With the eyes of faith one comes to see every human being, and especially those most desperate, repugnant or beyond help, as a child of God the Father, a sibling of the suffering Son and a Temple of the Holy Spirit, worthy not just of 'respect and care' but of a *mad* love akin in some ways to our reverence for the holy things. Indeed the 'weaker', the less 'respectable' and the 'low quality-of-life' people are precisely those for whom Christians are challenged to demonstrate particular sympathy and

---

[44] St Athanasius, *De Incarnatione* 54.3, cited in *CCC* 456. Likewise St Augustine, *In natali Domini* XII: 'Factus est Deus homo, ut homo fieret Deus.'

[45] MacIntyre, *Dependent Rational Animals*; S. Hauerwas, *Suffering Presence: Theological Reflections on Medicine, the Mentally Handicapped and the Church* (Notre Dame University Press, 1986).

protectiveness (cf. 1 Cor. ch. 12; *EV* 67). On this account directly killing or neglecting-to-death an innocent human being involves more than the loss of that person and all that he or she means to others, more than the harm it does to the killer and the community: it is also a kind of desecration of something or someone sacred, an attack upon the God in whose likeness both the killer and the victim are made. Accordingly, Paul, quoting the wisdom literature and recalling no doubt Jesus' command to love even your enemies, advises the church in Rome to avoid being overcome by evil by doing good: 'if your enemy is hungry, feed him; if he is thirsty give him drink' (Rom. 12:20; Prov. 21:25).

That, I think, is why the early Church put murder with apostasy among the most horrendous crimes: not just because both are very bad (for there are many, very bad sins), but because to kill another human being is not merely to do an injustice but directly to attack the Author of Life, to usurp the divine prerogative and so to sin against faith, hope and love, those virtues that unite us directly with God. Talk of sanctity of life tries, however limpingly, to capture something of the reverence or awe that religion has before the mystery of life and death, and something of the shudder down the spine that the Christian feels at the thought of killing or neglecting-to-death another human being, even one in desperate straits.[46]

SOME FINAL QUESTIONS

Spiritual acts personism

It would be naïve of course to pretend that the resources of Catholic moral theology are united and available to counteract those who hold that people lacking the exercise of rational autonomy do not matter or should not be fed. The Christian tradition suffers its own versions of liberalism, utilitarianism and autonomy-personism. These include situation ethics, some fundamental option theories, proportionalism and even some more traditional-sounding but ultimately dualistic approaches. John Paul II sought to counter some of these approaches in *Veritatis Splendor, Evangelium Vitae, Fides et Ratio* and his 2004 allocution. Earlier, in the section dealing with the Catholic engagement with modernity in Chapter 1, I suggested that such approaches are at last waning in theological circles, much

---

[46] John Paul II pointed out in *EV* 65 that depending on the circumstances euthanasia – by action or omission – 'involves the malice proper to suicide or murder'.

as their counterparts have been waning in the secular academy for decades. Nonetheless, theologians and pastors operating out of such paradigms have long advised not feeding and hydrating those who lack the exercise of rational autonomy,[47] and some of them are still advising this. Following the 2004 allocution some flatly denied its teaching authority, calling the Pope's position 'contrary to tradition', 'erroneous', 'irresponsible', 'insulting' and 'Vatican mischief'; some questioned who really wrote it and whether the Pope was well enough to know what he was pronouncing; some also recommended that people should just ignore the teaching and it would go away.[48] Others supported the Vatican position.[49] The confusion this caused led to a brief restatement of the papal position by the CDF in 2007. Ironically, the history of this kind of advice-giving by some Catholic ethicists means that some *Catholic* health, aged and palliative care providers may be *more* inclined than their secular counterparts to require rational autonomy (or the prospect of return to it) as a prerequisite for feeding.

The theological counterpart to 'autonomy-personism' might be called 'spiritual-acts-personism'. This view holds that the human person is capable of many acts but that those directed towards securing the goods of the body (nourishment, exercise, healthcare and so on) are intrinsically inferior to, merely instrumental for and entirely ordered towards specifically human spiritual acts (thought, contemplation, choice, worship and so on). Some go further, saying that only someone who can now or will in the future have spiritual experiences is fully a person or fully alive; others distinguish between personal/social/spiritual death and animal/biological death. According to these views, keeping someone alive when he or she can no longer perform spiritual acts or at least engage in relationships with others is pointless, because life has lost its point. It may even be cruel or blasphemous, as we are depriving the person of 'release' and delaying

---

[47] From many different starting points: Benedict Ashley, Edward Bayer, Thomas Bole, Philip Boyle, Daniel Callaghan, Arthur Caplan, Robert Craig, Jean deBlois, Richard Devine, Jason Eberl, Eileen Flynn, Norman Ford, Ronald Hamel, David Kelly, Kevin Kelly, Joseph Kukara, James McCarthey, Richard McCormick, Daniel Maguire, Thomas O'Donnell, Kevin O'Rourke, John Paris, Thomas Reece, Thomas Shannon, Andrew Varga, James Walter, Kevin Wildes and Anthony Zimmerman.

[48] For example those quoted in G. Kopaczynski, 'Initial reactions to the Pope's March 20 2004 Allocution', *NCBQ* 4(3) (2004), 473–82; D. Kelly, *Contemporary Catholic Health Care Ethics* (Washington, DC: Georgetown University Press, 2004), p. 194; Consortium of Jesuit Bioethics Programs, 'Undue burden? The Vatican and artificial nutrition and hydration', *Commonweal* 136(3) (13 February 2009); cf. P. Reilly, 'Teaching euthanasia', *Crisis Magazine* 23(6) (June 2005), 28–35.

[49] See for example the several articles in *NCBQ* 4(3) (2004) and in *Ethics & Medics* 34(6) (2009).

their entry into heaven. This view of the purposes of human bodily life obviously has implications for a much broader range of people than those who suffer persistent unresponsiveness.

The view that those incapable of spiritual acts should no longer receive life-sustaining care has something in common with an ancient line of thought that runs thus: if heaven is so good, why not go there now? The answer given by Schopenhauer, among others, was that suicide is an assertion of self at its strongest, hardly the kind of gentle acceptance of God's will that opens up heaven to us; assisted suicide and euthanasia mirror this wilfulness. Second, spiritual-acts-personism is often mind–body dualistic and élitist and amenable to many of the same criticisms which I have noted earlier in this chapter. Third, even if sub-spiritual goods serve spiritual ones, it does not follow that they lack any value in themselves: human life may also be good in itself and therefore worthy of protection and nurture even when it fails to serve higher 'spiritual' goods such as prayer.[50] Those who continue to value and sustain such an impoverished instance of human life may be doing so not out of an irrational attachment to biological life but rather out of love and respect for the person whose life it is, even if that person cannot consciously experience such acts of love.[51] Fourth, a concern to preserve the norm against killing – including killing by neglect – serves not only the person whose life is sustained but also the common good of the whole community, especially those most vulnerable and at risk of homicidal omissions of care.[52] Fifth, if heaven is the presumed end of the person with serious cognitive impairment – and that is a presumption – and if denying tube feeding to such a person is therefore a kindness, it is hard to see why spoon feeding should not also be stopped. Indeed, why not expedite heaven for them with more active measures? Sixth, can it be demonstrated that the persistently unresponsive have no 'spiritual experiences' or engage in no 'spiritual acts' – whatever these terms might mean? If John the Baptist leapt in Elizabeth's womb at

---

[50] Thus Augustine, *De doctrina Christiana* 1, 23.26, and Aquinas, in *ST* IIa IIae 25.4, 25.5, 25.12, argue that there is a duty to love one's own life and one's own body, even if these may at times properly resign oneself to losing one's (bodily) life (= 'sacrificing oneself') for the sake of God, neighbour or one's own eternal destiny.

[51] See G. Grisez, 'Should nutrition and hydration be provided to permanently unconscious and other mentally disabled persons?', *LQ* 57 (May 1990), 30–43; W. E. May, 'Tube feeding and the "vegetative state"', *Ethics & Medics* 24(1) (1999), 2–4.

[52] R. Barry, 'Feeding the comatose and the common good in the Catholic tradition', *The Thomist* 53 (1989), 1–30. Kopaczynski, 'Initial reactions', p. 478, notes a 1993 Lutheran document, *Christian Care at Life's End*, which supports continued feeding 'because it effectively blocks the temptation society may have solely to aim at the death of patients whose "biological tenacity" [the phrase belongs to Daniel Callahan] has become inconvenient and troublesome'.

the coming of the embryonic Jesus (Luke 1:44), spiritual experience may not be reserved to the rationally autonomous. Finally, can we assume that what such people undergo is purposeless for them and for others? Is no purgatory possible for people while on earth? Can the situations of such people not be a spiritual opportunity for others to demonstrate reverence, justice and care, which might contribute to their own good, too?

But no one wants to live that way!

Still we might say: but no one wants to live that way! Of course not. But there are countless awful situations that we would not want to be in or want others we loved to be in. No one would want to suffer double incontinence or progressive dementia or persistent unresponsiveness. No reasonable person would wish such things on others. The prospect or actual experience of living in such conditions, for ourselves or others, may well try our hope, courage, patience, perseverance, love. It may evoke in us repugnance, anxiety or fear. It may exhaust us physically, emotionally and spiritually. All this is a very different matter from saying that our life (or theirs) would no longer be 'worth living'; that our death (or theirs) would be no loss; that we (or they) would lose our 'dignity' or our life its 'sanctity'; or that others should then hasten our deaths or neglect to give us basic care.

To put it another way: is the action of a Teresa of Calcutta or a Catherine of Siena irrational, even cruel, if it lengthens 'the kind of life no one would want for themselves or those they love'? John Paul II in *Evangelium Vitae* (15) recognized that those who seek euthanasia may do so out of anguish, desperation or conditioning, thus lessening their subjective responsibility; those who engage in euthanasia may be motivated by pity rather than a selfish refusal to be burdened with the life of someone who is suffering. He nonetheless argued that euthanasia is 'false mercy', indeed 'a disturbing perversion of mercy'.

True *compassion* leads to sharing another's pain; it does not kill the person whose suffering we cannot bear. Moreover, the act of euthanasia is all the more perverse if carried out by those, like relatives, who are supposed to treat a family member with patience and love, or by those, such as doctors, who by virtue of their specific profession are supposed to care for the sick person even in the most painful terminal stages ... The height of arbitrariness and injustice is reached when certain people, such as physicians or legislators, arrogate to themselves the power to decide who ought to live and who ought to die ... Thus the life of the person who is weak is put into the hands of the one who is strong; in society the sense of justice is lost, and mutual trust, the basis of every authentic interpersonal relationship, is undermined at its root. (*EV* 66)

This 'false pity' is contrasted with 'the way of love and true mercy', which recognizes that in the face of 'the supreme confrontation with suffering and death', when all are tempted 'to give up in utter desperation', what is really called for is 'companionship, sympathy and support in the time of trial … [and] help to keep on hoping when all human hopes fail'.

Dying or as good as dead?

It has long been recognized that when someone is imminently dying treatments aimed at prolonging life are no longer appropriate and some forms of care should be scaled down, even as others might be increased. However, to label 'PVS' and similar patients as 'dying' or 'as good as dead' or as having a 'lethal pathology' and to call withholding nutrition and hydration from them 'allowing a natural dying process to proceed' is at best confused and inclines people to unethical behaviour.[53] No one denies that persistent unresponsiveness and such conditions are very serious ones, but can people like Terri Schiavo, who, if fed, will commonly live for years, honestly be tagged as 'dying'? 'Dying' in these circumstances becomes a tag we use for patients who, once so labelled, will be denied even basic care and so die sooner rather than later; it is a self-fulfilling prophecy, even a death sentence.

Every organism suffers from the 'life-threatening condition' of needing food and water: denied nutrition or hydration any living thing will undergo a 'natural dying process'. Some people (diabetics, babies, the disabled) are more dependent than others upon technology or other people's energies for the satisfaction of such basic needs. These people, like those in PVS who need help to achieve feeding and hydration, are *not* dying people, unless we choose to make them so: they are alive like any other organism, with the same basic needs, including food and water.

Food and death in contemporary culture

In this chapter I have offered the beginnings of a metaphysics and theology of food and feeding. I would like to offer one additional, somewhat provocative thought: that the last civilization we should trust about

[53] I argue this more fully in A. Fisher, 'Should we starve the unconscious?', *Australasian Catholic Record* 74(3) (1997), 315–29.

feeding issues is probably our own. While millions starve we have an eating crisis in the West; childhood obesity, adult obesity and diabetes are at epidemic proportions; we are unable to sit at table together at home and yet become compulsive diners as soon as we go out the door; for all the obsession with 'health food' our supermarkets and takeaways maximize the unhealthy; we are subject to diet fads, stomach stapling and more sinister pressures to anorexia or bulimia; fat-reducing gym regimes and fat-extracting surgery are now major household expenditures; Cher and Michael Jackson and countless others have their bodies remade, some even into the appearance of the opposite sex; we have trouble fitting into one airline seat while our 'models' starve themselves to death; binge drinking is a regular entertainment, especially for the young; alcohol and other substance abuse among adults breaks many bones, relationships and lives; and so we might go on.

Meanwhile the same consumer culture has a very strange relationship with death and dying.[54] There are countless signs of denial in this area: the futile attempts to delay or eliminate the signs of ageing (again, through cosmetic surgery, gyms, fantasies and techniques similar to those used to evade the implications of immoderate eating); attempts at cryopreservation, genetic enhancement and the like to obtain eternal mortal life; the relegation ('warehousing') of the frail elderly and dying to institutions where out-of-sight is often out-of-mind. Yet the same death-denying culture is often an actual 'culture of death', using death as an instrument of the strong against the weak and as a final solution to suffering of various kinds, whether by killing incalculable numbers through warfare, surgical abortion, abortifacient drugs, embryo exploitation or neglect of the disabled new-born. Our consumer culture now seeks to tame death when it can no longer be denied by controlling its time and quality. My thought here is that a civilization that is so dysfunctional when it comes to its own eating and drinking, death and dying, should be especially careful about initiating new life and death policies for withholding food and drink from the frail and dying.[55]

---

[54] See the very interesting analysis by Hayden Ramsay in a series of articles on death in *New Blackfriars* 86 (January to September 2005), and the sources cited therein.

[55] *EV* 64: 'In this context the temptation grows to have recourse to *euthanasia*, that is, *to take control of death and bring it about before its time*, "gently" ending one's own life or the life of others. In reality, what might seem logical and humane, when looked at more closely is seen to be *senseless and inhumane*. Here we are faced with one of the more alarming symptoms of the *culture of death*, which is advancing above all in prosperous societies, marked by an attitude of excessive preoccupation with efficiency and which sees the growing number of elderly and disabled people as intolerable and too burdensome. These people are very often isolated by their families and by

What else should we do for those lacking the exercise of rational autonomy?

In this chapter I have not considered all the complexities of applying the principle that we should *ordinarily* feed patients, even persistently unresponsive patients, and even when this requires some technical assistance such as a PEG tube. There will be questions about whether a person may ethically volunteer in advance not to receive such help, for what reasons and when; whether a surrogate may decide on behalf of the unconscious person to make such a 'sacrifice'; what should be done when health resources are limited and decisions must be made about who gets what; what role carers, family members, guardians, courts and the state should play in decisions about assisted feeding; and so on. I have been addressing a prior question: why would we even trouble ourselves about such matters if a patient can no longer exercise rational autonomy? Even resolving the why-people-matter issue and the assisted feeding dilemma will not be enough. We need to do more to show solidarity with those whom Christian faith and reason call us to love and protect.[56]

society, which are organized almost exclusively on the basis of criteria of productive efficiency, according to which a hopelessly impaired life no longer has any value.'

[56] John Paul II, *On Life-Sustaining Treatments* 6. Other recent writing on artificial nutrition and hydration and end-of-life care includes: E. Christian Brugger *et al.*, 'Reply to the Jesuit Consortium', *Ethics & Medics* 34(6) (2009), 3–5; G. Craig, 'Feeding via a percutaneous gastroscopy tube', *CMQ* 55(1) (2005), 6–15; FIAMC and the Pontifical Academy for Life, 'Considerations on scientific and ethical problems related to the Vegetative State', *NCBQ* 4(3) (2004), 580; G. L. Gigli and M. Valente, 'Quality of life and vegetative state', in E. Sgreccia and I. Carrasco de Paula (eds.), *Quality of Life and the Ethics of Health* (Libreria Editrice Vaticana, 2006), pp. 234–52; J. Haas *et al.*, 'A defense of the Vatican on ANH', *Ethics & Medics* 34(6) (June 2009), 1–3; J. Leies *et al.*, *Handbook on Critical Life Issues*, 3rd edn (Boston: NCBC, 2004), ch. 13; May, *Catholic Bioethics and the Gift of Human Life*, pp. 285–301; Thomas Pittre, 'Artificial nutrition and hydration for the PVS patient', in E. Furton (ed.), *Urged On by Christ: Catholic Health Care in Tension with Contemporary Culture* (Boston: NCBC), pp. 63–76; Anthony Port, 'The "allowed to die" game', *CMQ* 56(1) (2006), 31–4.

CHAPTER 9

Endings: suicide and euthanasia in the Bible

THE PROBLEM OF SUICIDE AND EUTHANASIA IN THE BIBLE

Contemporary readings

A complete study of what the Scriptures might say about end-of-life issues such as suicide and euthanasia would require a thoroughgoing exploration of themes such as life, ageing, disability, suffering, death and after-life, violence and non-violence, creation and stewardship, individual and community, responsibility and blame ... Rather than attempt that mammoth task in this chapter, I review the various reports of suicides in the Bible and some other texts, to see what they might say to us today. In doing so I recognize that there are many ways of reading the Scriptures and that each raises its own methodological problem. We must be wary both of an uncritical, fundamentalist reading and of a secularized, Bible-as-ordinary-literature treatment of the sacred text. There is a risk that we will import our previous conclusions to our reading of texts, finding our prejudices conveniently confirmed there. Moreover, it is far from clear how we are to bridge the gap between an ancient text with its particular form, language, audience and concerns and early twenty-first-century readers for whom words like 'suicide' are charged with considerable (if variant) descriptive and normative content. In addition to all these hermeneutical problems, there are others such as the specificity of Christian ethics, the rôle of Scripture vis-à-vis other sources of morality, the relationship between moral norms, situations and applications and the unique aspects of any particular case of suicide or euthanasia, attempted or actual, assisted or carried out alone.

Recently, there has, however, been some important scholarly literature on the subject. I examine three examples in this chapter: Arthur Droge and James Tabor's *A Noble Death: Suicide among Christians and Jews in*

Antiquity, James Clemons' *What Does the Bible Say about Suicide?* and several essays by Paul Badham.[1] Droge and Tabor's book comes with a back-cover accolade from Derek Humphry, founder of the Hemlock Society, and opens with a friendly reference to Jack Kevorkian, the infamous 'Dr Death', who until his imprisonment regularly assisted in the suicides of sick or depressed people. Droge and Tabor are very clearly exegetes *with a mission*: a mission to show that suicide and euthanasia were permitted to Jews and Christians, even commended, well into the first few centuries of the Christian era; that they therefore enjoy the warrant of Scripture and early tradition; that opposition to voluntary death is a late invention, the product especially of that archfiend of the Christian story, Augustine of Hippo; and that we should recover the purity of the Judeo-Christian revelation by supporting contemporary moves to permit voluntary death. Clemons, writing from a more pastoral perspective, is more moderate, but he too argues that the terminally ill should be able to choose death, and that the Christian community should offer them the latest and 'least violent, painful, messy, bothersome' methods.[2] Badham is a fan of Droge and Tabor's work and a campaigner for the view that 'Bible-believing Christians can legitimately choose death for themselves.' He believes that Christian leaders in Britain and elsewhere have been mistaken in holding out against the legalization of 'humane' killing. If the political advocacy of these authors gives cause for caution about their readings of the texts, it must be admitted that they are by no means alone in seeking scriptural warrant for their political ends. Nor are they alone in asserting that the Scriptures never forbid suicide or euthanasia.[3]

Droge and Tabor are aware of the dangers of reading contemporary views of suicide and euthanasia into the scriptural texts. 'In Western

[1] P. Badham, 'Should Christians accept the validity of voluntary euthanasia?', *Studies in Christian Ethics* 8(2) (1995), 1–12, 'Euthanasia and the Christian understanding of God', *Studies in Christian Ethics* 11(1) (1998), 1–12, and 'A final word on euthanasia', *Studies in Christian Ethics* 11(1) (1998), 24–7; J. Clemons, *What Does the Bible Say about Suicide?* (Minneapolis: Fortress 1990); A. Droge and J. Tabor, *A Noble Death: Suicide among Christians and Jews in Antiquity* (San Francisco: Harper, 1992). Droge first presented his views in 'Suicide', *Anchor Bible Dictionary* (New York: Doubleday, 1992), vol. VI, p. 225, but his joint work with Tabor is much fuller and more openly a work of advocacy. In the present chapter references in [square brackets] are to page numbers in each author's book or in Badham's case in his first article.
[2] Clemons, *What Does the Bible Say*, pp. 105 and 109.
[3] For example, A. Alvarez, *The Savage God* (New York: Random House, 1970), p. 51; M. Battin, 'Suicide', *Encyclopaedia of Ethics* (New York: Garland, 1992), 1215–19; D. Daube, 'Death as a release in the Bible', *Novum Testamentum* 5 (1964), 82–104; B. Harris, 'Suicide', *New Dictionary of Christian Ethics and Pastoral Theology* (Leicester: InterVarsity, 1995); E. Schneidman, *Definition of Suicide* (New York: Wiley, 1985), p. 30; G. Williams, 'Suicide', *Encyclopaedia of Philosophy* (New York: Macmillan, 1967), vol. VIII, pp. 43–6.

antiquity', they point out, 'the problem of voluntary death was conceived of altogether differently from the way it is understood today' [3]. Whether we can suspend our contemporary judgment when reading scriptural texts is another matter. As Francis Moloney argues, we inevitably bring our personal world 'in front of the text' to our exegesis of the world(s) 'in and behind the text'.[4] The text then commonly functions as a *mirror* of ourselves. The challenge, he suggests, is to allow the text also to be a *portrait* of a world created by the text itself, a *window* onto the actual experiences of the individuals and communities behind it. Holding in view our world, the text and the world behind the text enables the Word of God to speak to the believer. Only then can Scripture subvert and inform our views rather than merely confirm them. With these caveats in mind, I examine the scriptural texts in the company of some professional exegetes.

Searching for suicides in the Bible: some false starts

Droge and Tabor identify six instances of suicide or voluntary euthanasia in the Old Testament, as well as several other 'closely related' cases. I will examine these 'closely related' cases first, before dealing with the six genuine instances in the next section, 'Suicides and euthanasias in the Bible'.

Jonah, fleeing from his vocation, joins a boat bound for Spain, only to find it struck by storm. The crew divine that he is to blame. He owns up and suggests that they throw him overboard (Jonah 1:12). But the crew are reluctant to take innocent blood upon themselves, so reluctant in fact that they row on against the storm, risking their own lives (Jonah 1:13). Finally, in fear and trepidation, they do as Jonah suggests, throwing him overboard while making vows, prayers and sacrifices to God (Jonah 1:14–16). God famously sends a whale to swallow Jonah and in due course to vomit him up onto dry land.

Several scholars, including Clemons [22–3] and Droge and Tabor [60], read Jonah's call to be thrown overboard as a death-wish or failed suicide attempt, all of a piece with his repeated efforts to evade his vocation.[5]

---

[4] F. Moloney, 'Life, healing and the Bible: a Christian challenge', *Pacifica* 8(3) (Oct. 1995), 315–34 at 321.

[5] Likewise E. M. Good, *Irony in the Old Testament*, 2nd edn (Sheffield: Almond, 1981), p. 45; J. Limburg, *Jonah* (Louisville: Westminster John Knox Press, 1993), p. 55; M. Sweeney, *The Twelve Prophets* (Collegeville, MN: Liturgical Press, 2000), vol. 1, pp. 314–15; H. Wolff, *Obadiah and Jonah* (Minneapolis: Augsburg, 1986), pp. 118–24. Droge and Tabor also suggest it might have been a successful suicide, because Jonah might actually have died and been resurrected by the whale!

Of course, even if this *is* suicide, there is no hint of approval of Jonah's behaviour in the text: indeed it is overall quite critical of him. One might also question whether abandoning a sinking ship for the sake of others on board is really suicide.[6] Were this really a death-wish we might expect Jonah to have jumped overboard himself. Instead he consigns himself to the justice (and eventually mercy) of the God of land and sea.[7] On the question of attempted suicide Jack Sasson suggests that we 'best reject such an insidious notion, for whatever faults Jonah displays in this story, they do not include passivity or playing the sacrificial goat'.[8] Rather, the seamen are presented as reluctantly visiting a divine trial on Jonah by throwing him overboard. Exegetes and theologians may argue over what the Jonah story is really all about, but to read it as a divinely approved suicide seems to me as far-fetched as reading it as support for whaling.[9]

The second case is that of Job. His story is the classic treatment of 'innocent' suffering, which is the greatest mystery of life and the greatest challenge for religion. Job suffers acutely, and we are told he is close to despair. While Droge and Tabor admit that Job never attempted to take his own life, they attribute suicidal tendencies to him [64–6]. Certainly Job laments, time and again, and even curses his birth, longing for the grave and praying for death to come soon (Job 3:1–26; 6:8–13; 7:9–10, 21; 10:20–22). Yet his attitude seems the very opposite of Jonah's. There is no fleeing from God here and no hint he ever contemplated suicide. Job's resistance to any such thought, even in the midst of his plaint and maledictions, is the reason why we celebrate Job for his extraordinary patience, integrity and trust even amid unspeakable suffering.[10] Indeed, when his wife proposes that he curse God and die (2:9–10) – what S. L. Terrien called a 'theological method

---

[6] A. Lacocque and P.-E. Lacocque, *The Jonah Complex* (Atlanta: John Knox Press, 1981), p. 49.

[7] J. Sasson, *Jonah* (New York: Anchor-Doubleday, 1990), p. 124, notes that 'Jonah is not making it easy on his shipmates! He is not about to throw himself into the sea … The mediaeval exegetes who thought Jonah was contemplating suicide are way off the mark on this.' Likewise E. Achtemeier, *Minor Prophets I* (Peabody: Hendrickson, 1996), pp. 266–7, and É. Levine, *The Aramaic Version of Jonah*, 2nd edn (New York: Sepher-Hermon, 1978), p. 67.

[8] Sasson, *Jonah*, p. 127.

[9] Droge and Tabor describe the 'apocryphal' accounts of the Maccabees as historically questionable [71] but treat the tale of Jonah as forensic.

[10] Jas. 5:11; Clemons [34 and 46]; D. Clines, *Job 1–20* (Dallas: Word Books, 1989), pp. 83, 87 and 98; J. H. Eaton, *Job* (Sheffield Academic Press, 1985), p. 2; N. Habel, *The Book of Job* (Cambridge University Press, 1975), p. 20.

of committing euthanasia'[11] – Job is critical of her; her advice is foolish, a temptation to sin.[12] To the extent that it is relevant at all, the weight of the text is against suicide.[13] Nonetheless Droge and Tabor refuse to draw any such lesson.

A good New Testament parallel in some respects is Paul as he faces death. In 2 Corinthians he says he would rather be away from the body and at home with the Lord (5:6–10), which Droge and Tabor read as a Stoic 'fascination with death and desire to escape from life', indeed a death-lust [119–21]. In Philippians Paul recognizes that there are upsides both to being alive and to being dead and says 'which I should choose I cannot tell' (1:20–26). Our commentators take this not to mean 'I don't know which I'd prefer to happen but I will submit myself to God's will' (the usual interpretation) but 'it's _up to me to choose_ whether or not to kill myself' (a most unusual interpretation). Paul may regularly harp on about his troubles but, like Job, he does nothing to hasten 'the gain of death'. Droge and Tabor go on to assert not only that Paul was contemplating suicide himself, but that 'for Paul, an individual could kill himself and be "glorifying God with his body" by doing so' – a view which even they admit 'stands in sharp contrast to the view of most New Testament scholars' [123–4].[14] It also stands in sharp contrast to

---

[11] S. L. Terrien, _Job_ (Neuchâtel: Delachaux et Niestlé, 1963), quoted in Clines, _Job 1–20_, p. 51.

[12] Eaton, _Job_, pp. 2, 44 and 50–1; N. Whybray, _Job_ (Sheffield Academic Press, 1998), p. 34.

[13] J. Hartley, _The Book of Job_ (Grand Rapids, MI: Eerdmans, 1988), p. 92, observes: 'It should be noted that in his desire for death Job never entertains the option of suicide. Suicide was not acceptable for the person of faith, because it signified that one had lost all hope in God'; cf. pp. 83–4; R. L. Harris, 'The doctrine of God in the Book of Job', in R. Zuck (ed.), _Sitting with Job: Selected Studies on the Book of Job_ (Grand Rapids, MI: Baker, 1992), pp. 151–80 at 173. On the complexity of and ironies in the texts suggesting a Joban death wish see B. Zuckerman, 'The art of parody: the death theme', in _Job the Silent: A Study in Historical Counterpoint_ (Oxford University Press, 1991), ch. 11.

[14] Pauline scholars do not find that Paul is suicidal or believing he has the option to choose suicide. R. Martin, _2 Corinthians_ (Waco: Word, 1986), p. 112, observes: 'That Paul expressed his wish to depart from the body and be with Christ is not to say he developed a death wish. His ministry was important to him as a sacred trust from God (4:1; Thess. 2:1–8; 1 Cor. 9:23ff.; cf. 2 Tim. 4:7). This is seen especially in Phil. 1:21–26 where Paul, for the sake of the Philippians, views staying alive as a benefit, even though he desires to be with Christ.' See also P. Barnett, _The Second Epistle to the Corinthians_ (Grand Rapids, MI: Eerdmans, 1997), pp. 267–77; G. Fee, _Paul's Letter to the Philippians_ (Grand Rapids, MI: Eerdmans, 1995), p. 147; M. J. Harris, 'Paul's view of death in 2 Cor. 5:1–10', in R. N. Longenecker and M. C. Tenney (eds.), _New Dimensions in New Testament Study_ (Grand Rapids, MI: Eerdmans, 1974), pp. 317–28; J. Lambrecht, _Second Corinthians_ (Collegeville, MN: Liturgical Press, 1999), p. 89; G. Lee, _Paul's Letter to the Philippians_ (Grand Rapids, MI: Eerdmans, 1995), pp. 139–51; H. Marshall, _The Epistle to the Philippians_ (London: Epworth, 1991), pp. 32–4; P. O'Brien, _Commentary on Philippians_ (Grand Rapids, MI: Eerdmans, 1991), pp. 116–32; D. O'Mathúna, 'Did Paul condone suicide? Implications for assisted suicide and active euthanasia', in T. J. Demy and G. P. Stewart (eds.), _Suicide: A Christian Response_ (Grand Rapids, MI: Kregel, 1998), pp. 387–97.

so many of Paul's own words about perseverance in the face of external pressures and 'diabolical' internal struggles. For all his grumbles to the Corinthians about the various 'weaknesses, insults, hardships, persecutions and calamities' he had suffered, such that he was 'utterly, unbearably crushed' and 'despaired of life itself' (2 Cor. 1:8–10), he insists that these very afflictions became his strengths or at least the occasion for demonstrations of the power of God's grace in him (2 Cor. 12:7–10; cf. 2 Thess. 1:4). To the Philippians he brags that he has learnt to be content despite his privations (Phil. 4:11–13; cf. 3:10). To the saints in Rome he declares that the sufferings of this present time are as naught compared with the glory yet to be revealed to us (Rom. 8:18–25). He reminds the Ephesians that 'no one hates his own flesh, but nourishes and cherishes it, as Christ does the Church' (Eph. 5:29) and goes on to admonish them:

So be strong in the Lord and in the strength of his power. Put on the whole armour of God, so that you may be able to stand against the wiles of the devil. For our struggle is not merely against the enemies of blood and flesh … but the forces of darkness and evil. Therefore take the whole armour of God, that you may stand firm on the evil day. (Eph. 6:10–13; cf. 1 Pet. 1:6–9; Rev. 2:10–11)

Another set of cases Droge and Tabor bring forward as evidence of scriptural support for suicide and euthanasia are those of Moses, Aaron and Elijah who go to their deaths willingly or resignedly. We will see later that by adopting a strange definition of 'voluntary death' these exegetes manage to conflate resignation in the face of 'the inevitable', accepted as God's (permissive) will, with actively hastening one's death by acts or staged omissions. It is quite clear that submitting to death, and even wanting death, is not the same as deliberately intending to bring it about. Otherwise all deaths, apart from those which are strenuously, defiantly, indeed 'officiously' resisted, would be equivalent to suicide.

So we come to Jesus. According to the Synoptic Gospels, at the inauguration of his ministry Jesus was tempted by the Devil to throw himself off the pinnacle of the Temple: but he refused (Matt. 4:5–7; Luke 4:9–12). Soon afterwards he was driven out of town by his own people and led to the brow of a hill that they might hurl him off the cliff, but he evaded their grasp and went into hiding (Luke 4:29–30). One bent on self-destruction would hardly engage in such evasion. In John's Gospel, however, Jesus' repeated sayings that he is 'going away' are interpreted by the Jews as a threat of suicide (John 8:21–24), and he claims that when he is ready he will lay down his life (John 10:10–16, 18; 15:13).[15] Badham sees here a readiness to die comparable with that of Captain Oates of the Antarctic [4–5]. Droge and Tabor find evidence of a suicide-wish on Jesus' part [114ff.]. Later Christians were, they say, wilfully blind to the fact that the Jesus of the gospels actively chose to die and so misread him as merely resigning himself to go the way of a suffering servant or a ransom for many. If we are to imitate Christ, Badham argues, we must be willing to imitate him in his choice of death over life. More sophisticated exegetes have, however, concluded that far from being on a suicide mission, Jesus shares his Jewish contemporaries' abhorrence of suicide. In deliberately misinterpreting Jesus' words as a suicide-wish, the Jewish authorities were effectively consigning him to hell. They thereby revealed themselves to be enemies of the Author of Life and doomed to a spiritual death themselves. If Jesus will indeed lay down his life, it is *they* who will kill him. There is absolutely no hint of him seeking to escape suffering by shortening his life.[16]

I return to the case of Jesus later in this chapter. For now let me offer a counter-hypothesis to Droge and Tabor's: that the very example of Jesus may have played a crucial part in early Christian opposition to taking one's own life. In imitation of Christ's resignation and trust, his obedience and sense of belonging to God, Christians can (and do) pray that God's will be done even when they would rather the cup of suffering be taken from them. They can (and do) believe that they are called to take up their cross and endure it with patience and perseverance. They can (and do) do this without fatalism, morbidity or suicidal ideation, but with freedom, inner peace, even joy. Whether one likes this message or not, its originating *locus* in the manner of Jesus' death seems rather more plausible than the notion that the early Christians

---

[15] Droge and Tabor suggest that the Jews 'often speak more wisely than they know'. This ironic device is common enough in John, but usually in the context of Jewish *misunderstanding* of Jesus' sayings, whether about destroying and raising up the Temple (2:18–21), being born again (3:3–7), about his going away (7:33–36) or his setting them free (8:31–33).

[16] C. K. Barrett, *The Gospel According to St John*, 2nd edn (London: SPCK, 1978), p. 341; T. Brodie, *The Gospel According to John: A Literary and Theological Commentary* (Oxford University Press, 1993), p. 326; R. Bultmann, *The Gospel of John* (Oxford: Blackwell, 1971), p. 348; D. A. Carson, *The Gospel According to John* (Leicester: InterVarsity, 1991), p. 342; F. Moloney, *Signs and Shadows: Reading John 5–12* (Minneapolis: Fortress, 1996), p. 98; R. Schnackenburg, *The Gospel according to St John* (London: Burns and Oates, 1980), vol. II, p. 198; S. Williams, 'Christians and voluntary euthanasia: a response to Paul Badham', *Studies in Christian Ethics* 9(1) (1996), 134–9.

ignored Jesus' suicidal temper when creating a pro-life Augustinian ideology.

The 'assisted suicide' of Abimelech

The first account of an 'assisted suicide' or 'voluntary euthanasia' in the Bible is that of Abimelech son of Gideon (Judg. 9:50–57). Abimelech was the last of the Major Judges and an anti-hero or, as Lillian Klein puts it, an anti-judge,[17] who was a wicked adventurer and ruthless mass murderer. He started his career by killing seventy of his brothers, was cursed by the sole survivor, Jotham, and after reigning for three inglorious years himself came to a sticky end. During an abortive siege of a city a Gentile woman fatally wounded him by dropping a millstone on his head from a roof. Rather than suffer the disgrace of dying at her hand he directed his armour-bearer to draw his sword and kill him. 'As with all six accounts of voluntary death in the Hebrew Bible', Droge and Tabor conclude, 'this one is recorded without censure or condemnation' [54]. Clemons similarly concludes that: 'In the absence of any [statement that suicide is a sin], the author implies that the manner of Abimelech's death was of no serious consequence [22].

What does the text actually say? 'God sent an evil spirit between Abimelech and the lords of Shechem … Thus God requited the crime of Abimelech, which he committed against his father in killing his seventy brothers' (Judg. 9:23 and 56). Without censure or condemnation? Most exegetes read Abimelech's death as a manifestation of divine judgment on him for his fratricide and on the Shechemites for their support.[18] As Leslie Hoppe points out: 'the reader knows that neither the woman nor Abimelech's servant was responsible for his death. It was just the last act of a terrible drama which Abimelech himself directed.'[19]

Of course, behind the world in this story there is another world telling its story. The account of the life and death of Abimelech is part of the continuing polemic against Canaanite practices, the monarchy,

[17] L. Klein, *The Triumph of Irony in the Book of Judges* (Sheffield Academic Press, 1988), pp. 76–80.

[18] A. Cundall, *Judges* (London: Tyndale, 1968), 136; J. A. Soggin, *Judges* (London: SCM, 1981), p. 194.

[19] L. Hoppe, *Joshua, Judges with an Excursus on Charismatic Leadership in Israel* (Wilmington: Glazier, 1982), pp. 164–5. Likewise M. Brettler, *The Book of Judges* (London: Routledge, 2002), p. 112: 'He deserves his shameful fate of being killed by a woman.'

assimilation, intermarriage and reliance upon power, especially foreign power, rather than on the one king and God of Israel.[20] The message is: a monarchy founded on bloodshed will end in bloodshed and will take with it all those implicated in its inauguration.[21] While no specific message about 'assisted suicide' seems to be intended here, what is clear is that Abimelech got his just deserts: God saw to that.[22] The sacred author believes that God humiliated and brought about the death of Abimelech through the agency of the woman, the armour-bearer and Abimelech himself. Whatever we think of that picture of God, the assisted suicide of Abimelech, far from being lauded in these circumstances, would seem to be just one more part of his 'demeaning demise'.[23]

The alleged suicide of Samson

Not only did the last of the Major Judges die by suicide but on some readings of events so did Samson, the last of the Minor Judges (Judg. 16:23–31). The story of his death, like most of those about him, is that of the leading man in a *Boy's Own* tale. Let us relive the dramatic scene: now blind and without his former superhuman strength, our superhero is about to suffer his greatest humiliation by being paraded and tormented by his captors at a temple feast. He begs back his strength from the Lord that he might die bringing down the temple of Dagon and the Philistine rulers with it, so being avenged for all he has suffered. Like Abimelech – and, as we shall soon see, Saul – Samson was afraid of humiliation. However, unlike the other two he was not mortally wounded, only blind. Like Abimelech and Saul, Samson was assisted by a servant. God granted Samson the strength he sought: he bowed with all his might and pulled down the temple, dying with his captors and indeed killing more of the enemy in his death than he did during his life.

Is this suicide? Badham, Clemons, Droge and Tabor, think it is,[24] but there are other ways of reading the situation and I here note only a few. One is what philosophers call 'double effect': when an action (in this case

---

[20] R. Boling, *Judges* (New York: Doubleday, 1975), pp. 182–5; Hoppe, *Joshua, Judges*, p. 165; Klein, *The Triumph of Irony*, pp. 78–80; A. D. Mayes, *Judges* (Sheffield Academic Press, 1985), p. 26.

[21] Mayes, *Judges*, p. 26.

[22] J. Gray, *Joshua, Judges, Ruth* (Grand Rapids, MI: Eerdmans, 1986), pp. 309–10.

[23] Klein, *The Triumph of Irony*, p. 78: terrible and demeaning, it is 'exactly the disgraceful aspect of his death which is affixed to the name of Abimelech, as related in Joab's messenger report to David (2 Sam. 11:21)'. Likewise T. Schneider, *Judges* (Collegeville, MN: Liturgical Press, 2000), p. 148.

[24] So too V. Matthews, *Judges and Ruth* (Cambridge University Press, 2004), pp. 164–5.

destroying the pagan temple) has two effects, one intended (the deaths of the rulers), the other foreseen but not intended (Samson's own death).[25] On this account, adopted by Joseph Blenkinsopp, Samson's death was *not* suicide: while the act of pulling down the temple was chosen, the death itself was not.[26] If all the Philistines had died but Samson had lived to fight another day his action would not have been a failure. Alternatively, Samson might be seen as simply a dispensable instrument of divine justice in exacting vengeance against the Philistines: a casualty of 'friendly fire'. On both these accounts Samson's death was not the object of his temple-razing. If he volunteers it is not for death as such but for being a good soldier or a faithful Jew or God's avenging instrument, even unto death. Samson's death is no simple suicide – the moral landscape is rather more textured than our pro-suicide commentators allow.[27] Even when death is accepted, foreseen, desired, hoped for or permitted, there is no equivalence with the deliberate, intentional, premeditated choosing and causing of one's own death.

With respect to Samson's supposed suicide Droge and Tabor claim that God concurs, because 'the text gives no indication whatsoever that Samson's choice to take his own life was viewed with disapproval. On the contrary, the author relates the story with fascination and sympathy' [55]. Accordingly, even if Abimelech's end is dishonourable, Samson's was a *noble* death. Well, was it? The classic reading of Samson was as a simple superhero: or so thought Josephus, many of the Fathers and Milton. By contrast, most contemporary exegetes see him more as an anti-hero than a hero.[28] On these modern accounts, the scene at the Philistine temple is continuous with one in which Samson is punished because he did not take his Nazirite vows seriously. As Hoppe puts it: 'Samson's dalliance with foreign women brought him trouble, shame and finally death.'[29] Klein concludes that the death of the last judge is replete with irony: his victories are secondary to his overriding lust; like Abimelech he is brought low by foreign women; self-indulgently egocentric to the end, even in death

---

[25] This is not to suggest that the principle of double effect, as carefully formulated by modern and pre-modern philosophers, was known to the author of Judges; however, in this period there were already well-developed doctrines of causation and responsibility, intending and foreseeing.

[26] J. Blenkinsopp, 'Letter', *Bible Review* 6(3) (June 1990), 7.

[27] A similar case might be made out with respect to Eleazar (1 Macc. 6:44), Ptolemy (2 Macc. 10:12) and Razias (2 Macc. 14:41–46), and the 'suicides' at Masada recorded by Josephus in his *Wars of the Jews*.

[28] For example, J. L. Crenshaw, *Samson* (London: SPCK, 1978), pp. 137–9; Schneider, *Judges*, pp. 224–7; Soggin, *Judges*, pp. 258–9; G. von Rad, 'Die Geschichte von Simson', in *Gottes Wirken in Israel* (Neukirchen-Vluyn: Neukirchener, 1974), pp. 49–52.

[29] Hoppe, *Joshua, Judges*, p. 190.

he seeks personal revenge rather than freedom for his people or the vindication of God.[30] We can see clearly that in its context Samson's death, far from being a model 'noble death', is every bit as ambiguous and larger than life as the rest of his story. The lessons to draw from Samson's death are far from straightforward.

Even if we accept that the text is sympathetic or neutral towards Samson's 'suicide', does this amount to permission to emulate him? Should we mimic the rest of Samson's story, at least whenever the sacred author fails to criticize it? Are we too to take on roaring lions and foreign women, kill men for guessing our ribald riddles and take brazen hairdressers as mistresses? The point is that we cannot take short Old Testament portraits and conclude from the absence of an anathema that they endorse the actions they relate and authorize our imitating them. The Scriptures are liberally peppered with incidents such as Jeptha killing his daughter, the Israelites killing every woman, child and animal in banned towns, various characters offering their wives or virgin daughters to appease crowds, Jacob stealing his brother's birthright and so on, all told without negative comment. Without the context of the whole canon, and a lot more besides, we could draw some very strange conclusions about the behaviour endorsed by God and appropriate to believers!

The suicides of Saul and his armour-bearer

There are two traditions concerning the death of Saul. We are told that the Philistines overtook Israel's army including Saul and his sons: Saul was shot with an arrow and badly wounded. According to the first account (1 Sam. 31; 1 Chr. 10), Saul was afraid of being tortured and humiliated by his captors, as Samson had been. So he pleaded with his armour-bearer to kill him. In stark contrast with Abimelech's aide-de-camp, Saul's man refused, unwilling no doubt to kill the Lord's anointed.[31] So Saul fell on his own sword and his armour-bearer followed suit. Droge and Tabor read Saul's death as a noble death[32] – and thus as support for suicide [54]. Clemons gives a more neutral reading:

[T]here is no suggestion that Saul, or even his armour-bearer, were in any way to be condemned for their actions ... Those who had honoured and revered Saul

[30] Klein, *The Triumph of Irony*, ch. 7.
[31] H. W. Hertzberg, *I and II Samuel: A Commentary* (London: SCM, 1964), p. 232.
[32] Likewise J. Baldwin, *1 and 2 Samuel: An Introduction and Commentary* (Leicester: InterVarsity, 1988), p. 172, and Walter Brueggemann, *First and Second Samuel* (Louisville: Westminster John Knox Press, 1990), p. 207.

... were in turn respected and favoured by David (2 Sam. 2:4–7). By recording the story in this way, the biblical writer further shaped the idea in the minds of the Israelites that no condemnation was to be heaped upon those who treated suicides with respect. [17–18]

Badham likewise makes much of the lack of any hint of disapproval in the text [4].[33]

Yet again, the text itself is rather more nuanced and ambivalent than these commentators suggest. With the death of Saul 1 Samuel comes to a sudden end and we are left up in the air as to what will become of the House of Saul, Israel, David and the monarchy. It is true that there is no hostile obituary, but neither is Saul's a hero's death. Saul has become an anti-hero, indeed a villain, contrasted with David for theo-dramatic purposes within the story and for political purposes outside the story.[34] Saul has been repeatedly disobedient and unfaithful to the Lord (1 Sam. chs. 13, 15 and 28), and Samuel has declared the Lord's judgment against him: he is 'an enemy of God' (1 Sam. 13:14; 15:19–21; 27:16; 28:17–19). His death, like the latter part of his life, is 'inglorious' and his humiliation is emphasized by the subsequent desecration of his body (1 Sam. 31:8–10).[35]

The first tradition continues with the account of Saul's death in 1 Chronicles 10 following that in 1 Samuel in most respects but adding a theological conclusion: 'So Saul died for his unfaithfulness; he was unfaithful to the Lord in that he did not observe the Lord's command, and also in that he consulted a medium, seeking her guidance rather than the Lord's. Therefore the Lord slew him, and turned the kingdom over to David' (1 Chr. 10:13–14). Clemons [18–19], Droge and Tabor [54] dismiss the unsympathetic Chronicles version as 'late' and so a 'fabrication'. Other commentators are less confident about the priority of the Samuel version.[36]

---

[33] Similarly· C. Conroy, *1–2 Samuel, 1–2 Kings* (Wilmington: Glazier, 1983), 89; S. Japhet, *I and II Chronicles: A Commentary* (London: SCM, 1993), p. 224; R. Klein, *1 Samuel* (Waco: Word, 1993), p. 288; J. Mauchline, *1 and 2 Samuel* (London: Oliphants, 1971), p. 194.

[34] Good, 'Saul: the tragedy of greatness', in *Irony in the Old Testament*, pp. 56–80; R. Gordon, *1 and 2 Samuel* (Sheffield Academic Press, 1984), pp. 57–8; B. Halpern, *David's Secret Demons: Messiah, Murderer, Traitor, King* (Grand Rapids, MI: Eerdmans, 2001), p. 22; W. L. Humphreys, 'The tragedy of King Saul: a study of the structure of 1 Sam. 9–31', *Journal for the Study of the Old Testament* 6 (1978), 18–27, and 'From tragic hero to villain: a study of the figure of Saul and the development of 1 Samuel', *Journal for the Study of the Old Testament* 22 (1982), 95–117.

[35] Thus R. Gordon, *I & II Samuel: A Commentary* (Grand Rapids, MI: Regency, 1986), p. 202; R. Bergen, *1 & 2 Samuel* (Nashville: Broadman and Holman, 1996), p. 282.

[36] P. K. McCarter, *1 and 2 Samuel* (New York: Doubleday, 1980), vol. 1, p. 440, argues that the Chronicles version may well be the more primitive. H. G. Williamson, *1 and 2 Chronicles* (Grand Rapids, MI: Eerdmans, 1982), p. 92, argues that 'it is by no means easy to distinguish the one from the other'.

Early or late, it is hardly a panegyric for a noble soldier: God has got his own back, even using Saul's own hand against him.

The doomed king is not merely destroyed; he is self-destroyed, self-betrayed into a final act of self-destruction. By his wilful acts, he has locked himself into a course that leads to an inescapable fate. [Chronicles'] spare narrative excludes any sympathy or regret for Saul's degrading death: his theme is the doom of the disobedient and apostate king, whose end is deserved and inevitable. The piety and loyalty of his armour-bearer provide a grim foil to the impiety and disloyalty of his master.[37]

Once again, there is more going on in this story than just a forensic account of one man's sad end. The story of the fall of Saul and his house, and the interwoven and contrasting story of the rise of David and his dynasty, is the vehicle for many themes.[38] No specific teaching about suicide is intended here. In what Robert Polzin calls 'Saul's final abhorrent act of self-destruction' we find a complex and tragic figure – one who, though more worthy than Abimelech, is the vehicle for his own comeuppance.[39]

The 'voluntary euthanasia' of Saul

There is a second, somewhat different tradition concerning the death of Saul. In 2 Samuel 1 a young Amalekite reports to David that he had come upon the wounded Saul leaning on his spear – whether attempting suicide we do not know. Saul begged him, 'Stand beside me and slay me, for anguish has seized me and yet my life still lingers.' So the youth delivered the *coup de grâce* to the dying Saul in what today we might call an act of voluntary euthanasia or mercy killing.

We might note a few points about this story. First, in contemporary terms Saul was 'better off dead' or death was 'in his best interests': he reasonably hoped to die, to 'go to his fathers'. Second, everyone else was, more or less, better off with Saul being dead. Certainly David was: it

---

[37] W. Johnstone, *1 & 2 Chronicles* (Sheffield Academic Press, 1997), vol. 1, p. 134; likewise R. Braun, *1 Chronicles* (Waco: Word Books, 1986), pp. 150–2.

[38] Most commentators find Saul at this point a dark foil for the brilliance of the up-and-coming David; Saul's dynasty has been judged and, in retribution for his unfaithfulness, has to all intents and purposes come to an end; he is a paradigm for unfaithful Israel: R. J. Coggins, *The First and Second Books of the Chronicles* (Cambridge University Press, 1976), p. 64; Johnstone, *1 & 2 Chronicles*, pp. 134–6; G. Jones, *1 & 2 Chronicles* (Sheffield Academic Press, 1993), pp. 33–4; C. Mangan, *1–2 Chronicles, Ezra, Nehemiah* (Wilmington: Glazier, 1982), p. 27; Williamson, *1 and 2 Chronicles*, p. 93.

[39] R. Polzin, *Samuel and the Deuteronomist* (San Francisco: Harper & Row, 1989), p. 224; D. Gunn, *The Fate of King Saul*, rev. edn (Sheffield Academic Press, 1989), p. 57.

helped secure his throne and his own life. Third, the Amalekite who slew Saul seems to have done so with the best of motives. He was trusted by Saul and did nothing furtively: indeed he ritually mourned Saul's death, bringing the booty of his crown and armlet straight to David, as well as an account of all that had happened. Finally, if the lad is to be believed, he acted out of mercy: in his own words 'I stood beside him and slew him, because I was sure that he could not live after he had fallen.' So Saul died at the hand of a *merciful* man, a kind of ancient Near-Eastern Dr Death, having asked for euthanasia, being terminally ill and in great suffering at the time.

Notwithstanding all this, the undoubted conclusion of this story is that the killing was a wicked act, deserving the severest punishment. When the lad arrived to tell David the news, expecting jubilation and reward, David did not rejoice at the death of his enemy. Instead, he immediately rent his clothes asunder, wept and fasted in a ritual demonstration of non-complicity and genuine mourning. He had the youth punished for having killed his friend and the Lord's anointed (2 Sam. 1:11–27). Apologizing for the Amalekite, Mauchline argues that he was engaged in 'a humanitarian act' and that 'he was not in any way shortening Saul's life, he was shortening his dying'. He complains that David's zeal for the Lord 'took no account of the Amalekite's mercy killing or his honourable motives and humanitarian considerations'.[40] Whatever one's judgment of the Amalekite, Saul and David, this text is no endorsement of mercy killing. As David sings his beautiful lament 'O how the mighty have fallen', he does not celebrate Saul's manner of falling.

The suicides of Ahithophel and Judas

Later in 2 Samuel we read of the death of Ahithophel. He has been an esteemed adviser of King David but later joined Prince Absalom in his attempt to seize the throne. When his plans came to nothing, he was disgraced, crushed and doubtless afraid of David. He saddled his ass, went home, set his house in order and then hanged himself (2 Sam. 17:23). Unlike some of the other cases looked at here, no 'serves him right' judgment is made by the author of the text. So what are we to make of this story? Clemons concludes that there was at this time 'no stigma or other penalty' attaching to suicide, and that this was 'a prototype of a form of

---

[40] Mauchline, *1 and 2 Samuel*, p. 196. A. A. Anderson, *2 Samuel* (Dallas: Word, 1989), p. 7, says that Saul 'ordered his own mercy killing'.

suicide that has been repeated in many cultures since, the self-death of a trusted adviser when his or her best effort has been rejected' [20]. Droge and Tabor likewise determine that 'a good case can be made, based on this text, and on the account of Saul's death in 1 Samuel 31, that within Israelite society, as early as the period of the united monarchy, voluntary death, given the proper circumstances, was understood as honourable and even routine. The matter-of-fact way in which these events are recorded supports such a conclusion' [56].

Matter-of-fact reporting, however, tells us little about moral approval. Again we must look to the broader story. Ahithophel was an esteemed, even beloved adviser of the Lord's anointed; but he turned traitor, and David, weeping on the Mount of Olives, cries out to God (as will his greatest descendant, Jesus, when likewise betrayed). Not only did Ahithophel switch allegiance, he advised Absalom to 'go into his father's concubines in the sight of all Israel', thereby dishonouring both father and son, humiliating and provoking David. Then, to compound his treachery and his connivance in incest and dishonour, Ahithophel undertook himself to kill the king (2 Sam. 16:20–17:4). Are we to understand that all *this* 'matter-of-fact reporting' means the activities reported are natural, honourable, routine? Is not Ahithophel, like our other examples, clearly in God's bad books, awaiting his comeuppance? Is not his suicide the enacting of divine punishment for treachery, rather than a merciful release for a man who feared David's vengeance? Thus H. W. Hertzberg describes his death as 'the melancholy sign of divinely ordained failure',[41] and Walter Brueggemann observes that 'Ahithophel is left neither face nor honour ... He has risked everything in his defection and now he has been dismissed. His risk has yielded him nothing. He ends in ignoble suicide.'[42]

Matthew apparently had the death of Ahithophel in mind when he fashioned his report of the death of another notorious traitor to the line of David, Judas (Matt. 27:5).[43] There may have been several gruesome accounts of Judas' death circulating at the time,[44] and Matthew may have

[41] Hertzberg, *I and II Samuel*, p. 353.
[42] Brueggemann, *First and Second Samuel*, p. 315. Ahitophel is listed in the Mishna (Sanhedrin 10.2) among those who have forfeited their share in the world to come.
[43] Most commentators here follow P. Ackroyd, *The Second Book of Samuel* (Cambridge University Press, 1977), p. 162, and D. Senior, *The Passion of Jesus in the Gospel of Matthew* (Wilmington: Glazier, 1985), p. 106.
[44] In Acts 1:18–20 Judas stumbled and burst open, so that his insides spilled out. In Papias (fragment 3; mid-second century) Judas was afflicted with a loathsome disease, grotesquely swollen, blind, and died in great pain; the place where this took place was laid waste and 'to this very day' conveys such a stench than no one can pass unless holding his nose. Cf. Eduard Schweizer, *The Good News According to Matthew* (London: SPCK, 1976), pp. 502–3.

thought the suicide story the most credible after Judas' treachery.[45] Alan M'Neile concludes: 'Ahitophel the treacherous friend of David, and Judas the treacherous friend of the Son of David, meet a similar end.'[46] Surely no one would read this death as honourable: 'Judas gets what he deserves';[47] 'the betrayer's unhappy death recalls other stories of the terrible end of villainous persons';[48] it is 'a sober warning to the reader about the consequences when someone called to be a disciple of Jesus squanders that gift through greed, betrayal and despair'.[49] Despite the weight of contrary interpretation, Badham [4], Droge and Tabor [112] and Clemons [23] all assert that Matthew shows *no hint of disapproval* of the manner of Judas' death.

We might ask how suicide was regarded in Matthew's day. The Book of Tobit, one of the last composed before the Christian era, gives us a hint. After the death of seven consecutive husbands, Sarah is under a cloud and the subject of taunts even from the household staff. 'When she heard these things', we are told, 'she was deeply grieved, even to the thought of hanging herself. But she said, "I am my father's only child; if I do this, it will disgrace him, and I shall bring his old age down in sorrow to the grave." So she prayed to the Lord' (Tobit 3:10), and was in due course rewarded with a new husband with greater staying power. This text and Matthew's suggest that suicide was already regarded as dishonourable in the inter-testamentary period. Indeed by the time of Josephus the Jews were customarily exposing the corpses of suicides, leaving them unburied until after sunset and without public mourning.[50] Rabinowitz and Cohn note:

The duty of preserving life, including one's own, is one of the paramount injunctions of Judaism. The prohibition of suicide is a natural corollary to this ...

[45] Senior, *The Passion*, pp. 104–8; Schweizer, *Matthew*, pp. 502–5; R. V. Tasker, *Matthew: An Introduction and Commentary* (London: Tyndale, 1961), p. 258; A. Upton, 'The Potter's Field and the death of Judas', *Concordia Journal* 8 (1982), 213–19; W. C. van Unnik, 'The death of Judas in Saint Matthew's Gospel', *Anglican Theol Rev* Supp. 3 (1974), 44–57. These writers point out that Matthew presents Judas' suicide not as a sign of genuine repentance but as only compounding his sin of betrayal.

[46] A. M'Neile, *The Gospel According to St Matthew* (London: Macmillan, 1965), p. 497.

[47] C. Kenner, *A Commentary on the Gospel of Matthew* (Grand Rapids, MI: Eerdmans, 1999), p. 658.

[48] R. Schnackenburg, *The Gospel of Matthew* (Grand Rapids, MI: Eerdmans, 2002), p. 280.

[49] D. Senior, *Matthew* (Nashville: Abingdon, 1998), p. 319. Likewise K. Essex, 'Euthanasia', *Masters Seminary Journal* 11(2) (Fall 2000), 191–212 at 209; D. Hare, *Matthew* (Louisville: Westminster John Knox, 1993), p. 313.

[50] Josephus, *Wars* III, p. 375, quoted in Schnackenburg, *John*, p. 198: 'The souls of those whose hands have done violence to their own lives go to darkest Hades, and God, their father, will visit the sins of the evil-doers on their descendants.'

Post-Talmudic authorities considered suicide a most heinous sin, even worse than murder. It was thought to be a denial of the doctrines of reward and punishment, the world to come, and the sovereignty of God, and the opinion was expressed that the suicide forfeits his portion in the world to come. Suicide is sharply to be differentiated from martyrdom, which, under certain circumstances, is the greatest *mitzvah* of Judaism.[51]

Zimri and the suicide genre

Returning to the sequence of the suicidal judges and kings of Israel, the reader will by now be able to predict the likely outlines of the next suicide report, that of Zimri (1 Kgs. 16:18–20). Yet again we have a treacherous fellow – this time an assassin of the king and the whole royal family, a killer of all his rivals and even the friends of his rivals. (Indeed, by the time of Jezebel, Zimri has become the household name for a murderous traitor: 2 Kgs. 9:31.) After his *coup d'état*, Zimri reigned as king for a very short time indeed. Besieged by Ahab's father, he despaired and deliberately burnt down his palace with himself inside it. Once again, only those committed to exonerating suicide, such as Clemons [20], Droge and Tabor [59–60], would call this a *noble* death, evidence of biblical support for the practice of suicide, at least by defeated leaders. Yet the Deuteronomistic obituary candidly explains that all this befell Zimri 'on account of the sins which he committed, doing what was evil in the sight of the Lord, walking in the way of Jeroboam and leading Israel into sin' (1 Kgs. 16:19). As Richard Nelson concludes: 'Zimri's spectacular death was caused by his apostasy.'[52]

Some conclusions

At this point we might draw some preliminary conclusions regarding suicide and euthanasia in the Scriptures. First, we must beware anachronism. Many stories that might seem to involve elements of 'voluntary death' are not addressed to such questions and cannot fairly be cited either in favour of or against suicide or euthanasia: the stories are just not about such matters.

---

[51] L. I. Rabinowitz and H. H. Cohn, 'Suicide', *Encyclopaedia Judaica* xv, 490–1; cf. K. Kaplan and M. Schwartz, *A Psychology of Hope: An Antidote to the Suicidal Pathology of Western Civilization* (Westport: Praeger, 1993), chs. 3 and 6.

[52] R. Nelson, *First and Second Kings* (Atlanta: John Knox, 1987), p. 102. Likewise S. deVries, *1 Kings* (Waco: Word, 1985), p. 199; V. Fritz, *1 & 2 Kings* (Minneapolis: Fortress, 2003), p. 176.

Second, wherever suicide or assisted suicide appears in the Bible it is always a part of someone's tragedy: whether mad (Saul), dying (Saul), disgraced (Abimelech, Ahithophel), abandoned (Saul's armour-bearer, Ahithophel) or despairing (Zimri, Judas). In almost every case the person concerned is 'under a cloud', having committed some act of gross infidelity to God. His death (it is always a 'he') is viewed as part of his comeuppance, a divine judgment against him. However noble his earlier life, his death is part of his humiliation. Suicide in these several texts is in the 'death of the bad guy' genre. Of course the background images of providence, a vengeful God and human beings as instruments of divine judgment against themselves require careful interpretation.

Third, despite the searching efforts of some recent commentators, no biblical account can be found that celebrates suicide or euthanasia as godly or noble. If anything the examples point in the opposite direction.[53] In claiming scriptural warrant for these practices Badham, Clemons, Droge and Tabor have allowed 'the world in front of the text' – the contemporary debate over the legalization and practice of euthanasia – to determine their view of the worlds behind and within the text.

THE SCRIPTURAL BASIS OF JUDEO-CHRISTIAN OPPOSITION TO SUICIDE AND EUTHANASIA

Choose life

When Paul's Philippian gaoler discovered the prison doors open and the prisoners presumably all gone, he decided to fall upon his sword. Paul, seeing what the man was about to do, immediately cried out to stop him (Acts 16:25–34).[54] Ever since, Christian leaders have sought to protect the weak and vulnerable from attempting suicide and euthanasia.[55] What do our pro-euthanasia exegetes conclude? Predictably enough they say that

---

[53] Bergen, *1 & 2 Samuel*, p. 282 concludes: 'though the Bible does not explicitly prohibit such actions, each portrayal of this practice is replete with tragic overtones. The Bible seems to suggest that suicide or assisted-suicide is a desperate act by a deeply troubled individual. None of the individuals who resorted to this action is portrayed as a role model for the pious.' Likewise E. Larson and D. Amundsen, *A Different Death: Euthanasia and the Christian Tradition* (Downers Grove, IL: InterVarsity, 1998), pp. 103–15; D. O'Mathúna, 'But the Bible doesn't say they were wrong to commit suicide, does it?', in Demy and Stewart (eds.), *Suicide*, pp. 349–66.

[54] The argument of this section is more fully developed in A. Fisher, 'Theological aspects of euthanasia', in J. Keown (ed.), *Examining Euthanasia: Legal, Ethical and Clinical Perspectives* (Cambridge University Press, 1995), pp. 315–32.

[55] This point is well made in Alastair Campbell, 'A response to Paul Badham', *Studies in Christian Ethics* 11(1) (1998), 13–18 at 17.

Paul was not opposed to suicide or euthanasia; in this case he just thought it unnecessary. Unless we can point to a clear and repeated biblical prohibition of suicide and euthanasia, these writers insist, it follows that 'the Bible' permits them.[56]

This is an example of that legalistic and minimalist or tax-lawyer approach to morality identified in previous chapters. On a more holistic or canonical reading of the Bible, we find there a God who is presented time and again as one who communicates life to all living creatures, above all to the pinnacle of creation, human beings.[57] In the section on 'The perennial debate about abortion' in Chapter 6 I explored a number of scriptural passages in which human beings are accorded great dignity, as created uniquely in God's image and likeness, little less than gods, destined and oriented to God as their ultimate goal and saved by God becoming enfleshed in human history in the person of Jesus Christ. We saw that on this Christian view of things, life is not a free-for-all but a trust given into our stewardship by God. In a verse that Rabbinic Judaism reads as a direct prohibition of suicide,[58] God declares to Noah when pronouncing the terms of the covenant: 'For your own life-blood I will surely require a reckoning and from every person for the blood of another, I will require a reckoning for human life. Whoever sheds human blood shall have their own blood shed; for God made man in his own image' (Gen. 9:1–6).[59] Paul takes up this theme when writing to the Corinthians, giving it a specifically Christian significance: 'Do you not know that your body is a temple of the Holy Spirit within you? You are not your own; you were bought with a price. So glorify God in your body' (1 Cor. 6:19–20). Here we have something of the scriptural basis of the so-called 'sanctity of life principle',[60] which in turn has informed Christian opposition not only to murder and abortion, but also to suicide and euthanasia.

Taking the canon of Scripture as a whole, rather than relying upon doubtful readings of a few incidents within it, and admitting that there

[56] Badham [5]; Clemons [24–5]; Droge and Tabor [114].
[57] L. Bailey, *Biblical Perspectives on Death* (Minneapolis: Fortress Press, 1979); P. Sena, 'Biblical teaching on life and death', in D. McCarthy and A. Moraczewski (eds.), *Moral Responsibility in Prolonging Life Decisions* (St. Louis: Pope John Center, 1981), pp. 3–19.
[58] *Baba Kamma* 91b; *Yorah Deah* 345.
[59] Bailey, *Biblical Perspectives*, p. 100, cites this verse as a prime example of the high value placed on human life in the Scriptures and God's sole prerogative to create, sustain, end and restore life; the taking of human life without divine warrant is viewed as an arrogant usurpation of divine power.
[60] On the gradual evolution of the sanctity of life principle in Jewish religion and thus in the Old Testament, see John Paul II, *EV* 34–41. Its scriptural underpinnings are further explored by Moloney, 'Life, healing and the Bible', pp. 322–34.

is development and variation within that canon, the theological answer to the question 'Do the Scriptures endorse suicide and euthanasia?' is resoundingly: choose life not death; you shall not kill. Throughout the Bible killing demands justification, and the taking of innocent human life is repeatedly presented as contrary to God's law and to a sacred trust. Nor is this merely a superstitious taboo or perverse decree from on high. It is in fact well supported in Hippocratic medicine, natural law philosophy, the common law and other moral and legal traditions. All nations until very recently and almost all nations still today criminalize euthanasia and discourage suicide. Where suicide has been decriminalized, it is because the criminal law is not seen as helping with depression or despair. However, in those same places suicide itself is still abhorred and those who encourage or assist it are still punished. Likewise religions and communities that no longer exclude those who have committed suicide from funerals, sacred burial ground or inheritance rights demonstrate a greater understanding of the diminished responsibility of most suicidal people and a more merciful attitude to their grieving relatives. However, this does not represent any weakening of their opposition to all killing of innocent people, including self-killing.

The Passion of the Christ: liberal autonomy versus 'thy will be done'

The story of Christ's Passion begins with the Last Supper. While there are differences between what is included in the accounts and considerable post-Resurrection editing, the gospels suggest that long before that fateful night, Jesus had 'set his face toward Jerusalem', apparently resigned to fulfilling his destiny there (Matt. 16:21–23; 17:22–23; 20:17–19; 26:1–2; Luke 9:51). Jesus guessed that for all the adulation the crowd would turn and that his intimates would desert and even betray him (Matt. 26:20–25; Mark 14:27–31; John 10:18; 13:21–30; 15:13; 1 John 3:16). Yet as we have seen in several biblical cases, resigning oneself to the inevitability of death is not the same as intending, causing or being complicit in that death. Rather, it seems that Jesus had come to see God's will and his mission as intimately tied up both with suffering at the hands of sinful men and with Jerusalem. But ultimately it was violent men who would kill Jesus, not Jesus himself (Acts 2:23; 3:14–15).

The next scene in our story is that of the Agony in the Garden. Jesus, contemplating the horror ahead, is 'scared to death', falls to the ground shaking and even sweats blood (Luke 22:39–46). There is no calm stoicism here, no romanticizing of martyrdom. Jesus enters into the full horror of human suffering: the pain and torment, the loneliness and abandonment. Like any of us would, he prays that this cup be taken from him. Yet he does not finish his prayer like Saul or Abimelech, asking that if he cannot escape that he be killed quickly. He does not curse God and die, as Job's wife counselled. Instead he concludes with the daily prayer he had taught his disciples: 'Thy will be done.' Even the prospect of humiliation, pain and death does not dispense him from obedience to the Father. Such obedience in suffering can be redemptive. In his commentary on Job Francis Anderson observed:

> The heroes of faith in Hebrews 11 were all sufferers, and many died without deliverance. Now no suffering seems pleasant at the time, but *afterwards* 'it yields the peaceful fruit of righteousness to those who have been trained by it' (Heb. 12:11). This is not a thing for anyone to arrange for himself in order to gain spiritual benefits. God alone may send it. No one who has felt His rod would wish to go that way again; but no one who has come with Job to 'what the Lord is aiming at' (see Jas. 5:11) would ever wish not to have trodden his path. The body of Jesus for ever bears the scars of crucifixion, and they are its chief glory. If the passion of Job was an early sketch of the greatest Sufferer, it remains for His later followers to enter into 'the fellowship of His sufferings' (Phil. 3:10) and joyfully to supply what is still needed to complete the sufferings of Christ (Col. 1:24) ... What Job longed for blindly has actually happened. God Himself has joined in our hell of loneliness ... all the 'meanings' of suffering converge on Christ.[61]

Christ's obedience, even unto death on a cross, brings us to a crucial issue in liberal philosophical advocacy for suicide and euthanasia: is suffering meaningless and autonomy what matters? These issues have been explored at several points in this book. Suffice it here to say that the scriptural notions of stewardship, community and law point us in a rather different direction. As Christ's agonizing in the garden demonstrated so graphically, we are not free to do 'whatever we please' with our bodies, lives and talents. We too must hear God's call, consider what our choices make us and say about us and consider also their effects on others. Instead of 'I did it my way' his swan-song and ours must be 'Thy will be done.'[62]

---

[61] F. Anderson, *Job: An Introduction and Commentary* (Downers Grove, IL: InterVarsity, 1976), p. 73.
[62] Cf. G. Meilaender, *Bioethics: A Primer for Christians* (Grand Rapids, MI: Eerdmans, 1996), ch. 1; C. Vogt, *Patience, Compassion, Hope and the Christian Art of Dying Well* (Lanham, MD: Rowman and Littlefield, 2004).

The com-passion of Mary: the duty to keep on caring

Next in the Passion narrative comes the arrest, trial and execution of Jesus. As the drama unfolds we are each confronted with the question: how do I respond to the suffering and impending death of others? Jesus is abandoned by his disciples, even by Peter, who had pledged to lay down his life, but a stranger from Cyrene is pressed to help carry his cross and Jesus' mother and beloved disciple wait by his deathbed, the Cross.

Time and again the Scriptures and the Christian tradition call us to join Simon of Cyrene in caring generously for those heavy-burdened or in need. Compassion expressed in active engagement with those who suffer was central to Christ's own mission and is his litmus test for ours: what did you do for the little ones, the hungry, thirsty, sick, imprisoned (Matt. 25:31–46; cf. Luke 10:30–37)? For care we can, even when we cannot cure. Good therapeutic, palliative and spiritual care is a real alternative to the 'exit' of euthanasia.[63]

On the other hand we know that even with the best of care, pain and death cannot be eliminated from this life. Some problems in this life have no solution. Then comes the really hard loving: the loving of a family surrounding their comatose child, of a husband whose wife's Alzheimer's disease means she no longer recognizes him, of siblings playing patiently with their profoundly disabled brother, of a mother watching and weeping at the foot of the Cross. Sometimes the best we can do is invest ourselves – our time, companionship, prayer, hope – in the suffering, the persistently unresponsive and the dying. This is a kind of respecting and loving that no one should pretend is easy.

Suffering must be faced, despite the pervasive temptation to demand a quick fix, to marginalize those who suffer so others can remain undisturbed or to flee the scene with Peter and the others. Faith recalls the profounder possibilities for good occasioned by illness and pain: for the sufferer, there is a chance for re-evaluation, conversion, growth in virtue, setting things right with God and others; for onlookers, there are opportunities for compassion and selfless behaviour, perseverance in generosity even when exhausted. Job is one of our models of this and so is

---

[63] Badham, while nodding in the direction of palliative and hospice care [2] presents the debate in terms of 'whether a swift death at one's own choosing can be legitimate for a Christian when the alternative is an agonising, long-drawn-out, and ultimately futile battle with a terminal illness' [5]. In 'Euthanasia and the Christian understanding of God', p. 12, he goes further, quoting with approval authors who describe contemporary end-of-life care as 'torture'. This receives critical attention in Campbell, 'A response to Paul Badham', pp. 15–16.

our crucified God. Christ points to the redemptive potential of suffering and invites us to unite our suffering with his (see e.g. Matt. 27:34; Rom. 8.17–18). We are promised the Holy Spirit to help us in our weakness (Rom. 8:26) – but there is no shortcut to glory. In the end, as we humbly admit our incomprehension before the mystery of suffering, we must trust that the One who has gone before us through pain and death into new life will bring us with him. 'O death, where is your victory? O death, where is your sting? ... Thanks be to God, who gives us the victory through our Lord Jesus Christ' (1 Cor. 15:55–57). 'The Lord of hosts will destroy the shroud that is cast over all peoples ... He will swallow up death forever. Then the Lord God will wipe away the tears from all faces ... It will be said on that day, "Let us rejoice and be glad for the Lord has saved us"' (Isa. 25:6–9).[64]

Divine mercy and suicide

Taken as a whole and read in the light of Christian tradition, the Scriptures do not countenance suicide and euthanasia: those who kill innocent others or even themselves are under the censure of that text and tradition. Dare we hope, however, for a merciful judgment for those who commit suicide? I have suggested that the biblical witness is in places hostile to suicide and in others silent but that its overall thrust is life-affirming even in the depths of suffering and despondency. Yet Christians hold that 'we should not despair of the eternal salvation of persons who have taken their own lives'. Indeed, as the *Catechism of the Catholic Church* (2283) goes on, 'By ways known to God alone, God can provide the opportunity for salutary repentance. The Church prays for persons who have taken their own lives.' Why is that?

Clemons suggests that at its root is a biblical confidence in God's omnipresence, his abiding love and our hope against hope in eternal life. 'If I ascend to heaven, you are there; if I lie down in the underworld, you are there! If I take the wings of the morning and settle at the farthest limits of the sea, even there your hand shall lead me, and your right hand hold me fast' (Ps. 139:8–10) This omnipresent, leading, holding God so loved the world that he gave his only Son that we might have eternal life (John

---

[64] See also N. Biggar, 'God, the responsible individual, and the value of human life and suffering', *Studies in Christian Ethics* 11(1) (1998), 28–47, and *Aiming to Kill: The Ethics of Suicide and Euthanasia* (London: DLT, 2004); S. Hauerwas, *Suffering Presence: Theological Reflections on Medicine, the Mentally Handicapped and the Church* (Notre Dame University Press, 1986); John Paul II, *Salvifici Doloris: Apostolic Letter on the Christian Meaning of Human Suffering* (1984).

3:16). 'I am convinced', declares Paul, 'that neither death, nor life, nor any power ... can separate us from the love of God in Christ Jesus our Lord' (Rom. 8:38–39).

None of this is to deny the terrible possibility that is hell: Jesus is quite clear that people may turn against God in their free choices and that God respects us enough to let us make such choices, even for all eternity (Matt. 5:22–30; 10:28; 18:8–9; 23:33; 25:31–46; Luke 13:22–30, etc.). Love cannot be forced – there is no heaven against our wills. It is self-delusion or romanticism to suggest, as Badham does, that those who commit suicide do so as a declaration of faith and hope.[65] Some may of course kill themselves while still hoping for a merciful judgment. Others may die obstinately preferring self-imposed exile from God to repentance of their disobedience. If Christians today are less willing to consign suicides to hell, it is not because they deny that such choices can be made. Rather, we now recognize the complexities of psychology and causation in these circumstances and that there is space for the Holy Spirit's work in converting and healing, even at the moment of death. The Christian Scriptures and tradition recognize how depression, pain, fear, anxiety, grief, shame and madness can overwhelm some people and reduce their moral freedom and culpability.

For the survivors of a loved one who has committed suicide, the Scriptures also have their words of sense-making and consolation. Amid the incomprehension, denial, horror, righteous indignation, shame and extended grief suffered by the survivors the New Testament speaks its shortest verse: 'Jesus wept' (John 11:35).[66] The weeping God has gone before us through despair, torment and death. In the very moments when all seemed most hopeless a dying thief was promised paradise, Lazarus was given new life and he who took all our weaknesses and sins upon himself rose triumphant from the grave. So, yes, we dare to hope for those who die in tragic circumstances, even at their own hands, trusting in the One who came that we 'might have life, and have it to the full' (John 10:10).

---

[65] In his several articles. See Williams, 'Christians and voluntary euthanasia', p. 138.
[66] Cf. G. L. and G. C. Carr, *After the Storm: Hope in the Wake of Suicide* (Leicester: InterVarsity, 1990).

PART IV

Protecting life

CHAPTER 10

Identity: what role for a Catholic hospital?

A TALE OF TWO HOSPITALS

St Mary Magdalene's

St Mary Magdalene's Hospital is a large modern acute-care hospital in the middle of a major city. Founded in 1880 as a hospice for the poor, 130 years of devoted service by religious women and their collaborators have seen 'the Mag' grow into one of the most highly regarded hospitals in the country. It offers state of the art medical technology in 'hotel-style comfort' and is favoured by politicians and society leaders.

Originally staffed by heroic sisters and a few lay staff, the Mag now employs over a thousand people in various capacities. In 1995, on advice from health management consultants, the hospital was independently incorporated, and an expert health administrator, Jack Tecknay, was appointed as CEO. Mr Tecknay has no religious affiliation but is well disposed to the hospital's Christian ethos and the congregational history. He promised to lead the hospital into the new century with top-of-the-range services at competitive prices, maximum throughput, big efficiency gains, tough labour relations and greater public profile. There are no longer sisters on the hospital board or in administrative or nursing positions; the congregation has established a 'public juridic person of pontifical right' to own and oversee its hospitals now and into the future, when it is presumed there will be few or no religious to do so; this guarantees a large measure of independence from the local bishops but allows for the 'passing on of the congregational charism' to the new lay leaders. The sisters still have some role in mission statements and senior appointments. Two sisters are still employed by the hospital: Kay, who is the chaplain, and Beth, the mission officer.

Kay and Beth both have modest budgets, but ever since the cutbacks to all departments (except administration) the chaplaincy team – formerly

a priest, two sisters and two lay people trained in clinical pastoral education – has been reduced to Kay working with the occasional volunteer. Social workers have taken up some of the slack, such as bereavement
counselling. Kay visits patients and is keen to try pastoral strategies such
as the enneagram. Beth has been especially active in regularly revising the
policy statements on mission, vision, patient empowerment and affirmative action in employment. She consults widely with other hospital staff
with a view to keeping such statements up to date, relevant and inclusive. She is very conscious of the need to maintain mission and values
and so has conducted formal seminars and informal conversations with
staff about how they might better integrate policy and practice. Kay and
Beth have helped preserve some tangible signs of the congregation's traditions despite the massive redevelopments and relocations of the hospital
complex in recent times. Some new religious symbols have been com-
missioned for the prayer room and a sculpture of the foundress for the
lobby. The former convent and chapel have been turned into offices, but
provision has been made for an interfaith 'quiet space', with a welcoming
decor, some encouraging posters and refreshment facilities.

Like all hospitals, the Mag has lately felt the pinch of resource constraints, but it has fared better than most. It is on a firm financial foot-
ing, has significant endowments and has entered a series of cooperative
arrangements with various secular providers to ensure that it maintains
its competitive advantage. It enjoys particularly close cooperation with
Mr Tecknay's former employers, the City General Hospital, with whom
it operates an 'integrated service delivery network' and health maintenance organization. For example, the two hospitals operate a joint reproductive services programme, with City General providing any human
embryo work such as IVF and the Mag offering 'GIFT', widely regarded
as 'Catholic IVF'. The Mag also has a large prenatal diagnosis and genetic counselling programme, and this is one of its principal research
strengths.

The Mag's reproductive and prenatal services are part of its 'top-of-
the-range women's services'. Church strictures in this area are in general
accepted with good humour, if not entirely understood by staff. The hospital's lawyers and ethics consultants are skilled in finding ways around
some of the harsher rules. Patients wanting forbidden procedures such as
genetic abortions are commonly passed on to City General for treatment.
The Mag has an official 'no abortion' policy, but occasionally severely
disabled children are induced early and the hospital is less squeamish
than some other facilities about potentially abortifacient interventions,

especially after rape or in tubal pregnancy. Again, despite the 'no sterilization' policy, some women, several of whom were living with intellectual disabilities, have been sterilized in association with some other
operation or for some clinical indication such as menstrual regulation.
The 'no contraception' policy is applied flexibly, especially where pregnancy poses a threat to health, where natural methods of family planning
have proved difficult or as prophylaxis against diseases other than pregnancy. None of these 'exceptions', it should be said, is trumpeted abroad:
the hospital avoids public scandal, does not want to embarrass Church
officials or the sponsor congregation and insists that it provides only 'life-
affirming' services.

St Norbert's

At the opposite end of the city is St Norbert's Hospital, founded around
the same time as the Mag by an order from somewhere in the Austro-
Hungarian empire. It is showing its age rather more than its big sister,
with its buildings, religious decor and (people claim) even its staff little changed. Originally an asylum for lunatics, waifs and disgraced girls,
St Norbert's became a hospital in the modern sense and diversified in
various ways. Yet it resisted expansion into every medical specialty or
technology, and so never achieved the size or status of the Mag, remaining a much more local concern. The hospital relies on an unpredictable
mix of bequests, benefactions, government grants, fundraising activities
and user and insurer contributions. Staff and community relations are
very good, but only prayer and a series of Mother-Administrators with a
talent for fundraising have kept the hospital from bankruptcy to date.

The smaller scale of St Norbert's made it easier for the sisters to hold on
to its management – with the help of an advisory board of local Catholic
worthies and grateful former patients. The sisters provide several of the
nurses, and semi-retired nuns are encouraged to chat with patients and
staff and generally be obvious and welcoming. The favourite of all is
Sister Mary Philomena, who, it seems, attended the births of everybody's
grandparents and wanders around the wards distributing rosaries and a
kindly word to all – Muslims and atheists included. The sisters are ageing
and professing too few to replace those who die on the job, and so must
employ a significant number of lay staff. Nonetheless the sisters are sufficiently numerous to communicate their Catholic beliefs and their congregation's particular inspiration unselfconsciously to the rest of the staff.
They continue to prefer staff with a strong faith, although this has landed

them in a few scrapes with the unions and the Anti-Discrimination Board; they require all staff to undertake professional development in Catholic bioethics and invite them to take part in retreat days.

Pastoral care is perhaps the most distinctive feature of the hospital. In addition to Sister Philomena's attentions, patients are guaranteed regular visits from a pastoral care team (which includes sisters, a priest and others) and ready access to the sacraments, daily Mass, daily prayer and other devotions. In addition to its particular identification with the local ethnic communities, St Norbert's is chosen by many non-Catholics because they think it is *different*: they report that it is 'a peaceful place', 'prayerful', 'personal', 'a real community hospital'. Responding to developments in the surrounding society, the sisters have decided to focus their energies on the most neglected people and those most at risk of harm in other hospitals and on areas of healthcare unfashionable in most institutions. To the extent that it is possible, preference is given to poorer patients; more affluent ones are asked to consider sponsoring an underprivileged patient with the same condition as their own, and some do so willingly. Other hospitals regularly divert patients who are unlikely to meet their bills to St Norbert's, and this is certainly putting a strain on the finances. In conjunction with some friendly parishes and reporters, the hospital has been active in promoting a Christian health maintenance organization; it has also actively sought greater cooperation among like-minded services with a view to establishing an 'integrated Christian healthcare network'.

The jewel in St Norbert's crown is its hospice for the dying. Highly regarded throughout the city, it has successfully tendered to provide palliative care services to other hospitals and to homes in the district. A number of its patients are dying from AIDS. All are treated with special love and respect, and assisted to live their last days in comfort, surrounded by those they love and well prepared for death both emotionally and spiritually. The hospice stands resolutely against the contemporary tendency either to withdraw all care which might in any way extend the lives of patients thought better off dead or deliberately to overdose them. It is equally resistant to the trend to ration limited resources on the basis of so-called 'quality of life' judgments which, the sisters observe, always seem to put their 'favourites' at the end of the line. Not that St Norbert's is inclined to over-treatment either: the technological imperative and immoderate expectations of medicine are discouraged by the sisters as is intemperance with liquor.

Less well known than the hospice is St Norbert's fertility clinic, which provides natural alternatives not only to the contraceptive pill but also to the reproductive technologies offered to the infertile elsewhere in the city. The hospital is also involved in several community and home-care programmes: shelter and support for women with unplanned pregnancies, for recovering drug addicts and for street kids; physiotherapy and special education for children with disabilities; a rescue and support service for mental health patients abandoned to 'care in the community'; home visitation and community nursing for the housebound; a state-of-the art hospice-in-the-home programme; and respite for families over-burdened with the care of a dependant. Despite its old-fashioned ethos these particular specialties have attracted some research projects to the hospital, some benefactors and a great many volunteers willing to help extend the labour budget and skills base.

CURRENT CHALLENGES FOR CATHOLIC HOSPITALS

Achievements

My two hospitals are of course fictional, collages of various institutions in several countries and caricatures of different aspects of them. Neither is a description of any actual hospital – though when I first sketched the Mag and St Norbert's in a conference paper in 1997 people from several institutions were convinced I was talking of them. My purpose was to highlight some of the challenges for Catholic identity presented by modern institutionalized medicine and to outline two kinds of response: one has been to offer top-quality healthcare on competitive terms but at some cost to 'Catholic identity'; another maintains religious traditions and particular, often fairly low-tech, forms of care but at the risk of becoming rather marginal. No one should doubt the enormous contribution which both styles of hospital have made over the past century or so and still make today, and the extraordinary self-spending by their staff, especially religious women, almost always without having enjoyed the opportunity of studying theology, philosophy or even 'healthcare ethics'. Many Catholic hospitals have moved in directions that involve elements of both these imaginary hospitals or sometimes different directions altogether, and no one pretends that either is ideal. Both styles are in danger of extinction: why is that?

The Catholic Church is the oldest and largest provider of healthcare in the world. From the time the apostles healed a paralytic at the Beautiful Gate in Jerusalem (Acts 3:1–10), Christians have cared for the sick as part of *hospitality*. St John Chrysostom (d. 407) records that already in his day the sick and the convalescent in Antioch were nursed in Christian hospitals.[1] Monks established hospices and welcomed sick pilgrims and neighbours. In the medieval period there were fraternities and orders of hospitallers. In the early modern and modern periods, many new nursing congregations were founded, and hospitals such as St Mary Magdalene's and St Norbert's evolved as part of an extraordinary network of institutions established largely by religious women and their benefactors.[2] Today there are over 5,000 acute care hospitals, over 15,000 nursing and long-term care centres, over 9,000 orphanages and over 11,000 nurseries operating under Catholic auspices throughout the world. The USCCB *Official Catholic Directory 2008* reports that in the United States alone there were 557 Catholic hospitals, which treated nearly 84 million patients in 2007; there were also 417 other healthcare centres, which treated another 7 million patients, and 1,538 other specialized homes, including many nursing homes, with over 750,000 residents. Together they employed the best part of a million people and spent in excess of $85 billion per annum. The Church has an even bigger proportion of the health and aged care services in some countries, but in others its principal contribution is at the level of nursing home care or basic clinics. This means that the role of a Catholic hospital will vary enormously from community to community, and much of what I say in this chapter would have to be modified to apply, if at all, to some of them.

Overall, the past century and a half has seen a huge growth in the scale and activities of all hospitals, Church ones included, with a parallel growth in public expectations.[3] Catholic hospitals have commonly

[1] *In Mat. Hom.* 66, 3; *Ad Stagyr. Conc.* 3, 13; *In Act. Hom.* 45, 4. On the history of Christian-Catholic healthcare see: J. A. Gómez, 'The care of the sick in the history of the Church', *Dolentium hominum* 31 (1996), 45–7; A. Richardson, 'Compassion and cures: a historical look at Catholicism and medicine', *JAMA* 226(21) (December 1991), 3063.

[2] See Christopher Kauffman, *Ministry and Meaning: A Religious History of Catholic Health Care in the United States* (New York: Crossroad, 1995).

[3] In addition to works cited in this chapter, examples of recent writing on the historical, economic and cultural developments which challenge the identity of Catholic hospitals include: H. Aaron, *Serious and Unstable Condition: Financing America's Healthcare* (Washington, DC: Brookings Institution, 1991); J. Amos et al., *The Search for Identity: Canonical Sponsorship of Catholic Healthcare* (St. Louis: CHA (US), 1993); B. Ashley, 'Does the "Splendour of Truth" shine on bioethics?', *Ethics & Medics* 19(1) (January 1994), 3–4, and 'The documents of Catholic identity', in Russell Smith (ed.), *The Gospel of Life and the Vision of Health Care* (Braintree, MA: Pope John Center, 1996), pp. 10–6; B. Ashley, J. deBlois and K. O'Rourke, *Health Care Ethics: A Catholic Theological Analysis*, 5th edn (Washington, DC: Georgetown University Press, 2006), pp. 227–37; Catholic Health Association of the United States, *No Room in the Marketplace: The Healthcare of the Poor* (St. Louis: CHA (US), 1986), and 'How to approach Catholic identity in changing times', *Health Progress* (April 1994), 23–9; R. Cessario, 'Catholic hospitals in the new

evolved from 'family businesses' into something more like 'franchise operations'.[4] The very Catholic sub-culture in which they were founded has largely vanished, and declining vocations and new priorities have meant their founder congregations no longer lead or staff the hospitals. Day-to-day management has been handed over to lay trustees, administrators and clinical staff with a wide range of perspectives on faith and morals. Relying less and less on the Church and benefactors for finance and increasingly upon patient fees, government grants and private insurers, these institutions have achieved a much greater resource base but at some (often considerable) cost to their financial and administrative independence.

Pressures

In recent decades, escalating healthcare costs have led governments, insurers and hospitals to engage in budget caps, aggressive cost containment, rationalization such as closures and mergers and rationing of services. In some places, the very survival of religious and other charitable hospitals is threatened by such cutbacks and by competition from for-profit hospitals. By the 1980s technology and the free market were increasingly shaping healthcare relationships, as healthcare came to be seen as a high-tech service, supplied for a fee by 'healthcare providers' to 'healthcare consumers' under the direction of 'healthcare managers', rather than as a priceless form of compassionate service between a professional and a patient. 'No margin, no mission' became the catch cry for the not-for-profits.

As a result in the 1990s there was some radical questioning of the goals and usefulness of Catholic hospitals. For instance, towards the end of his life Richard McCormick argued that hospitals must sustain an appropriate culture to be genuinely Catholic; however, that goal, he thought, is deeply compromised today by the depersonalized atmosphere in which medicine is practised, by the trend to viewing it as a mere business and

---

evangelization', *NCBQ* 5(4) (2005), 675–86; O. Griese, *Catholic Identity in Health Care: Principles and Practice* (Braintree, MA: Pope John Center, 1987); D. Guillen, 'The Hippocratic Oath in the development of medicine', *Dolentium hominum* 31 (1996), 22–8; J. B. Hehir, 'Identity and institution', *Health Progress* (December 1995), 17–23; D. Maher, 'Catholic identity in health care', in E. Furton (ed.), *Ethical Principle in Catholic Health Care* (Boston: NCBC, 1999), pp. 9–12; E. Pellegrino, 'Catholic health care ministry and contemporary culture: the growing divide', in E. Furton (ed.), *Urged On by Christ: Catholic Health Care in Tension with Contemporary Culture* (Boston: NCBC), pp. 13–32.

[4] J. Beal, 'Catholic hospitals: how Catholic will they be?', *Concilium 1994–5: Catholic Identity* (1995), 81–90.

by the pressures to 'exit' patients more quickly. That same surrounding culture 'tries to transcend mortality, investing bigtime in sick-care and medicalizing more basic human problems'. Meanwhile some healthcare is moving away from major institutions towards out-patient or community-based care. With respect to their specifically Catholic *raison d'être*, McCormick thought that Catholic hospitals had become 'practically dysfunctional'. His conclusion was unusually gloomy: 'The heart of the Catholic healthcare culture is gone. The mission has become impossible.'[5]

In response to this mission impossible – or, at least, 'mission very difficult' – healthcare providers reorganized into horizontally and vertically integrated systems, becoming part of what Joseph Piccione called a 'healthcare ecosystem' instead of continuing as relatively self-contained, stand-alone institutions.[6] Catholic and secular providers also co-sponsored joint delivery networks or health maintenance organizations in the hope that these could better provide a full spectrum of services while competing for the business of third-party payers and for market share. This survival strategy was not, of course, without its own difficulties. Benedict Ashley and Germain Grisez argued that such arrangements often came at a major moral cost: they required providers to engage in wrongful cooperation in evil, whether formal or material.[7] When such arrangements lead Catholic hospitals to engage in wrongful practices, Ashley and Grisez suggested that this radically erodes their Catholic identity while doing no real service to the poor, sick and dying. They concluded that those responsible for Catholic hospitals must never subordinate their mission

[5] R. McCormick, 'The Catholic hospital: mission impossible?', *Origins* 24(39) (16 March 1995), 648–53; cf. John Cardinal O'Connor, 'The temptation to become just another industry: healthcare', *Origins* 25(27) (21 December 1995), 452–4.
[6] J. Piccione, 'Catholic healthcare: justice, fiscal realities and moral norms', in Smith (ed.), *The Gospel of Life*, pp. 95–108 at 97.
[7] G. Grisez, *The Way of Our Lord Jesus*, vol. III, *Difficult Moral Questions* (Quincy, IL: Franciscan Press, 1997), pp. 391–402, argues that unlike hoteliers, hospital administrators *do* sponsor any immoral healthcare activities that take place in their institution or are carried out by associated providers because they ordinarily intend each and every procedure carried out by the parties or at least that any such procedures, if and when they occur, are performed well and with consent. Even if considerable care is taken to 'isolate' the hospital from the immoral activities of one of its collaborators, the negotiators and subsequent managers will, he thinks, probably intend that those services are indeed provided, if only by the collaborators; such strategies to avoid formal cooperation are often impractical. 'In sum, entirely avoiding formal co-operation in immoral practices will be difficult indeed. It can arise in ways that are not obvious and it seems unavoidable in any arrangement that would satisfy a mandate to provide all services.' Grisez further argues that the material cooperation of Catholic hospitals in the immoral activities of others is often an occasion of formal cooperation, leads others to sin (scandal in the theological sense), impairs the hospital's capacity to give credible witness against evil and/or is unfair to injured parties.

to their (otherwise quite necessary) concerns for economic stability, professional reputation and cultural acceptability. 'When to do good by evil means is the only option our culture and our government seem to allow us, we should create new channels for our service to the poor, remembering the admonition of the Lord: "If they will not hear you, shake the dust from your feet and go elsewhere" (Luke 9:5).'[8] After examining various strategies used in the 1990s to avoid this grave result, Grisez also concluded that if Catholic hospitals cannot remain financially viable without engaging in wrongful cooperation, the Church ought to be prepared to give them up. 'Institutions like hospitals are only means for carrying out a healthcare apostolate. Like other means, their usefulness is limited. Remaining attached to them as their usefulness diminishes will entail infidelity to the good they formerly served.'[9]

The views of McCormick, Ashley and Grisez have been contested by several authors, and ways of maintaining identity and moral integrity proposed, even within integrated delivery networks.[10] Clearly very careful thought must be given to any such arrangements in advance, various procedural safeguards put in place and eternal vigilance exercised by all concerned if a specifically Catholic-Christian character is to be maintained and strengthened.

The Catholic-Christian difference

Is there such a thing as a specifically Christian institutional character? Should Catholic hospitals be different from secular institutions? I suspect

---

[8] B. Ashley, 'The documents of Catholic identity', in Smith, ed., *The Gospel of Life*, pp. 10–16 at 15–16.

[9] Grisez, *Difficult Moral Questions*, p. 401. The US Conference of Catholic Bishops (in *Ethical and Religious Directives for Catholic Health Care Facilities*, 5th edn (Washington, DC: USCCB, 2009), introduction to part 6) though more optimistic, points out that 'new partnerships can pose serious challenges to the viability of the identity of Catholic healthcare institutions and services, and their ability to implement these directives in a consistent way, especially when partnerships are formed with those who do not share Catholic moral principles. The risk of scandal cannot be underestimated when partnerships are not built upon common values and moral principles. Partnership opportunities for some Catholic healthcare providers may even threaten the continued existence of other Catholic institutions and services, particularly when partnerships are driven by financial considerations alone. Because of the potential dangers involved in the new partnerships that are emerging, an increased collaboration among Catholic-sponsored healthcare institutions is essential and should be sought before other forms of partnerships.' Cf. Catholic Health Australia, *Code of Ethical Standards for Catholic Health and Aged Care Services in Australia* (Canberra: CHA, 2001), 7.10–7.15.

[10] M. C. Kaveny and J. Keenan, 'Ethical issues in healthcare restructuring', *Theol Studies* 56(1) (1995), 136–50; K. O'Rourke, 'Making mission possible', *Health Progress* (July–August 1995), 45–7; R. Smith, 'Ethical quandary: forming hospital partnerships', in Smith, *The Gospel of Life*, pp. 109–23.

a resounding 'yes' would be given by almost anyone uneducated in (or uncorrupted by) moral theology. Ever since the Second Vatican Council celebrated a new 'openness to the world' (*LG* 21, 36–7; *GS* 36, 41–6), there has been a heated theological debate over the specificity of Christian ethics. In some ways it replays age-old matches between philosophy and theology, between Catholics and Protestants and between fans and foes of the Enlightenment. Indeed the debate goes back at least to Deuteronomic and prophetic utterance against false gods, their devotees and practices and St Paul's suspicion of the wisdom of this world and his call to put on instead the mind of Christ. This is an ancient quarrel, yet as Servais Pinckaers observes:

> The question has become particularly acute in the discussion of concrete moral problems presented to public opinion in a pluralistic society. Christians have been struggling to establish renewed bases for friendly collaboration with those who do not share their faith. Faced with the difficult problems of contraception, abortion, euthanasia [and so on] … may Christians follow their own lights, norms, and criteria implying special standards, or should they remain on the same level with others and form their judgments according to merely rational criteria, with the help of philosophy and the behavioural sciences? If the second alternative were preferable, could they go still further and reinterpret Christian morality in its entirety according to purely human values?[11]

In the 1970s and early 1980s this debate took the form of the impasse between those who proposed an 'autonomous ethics' common to people with and without faith and those who proposed a 'faith ethic' particular to Christians. Influential authors such as Josef Fuchs argued that Christian ethics is 'a morality of authentic humanness' and that its values are 'not specifically Christian values but universal, human ones'.[12] As Charles Curran concluded in his review of the literature on Catholic institutional identity: 'what Catholics are obliged to do in this world is at the very least not that much different from what all others are called to do'.[13] A Catholic hospital in a pluralist society would thus aim to be the humanly best hospital, demonstrating the greatest respect for human dignity, life and health, and the technically best hospital, demonstrating the highest standards of rescue, healing and care.

[11] S. Pinckaers, *The Sources of Christian Ethics* (Washington, DC: Catholic University of America Press, 1995), p. 98.
[12] See Fuchs and others in C. Curran and R. McCormick (eds.), *The Distinctiveness of Christian Ethics* (New York: Paulist, 1980).
[13] C. Curran, 'The Catholic identity of Catholic institutions', *Theol Studies* 58 (1997), 90–108 at 92.

Where, we might ask, is Christ in all this? In Chapter 1 I outlined at length the move of several contemporary theologians and pastors to recover what is distinctively Christian and Catholic in ethics. They suggest that Christian faith makes special demands upon the disciple; it subverts mere human reasoning in ethics, often puts believers in a position *contra mundum*, and so Catholic institutions must offer a pluralist society something rather different. Cardinal Kasper suggests that the autonomy of secular disciplines and affairs proposed anew by the Second Vatican Council has been commonly misread as reducing the field of the specifically religious to certain spiritual tasks (such as worship, narrowly defined) and to the Church's internal problems. As a result there has been an 'over-adaptation' of Christian morality 'whether to secularized bourgeois civilization or to revolutionary liberation movements'. Kasper asks whether *Christianity* cannot make some particular contribution to the transformation of our life and our world?[14]

While it is true to say that the sublime teaching and example of Christ adds to the clarity of believers, and that the Gospel's transcendent hope and love adds to their motivation, Catholic identity requires more than this. Because revelation affects the whole way we understand God, our fellows, the world and ourselves, it will colour the application even of 'natural' principles of morality and offer some 'supernatural' norms as well. While Christian faith does not annul or contradict natural law and virtue, it inwardly transforms Christ's disciples and calls them to be what they can be and to do what they can do by virtue not only of being human (and therefore free, reasoning and loving) but also because they are children of God (and therefore graced with Word and sacraments, magisterium and ecclesial community). How else could we make sense of the consecrated celibacy, the total self-giving, the particular priorities and the way of relating to patients demonstrated by the sisters of St Mary Magdalene's or St Norbert's down the years? Any description of their vocation as merely one more 'mode of authentic humanness' seems rather to limp. Like other institutional apostolates and activities of Christians, a Catholic hospital might be expected to have much in common with others but also much that is different.

The Second Vatican Council described the Church as a sacrament – a sign and instrument of our union with God (*LG* 1, 9, 48; *GS* 42, 45). In his encyclical *Deus caritas est* Pope Benedict XVI says that 'The Church's deepest nature is expressed in her threefold responsibility: of proclaiming

---

[14] W. Kasper, *Faith and the Future*, trans. R. Nowell (London: Burns and Oates, 1985), p. 86.

the word of God (*kerygma-martyria*), celebrating the sacraments (*leitour-gia*), and exercising the ministry of charity (*diakonia*). These duties pre-suppose each other and are inseparable.'[15] In so far as healthcare ministry is an expression of this broadly sacramental character of the Church,[16] Catholic hospitals should be signs and instruments of union with God effected by service of the sick, witness given to Gospel truth and wor-ship offered in prayer and pastoral care. In what remains of this chapter I will explore what these three 'sacramental' aspects of healthcare might say about the distinctive role of the Catholic hospital in a pluralist society.

CATHOLIC HOSPITALS AS *DIAKONIA*

Preferential option for the poor and marginalized

The Old Testament is replete with references to God's siding with the disadvantaged and the requirements of justice towards them. The Torah requires special provision to be made for the poor, the weak and the out-cast and for widows, orphans and refugees (e.g. Exod. 22:25–27; 23:6, 10–11; Lev. 19:10; 23:22; Deut. 24:14–15, 19–22). 'Since the poor will always be with you', says the Lord, 'I command you to open wide your hand to the poor and needy' (Deut. 15:11). When Israel fails in this regard God rages in the prophet's voice: 'What do you mean by crushing my people, by grinding the face of the poor?', says the Lord of Hosts (Isa. 3:15; cf. 10:1–2; 11:4; 14:30; 25:4–6; 32: 7; 58:3–7; Jer. 2:34; Amos 2:6–8; 4:1–2; 5:11; 8:4–6; Zech. 7:10). In his programmatic reading from the same prophet at the beginning of his ministry, Jesus declares himself anointed to bring good news to the poor (Luke 4:17), and later in the same Gospel he beati-fies them (Luke 6:20; cf. 14:13–23; 16:19–31; 19:8).

Much has been written in recent decades, not least by Pope Benedict XVI, about the Church's preferential love for the poor and the marginalized,[17] which has a long history in Christian social teaching and practice, especially in institutional apostolates such as hostels, orphan-ages, schools and soup kitchens. This same inspiration was behind the

---

[15] Benedict XVI, *Deus Caritas Est: Encyclical Letter on Christian Love* (2005) 25; cf. Kasper, *Faith and the Future*, p. 95.

[16] J. Curley, 'Catholic identity, Catholic integrity', *Health Progress* (October 1991), 56–69 at 57.

[17] For example, Benedict XVI, *Deus Caritas*, and *Caritas in Veritate: Encyclical Letter on Integral Human Development in Charity and Truth* (2009); see also John Paul II, *Sollicitudo Rei Socialis: Encyclical Letter on Social Concerns* (1987) and *Centesimus Annus: Encyclical Letter on the Centenary of 'Rerum novarum'* (1991); Pontifical Council for Justice and Peace, *Compendium of the Social Doctrine of the Church* (2004).

foundation of hospitals like St Mary Magdalene's and St Norbert's. One of the principal reasons given by Church leaders and agencies for the Church's continued commitment to hospitals is that Catholic institutions pay particular attention to the needs of the sick poor. This is perhaps most obvious in those countries where universal access to healthcare is yet to be achieved, but even in places where such access is more or less guaranteed, there will be those who 'slip through the safety net', and there will be pressures to limit some people's access even to reasonable care, whether out of partiality, cost containment or other reasons. 'Charity' hospitals will always have their place.

The preferential option for the sick and the disabled

In the Old Testament God's preferential care is not reserved to the financially poor but to a larger group of those disadvantaged in various ways. Thus the prophet Ezekiel rails against the pastors of Israel: 'You eat the fat, you clothe yourselves with wool … but you do not feed the sheep. You have not strengthened the weak, you have not healed the sick, you have not bound up the injured, you have not brought back the strayed' (Ezek. 34:1–6) The Psalmist and the prophets respond, as it were, with the promise that the Lord God himself will 'gather the outcasts of Israel, heal the broken-hearted and bind up all their wounds' (Ps. 147:2–3).

This divine physician came among us in Jesus Christ – and heal he did, serving people not only by preaching and absolving but also by curing them. He restored sight to the blind (Mark 8:22–26; 10:46–52; Matt. 20:29–34), hearing to the deaf (Mark 7:32–37; Matt. 11:5) and speech to the mute (Matt. 9:32–3; 12:22; Luke 11:14). He cured the woman with a haemorrhage (Mark 5:25–34), lepers (Mark 1:40–45; Luke 17:12–19), the paralyzed and lame (Mark 2:3–12; Matt. 8:6–13; 21:14; John 5:3–8). He even restored the dead to life (Mark 5:35–43; Luke 7:12–17; John 11; cf. Mark 9:17–29). In Mark's Gospel, Jesus is very much the exorcist-healer. Luke records Jesus' declaration that he had been anointed not only to bring good news to the poor but also sight to the blind (Luke 4:17) and that he later compared himself with a physician of bodies and souls and (via the parable of the Good Samaritan) to a nurse of a man mugged and left for dead (Luke 5:31; 7:22–23; 10:29–37). Luke sums up his many cures: 'Now when the sun was setting, all those who had any sick with various diseases brought them to him; and he laid his hands on them and healed them' (Luke 4:40; cf. 6:17–19). Likewise Matthew tells us: 'Great crowds came to him, bringing with them the lame, the maimed, the blind, the mute, and many others. They put them at his feet, and he cured them, so that the crowd was amazed when they saw the mute speaking, the maimed whole, the lame walking, and the blind seeing. And they praised the God of Israel' (Matt. 15:30–31; cf. 9:35; Mark 7:37). Indeed so replete was his life with cures of every kind that Matthew interpreted Jesus' mission as the fulfilment of the prophecy of Isaiah: 'He took away our infirmities and bore our diseases' (Matt. 8:17; cf. Isa. 53:4).

Why have Christians always engaged in healthcare and institutionalized it? The most obvious reason is to restore people to health, which is self-evidently choice-worthy. By providing hospitals and other services the Church has made many people well and cared for them while unwell, reflecting respect for human dignity, active compassion in suffering and service of the common good. There is, however, more to it than this: Jesus told his disciples *to continue his own healing mission*: he commanded them to 'heal the sick, raise the dead, cleanse lepers' (Matt. 10:8) and to embrace the likes of these sick people as part of the kingdom (Luke 14:12–14). In all their tasks he promised them his divine assistance: 'Truly, truly, I say to you, whoever believes in me will also do the works that I do; and even greater works than these will that one do' (John 14:12; cf. Luke 10:17–20). This the disciples set about doing even before Christ's Resurrection and very regularly after it (e.g. Mark 6:7–13; Acts 3:1–10; 5:12–16; 8:5–8; 28:7–9). Thus, in serving the sick, Christians claim to be engaging not merely in a job but an 'apostolate', 'ministry' or holy service, mediating the healing compassion of God to a broken world, serving the suffering Christ in their patients.[18] Even if much of what a Catholic hospital does is very similar to what occurs in other hospitals, the commitment of sponsors, administrators and personnel to healthcare as *diakonia* to the poor and sick should colour its whole life. Embracing the whole person – body, mind and spirit – with compassion, Catholic hospitals say to the sick, infirm and all those in need of healthcare: 'As Christ would reach out to touch and heal you, so too do we.'[19]

Preferential option for the suffering and the dying

A third group to whom the Christian tradition directs preferential love and care is the suffering and the dying. Even as he was dying himself,

---

[18] For example, Pontifical Council for Health, *Charter for Healthworkers* (1994; English trans. 1995) 4–5.

[19] Administrative Committee of the National Conference of Catholic Bishops, *The Bishops' Pastoral Role in Catholic Healthcare Ministry* (Washington, DC: NCCB, 1997).

Christ showed his care for a dying thief, as for his Blessed Mother and the Beloved Disciple, for the women of Jerusalem and even for his captors (Luke 23:27–31, 34, 42–43; John 19:26–27). The task of healthcare is to care even when it cannot cure. Christians have been at the forefront of the hospice movement, in specialized care for the suffering and the dying, including but not limited to the increasingly effective science of pain management. As the US bishops suggested:

Christ's redemptive and saving grace embraces the whole person, especially in his or her illness, suffering and death. Catholic healthcare ministry faces the reality of death with the confidence of faith. In the face of death – for many, a time when hope seems lost – the Church witnesses to her belief that God has created each person for eternal life. Above all, as a witness to its faith, a Catholic healthcare institution will be a community of respect, love and support to patients or residents and their families as they face the reality of death.[20]

The task of caring well for the terminally ill is especially challenging in a world increasingly inclined to discrimination, abandonment, even homicide of the frail elderly and dying, in the guise of efficiency or mercy. As John Paul II proposed, we must try to rebuild the 'covenant between the generations' so that the elderly and the dying can trust that they will be treated with *pietas*, reverence and genuine compassion, even unto death (*EV* 94).

No one should underestimate the difficulty of this task. The late Cardinal John O'Connor of New York related a disturbing example:

Our own Calvary hospital is considered, I believe, by professional observers to be one of the very finest hospitals in the US for those who are currently ill with cancer, from a human perspective incurable. Until not too many years ago, patients referred to Calvary from acute-care hospitals had an average length of stay of approximately six weeks. They lived for those six weeks in great comfort and in love, given tender, gentle care by incredibly warm and dedicated doctors and nurses, administrators and staff. Now, because of various new wonder drugs, patients may live six months or longer in the same loving and virtually pain-free environment, with added time to prepare both materially and spiritually for the death they know is coming, often strengthening bonds with their families, finding peace at the end. I have never known a relative or friend of a Calvary patient who has not been deeply grateful for the extraordinary care given their loved ones. Some time back, however, the storm clouds gathered. A major insurance carrier, I am told, called the leadership of Calvary hospital to say: 'You are keeping your patients alive too long. If you continue to do this, we will discontinue your insurance.'[21]

---

[20] USCCB, *Ethical and Religious Directives*, introduction to part 5; CHA, *Code*, 7.
[21] O'Connor, 'The temptation', p. 453.

As O'Connor noted, that sort of thing has 'a chilling effect' on 'people trying to do good'.

Against such opposition, institutional and communal support is crucial. Resources are not all that are at issue here. Stanley Hauerwas argues that in the face of the grave demands put upon healthcarers today – to rescue, to respond to pain and sickness, to engage in the 'hard slog' of caring for chronic and dying patients, to give of self not just with great physical energy and technical skill but from the heart – something very much like a *church* is necessary. Human sympathy and high ideals, important as they are, will not, he thinks, be sufficient to sustain such care. Nor will the technical, ethical and people skills required for this kind of care simply come 'naturally': they must be acquired in a community of care. 'Medicine needs the church not to supply a foundation for its moral commitments, but rather as a resource of the habits and practices necessary to sustain the care of those in pain over the long haul.'[22]

Fundamental, then, to what Catholic hospitals offer a pluralist society is the alternative of healthcare institutions committed to a preference for the poor and marginalized, the sick and disabled, the suffering and dying. How such vulnerable persons are treated is a litmus test for any civilization.

CATHOLIC HOSPITALS AS *MARTYRIA*

Healing as evangelization

The widening rift between secular and religious thought – described in Chapter 1 – is apparent not only in academic theology but also in the lived theology of institutions such as hospitals. Religious assumptions and categories still play a large part in medical and nursing practice, form the backdrop to any secular alternatives and have a distinctive wisdom to offer. However, Catholic hospitals must re-establish that they 'have something to say', so to speak, that they have an approach to healthcare worthy of being a competitor in the market of ideas, a rival not just for resources but for people's commitment, in short for their souls. If we *over-adapt* Christian morality to secularized bourgeois civilization – as Kasper put it – we may be selling our birthright for 'a mess of pottage'

---

[22] S. Hauerwas, 'Salvation and health: why medicine needs the Church', in E. Shelp (ed.), *Theology and Bioethics: Exploring the Foundations and Frontiers* (Dordrecht: Reidel, 1985), pp. 205–24 at 222.

(Gen. 25:29–34; Heb. 12:16). Social acceptability, real or imagined, may cost us our values, even our souls. Are we really the movers and shakers we imagine we are or are small apparent victories such as external funding for some Catholic hospitals tolerated only as long as this serves an ultimately very different, non-Christian agenda? Is that agenda hidden from our eyes or have we become blinded to it by consorting for so long with those who set it? Without courting unpopularity, should a prophetic people not expect sometimes to be at odds with a healthcare world that does not always share its faith and morals?[23]

If Catholic hospitals enable *diakonia* to large numbers of people, especially the poor, sick and dying, they also allow such holy service to be integrated with the proclamation of the Gospel. 'Jesus', in Matthew's gospel, 'went about Galilee, teaching in the synagogues, preaching the gospel of the kingdom, and healing every disease and infirmity among the people' (Matt. 4:23; 9:35). Sometimes the healings preceded and evoked faith; at other times the cure was a response to faith. When the leper was cured it was 'as a testimony [*marturion*] to them' (8:4), and when the blind, the mute and even the dead were healed, it evoked human and religious awe among the people (9:26–33). On the other hand, when the centurion's servant was saved, the woman with a haemorrhage cured and other blind men restored to sight, it was in response to faith and the prayer of faith (8:5–13; 9:20–30). Thus Jesus' *diakonia* and *martyria* were intimately related. The linking of these two ministries is extended to his disciples: 'As you go', he tells them, 'proclaim the good news that the kingdom of heaven is at hand. Heal the sick, raise the dead, cleanse lepers, cast out demons' (10:7–8). Whether for Jesus or for his disciples, healing and preaching are, as it were, two sides of the same redemptive coin.

Witnessing to what?

Catholic healthcare, then, must be not only *diakonia* but also *martyria*, a lived proclamation of the Gospel. John Paul II described healthworkers as '*servants* and guardians of life, *witnesses* to the Church's presence alongside sick and suffering people'.[24] Leaders and staff must therefore have a genuine appreciation not merely of some ethical rule book but of the

---

[23] Sectarianism, too, has its own temptations. How comforting it might be to retire to the relative safety of a Catholic ghetto on the margins of political and social life, sneering at outsiders as damned or invincibly ignorant. However, such sectarianism involves the abandonment of any attempt to be the leaven in the loaf, to evangelize all nations and be the servants of all.

[24] John Paul II, *Message for the Fifth World Day of the Sick*, 11 February 1997, 7.

fundamental commitments of their institution as one that (a) is heir to the Hippocratic and Catholic traditions, the charism of the founders and the teachings of the Church; (b) has certain financial resources and, above all, certain human and spiritual gifts; and (c) has particular opportunities to serve the surrounding community and beyond. In the face of pressures of secularism, bureaucracy and the market and the perennial temptation to 'jump into bed with the *Zeitgeist*', the Church since the 1990s has been sounding a state of ethical alert, calling on Catholic hospitals to regain their sense of identity and fight back. Central commitments will include: respect for the dignity of every human person as made in the image of God; reverence for life from conception to death as a sacred trust; love of neighbour and a concern for the common good, including universal access to a reasonable level of care and the just allocation of resources; a desire to humanize medical practice; and a preferential option for the disadvantaged.[25]

Catholic hospitals give *martyria* to the Gospel the more consistently and luminously they exemplify Christian morality; they obscure and ultimately abandon their *raison d'être*, the muter and more compromised becomes their moral witness. Stanley Reiser identifies several cases of 'ethical bifurcation' now commonplace in hospitals.[26] First, major differences between the goals of the founder-sponsors and those of the current administrators and staff. Second, the growing chasm between the traditional professional ethic of healthworkers and the new bureaucratic-commercial mindset of health administrators. Third, inconsistencies between official ethical commitments and the array of organizational policies never subjected to explicit ethical analysis. Fourth, the gap between official rhetoric and actual practice.

Catholic hospitals must be especially aware of the scandal, both in the theological and the ordinary senses, that some actions occasion, whether engaged in by the institution or particular staff, whether alone

[25] For example, Administrative Committee of the National Conference of Catholic Bishops, *Bishops' Pastoral Role*; Joseph Cardinal Bernardin, 'Crossroads for the Church's health care ministry', *Origins* 22(24) (26 November 1992), 409–11, and 'AMA address: medicine's moral crisis', *Origins* 25(27) (21 December 1995), 454–7; CDF, *On Certain Bioethical Questions* (2008), and *On Respect for Human Life and Procreation* (1987) ii, B, 7; CHA, *Code*; John Paul II, *EV* 27, 74 and 87–90; O'Connor, 'The temptation'; Paul VI, *HV* 27; Pontifical Council for Health, *Charter for Healthworkers*; USCCB, *Ethical and Religious Directives*. See also K. O'Rourke and P. Boyle (eds.), *Medical Ethics: Sources of Catholic Teachings*, 3rd edn (Washington, DC: Georgetown University Press, 1999).
[26] S. Reiser, 'The ethical life of healthcare organizations', *Hastings Center Report* 24(6) (November–December 1994), 28–35.

or with other providers, and either with or without official permission.[27] Practitioners, managers and ethicists who use theology or ethics as vehicles to accommodate dubious practices rather than as a standard against which they should be judged do no service to the Gospel, their patients or their profession. Benedict Ashley suggests that some Catholic hospitals have wrongfully cooperated in

intrinsically evil means, as these have been defined by magisterial instructions, some of which are common practices in today's culture (abortion, contraception, sterilization, reproduction in the laboratory, and euthanasia), on the mistaken view that these are pragmatically necessary ways of promoting human health. The various efforts to justify these intrinsically evil practices in hardship cases or by wrong application of the notion of material co-operation under duress has already gone far to erode Catholic identity in our healthcare facilities and medical education ... When seeming conflicts arise between the concern for the poor, [the sick and the dying] and the ethical limitations on the means that can be used, Catholics should remember that it is no real service to the poor to help them abort, contracept, sterilize themselves, or commit suicide.[28]

Faithful witness requires vigilance on the part of sponsors and administrators to ensure not only that nothing unethical occurs in the hospital but also, more positively, that its whole approach accords with the core commitments and values of the hospital. In recent years Church leaders have repeatedly recommitted the Church to the healthcare ministry but only if it enacts Catholic morality as articulated by the Church's magisterium. The US bishops, for instance, have ordered that all Catholic healthcare services in that country adopt their published directives as *policy*, 'require adherence to them within the institution as a condition for medical privileges and employment, and provide appropriate instruction

---

[27] J. Provost, 'Approaches to Catholic identity in Church law', *Concilium 1994–5: Catholic Identity* (1995), 15–25, argues that any institution that works at cross purposes to those of the official Church 'lacks the very inner reality to be considered "Catholic", whatever its formal title'. Grisez, *Difficult Moral Questions*, pp. 399–400, suggests that the compromised witness and scandal given by some Catholic hospitals may not only lead people into sin but mean that some individuals die or otherwise suffer in ways that might have been prevented 'if those who profess the sacredness of life and the dignity of persons consistently avoided complicity in wrongful behaviour. Accepting these bad consequences is likely to be unfair unless the victims themselves freely consent to what they suffer.'

[28] Ashley, 'The documents of Catholic identity', pp. 15–16. Likewise Piccione, 'Catholic healthcare', p. 101: 'The instinct of the Catholic provider is to serve the poor, yet our concern to meet the needs of the underserved cannot exclude Catholic moral norms, otherwise we would formally co-operate with, or even do, evil for the sake of other goods. The charitable instinct is not served by performing services that are not truly charitable, denying the dignity of the human person, marriage, or life itself. Catholic healthcare cannot provide morally objectionable services as if healthcare were simply a commodity, driven by market needs or state mandate.'

regarding the directives for administration, medical and nursing staff and other personnel'.[29]

Apart from giving the example of Catholic moral teaching in action, Catholic hospitals can also be appropriate places for more overt evangelization. Catholic teaching hospitals should never be merely providers of 'value-free' technology and art: rather, they offer in a pluralist society the real alternative of a training in full accord with a particular tradition. We should not shy away from this for fear of losing funding, patients, staff, students or respectability. Indeed, I suspect that it is precisely as a high-quality *alternative* to the run-of-the-mill that Catholic hospitals will best be able to justify continued tolerance and support of funding bodies and regulators. Unashamedly Catholic codes of ethics and practice, ethics committees, staff education programmes and so forth will not only help ensure that the hospital fulfils its primary mission of providing sound care but will also offer it a 'market niche'.[30] This will have its attractions not only for many patients but also for many staff. It is already the case in some countries that trainees and practitioners in certain specialties such as ob-gyn, family planning, genetics, paediatrics, geriatrics and intensive care, are pressured to conform to immoral practices and are even refused positions if they will not. Without Catholic hospitals in which to train and work, some healthworkers might either compromise their consciences and objective morality or have to quit their speciality. In such a world Catholic hospitals offer not only a place for a distinctively Christian healthcare vocation but also a refuge for those still committed to genuinely Hippocratic medicine.

In fact both staff and patients are appropriate targets of evangelization. This should not involve 'forcing the Gospel down people's necks' or exploiting the vulnerability of the sick and the employed. A simple word of encouragement or explanation, coming from hospital staff, may well be the occasion of enlightenment and even perhaps a deeper conversion. Staff induction and ongoing professional development will naturally include discussion of ethos, ethics and faith.

Another respect in which Catholic hospitals can give *martyria* to the faith is in advocacy of Christian values to the wider society. Large institutions often have a voice that individuals and smaller groups do not.[31]

[29] USCCB, *Ethical and Religious Directives*, p. 5.
[30] Pontifical Council for Health, *Charter for Healthworkers* 8.
[31] T. Murphy, 'What is the bottom line in Catholic healthcare?', *Origins* 26(4) (13 June 1996), 56–60 at 58; F. Sullivan, 'Dreaming the impossible dream', *Australasian Catholic Record* 73(2) (1996), 131–5 at 135.

In *Evangelium Vitae* John Paul II exhorted healthcare institutions to take every opportunity to make 'impassioned and unflinching affirmations' of the sacredness and inviolability of every human life (87–9). In a world where recourse to medical homicide is increasingly common, Catholic hospitals must represent a stark contrast and help to unmask the ideologies which banalize such killing. Among the latter identified in the encyclical are: individualism, materialism, consumerism, hedonism, Prometheanism, pragmatism and ethical scepticism, all of which contribute to what John Paul II immortally labelled 'the idolatry of the market' and 'the culture of death' (*EV* 12). Testimony to higher values, to better ways of relating and to the culture of the Kingdom is crucial to the distinctive role of the Catholic hospital in a pluralist society.

More than rules of the Catholic club

Catholic hospitals must address themselves not only to promoting fidelity to norms but also to cultivating certain kinds of character. Among staff these include: respectfulness, *pietas*, compassion, understanding, benevolence, spontaneity, honesty, fidelity, thoroughness, patience, humility – virtues exemplified in the Good Samaritan. Among patients they include virtues such as patience, courage, moderation in expectations and hope.[32] Leaders and staff of Catholic hospitals should be especially wary of the institutionalization of vices such as cavalier disrespect for persons, indifference to the effects of policy on particular groups of people, avarice for market share or particular specialties, ageism and the technological imperative. They will promote a certain asceticism in response to the drive to medical maximization and a certain reflectiveness in response to the busyness of the average hospital.

All in all, Catholic hospitals must not allow the scope of their moral concerns to be narrowed to the stereotypical 'Catholic club rules' against contraception, sterilization, abortion, IVF and euthanasia – important as those are in themselves and as litmus tests for professionalism and for the Catholicity of the institution. Rather, Catholic hospitals should see as one

[32] See R. Cessario, 'From casuistry to virtue ethics', *Ethics & Medics* (October 1994), 1–2; A. Di Noia, 'The virtues of the Good Samaritan: healthcare ethics in the perspective of a renewed moral theology', *Dolentium hominum* 31 (1996), 211–14; G. Meilaender, 'Are there virtues inherent in a profession?', in E. Pellegrino, R. Veatch and J. P. Langan (eds.), *Ethics, Trust, and the Professions* (Washington, DC: Georgetown University Press, 1991), pp. 139–55; E. Pellegrino, 'Toward a virtue-based normative ethics for the health professions', *Kennedy Institute of Ethics Journal* 5 (1995), 253–77; E. Pellegrino and D. Thomasma, *The Virtues in Medical Practice* (Oxford University Press, 1993).

of their fundamental purposes a conversion of patients and health professionals, community and culture – spiritual heart transplants to match the physical, health of soul paralleling health of body, the goal of eternal life beyond any extension of earthly life.

CATHOLIC HOSPITALS AS *LEITOURGIA*

Dulia without idolatry

Just as Jesus' healing miracles at once expressed the healing compassion of God and provided foretastes of the coming of God's Kingdom, so Catholic hospitals 'see their ministry not only as an effort to restore and preserve health but also as a spiritual service and a sign of that final healing, which will one day bring about the new creation that is the ultimate fruit of Jesus' ministry and God's love for us'.[33] The life of Catholic hospitals should thus testify to more than just Christian morality, even richly understood. Christian beliefs about a loving, provident God, about creation and anthropology, about sickness and death, the communion of saints, the forgiveness of sins, the resurrection of the body and life everlasting: all these should inform and be proclaimed by Christian healthcare.

Of course, Christians have no monopoly on beliefs such as the dignity of the human person, the importance of community or values such as care and respect. Yet their faith means that they see the person as much more than an autonomous agent, a locus of rational preferences or the like: the human person is the image of God, and the human community can be an image of the Trinity. We are, therefore, brothers and sisters in the Lord and we are our brothers' and sisters' keepers; 'care and respect' are words too lame to describe that sacred relationship and trust. Reverence, wonder, what St Thomas called *dulia*,[34] should mark our relating. How that is realized in the particulars of day-to-day hospital care is not easy to identify: perhaps it manifests in the courtesy and compassion, the patience, perseverance and hopefulness, the willingness to engage in apparent inefficiencies such as listening, a reverential language and touch not unlike the way we treat the holy things.

Catholic hospitals might, on this basis, be said to engage in a kind of liturgical drama as they invoke the presence of God, retell the sacred stories, apply revelation to daily life, proclaim their creed, intercede for

---

[33] USCCB, *Ethical and Religious Directives*, Conclusion.
[34] *ST* IIa IIae 25, i; 103–9; IIIa 25, ii.

the sick and dying, deliver God's healing mercy, stand in wonder before the mysteries of birth, suffering and death, celebrate the sacredness of life and recall the promise of a life beyond. Words such as 'vocation', 'mission' and 'apostolate', which roll so easily off the Christian tongue, must mean more than 'job' or even 'profession' here: they must bespeak a kind of 'liturgical' ministry of mediating and praising the God who is the lover of life and health (Wisd. 11:26).[35]

If Catholic healthcare is so high a calling, those charged with it must be wary of secularization and compromise, and wary too when medicine exceeds its legitimate sphere, colonizing the whole of reality, promising to solve every human problem, offering false hopes of earthly immortality, engaging in therapeutic overkill, making death part of the medical armoury or pretending that health is salvation. Like the anathemas against witch-doctors in the Old Testament (Lev. 20:27; Deut. 18:10–14; 1 Chr. 10:13–14; cf. Acts 13:6–12) and potion dealers in the New (Gal. 5:20; Rev. 9:21; 21:8; 22:15), worshippers of true religion must always be ready critics of healthcare messianism and medical idolatry. Whatever the values of Hippocratic medicine, we do not swear by Asclepius, Hygienia, Panacea or even Apollo the Great Physician.[36]

Pastoral care

Jesus healed whole persons, body and soul. When he cured the paralytic he first forgave him his sins (Luke 5:17–26; cf. Mark 2:1–12). The links between physical and spiritual sickness, and between physical and spiritual healing, have long been appreciated by Christians and other believers. Yet already by Aquinas' time different monks dispensed the medicaments and the absolutions. Aquinas recognized the connection, however, when he compared the duty of the sinner not to delay seeking a priest for confession with the duty of a sick man not to delay sending for a physician.[37] As the US bishops observed, 'without health of the spirit, high technology focused strictly on the body offers limited hope for healing the whole person. Directed to spiritual needs that are often appreciated more

---

[35] B. Honings, 'The Charter for Healthcare Workers: a synthesis of Hippocratic ethics and Christian morality', *Dolentium hominum* 31 (1996), 48–52 at 49.
[36] See M. Lütz, 'The religion of health and the new view of the human being', in E. Sgreccia and I. Carrasco de Paula (eds.), *Quality of Life and the Ethics of Health* (Libreria Editrice Vaticana, 2006), pp. 128–35.
[37] *ST* Supp. 6, v, ad 2.

deeply during times of illness, pastoral care is an integral part of Catholic healthcare.'[38]

A strong, well-prepared pastoral care team is clearly desirable in any large hospital. *Catholic* pastoral care to the sick is, of course, different from social work, counselling and other human supports, even if it includes elements of these things: it is first and foremost about the sacraments. Priests, supported by pastoral teams and cooperative clinical staff, must be ready to engage with people at some of the most vulnerable and receptive moments of their lives with the sacraments of God's love. Ever since St James counselled that the presbyters be called to pray over, anoint and absolve the sick (Jas. 5:14–15), Church leaders have properly been solicitous to ensure that the sick and dying have access to the sacraments.[39] The sacrament of Anointing of the Sick is obviously central here, but this ministry also includes: Baptism, Confirmation and/or reception into the Church for those in danger of death; sacramental Confession, with the apostolic pardon for the dying; the Eucharist and Holy Communion, especially viaticum for the dying; regular opportunities for communal prayer and worship both for patients and staff; blessings, sacramentals, religious art and devotions of various kinds, perhaps most fittingly crucifixes and the stations of the cross. Obviously such spiritual care, like the rest of hospital care, will have to be tailored to the particular needs of the patients: non-Christians, non-Catholics, non-practising Catholics and more 'regular' Catholics will have rather different needs. Few non-Catholics will be offended, though, by encountering something spiritually distinctive in a Catholic hospital, and we ought not to be afraid of 'showing our true colours'.

In addition to the sacraments, pastoral care of the sick 'encompasses the full range of spiritual services, including a listening presence, help in dealing with powerlessness, pain and alienation, and assistance in recognizing and responding to God's will with greater joy and peace'.[40] The goal here is to confirm brothers and sisters in the Lord so that they may live, suffer and die well. Seeking to humanize and Christianize sickness, dying and healthcare itself, and offering cause for hope even when medicine can do no more, are crucial ways in which pastoral care complements clinical care. As Hauerwas has observed:

---

[38] USCCB, *Ethical and Religious Directives*, introduction to part 2; cf. CHA, *Code* 1, 2.
[39] For example, CHA, *Code* 11, 7.16–7.17; *CIC* 998ff.; Pontifical Council for Health, *Charter for Healthworkers* 108–13; USCCB, *Ethical and Religious Directives*, pp. 12–20.
[40] USCCB, *Ethical and Religious Directives*, introduction to part 2.

No matter how powerful [medicine] becomes, it cannot in principle rule out the necessity of prayer. For prayer is not a supplement to the insufficiency of our medical knowledge and practice; nor is it some divine insurance policy that our medical skill will work; rather, our prayer is the means that we have to make God present whether our medical skill is successful or not. So understood, the issue is not whether medical care and prayer are antithetical, but how medical care can ever be sustained without continued prayer.[41]

Of course, much of all this can be done by pastoral workers who are part of or visit secular hospitals. In a Catholic hospital what should be different is that *leitourgia* is central to people's understanding of patient care and staff support, not merely 'icing on the cake'.

CONCLUSION: SIX TASKS FOR A NEW CENTURY

Richard McCormick observed:

Catholic hospitals have beautiful mission statements. We read references to continuing the health mission of Jesus ... caring services for each individual, personalised patient care, the holistic approach which weds competence and compassion ... [and] the option for the poor ... [Yet] everywhere I go I see Catholics involved in healthcare doubtful, perplexed, wondering whether they are viable, whether they ought to be in healthcare, asking about their identity, how they differ from non-Catholic institutions. There is a great deal of institutional navel-gazing ... [about] rediscovering or re-creating mission in changing circumstances. In sum, there is a gap between institutional purpose and aim, and personal conviction and involvement.[42]

Various responses to these challenges have been proposed and attempted. Sponsorship, mission and vision statements, mission effectiveness programmes and ethics committees have been in the forefront of strategies to maintain Catholic identity.[43] Far more crucial, in my view, are six matters.

First, like individuals discerning their personal vocations or reassessing their commitments, the sponsors of Catholic hospitals must consider seriously the materially and morally available options, neither engaging in a simple maintenance operation nor abandoning the trust received from

---

[41] Hauerwas, 'Salvation and health', p. 81.
[42] McCormick, 'The Catholic hospital: mission impossible?', p. 648.
[43] Developed through institution-wide discourse and revised periodically, these documents and programmes are supposed to articulate the traditions, values and no-go areas for the hospital community, clarifying what the institution stands for, instructing members about their goals and responsibilities and eliciting commitment-in-action; mission officers and ethicists are charged with promoting understanding and living of these. Cf. Reiser, 'The ethical life', pp. 33–5.

their predecessors and the Church today. They must, for instance, ask themselves: what healthcare and other needs are now unmet and likely to remain unmet by others? Are we more ready, willing and able to meet some of those needs than others? If Catholic healthcare *is* thought still to be worthwhile and possible, there must be a conscious reappropriation of the distinctively Christian and Catholic in healthcare.

Second, with this in view, a 'critical mass' of strategically located care-givers, administrators and policymakers, practising their Catholic faith and dedicated to the hospital's mission and values must be selected, trained and appropriately supported. There must be no 'ethical bifurca-tion' between the goals of the Church and religious sponsors and those of the current administrators and staff.

Third, there must be far greater cooperation within the Catholic (and any other Christian) healthcare sector, moving perhaps towards providing integrated delivery networks or towards less comprehensive alliances.[44]

Fourth, if Catholic hospitals are to survive and thrive, this will require considerable astuteness on the part of sponsors and managers so that they can respond effectively to the political and financial pressures of the con-temporary healthcare 'ecosystem' in ways that promote rather than com-promise mission and ethics.[45]

Fifth, organizational policies, the stances of ethics advisers and com-mittees, and especially clinical, nursing and administrative practice, must be assessed (and, if needs be, revised) against any approved mission, vision and ethics statements of the institution, the tradition of health-care ethics and the Church's magisterium. Studied ambiguity or eva-sion must be honestly addressed and corrected. Leaders and staff need ongoing professional development in Catholic bioethics, which cannot be the preserve of professional ethicists, committees or clerics. A range of educational modes is required: the preparation and dissemination of clear codes of conduct and other essential materials, seminars, case stud-ies, debates and so on.

---

[44] P. Cahill, 'Collaboration among Catholic health providers', *Origins* 24(12) (1 September 1994), 212–13; T. Murphy, 'What is the bottom line in Catholic healthcare?', *Origins* 26(4) (13 June 1996), 56–60; Sullivan, 'Dreaming the impossible dream', p. 134.

[45] Piccione, 'Catholic healthcare', p. 102: 'Certainly we should utilize the skills presented for good and efficient stewardship of our resources, but must resist the model of corporate life and cor-porate culture ... If we talk like business leaders and think like business leaders and structure personal rewards like business leaders, we will not be effective models of the ministry of service. As laypersons take the leadership roles of religious sisters and brothers, the laity must under-stand that they, too, are now symbols of this service, and their concerns for the conduct of the service must extend beyond financial performance.'

Finally, local bishops, in conjunction with leaders of religious congregations and others, must vigorously oversee, coordinate and plan in this area to ensure that the hospitals for which they are responsible do indeed fulfil the functions of service, witness and pastoral care. The tasks of Church leaders here include: to initiate and help coordinate collaboration among various Catholic institutions, parishes, programmes and people; to challenge the faithful to take greater responsibility for health and healing; to teach Catholic faith and morals in the healthcare context and to insist upon the doctrinal and moral integrity of each institution; to examine carefully any partnerships with non-Catholic providers that may affect the mission or identity of Catholic providers; to make provision for good pastoral and sacramental care; and to ensure the preservation and deepening of the Catholic identity, apostolic zeal and effectiveness of the institutions and when appropriate withdraw formal recognition of a particular hospital as a Catholic institution.[46]

Is all this, as some have suggested, 'mission impossible'? This much is clear: even Jesus could not call the uncallable, forgive the unrepentant, teach the unteachable or heal those who refused to be healed (Matt. 13:13–15; 19:20–22; Mark 3:29; 6:1–6; 13:32). If even he was bound by the limits of logical and moral possibility and above all the receptivity of those he dealt with, so too Church institutions and members cannot expect to do everything they would like. Perhaps Catholic healthcare on the institutional scale to which we have become accustomed is no longer possible – though we should be very reluctant to retreat from what has been achieved or could yet be achieved through such institutions. What is certain is that whether big or small, Catholic healthcare is challenged today to rediscover and deepen its *diakonia, martyria* and *leitourgia*. If it does so, Catholic healthcare may discover that many apparently impossible things are indeed possible with God (Matt. 19:26).

---

[46] Ad Hoc Committee on Healthcare Issues and the Church of the National Conference of Catholic Bishops, *The Responsibility of the Diocesan Bishop for Strengthening the Health Ministry* (Washington, DC: NCCB, 1996); Administrative Committee of the National Conference of Catholic Bishops, *Bishops' Pastoral Role*; Provost, 'Approaches to Catholic identity'; chapters by Wuerl, Cahill, Cafardi and Jennings in D. Maher (ed.), *The Bishop and the Future of Catholic Health Care: Challenges and Opportunities* (Boston: Pope John XXIII Center, 1997); cf. *CIC* 216, 217 and 305.1.

CHAPTER II

Regulation: what kinds of laws and social policies?

A TALE OF THREE POLITICIANS

Ethical principles, as discussed in previous chapters, are one thing; how to turn them into real-life laws and practices is quite another. I begin this chapter with the stories of three fictional politicians dedicated to the 'culture of life' and their attempts to improve the situation in their part of the world.

Nightingale Singh battles infanticide in Asia

A politician and mother of seven girls has introduced a bill to ban female infanticide in India. While all homicide, at least after birth, is already technically illegal in her country, the law has long been ineffectual, being applied only to boy children; thousands of infant girls are killed with impunity each year. Mrs Nightingale Singh's plan is to make it clear by legislation – followed by pressure upon the police and prosecuting authorities – that to kill a healthy child, simply for being a girl, is a crime. She realizes that this will leave unaffected the many hundreds of *disabled* babies of both sexes who are smothered each year – a tragedy in her eyes, though possibly less cruel than the lethal neglect called 'nursing care only' and 'demand feeding' suffered by children with disabilities in the (more ethically primitive) hospitals of the Western world. Her own opposition to all infanticide is well known, but she realizes that there is at present no realistic hope of getting an effective universal ban on the practice in her country.

Mrs Singh is untroubled by the predictable opposition of the anti-population lobby and certain other 'conservatives'. She is more perplexed that some people might think that by seeking to ban sex-selection infanticide she is implicitly conceding the legality and morality of killing infants on other grounds such as disability. Would she be sacrificing some children's lives in order to save others? She is concerned to avoid the bad

energy that comes from doing evil even in the hope that good may come
of it and from collaborating in the evil acts of others. She also knows that
the law, as it presently stands, even if it is regularly flouted, still officially
says 'no infanticide' and she does not want to make the situation worse.
She wonders if she should just give up on this matter altogether.

Muhammed Mboembe confronts cloning in Africa

Meanwhile Muhammed Ignatius Mboembe, a Ugandan representative
in the recently formed African Union Parliament, is promoting a bill to
ban human cloning and embryo experimentation in Africa and to promote more positive alternatives. While cloning is being attempted for
some extinct game animals and genetic engineering is being used to produce a low-cholesterol hippopotamus for the table, these technologies have
not yet been applied to humans in Africa. Mboembe is aware, however,
that in some countries such experiments on humans already occur and he
fears some foreigner may set up shop in Africa where there is little regulation and a readier supply of poor women to provide eggs. He thinks
there is a very good chance of getting an Africa-wide ban on so-called
'reproductive' cloning (cloning intended to produce a live-born child) but
is less confident of also achieving a ban on 'therapeutic' cloning (the even
more unethical kind of cloning, where embryos are created in order to be
cannibalized for experimental purposes). There is even less likelihood of
achieving a total ban on human embryo experimentation, which is what
he would really like.

Dr Mboembe plans to put up a bill banning all three practices but is
willing to fall back to a ban on cloning or even to a ban on only reproductive cloning, depending upon the vicissitudes of the political debate.
He had also considered going for a ban on all reproductive technologies,
but this might kill his bill altogether. He finds he is opposed not only by
those who favour a laissez-faire policy in this area, but also by a group
calling themselves the Defenders of the African Family Today. DAFT
declare that they cannot support any bill that does not also ban contraception, artificial reproduction, sex education in schools and the public
dissemination of the theory of evolution.

Don Vidal tackles euthanasia in Spain

Meanwhile in leftist Spain a physician-assisted suicide bill has widespread
popular support and is likely soon to be passed with similar majorities

to the recent same-sex marriage and abortion laws. Provincial MP Don Miguel-Angel Vidal thinks he will vote against the PAS bill in any case but is toying with moving an amendment requiring a one-week 'cooling off period' between the consent to assisted suicide and its implementation and also requiring that good palliative and pastoral care be offered first.

Don Vidal is uncertain, however. He wonders about the prudence of amendments that might seem to lend some credibility to the PAS bill and the wicked practice it condones. He also wonders whether the consciences of a few weaker MPs may be appeased, with the 'safeguards' enabling them to vote in favour of assisted suicide. Furthermore, Vidal's proposal might itself be amended by his opponents, making a bad law worse. Perhaps it would be best to take an absolute stand against the bill or even just to let sleeping dogs lie and hope the bill will fail. He asks his elderly parish priest what he should do. The monsignor suggests prayers to San José, Patrón de la Muerte Feliz, and refers the question to a classmate who lectures at the seminary. The response – advising that Don Vidal should follow his conscience – arrives three days after the final vote on the bill.

CATHOLIC PRINCIPLES FOR POLITICIANS

The noble art of politics

The complementary roles of pastors and laity in the formulation of public policy were described by the Second Vatican Council:

> Secular duties and activities belong properly although not exclusively to the laity … Lay-people should know that it is generally the function of their well-formed Christian conscience to see that the divine law is inscribed in the life of the earthly city; certainly the laity can expect from priests spiritual light and strength. Let the laity not imagine that their pastors are always such experts, that to every problem which arises, however complicated, they can readily give a concrete solution, or even that such is their mission. Rather, enlightened by Christian wisdom and giving close attention to the teaching authority of the Church, let the laity take on their own distinctive role. (*GS* 43)

Regarding what they called 'the difficult but very noble art of politics', the Fathers of Vatican II praised 'the work of those who for the common good devote themselves to the service of the state and take on the burdens of office'. They taught that 'with integrity and wisdom, [politicians] must take action against any form of injustice and tyranny'. Lawmaking has an important role to play in such action against injustice: by formally recognizing the duties and protecting the rights of all persons, families and groups in the community and prescribing any attacks upon those rights and persons (*GS* 75). In this context the responsibility of lawmakers and those who influence them to protect the life of all members of the community from conception until natural death was reaffirmed by the Council (*GS* 27 and 51) and has since been repeated very often by popes and bishops, as well as by many other faithful Christians, clerical and lay.

Of course, as politicians such as those in the first section of this chapter know only too well, no leader can do everything, and good laws will take us only so far in building up a civilization of life and love. Morally sensitive lawmakers also face many dilemmas about what kinds of laws to seek, which to oppose, how to ameliorate bad proposed laws by amendment and what are the best means to such ends. This chapter will focus on a particular group of *causae conscientiae* (matters of conscience) often encountered in the conventional political struggle in defence of innocent human life: the duties of a politician with respect to laws in the area of abortion, infanticide, embryo destruction, euthanasia or other crimes against life, especially in those situations where the laws are not presently, and are not likely in the near future to be, as 'perfect' as the pro-life politician would desire.[1] These questions are all the more important in the context of recent debates about whether and when a Catholic politician might be formally excommunicated for his or her position on laws in this area.

In considering such questions I cannot elaborate a full political ethic here or articulate all the principles to be followed or all the qualities to be cultivated in civic leaders; neither can I describe the complex process of discernment appropriate in any political judgment. While relying upon the authoritative teachings of the Catholic Church, I cannot elaborate as fully as I would like all the theological presuppositions that underpin those teachings, the levels of authority with which they have been proposed or the common ground such teachings have with the positions of many other Christians, pro-lifers and persons of good will. While I will often refer to abortion legislation in particular to illustrate the principles that I elaborate here, many of them will apply, other things being equal,

[1] The language of 'perfect' and 'imperfect' bio-legislation has been common in ecclesiastical circles at least since the symposium held by the CDF in Rome, 9–12 November 1994, 'Catholics and the pluralist society: the case of imperfect laws' (*I Cattolici e la società pluralista: Il caso delle 'leggi imperfette'*, Bologna, 1996). I use the category 'pro-life' to cover not only Catholic and like-minded Christian politicians, but all those opposed to all abortion, euthanasia and so forth. Much of what I say will apply, suitably adapted, to those who advise, lobby and support them.

to other areas of bio-legislation such as those I outlined in my opening examples.

Negative norms governing acceptable bio-legislation policy

Since the Second Vatican Council, a series of documents have offered some counsel to Christian politicians on the positive course reasonably to be taken with respect to the protection of human life. These have included speeches of Pope John Paul II, declarations of the Congregation for the Doctrine of the Faith, interventions by the Holy See at UN meetings, statements by national bishops' conferences, responses of individual bishops to Catholic politicians – and much else besides – all culminating in the great encyclical *Evangelium Vitae*. A number of positions, not uncommon in contemporary discourse and practice, have also been authoritatively rejected. Rather than rehearse the substantial argumentation offered in those texts or offered by theologians who support those teachings, it must suffice for present purposes to summarize six positive conclusions regarding bio-politics:

- It is the duty of politicians to ensure that civil law serves the common good and reflects fundamental moral norms (especially those regarding basic human rights), and that civil law protects from unjust attack the vulnerable (including the unborn, disabled, frail elderly, sick and dying) (John Paul II, *EV* 4, 20 and 68–72; *CCC* 2273; CDF, *On Abortion* 20; *On Respect for Human Life and Procreation* 3).[2]
- It is likewise the duty of politicians to lead rather than merely follow public opinion in such crucial matters (CDF, *On Respect for Human Life and Procreation* 3).
- Far from being an imposition upon the consciences of others, laws that protect the vulnerable from the impositions of the strong reflect a healthy respect for human rights and fundamental moral norms, and assist people to grow in virtue (*EV* 71; CDF, *On Abortion* 20; *On*

---

[2] St Thomas Aquinas taught that not all immoral activities can or should be proscribed by law: thus the Church does not counsel politicians to enact laws against adultery or lying even though such activities are wrong. Even so, if the law should not seek to prohibit all vices, it should at least prohibit the more serious (e.g. lethal) ones: 'human laws do not forbid all vices, from which the virtuous abstain, but only the more grievous vices, from which it is possible for the majority to abstain; and chiefly those that are to the hurt of others, without the prohibition of which human society could not be maintained: thus human law prohibits murder, theft and suchlike' (*ST* 1a 11ae 96, ii). Several recent magisterial documents have insisted that it is a primary function of the criminal law to ensure that all members of society enjoy respect for their fundamental rights, such as the right to life.

Respect for Human Life and Procreation 3); those whose religion part-motivates their political struggle in this area are thus not guilty of religious intolerance or imposition but merely assuming their proper role as believers within a democracy.

- On the other hand, laws that attack or deny protection to certain classes of human beings undermine the common good and expose even the supposedly democratic state as tyrannical (*EV* 20 and 70; *CCC* 2273; CDF, *On Respect for Human Life and Procreation* 3); such laws are not morally binding and must not be obeyed (*EV* 69, 72, 73 and 90).[3]

- Direct abortion and euthanasia are intrinsically and gravely evil, since they are the deliberate killing of innocent human beings and no circumstance, purpose or law can ever make them right (Vatican II, *GS* 27 and 51; Paul VI, *HV* 14; John Paul II, *EV* 57, 62 and 65; *CCC* 2268–79); they also damage family and community (*EV* 42–5 and 53–67); the prohibition on killing the innocent is a conclusion of well-informed natural reason, even unaided by faith, and is therefore proper ground for political action even in an avowedly 'secular' society; revelation mediated by the Church clarifies and confirms this conclusion[4] and gives additional grounds for political action in any self-consciously Christian

---

[3] In his important reflection upon the implications of grievously unjust laws, John Paul II concludes that 'Laws which authorize and promote abortion and euthanasia are therefore radically opposed not only to the good of the individual but also to the common good; as such they are completely lacking in authentic juridical validity. Disregard for the right to life, precisely because it leads to the killing of the person whom society exists to serve, is what most directly conflicts with the possibility of achieving the common good. Consequently, a civil law authorizing abortion or euthanasia ceases by that very fact to be a true, morally binding civil law' (*EV* 72). Here he is in the tradition of St Thomas, who taught that 'a tyrannical law, through being contrary to reason, is not a law, strictly speaking, but rather a perversion of law' and 'an act of violence' (*ST* 1a 11ae 92, i, resp. 4; 96, 4).

[4] There is some dispute about the status of the three definitions in *EV*, and in particular whether they are proposed as an exercise of the 'ordinary' and/or the 'extraordinary' magisterium of the Church, whether of the papal and/or episcopal magisterium and/or the *sensus fidelium*. *All* of these kinds of authority seem to me to have been appealed to in *EV* (and the tradition behind it), and for these reasons and others I believe that Catholic teaching on the intrinsic evil of all direct abortion is proposed *infallibly*. The later publication of John Paul II, *Ad Tuendam Fidem* (1998) and of the CDF's accompanying *Explanatory Note* seemed to confirm that this teaching is an example of one 'definitively proposed by the Church regarding faith and morals' and 'necessary for faithfully keeping and expounding the deposit of faith, even if they have not been proposed by the magisterium of the Church as formally revealed'. Following Vatican II these documents suggest that the Catholic faithful are required to give 'firm and definitive assent to these truths' and that 'whoever denies them would be rejecting a truth of Catholic doctrine and would therefore no longer be in full communion with the Catholic Church'.

society or any pluralist democratic society with some Christian voters and leaders.[5]

- Politicians must act individually and in concert to ensure that the law prohibits all homicide, including abortion, embryo destruction, infanticide and euthanasia (*EV* 68–74, esp. 72).

The arguments that the Catholic Church and others present for these six claims are sophisticated, persuasive and, I believe, conclusive. Various things follow. Commonly heard counterproposals that are *incompatible* with Catholic teaching on bio-politics include:

- that abortion, euthanasia and so forth are morally permissible;[6]
- that attitudes to abortion, euthanasia and the like are matters of 'private morality' or 'personal religion' and therefore should not influence public policy;[7]
- that respect for the consciences of constituents, including those who do not believe abortion or euthanasia is wrong, requires their elected representatives make no laws that interfere with their right to exercise their conscientious beliefs in this area;
- that politicians must respect and enact majority opinion on such matters, whatever it is;
- that a politician may initiate or should support (and a citizen may support or obey) a law that admits in principle the licitness of abortion or euthanasia.

In addition to the range of things that a politician might not reasonably initiate, sponsor or by his affirmative vote legislate, there are also

---

[5] Catholic teaching on abortion, euthanasia and so forth, while amenable to reason unaided by faith, is *also* a matter of faith, since it is believed by Catholics not only on the basis of persuasive philosophical and sociological reasons but also on the authority of the Scriptures, the Christian tradition and the living magisterium of the Church. The gravity of the matter is all the greater when it is realized that such acts involve the killing of a being *made in the image of God*, that they are *contrary* not only to practical reason but also to *God's will* and that they involve not only an attack upon a basic human value (life) but also *the renunciation of a sacred trust*. On the complex relationship between faith and reason in such matters see John Paul II, *Fides et Ratio: Encyclical Letter on Faith and Reason* (1998). On the implications of a more self-conscious focus on building a Christian society see Aidan Nichols, *Christendom Awake* (Edinburgh: T&T Clark, 1999).
[6] Some Catholics or other Christians openly declare themselves opposed to the Church's teaching on abortion or euthanasia and yet claim they are believing and practising members of their church. On the problems with this position, see Chapter 2. Given the consistency and gravity of Church teaching in this area, '(conscientiously) Catholic and pro-abortion' makes about as much sense as '(conscientiously) Catholic and anti-Eucharist' or 'Catholic and pro-rape'.
[7] Catholic teaching on human rights questions such as abortion is no more mysteriously religious or sectarian than Catholic teaching against slavery, apartheid or unjust wars. To characterize these matters as 'private morality' or 'personal religion' is an evasion amounting to ethical relativism: cf. R. George, *Political Action and Legal Reform in 'Evangelium Vitae'* (Washington, DC: US Conference of Catholic Bishops, 1996); John Paul II, *EV* 70; Vatican II, *GS* 43.

those actions that have the effect of assisting others in the liberalization of abortion laws and thus in the practice of abortion. Such assistance may amount to cooperation in another's evil, a matter addressed more fully in Chapter 3. Suffice it to say that a legislator who favours permissive abortion and therefore actively supports someone else's permissive bill or actively blocks someone else's restrictions to such a bill engages in formal cooperation in the evil of the sponsor of the legislation. So too does one uninterested in the abortion issue who nonetheless supports such a bill or blocks such restrictions, hoping thereby to gain something else, such as appeasing certain opponents, keeping his or her seat or horse-trading support for some other (possibly better) legislative objective. In such cases politicians can be guilty of formal cooperation in evil even if they disapprove of abortion and say so publicly. Some of the worst collaborators in permissive abortion regimes in recent decades have been politicians ostensibly opposed to abortion.

Positive norms governing acceptable bio-legislation

Having reviewed some commonly espoused positions that are inconsistent with the Catholic notion of a politician's vocation, I will now consider what (Catholic) politicians *can* do. The applicable moral principles in this area are those concerning the intended object of the moral act, and concerning formal and material cooperation in an evil instigated by another person(s). There are also several virtues at issue that I treat at the end of this chapter.

In situations where abortion, infanticide, embryo experimentation, euthanasia and the like are already clearly illegal, leaders must remain vigilant lest such laws are flouted or diluted by permissive judgments in *causes célèbres* or eroded by non-enforcement; they must seek to educate the public about the values underpinning and the benefits of maintaining such laws; they must counter those forces that will always be at work to undermine the civilization of life and love. Above all, perhaps, politicians must work to minimize not just the supply but also the demand for abortion and the rest: to ensure that public values education, financial and social support, counselling and the like are more than adequate, so that unwanted pregnancy rates are as low as possible and those who are troubled by their pregnancy are as fully supported as possible. Likewise the frail elderly, sick and disabled must not only be protected by laws but be so loved and cared for by communities that killing them becomes unthinkable.

If only the concern in most countries was about moves to weaken a legislative regime that protects human life in most circumstances! The tragedy is that most of the Western world, at least, now operates under systems tolerant of huge numbers of abortions per year and increasingly tolerant of embryo destruction and euthanasia at least by neglect. The 'culture of death', so tellingly identified by Pope John Paul II, is now predominant in the West and means that violence has become so commonplace that even practising Christians rarely reflect on just how bloody are the supposedly enlightened institutions and practices of their community.

Here we might distinguish several kinds of unjust bio-legal situations:

- where killing the innocent is presently constitutionally permitted or protected in some situations – as is the case with respect to abortion in the USA (according to a series of Supreme Court decisions that were arguably judicial legislation rather than genuine constitutional interpretation);
- where killing is presently legal in some situations under statute law – as is the case with euthanasia or physician-assisted suicide in a few jurisdictions and abortion and embryo experimentation in many more;
- where killing the innocent is formally permitted by law in some situations as a result of judge-made common law or statutory interpretation – as with abortion in several jurisdictions and, as we saw in Chapter 8, with euthanasia by court-sanctioned withdrawal of feeding in some places;
- where killing the innocent is presently de facto permitted in some situations either because any law against killing is not enforced by the police, the prosecuting authorities and/or the courts, or because, while killing the innocent is still formally illegal, experience and present circumstances indicate that any conviction is unlikely or impossible – as is the case throughout much of the Western world today with respect to much bio-legislation.

In these situations the question immediately arises: are politicians bound to seek to change constitutions or to pass laws to make practices such as abortion illegal in all circumstances? The examples given in the opening section of this chapter highlight this very real question for politicians. If the passage of such constitutional amendments or statutes is, for the time being, politically impossible, are they bound, or at least permitted, to sponsor or support bills to mitigate the evil in some way, so that the rate of abortion, infanticide, embryo destruction or euthanasia is decreased? Such a course of action has in fact been tried, and has sometimes succeeded, in some places.[8] If such a restrictive yet still permissive bill is proposed, are pro-life politicians bound to support it, oppose it or take some middle course?

What happens if someone from 'the other side' sponsors a bill to make access to abortion or euthanasia more clearly or more broadly legal? Suppose that the passage of such a bill seems very likely. Should or may a pro-life politician oppose such a bill at all stages, or support the bill at certain stages of the legislative process but not at others, in the hope of gaining some concession? Should such a lawmaker, while opposing the bill as a whole, propose or support amendments to the bill that would, at least, tighten up the regime envisaged by the bill so that at least some abortion or euthanasia is not visited upon at least some innocent human beings?

In *Evangelium Vitae* 73 Pope John Paul II wrote:

A particular problem of conscience can arise in cases where a legislative vote would be decisive for the passage of a more restrictive law, aimed at limiting the number of authorized abortions, in place of a more permissive law already passed or ready to be voted on. Such cases are not infrequent. It is a fact that while in some parts of the world there continue to be campaigns to introduce laws favouring abortion, often supported by powerful international organizations, in other nations – particularly those which have already experienced the bitter fruits of such permissive legislation – there are growing signs of a rethinking in this matter. In a case like the one just mentioned, when it is not possible to overturn or completely abrogate a pro-abortion law, an elected official, whose absolute personal opposition to procured abortion was well known, could licitly support proposals aimed at limiting the harm done by such a law and at lessening its negative consequences at the level of general opinion and public morality. This does not in fact represent an illicit co-operation with an unjust law, but rather a legitimate and proper attempt to limit its evil aspects.[9]

---

[8] For a review of various attempts to ameliorate or enforce British abortion laws and the almost impenetrable obstacles to the passage of such laws, see J. Keown, *Abortion, Doctors and the Law* (Cambridge University Press, 1988).

[9] This is repeated in CDF, *On Participation of Catholics in Political Life* (2002) 4. Likewise the then-Cardinal Ratzinger wrote in May 1982 in response to a request from the US bishops regarding the Hatch amendment: 'according to the principles of Catholic morality, an action can be considered licit whose object and proximate effect consist in limiting an evil insofar as possible. Thus, when one intervenes in a situation judged evil in order to correct it for the better, and when the action is not evil in itself, such an action should be considered not as the voluntary acceptance of the lesser evil but rather as the effective improvement of the existing situation, even though one remains aware that not all evil present is able to be eliminated for the moment.' Cited in R. G. Peters, 'Stopping abortion: the pragmatist's view', *Catholic Twin Circle*, 17 September 1989.

Following this text the then-Secretary of the Congregation for the Doctrine of the Faith, Archbishop Tarcisio Bertone, argued that by virtue of their specific vocation, it is largely up to the laity to engage with 'imperfect laws' and that three attitudes are possible here:

1 *Prophetic resistance* … may be justified in the Church if a lay Christian prefers to opt for the value placed in question by the law [here: absolute respect for life] rather than opt for the lesser evil [here: a less 'imperfect' abortion law, etc.].

2 *Collaboration.* A less radical attitude, or one involving greater collaboration, is permitted by the Church if it is possible to promote a lesser evil than that proposed by the law … It is not the [lesser] evil as such that is at issue here, but the good, more specifically the good necessary to defuse or reduce the evil … It is never permitted to do evil or use evil means to produce a good end; nonetheless each value, by the very fact that it belongs to what is good or what is true, asks to be respected … [Because this strategy] may be difficult to understand for those not directly involved in the political experience and unfamiliar with its very complex ramifications … [it] must be publicly explained by those who take such a decision on grounds of conscience. Once this effort has been made with all the necessary seriousness, the legislator must not let himself be tormented, or [pressured into] changing attitude, as a result of the false interpretation that may be given to his gesture.

3 *Toleration* … of evil expressed through an unjust law … can only be possible if resistance to the evil would involve a yet greater evil.[10]

This important teaching has already occasioned considerable debate among faithful Catholics and their pro-life friends.[11] To some it appears

---

[10] T. Bertone, 'Catholics in a pluralist society: "imperfect laws" and the responsibility of legislators', in J. Correa and E. Sgreccia (eds.), *'Evangelium Vitae' – Five Years of Confrontation with the Society* (Libreria Editrice Vaticana, 2001), pp. 206–22. Likewise R. George, 'The gospel of life: a symposium', *First Things* 56 (October 1995), 32–8; A. R. Luño, '*Evangelium Vitae* 73: the Catholic lawmaker and the problem of a seriously unjust law', *L'Osservatore Romano*, 18 September 2002, 3–5; W. E. May, '*Evangelium Vitae* 73 and the problem of the lesser evil', *NCBQ* 2(4)(2002), 577–9, and 'The misinterpretation of John Paul II's teaching in *Evangelium Vitae* n. 73', *NCBQ* 6(4) (2006), 705–18; N. Tonti-Filippini, 'Public policy and abortion: bad but better law', in J. Fleming and N. Tonti-Filippini (eds.), *Common Ground? Seeking an Australian Consensus on Abortion and Sex Education* (Sydney: St Paul's, 2007), ch. 10.

[11] For example, C. Harte, 'Challenging a consensus: why *Evangelium Vitae* does not permit legislators to vote for "imperfect legislation"', in L. Gormally (ed.), *Culture of Life – Culture of Death* (London: Linacre Centre, 2002), pp. 322–42; his exchange with Finnis in H. Watt (ed.), *Cooperation, Complicity and Conscience: Moral Problems in Healthcare, Science, Law and Public Policy* (London: Linacre Centre, 2005); 'Inconsistent papal approaches towards problems of conscience?', *NCBQ* 2(1) (2002), 99–124; and *Changing Unjust Laws Justly* (Washington, DC: Catholic University of America Press, 2005).

a contradiction: how can anyone who believes all abortion is wrong support 'just a little abortion'? Is a spirit of appeasement or pragmatism being manifested in Vatican politics? Are we engaging in evil in the vain hope that good may come, trading some lives for others? Has despair of ever having sound laws and practices in this area resulted in a sell-out?[12]

I think not, but I recognize that understanding Catholic teaching and its implications in this area, like understanding the Christian Gospel on many topics, requires a certain amount of arduous and dispassionate thinking. Given the heat of political debate, the urgency of these issues, the unhelpfully simplistic or plainly hostile media, and politicians and public poorly versed in the nooks and crannies of ethical theory, it is easy to see why people may dismiss such thinking as a luxury or as unnecessarily convoluted. I believe this view is wrong, if understandable. A parallel might usefully be drawn, perhaps, with respect to Catholic teaching on the just war. It is complex and will not always deliver up a single clear answer on which wars are just ones and which ways of fighting them are just. Some will, however, be clearly unjust. The complexities of the argument are no excuse for not doing the hard thinking. Too much is at stake simply to embrace 'my country right or wrong' or a dogmatic pacifism. The same in true in our present discussion.

John Finnis explained the application of these principles to abortion law reform as follows:

[According to *Evangelium Vitae*] the always illicit vote is one for a law *as permitting*, precisely *to* permit, abortion. This is always illicit, even if one is personally opposed to abortion and is voting for it only to keep one's seat and prevent euthanasia or genocide laws, or only to equalize the position of the poor and the rich. The kind of vote which … [*Evangelium Vitae*] judges can be licit has as its object not: *to permit* abortions now illegal but rather: *to prohibit* abortions now legal or imminently likely otherwise to become legal. (Say: the existing law or the threatened alternative bill says abortion is lawful up to 24 weeks, while the law or bill for which the Catholic legislator is voting for says abortion is lawful up to 16 weeks.) Even though it is a vote for a law which does permit abortion, it is chosen by this legislator as a vote for a law which restricts abortion. That this restrictive law also permits abortion is only a side-effect – when we consider the act of voting in the perspective of the acting person – even though the side-effect of permission is as immediate as the object of restriction.[13]

[12] An example of a commentator who is sceptical of incremental strategies to limit abortion is C. Rice, *The Winning Side: Questions on Living the Culture of Life* (Mishawaka, IN: St. Brendan's, 1999), pp. 225–33.
[13] J. Finnis, 'The Catholic Church and public policy debates in Western liberal societies: the basis and limits of intellectual engagement', in L. Gormally (ed.), *Issues for a Catholic Bioethic* (London: Linacre Centre, 1999), pp. 261–73 at 268–9.

The ink of these words was barely dry when lawmakers and pro-lifers in two different Australian jurisdictions were debating their implications for new laws: Western Australia and the Australian Capital Territory. In both cases pro-life politicians achieved some limited success in a very hostile environment and were vilified by both the pro-abortionists and also some of their pro-life friends. What were the points of contention? Four are worth mentioning here because they have wider ramifications.

Does Evangelium Vitae *73 apply only to existing laws or only to bills being debated or to both?*

During the debate over abortion laws in Western Australia there were some who asserted that *Evangelium Vitae* 73 applied only to the introduction by pro-life MPs of new laws aimed at restricting abortion in a permissive regime, not to attempts to ameliorate by amendment permissive bills introduced to a legislature by someone else. (On this view Dr Mboembe, and possibly Mrs Singh, might be justified in their actions but not Don Vidal.) During a similar debate in the Australian Capital Territory, on the other hand, some people asserted the opposite: *Evangelium Vitae* sanctioned attempts to ameliorate by amendment other people's pro-abortion bills but did not allow the introduction of new laws in a permissive regime that would restrict but not prohibit abortion. Yet in praising efforts 'aimed at limiting the number of authorized abortions' the encyclical clearly refers *both* to promoting new, more restrictive laws in place of permissive ones already in place ('laws already passed') and to promoting restrictive amendments to other people's permissive bills ('laws ready to be voted on'). Either way, Pope John Paul II explained, when it is not possible to defeat a pro-abortion law or bill, a politician could in certain circumstances licitly support a proposal aimed at 'limiting the harm done', without thereby being responsible for the far from perfect state of the law. Even had the Pope not drawn this conclusion so explicitly, his principles (and those of the tradition for which he spoke) clearly apply equally to existing and to proposed laws.

Where is 'existing law' to be found?

Another dispute in this context was over whether, in considering what *is* the present state of the law (the 'law already passed'), one must refer only to a plain reading of existing statutes. The reason this was so important is that throughout much of Australia abortion has not yet been legalized by statute as it was in the UK in 1967; rather, courts had given permissive interpretations of prima facie restrictive abortion statutes and law 'enforcement' agencies had done little to enforce even those very liberal interpretations of the law. This led to de facto abortion on demand in Australia despite the officially restrictive statutory regime: in fact Australia had a significantly higher abortion rate than countries such as Britain with more permissive laws.

Of course, all laws, whether common law or codified, require authoritative interpretation and application. In jurisdictions where customary law plays some role, it is even clearer that the courts make the law, at least in part. Even statute law is not self-interpreting or self-applying. Indeed the ordinary reader easily misses the import of some legal provisions. With respect to abortion this is very much the case. Activist courts in the English-speaking world discovered either exceptions to the laws against abortion or rights to abortion that were hidden in words where no plain reader could find them. Likewise courts in several countries have allowed euthanasia by neglect of certain patients. However ideologically driven these readings of the law may be, until a superior court or legislator overrules them they set the precedent for subsequent cases.

Even accepting a plain reading of the statutes then forbidding abortion in West Australia and the Australian Capital Territory, such statutes were manifestly not enforced by police, prosecutors or courts. It could well have been argued that by the turn of the twenty-first century those statutes had been annulled by desuetude.[14] Several facts supported this view. First, 'the average man in the street' thought that abortion was already legal, and the practice of governments, police and prosecuting authorities suggested nothing to the contrary. Abortions were financed under the national health scheme or by insurers, advertised in the media, approved by medical colleges, referred for and performed by doctors 'in good standing' and recommended by school counsellors. Furthermore, the first attempt in many years to initiate a case against a doctor who flagrantly broke the West Australian abortion statute led to the prompt repeal of that technical prohibition.

So what are we to make of an ineffectual law, ineffectual indeed for several generations? Catholic theology going back at least to St Thomas

---

[14] This raises the complex jurisprudential question of whether and when a law ceases to be such by virtue of desuetude. Such assessments are made on different bases in different jurisdictions and are provisional until an authoritative pronouncement of desuetude has been made by a superior court or the original law has been rescinded by the legislator. It might also be argued that some laws are ineffective for their primary purpose (in this case, protecting unborn human beings and their mothers from abortion) but effective for some other purpose (e.g. protecting the right of some institutions and individuals to refuse to provide such 'services').

Aquinas has been well aware that black-letter laws are necessarily adapted 'to time and place'. As Aquinas observed, 'consuetude et habet vim legis, et legem abolet, et est legum interpretatrix' (custom makes, unmakes and interprets laws).[15] Thus the Law, taken in the broad, capital-L sense of the restrictions and permissions that a particular legal system effectively brings about, can be more or less than the sum total of small-l laws (statutes and precedents). A lawmaker will properly take into account what the Law effectively achieves, or can be expected effectively to achieve, in making decisions about whether legal reform is desirable and so will then decide which particular laws to support or seek to change.

The prudence of ameliorative measures

A third point of dispute has been over the prudence of particular ameliorative measures proposed in specific contexts – a matter about which morally and factually well-informed people may disagree even in ideal circumstances. During debates over abortion laws in Australia over the past two decades some pro-lifers have feared that any attempt to improve the law was doomed to fail, might lend respectability to bad laws and might make the laws even worse. Some feared causing scandal either by action or inaction in these circumstances; others were concerned about the political minutiae of how to word bills or amendments, when to move and in concert with whom and so on. Some critics thought any such measures so imprudent as to be morally culpable – a claim that deserves a little more attention here.

I have already dealt with immoral initiation and cooperation in the evil of legalizing or otherwise permitting offences against innocent life. *Evangelium Vitae* 73 makes it clear that support for imperfect laws is sometimes permissible, despite the material cooperation it might lend to offences against life. What reasons could persuade a pro-life lawmaker to risk such material cooperation? One must examine these risks carefully and honestly, taking them seriously without overstating them. The most important risk will be to any unborn, disabled or dying people who the legislator believes might be saved, and any others (such as pregnant women) who might also benefit, even if not all can be saved or assisted. Politicians themselves may also have much at stake, as might those who rely upon them. They might have various prior commitments and other

[15] *ST* 1a 11ae 97, iii. cf. R. George, *Making Men Moral: Civil Liberties and Public Morality* (Oxford University Press, 1993), ch. 1.

responsibilities to take into account. So before supporting an imperfect bio-law the politician must ask: how important are the benefits expected from this activity, how extensive, how certain and for whom?

What would count against such potential material cooperation? Again, politicians must examine these carefully and honestly, not ignoring them simply because they are unintended or minimizing them because of their enthusiasm for the good they hope to achieve. The most obvious ill-effect of material cooperation in an ameliorative amendment to a law that permits abortion would be that it might assist the passage of that law. Thus the legislator must ask: what kind of loss or harm will result from the liberalization of abortion with which I may unintentionally be cooperating or from the other foreseeable side-effects of my activities? How extensive will the harm be, how certain is it to occur and who will suffer it? Will my refusing to cooperate in any way help prevent the wrong – or will it go ahead regardless? Am I in a position to stop it or at least reduce the harm done? In what ways can I at least express my disapproval and try to convert hearts and minds to my way of thinking?

A second bad side-effect of material cooperation is that it may corrupt the politician concerned. A person may find their strength of will on these matters affected by having, even once, cooperated materially in the evil of liberalizing abortion. They may become blasé about it, dulled to the evil side-effects and happy enough to admit them as their own intention in the future; they may find themselves trapped in the company and schemes of others they thought allies who do not in fact share their scruples; the desire for solidarity and success may then carry such a person along into formal cooperation with evil in the future, whether with respect to bad bio-law or some other moral 'compromise'.

A third ill-effect of such material cooperation can be that it corrupts others. Pro-life politicians who support imperfect bio-legislation may be misunderstood by others to be abandoning their pro-life position; they might thereby 'give scandal' to others who do not appreciate the distinctions between intentional ends and foreseen side-effects, formal cooperation and material cooperation and so forth. This might seriously impair the witness they could and should be giving to others. Moreover their example might encourage others not only to cooperate materially, but even to cooperate formally, i.e. to advance even more permissive abortion laws or to regard abortion less seriously. Pro-life politicians must be prepared at times to take a stance against an activity by privately or publicly refusing to cooperate even materially in a particular evil, even at the risk of their political career; or, if they *are* cooperating materially, at least to take as active a part as is practicable in otherwise protesting against the evil practice they are unwillingly facilitating.

Underlying intentionality

The characterization of acts is a fourth area of difference in debates over imperfect laws. In Chapter 3, I suggested that contemporary Church teaching would seem to allow at least two accounts of the human act: first, a *natural meanings* account wherein acts have a certain meaning by virtue of their intrinsic object or proximate end, whatever the private intentions or motives of the agent; and, second, an *intended acts* account wherein acts can be assessed only 'from the perspective of the acting person' and the proximate ends deliberately willed. This is part of why, even from within the camp of those who support traditional Catholic moral teaching, there can be different conclusions on particular questions. To give three examples: some years ago the British bishops taught that the victim of rape is entitled to defend herself against the continuing effects of such an attack, including protecting her eggs from union with the rapist's sperm by taking 'the pill' to prevent ovulation.[16] Interventions aimed at causing abortion after rape were, of course, excluded.[17] However, some thought this amounted to condoning contraception, at least in certain cases, and that it promoted the doing of evil that good may come of it. The bishops explained that contraception is an act of deliberately sterilizing one's chosen sexual acts in prospect or retrospect, whereas ovulation suppression in this situation is merely protecting oneself from continuing attack by the rapist, i.e. self-defence. In this respect taking the pill is no more an act of contraception than would be the woman pushing the rapist away just as he was about to ejaculate. Some critics remained unpersuaded. Their objection would seem to have been that the object of an act can be seen from the outside, as it were: taking the pill is obviously engaging in contraception; contraception is an intrinsically evil act that cannot be ordered to

---

[16] British Bishops' Joint Committee in Bioethical Issues, 'Use of the "morning after pill" in cases of rape', *Origins* 15(39) (31 January 1986), 633–8, and 'A reply', *Origins* 16(13) (11 September 1986), 237–8; cf. Catholic Health Australia, *Code of Ethical Standards for Catholic Health and Aged Care Services in Australia* (Canberra: CHA, 2001), 3.8 and 3.9; Pennsylvania Catholic Conference, 'Guidelines for Catholic hospitals treating victims of sexual assault', *Origins* 22(47) (6 May 1993), 81.

[17] It follows that measures such as the 'morning-after pill' may only be used after rape when they involve no significant risk to the life of a developing embryo. See N. Tonti-Filippini and M. Walsh, 'Post-coital intervention: from fear of pregnancy to rape crisis', *NCBQ* 4(2) (2004), 275–88.

the good; 'subjective' intention may affect culpability but it cannot affect the object that is 'objectively' known.[18] There has been a similar debate among reliable Catholic theologians over whether condomized intercourse is always contraceptive, even when a couple are infertile and/or their goal is prophylaxis against HIV transmission.[19]

Another example also hails from the UK: the teaching, some years ago, that the Rubella vaccine might licitly be used even though it is routinely grown upon a cell line originally derived from an aborted foetus.[20] Despite the arguments of those who stressed the remoteness of the abortion from the vaccinations, the difference of intended object and the lack of any formal cooperation in the evil of abortion on the part of those giving or receiving the vaccine, some thought it intrinsically wrong to use such a vaccine. This question recurs in the pro-life literature and periodically comes to the surface among parents and schools.

A last example occurs at the other end of life. Advocates of euthanasia often suggest that intentionally killing a patient thought better off dead, withdrawing life-sustaining treatments because they are too burdensome and giving high doses of pain-relieving agents at the risk of suppressing respiration are all the same. However, it is not only the pro-euthanasia lobby that assesses these acts as all of a piece: some 'perfectionists' also assert that removing a ventilator from someone who is ventilator-dependent or giving a high dose of morphine is killing. Talk of double effect and good intentions – these critics suggest – allows health professionals literally to get away with murder, even if for some merciful end.[21]

---

[18] They referred especially to *HV* 14 on the intrinsic evil of contraceptive agents whatever the motives. However, the very next paragraph of the encyclical notes: 'The Church, on the contrary, does not at all consider illicit the use of those therapeutic means truly necessary to cure diseases of the organism, even if an impediment to procreation, which may be foreseen, should result therefore, provided such impediment is not, for whatever motive, directly willed.' This statement makes little sense if contraceptive agents are themselves (or their use always and everywhere) evil whatever the agent's intention.

[19] A. Fisher, 'HIV and condoms within marriage', *Communio* 36(2) (2009), 329–59, and sources therein.

[20] See *The Tablet*, 29 October 1994, 1391. Continuing debate on this matter includes Pontifical Academy for Life, *On Vaccines Prepared from Cells Derived from Aborted Human Fetuses* (2005), which appears with essays by Grabenstein, Leiva, Luño and Pruss in *NCBQ* 6(3) (2006). See also E. Furton, 'Vaccines and the right of conscience', in E. Furton (ed.), *Live the Truth: The Moral Legacy of John Paul II in Catholic Health Care* (Washington, DC: NCBC, 2006), pp. 279–92.

[21] This is despite the clear teaching in: *CCC*; CDF, *On Euthanasia* (1980); and John Paul II, *EV*; cf. G. Grisez and J. Boyle, *Life and Death with Liberty and Justice* (Notre Dame University Press, 1979). Several palliative care experts have assured me that there is rarely if ever a risk that pain-relieving agents will suppress respiration: indeed, a failure to provide adequate pain relief may well be more likely to shorten life.

My point in raising these controversial examples is that debates over imperfect or ameliorative laws sometimes rehearse the same divides. On the face of it, it is a difference over how 'hard-line' one is about principle and how willing to compromise in order to achieve results such as saving babies' lives or relieving people's misery. Much more importantly, however, and often unbeknown to the disputants, there is often a more fundamental meta-ethical difference between them, a difference not of seriousness about principles but of the most basic principles themselves. For my own part I think Church teaching on the withdrawal of treatment, palliative care, care of victims of sexual assault, the permissibility of using 'the pill' for some genuinely therapeutic purpose, the acceptability of certain vaccinations and the permissibility of certain less-than-perfect abortion laws makes sense only if one accepts an account of the object of the moral act that clearly distinguishes between intending and foreseeing.

REASONABLE STANCES FOR A PRO-LIFE POLITICIAN

Opposition to permissive bio-laws at all stages

Should a pro-life lawmaker support an imperfect bio-law? Sometimes politicians will form the view that any bio-legal reform in our current circumstances is likely to have the net effect of making abortion even more accessible and common or, at least, of confirming and codifying an already shameful situation. They might believe that the present official restrictions (such as they are) are the best achievable at this time and that any new restrictions will be ignored in practice or will create new loopholes that will put more people's lives at risk. They might judge that a restrictive bill or restrictive amendments would be unlikely to be passed or would only be passed at the expense of some other, very unhelpful changes. They might suspect that by giving support to an imperfect bio-law their witness against abortion and so on would be severely impaired and people would be scandalized. Or they might conclude that by refusing to be party even to ameliorative amendments to a bad bio-law they will help to ensure the defeat of that law altogether. While recognizing that they have a prima facie duty to ensure that at least *some* babies are saved (where no more is practicable) and that others might in good faith support imperfect but restrictive bills or amendments, some politicians may nonetheless judge such actions imprudent in a particular situation and oppose them throughout their legislative progress.

Those pro-lifers who oppose restrictive but imperfect bills on these prudential grounds should be absolutely clear in their own minds (and possibly in their statements) that they are neither opposing all imperfect abortion legislation per se nor accusing all supporters of such bills or amendments of intending permissive abortion, of formal cooperation in evil or of being willing to trade life for life. Rather, they make their own best judgment that by refusing to be party even to such efforts they will serve best the ultimate goals of creating a just and loving society, of saving babies and their mothers, of opposing the further corruption of our culture and so on.

Support for some (restrictive) bio-law reform in a permissive situation

An alternative strategy for pro-life politicians, one which falls within the terms of *Evangelium Vitae* 73, is to initiate or support a bill that, while continuing to allow some abortions, restricts it in some new ways – thereby protecting at least some babies and mothers who are presently at risk. Leaders have a strong prima facie duty to seek to protect the most vulnerable members of their community, but sometimes that can only be achieved by the gradual correction of a de jure or de facto permissive abortion regime.[22] While maintaining their ultimate goal of protecting the lives of all and being careful not to conclude too hastily that this is presently impossible, pro-life politicians will sometimes conclude that protecting *some* babies is all that they presently can do.

There are many kinds of restrictions to permissive bio-laws that pro-life politicians may support if they have reason to believe such restrictions will, if passed, be effective and not do more harm than good. Some examples in the area of abortion laws (that would apply suitably modified to other areas of bio-lawmaking) include:

---

[22] As St Thomas observed, 'it seems natural to human reason to advance gradually from the imperfect to the perfect' (*ST* 1a 11ae 97, 1). In unpublished advice offered to some pro-life groups during the Western Australian controversy, John Finnis suggested that if a legislator judged Western Australian law already widely permissive of abortion because it would be read as such by superior courts were it ever tested, the politician could in good conscience vote for a bill which, if enacted, 'would accord real legal protection to some class of unborn babies who today are without that protection, even though the same Bill openly and plainly affirmed and ensured that some (perhaps many or most) other unborn babies remain unprotected (and are stripped of even "paper" legal protection). That is to say, members holding the view I have described could cast such a vote (and agree in advance to do so) without immorally co-operating in the use of the legislative process to deprive human persons of their inalienable moral and human right to life.'

- restricting *the stage* of foetal development up to which abortions may be performed and beyond which no abortions are permitted (e.g. twelve weeks);
- restricting *the reasons* for which abortion is permitted or specifically prohibiting abortion on certain other grounds (e.g. no sex-selection abortion);
- restricting *where* abortions may be performed (e.g. only in public hospitals) and *by whom* (e.g. only doctors) and licensing or otherwise restricting the number and activities of abortion providers;
- restricting government *funding* or private insurance for abortion;
- restricting access to particular *methods* of abortion (e.g. banning 'partial birth' abortion or RU486);
- requiring *counselling* of women considering abortion;
- instituting strict *information-giving* provisions, including information about the unborn child, the risks of abortion and alternatives to abortion, by any doctor giving any information about abortion;
- requiring *parental or guardian* notification of abortion performed on under-aged girls and court consent to abortion performed on women living with intellectual disability;
- imposing a '*cooling off period*' between the time a woman first seeks an abortion and the actual abortion;
- provision for *exemption* on conscientious grounds of doctors, nurses, pharmacists and counsellors from any requirement that they perform, refer for, prescribe, dispense or otherwise cooperate in abortion;
- provision that no Church institution can be required to provide such procedures on its premises or to otherwise cooperate in such provision.

Support for restrictive amendments to permissive bio-legislation but opposition to an unjust bill as a whole

A third strategy consistent with *Evangelium Vitae* 73 that a pro-life legislator may reasonably adopt would be: publicly opposing an unjust bill from the beginning, on the basis that it is aimed, for instance, at permitting abortion on demand; then voting *for* various amendments in the committee stage involving restrictions much like those proposed in the previous section; but opposing the final bill (even as amended) because it will, *in toto*, liberalize or confirm the permissive situation regarding abortion. Here the politician is facing a law 'ready to be voted on' and does his or her best to improve that law.

As with the legislator who votes for a new, more restrictive but still imperfect law, politicians who support restrictive amendments must aim neither at permitting abortion in all other circumstances (even though this is a foreseen side-effect) nor at lending respectability to abortion performed within these restrictive circumstances. Rather, their goal must be to place some obstacles in the way of abortion on demand in the hope that some abortions will thereby be prevented. The elimination of *all* induced abortion remains their goal, but in the meantime, they propose or support amendments to a very permissive bill likely soon to be passed, with the goal of 'tightening up' that new law, hoping thereby to protect at least some unborn children who would not otherwise have the benefit of legal protection.

Of course, some supposedly pro-life politicians may disingenuously support such provisions with the real goal of permitting a 'moderate' or 'morally respectable' amount of abortion or as a way of evading taking an open stand for or against abortion or because they are willing to trade some lives for others. Genuinely pro-life supporters of such moves, however, will support them only if they are convinced that the net effect will be to increase, not diminish, the present protection of the lives of unborn children. Here there are important prudential judgments to be made about what actions will actually save lives, whether the amendments will have any real (positive) effect, who else will be affected,[23] what messages will be conveyed to a morally unsophisticated public (by an often unhelpful media) and what overall effect such moves will have upon culture and society. Supporters should voice a clear and public opposition to all abortion and make it clear that in supporting such amendments they are not retreating from their judgment that the present permissive situation with respect to abortion is a serious violation of human rights.

I noted above that one matter of contention among pro-life lawmakers is the stage in the political process at which politicians should engage privately in canvassing amendments or announce publicly their willingness to discuss or support restrictive amendments. Sometimes the earlier amendments are canvassed, the greater the likelihood that they will eventually be accepted, that other helpful amendments will be proposed or that the promoters of a bill will be discouraged from persevering altogether. At other times, the earlier such amendments are proposed, the more likely

---

[23] For example, an undesired effect of such moves might be that doctors who at present can plead the de jure prohibition of abortion against claims in tort or professional misconduct for failure to provide an opportunity for an abortion find themselves without such protection.

they are to generate organized opposition from the proponents of a more permissive regime and the more likely they are to grant some respectability to the bill as a whole. These are again matters of prudent judgment for the politicians concerned, taking into account their best assessments of the present and likely future situation, the principles enunciated so far and the process of discernment sketched briefly below.

SOME VIRTUES OF A PRO-LIFE POLITICIAN

The virtues of faith, prudence and courage

This chapter has focused on some very particular dilemmas for pro-life politicians in the area of imperfect bio-legislation. I have argued that many commonly espoused positions are ruled out for the faithful and prudent political leader but that several remain as possible. Which of these is to be preferred will depend upon the opportunities that present themselves and the fine detail of particular legal and political situations. Each legislator must make his or her best prudential judgment of what will work without, on the one hand, adopting a perfectionist position that fails to try to make a bad situation better or, on the other hand, adopting immoral means even to achieve good ends. Whichever course be chosen, it should follow upon discussion with pro-life friends and allies. One would not be surprised if people of 'good faith, moral probity, and legal competence' honestly disagreed about aspects of the current situation or about the prospects of real gains from imperfect legislation.[24]

At several points in this chapter I have appealed to that earthly wisdom, which is the virtue of prudence, and that supernatural wisdom, which is a gift of the Holy Spirit. Only with these can a person quickly and reliably apply principles with sensitivity to the range of people and values at stake. I have outlined several important principles here that virtuous lawmakers must bear in mind in their noble task. Two more that I have hinted at along the way would be these: we must never be willing to do even a little evil in order to bring about even a very great good; and we must with imaginative impartiality apply the Golden Rule to our situation, asking ourselves, for instance: were I one of the babies at risk, one of the mothers seeking an abortion, one of the old people marked for euthanasia, some of the other politicians engaged in this great debate, some of the voters I represent or people I influence, would I reasonably regard my action or inaction as fair?

---

[24] This latter observation was made by Finnis in his advice already cited.

Finally, having tried one's best to think these matters through and exclude thereby all unreasonable choices, politicians might conclude that there are still two or more paths open to them. Having done this, they then must go for what seems best to them in the context of their particular temperament, gifts, opportunities, commitments and vocation.

If we are to have faith and prudence ourselves, we must cultivate certain attitudes of heart and mind: prayerfulness above all; a willingness to take counsel; humility and docility to truth; respect for allies and an eagerness to learn from them, work with them and console them; self-criticism, imaginative impartiality and love for all. Of these habits of the heart St James wrote:

> Who among you thinks he is wise and understanding? Let him demonstrate this by a good life in the humility that comes from prudence ... The wisdom which comes from above is first of all pure, then peaceable, gentle, compliant, full of mercy and good fruits, without inconstancy or insincerity. And the fruit of righteousness is sown in peace for those who cultivate peace. (Jas. 3:13–18)

In addition to faith and prudence, the task of the Christian legislator requires a great deal of fortitude: whichever of the various reasonable positions outlined above politicians take, they may meet a great deal of hostility from foes and even erstwhile allies. Taking a conscientious stance can come at great personal cost, including some cost to prospects in one's party or electorate. This should not, perhaps, be overestimated: even political opponents and voters who hold a different view are likely to respect a stance taken out of conviction rather than political ambition. A degree of heroism may nonetheless be called for, and Christians will naturally turn to God, their Church, their friends and families for support in such situations; in the meantime, the politician must cultivate the virtue of courage.

Being called to serve the common good, political leaders must make courageous choices in support of life. In a democratic system, where laws and policies are made on the basis of the consensus of many, the sense of personal responsibility of individuals invested with authority may be weakened. Even so, in democracies leaders must answer to God, to their own conscience and to the whole community for choices contrary to the common good (*EV* 90).

Unity of purpose; diversity in strategies; charity in everything

The Second Vatican Council taught that Christians 'must recognize the legitimacy of different opinions' in political matters.

Often enough the Christian view of things will itself suggest some specific solution in certain circumstances. Yet it happens rather frequently, and legitimately so, that with equal sincerity some of the faithful will disagree with others on a given matter. Even against the intentions of their proponents, however, solutions proposed on one side or another may be easily confused by many people with the Gospel message. Hence it is necessary for people to remember that no one is allowed in the aforementioned situations to appropriate the Church's authority for their own opinion. They should always try to enlighten one another through honest discussion, preserving mutual charity and caring above all for the common good. (*GS* 43; cf. 75)

No politician or lobby group can rightly claim for themselves a monopoly on prudence or on the authentic interpretation or application of principles about which there has as yet been no definitive clarification. We must therefore avoid the tendency to consider a person or a group less goodwilled or less committed to the pro-life effort because of a different legislative strategy from our own. In this context the then-Archbishop Bertone criticized those who too readily brand the supporters of imperfect bio-laws as persons of faint heart or weak character and those who write off the opponents of less-than-perfect bio-laws as extremists or extraterrestrials.[25] He suggested that the Church and the pro-life movement ought to be capable of generating diverse approaches to these matters while remaining, despite all the differences, within the bond of communion.

Humility and hope

I have suggested that humility is an important virtue for the politician in this area. Legislators must be aware that there is only so much they

[25] Bertone, in 'Catholics in a pluralist society', pp. 219–20, noted that collaborations with less-than-perfect but better laws are not necessarily 'idle compromises with evil' but rather pursue 'different ways of affirming truth and goodness in the world, bearing in mind their concrete and often complex co-ordinates. In this respect, they are revealed as belonging to the same nature as the first attitude [of prophetic resistance], i.e. they form part of the dynamism intrinsic to the truth that tries to affirm itself in the world in order to redeem it and lead it definitively to Trinitarian fullness. It follows from this that the person who tolerates "imperfect laws" or the person who collaborates with them [in the particular sense discussed above], must not be judged by his fellow-Christian, who actively resists them, as a person of faint heart or weak character, but as a brother who tries to bury in the infinitely diversified soil of the contemporary world "a mustard seed" (cf. Matt. 13:31–32 *et par.*) that could become … a great tree.

'Contrariwise, the person who resists "unjust laws" must not be considered by his fellow-Christian who tolerates them or collaborates with them, in the sense discussed above, as a brother who has sprung from another planet or as a extremist cut off from reality, but rather as a true champion of truth in the world. Here the Pauline idea of the different charisms in a single Body might apply (cf. 1 Cor. 12:1ff.) … The Church ought to be capable of generating [diverse] heralds of truth and ensuring that they remain, despite all their differences, within the bond of communion.'

can do, especially with the blunt instruments at their disposal. As the Church's critiques of communism, fascism and some liberation theologies made clear, the Enlightenment notion of salvation by law and policy is misguided. Vices like disrespect for innocent life certainly require the best efforts of the state to 'make men moral',[26] but in the end these will not suffice.

John Finnis has observed that at the root of the present disarray and demoralization in Western Church and society is the practical elimination of transcendent hope. 'It is obviously a precondition of sustainable engagement in public policy debates that one keep bright one's hope, and keep clear and firm the presuppositions of that hope.'[27] We must pray that, in living out the imperative to be 'unconditionally pro-life' in a new century and millennium, politicians, pro-life activists, lobbyists and their sympathizers will always hold fast to that hope, even when the political scene is difficult to negotiate and potentially demoralizing.

The entire creation has been groaning till now in an act of giving birth, as it waits for the glory of the children of God to be revealed (Rom. 8:22). Let Christians therefore be convinced that they will yet find the fruits of their own nature and effort cleansed of all impurities in the new earth which God is now preparing for them, and in which there will be the kingdom of justice and love, a kingdom which will be fully perfected when the Lord will come himself.[28]

---

[26] 'The purpose of law is to make men moral': *ST* 1a 11ae 92, i, *sed contra*, citing Aristotle, *Ethics* 2, i.

[27] Finnis, 'The Catholic Church', p. 266.

[28] Synod of Bishops, *Justice in the World* (1971) 75–6.

Index

Abbott, Hon. Tony, 169
abortion, 152–81
    Benedict XVI, Pope, 145, 157
    Catechism of the Catholic Church, 157
    challenges to pro-abortion consensus, 169
    children with disabilities, 165
    Christian theology, 152–7
    Congregation for the Doctrine of the Faith,
        157
    counselling, 179
    culture of death, 19–20
    demographic effect, 176
    duties of a pro-life politician, 302–27
    early Christians, 155
    effect on community, 177–8
    grief, 175
    'holocaust', 19
    John Paul II, Pope, 56, 84–5, 156, 173
    knowledge of after-effects, 173, 175
    and new eugenics, 168
    and new genetics, 160
    prejudice or compassion?, 167–8
    pre-natal diagnosis, 160–9
    providers of, 14, 175, 176
    psychological complications, 172
    rates of, 19, 158
    response, 178–81
    sanctity of life principle, 157–9
    support for improving laws, 85
    twentieth century, 19
    Vatican II, 155
    women's experience, 171
AIDS
    condoms against HIV, 77
    'safe' sex, 18
Anderson, Francis, 268
Annas, George, 210
Anscombe, G. E. M., 29, 88, 89
antenatal screening, *see* pre-natal screening
Aquinas, St Thomas, 40, 44, 45, 48, 49, 112, 115,
    216, 220, 296, 297, 316

Aristotle, 45, 112, 113, 115, 216, 220, 227
artificial nutrition, 213–41
    autonomy-personism, 214–16
    care vs treatment, 227
    Catholic teaching, 216–18, 229–41
    critics, 218
    dignity and inviolability, 218–23
    feeding and caring, 224–7
    John Paul II, Pope, 216–18, 230–2, 241
    Schiavo, Terri, 213
    spiritual acts personism, 241–4
Ashley, Benedict, 28, 197, 282, 283, 293
assisted suicide, *see* suicide
Augustine of Hippo, St, 44, 216, 249

Baby Fae case, 199
Badham, Paul, 248–71
Basil the Great, St, 3
Beauchamp, Thomas, 193
Benedict XVI, Pope, 24, 28, 34, 36, 145, 150,
    178, 196, 208, 217, 226, 286
    abortion, 142–3, 157
    conscience, 2, 26, 38, 42, 60–1,
        65–6, 142
    cooperation in evil, 77–82
    Deus Caritas Est, 285
    Verbum Domini, 27
Bertone, Cardinal Tarcisio, 85, 312, 326
Black, Julia, 169
Blenkinsopp, Joseph, 257
Bloom, Allan, 18, 41
Bohr, David, 42
Bonaventure, St, 44, 45
Boyle, Joseph, 29
brain-death, 197–8
Brueggemann, Walter, 262

Catechism of the Catholic Church, 39, 46, 65, 81,
    96, 142, 270, 306, 307
Catherine of Siena, St, 239
Catholic bioethics summary, 4–5

Catholic bishops of England and Wales, 147,
    318, 319
*Catholic Health Australia, Code of Ethical
    Standards*, 70, 229, 283, 318
Catholic hospitals, 275–99
    advocacy of Christian values, 294
    Catholic identity
        challenges, 275–83, 301
        responses to challenges, 279, 283–6
        scandal vigilence, 294
    character cultivation, 295
    diakonia (ministry of charity), 286–90
    evangelization, 294
    fundamental commitments, 292
    healing as evangelization, 290–1
    leitourgia (celebrating the sacraments),
        296–9
    martyria (proclaiming Word of God), 290–6
    pastoral care, 297–9
    preferential option for poor and
        marginalized, 286–7
    preferential option for sick, disabled,
        suffering, dying, 287–90
    pressures, 281
    providers, Catholic Church, 279–80
    sacraments, 298
    spiritual service, 296–7
Catholic sexual teaching summary, 5–6
CDF, *see* Congregation for the Doctrine of
    the Faith
Centre for Bioethics of the Catholic University
    of the Sacred Heart, 122
Cessario, Romanus, 29, 31, 280, 295
children
    burdensome, 16
    consumer items, 14–15
    propaganda against child-bearing, 18
Childress, James, 193
Clancy, Cardinal Edward, 81
Clemons, James, 248–71
Cohn, Haim, 263
Condic, Maureen, 107, 139
Congregation for the Doctrine of the Faith
    artificial nutrition, 217, 230, 242
    Christians rôle in politics, 86
    conscience, 59–60
    drug-injecting rooms, 81–3
    embryo/human being, 143
    On Abortion, 157, 306, 307
    On Certain Bioethical Questions, 157
    On Respect for Human Life and Procreation,
        157, 306, 307
    sterilizations in Catholic hospitals, 75, 89
Connell, Richard, 114
conscience

authority of, 50–2
Benedict XVI, Pope, 2, 26, 38, 42, 60, 61,
    65, 66, 142
    communitarian account, 62–4
    continuing division over moral conscience
        and authority, 60–2
    history of idea, 42–7
    John Paul II, Pope, 2, 3, 24, 31, 35, 42, 49, 51,
        59, 195, 217, 222, 307, 311
    and magisterium, 52–62
    practical reason account, 64–6
    three dimensions of, 47–50
contraception
    'recreational sex', 14
    providers of, 14
Cooper, Adam, 14
cooperation in evil, 69–98
    different moral worldviews, 93–4
    duress, 89–90
    examples in healthcare, 73–4
    formal, 72
    human act, 86–8
    intended end, 88
    and love of God, 94
    and love of neighbour, 95–6
    and love of self, 96–7
    material, 72
    modern examples
        condoms against HIV, 77–80
        counselling pregnant women, 83–5
        drug-injecting rooms, 80–3
        sterilization in Catholic hospitals, 74–6
        support for improving abortion laws, 85–6
    pluralism, 90
    reasons to cooperate materially, 91
    reflection on, 71
culture of death, 5, 19, 20, 35, 37, 171, 230, 246,
    295, 310
culture of modernity, 13–21
    Catholic engagement with, 21–7
    moral theology, 27–37
Curran, Charles, 22, 57, 284

Daly, Tom, 103, 126, 129
Daniel, William, 129
Davis, Henry, 70, 89
death, moral certainty, 207
Delmonico, Francis, 205
Di Noia, Augustine, 295
Donagan, Alan, 197
Donceel, Joseph, 104
Donne, John, 175
Droge, Arthur, 248–71
drug-injecting rooms, 80–3
Dworkin, Ronald, 214, 215, 240

embryo
  as human being, 102, 129, 138
  beginning of individual, 101–30
  Catholic teaching, 140–3
  classical and contemporary metaphysics,
    112–19
  cloning, 14, 120, 125, 134, 136, 137, 138, 147,
    148, 149, 150, 151
  delayed hominization, 102, 104, 114, 118
  early human development, 104–12
  experimentation, liberalization, 103
  fertilization, 107–8
  fourteen-day rule, 102, 111
  frozen generation, 137
  Hippocratic oath, 144
  indiviuality criteria, 119–29
  monozygotic (identical) twinning, 109
  soul
    Aquinas, St Thomas, 114–15
    Aristotle, 114
    Ford, 102, 115
    hylomorphism, 114
    magisterial teaching, 116
  syngamy, 106–8
Engelhardt, Tristram, 193
euthanasia, 248–65
  by removal of feeding and hydration,
    213–47
  campaigns for, 20
  culture of death, 20–1
  duties of pro-life politician, 302–27
  dying or as-good-as-dead, 245
  false pity vs true love, 244–5, 269–70
  food and death in contemporary culture,
    245–6
  John Paul II, Pope, 56, 230–2, 244–5
  magisterium, 230–3
  and Scripture, 248–71
Ewing, Selina, 159

Filice, Francis, 121
Finn, Richard, 7
Finnis, John, viii–x, 7, 29, 30, 39, 42, 45,
    85, 103, 112, 160, 193, 312–13, 321,
    324, 327
Fleming, John, 159, 168, 179, 221
Fletcher, Joseph, 22, 193
food and drink
  Christ, 235
  in contemporary culture, 245–6
  theological significance, 235–8
Ford, Norman, 101–30
Freud, Sigmund, 41
Fuchs, Josef, 22, 77, 284
Fuller, Jon, 77

genetic screening, *see* pre-natal screening
George, Robert, 29, 218
German Catholic bishops
  counselling pregnant women, 84
Gilson, Étienne, 29
Glover, Jonathan, 19
Gormally, Luke, 8, 9, 31, 211, 218, 312, 313
Gracia, Jorge, 113
Green, Michael, 201
Greer, Germaine, 174
Griese, Orville, 75
Grisez, Germain, 7, 29, 65, 71, 75, 76, 80, 95,
    223, 282, 283

Haas, John, 198
Hamel, Ronald, 90
Häring, Bernard, 28, 90, 91
Harris, John, 200, 201
Hauerwas, Stanley, 32, 240, 290, 298, 299
Hertzberg, Hans, 262
Hippocrates, 158, 227
HIV/AIDS, *see* AIDS
Holy See
  Charter of the Rights of the Family, 307
Honings, Bonifacio, 297
Hoppe, Leslie, 255, 257
human dignity, 46, 86, 147, 150, 152, 218–28,
    284, 288
Humber, James, 121
Humphry, Derek, 249
Hwang, Woo-Suk, 148

in vitro fertilization, *see* IVF
IVF, 20, 176
  'made-to-order babies', 14
  market, 136
  providers of, 14

Janssens, Louis, 22
John XXIII, Pope, 140
John Paul II Institute for Marriage and the
    Family, 7, 26
John Paul II, Pope, 28, 29, 37, 171, 178, 205, 206,
    217, 219, 291, 314
  abortion, 56, 84, 85, 140–2, 156, 173
  Ad Tuendam Fidem, 60
  artificial nutrition, 217, 230–2, 241
  conscience, 2, 24, 31, 35, 42, 49, 51, 59, 195,
    217, 222, 307, 311
  cooperation in evil, 84
  dignity of human person, 219
  embryo experimentation, 145
  euthanasia, 56, 230–2, 244–5
  Evangelium Vitae, 1, 2, 4, 26, 33, 46, 51, 55,
    56, 60, 67, 76, 85, 86, 140, 142, 145, 156,

165, 173, 202, 207, 217, 222, 228, 230, 232, 235, 241, 244, 245, 289, 295, 306, 307, 308, 311, 313, 314, 316, 321, 322, 325
Familiaris Consortio, 5, 26, 33
Fides et Ratio, 241
healthcare, 289–95
Love and Responsibility, 26
Novo Millennio Ineunte, 2, 3
prenatal diagnosis, 165
response to culture of modernity, 23–7
Theology of the Body, 1, 2, 5, 26, 188
transplantation, 185, 188, 198, 203, 204, 206, 207, 208, 211
Veritatis Splendor, 24, 26, 31, 35, 39, 42, 50, 56, 59, 64, 65, 67, 76, 87, 195, 202, 217, 241
Jones, David, 103, 112, 171

Kant, Immanuel, 216
Kasper, Cardinal Walter, 285, 290
Kass, Leon, 3, 33, 147, 148, 197, 199
Kaveny, Cathleen, 70, 71, 96, 97
Keane, Philip, 57
Keenan, James, 77, 78, 82, 83, 89, 90
Kelly, Kevin, 77
Kevorkian, Jack, 249
Klein, Lillian, 255, 257
Knauer, Peter, 22
Knox, Elizabeth, 13, 20, 21
Kolbe, St Maximillian, 226
Kopfensteiner, Thomas, 89, 90
Küng, Hans, 57

Langton, Stephen, 44
Lasch, Christopher, 16
Lawler, Philip, 24
Lawson, Dominic, 161
Lee, Patrick, 29, 112, 129, 160, 187, 220
Leo XIII, Pope, 29
Levin, Yuval, 133
Lewis, Brian, 90, 91, 135
Ligouri, St Alphonsus, 45
Lombard, Peter, 44, 45

M'Neile, Alan, 263
McCabe, Herbert, 29
McCormick, Richard, 22, 77, 200, 281, 282, 283, 299
McDonagh, Enda, 77
McInerney, Ralph, 29, 48
MacIntyre, Alasdair, 32, 63, 105, 195, 218, 220, 240
McKenna-Vout, Brigid, 174
magisterium, 52–6
Mahoney, John, 200

Manne, Anne, 24, 25
Maritain, Jacques, 29
May, William E., 29
Meilaender, Gilbert, 129, 193, 197, 220, 268, 295
Mill, John Stuart, 215, 240
Moraczewski, Albert, 103
moral theology, 27, 36, 60
cooperation in evil, 69–97
human freedom and conscience, 22
renewal, 22, 34–7
Scripture, emphasis post-Vatican II, 27–9

natural law theory, 29–31
Nelson, Richard, 264
Newman, Cardinal John Henry, 38, 39, 41, 45
Nietzsche, Friedrich, 14

O'Connell, Timothy, 58
O'Connor, Cardinal John, 289
O'Neill, Onora, 197
Ockham, William of, 40, 41
oocytes, 134, 135
reluctance to donate, 136
Orsy, Ladislau, 55

Paul VI, Pope, 140
Humanae Vitae, 22, 57, 140, 307
Paul, St, 241, 265, 266
conscience, 51
Pell, Cardinal George, 9, 39, 67
Pelosi, Nancy, 101
Philip the Chancellor, 44
physician-assisted suicide, *see* euthanasia
Piccione, Joseph, 282
Pieper, Josef, 29, 48
Pinckaers, Servais, 23, 27, 28, 29, 41, 45, 284
Pius XII, Pope, 200, 206, 207
Planned Parenthood v. Casey, 21
politics, 302–24
Catholic teaching, 306–10
Christians' role, 86
cooperation in evil, 309
documents of counsel, 306
imperfect laws, 314–18
material cooperation, 317–18
pro-life politician
legitimacy of different opinions, 325
reasonable stances, 320–4
virtues of, 327
Pontifical Academy for Life, 149
Pontifical Biblical Commission, 27
Pontifical Council for Health
Charter for Healthworkers, 81, 157, 189, 200, 204, 206, 212, 230, 288, 294
pre-natal screening, 160–9

Prümmer, Dominic, 29

Rabinowitz, Louie, 263
Rahner, Karl, 56, 57, 58
Ramsay, Hayden, 7, 29, 246
Ramsey, Paul, 128, 197
Ratzinger, Cardinal Joseph, *see* Benedict XVI,
   Pope
Regan, Tom, 199
Reiser, Stanley, 292
Riordan, Marcia, 174
Rorty, Richard, 220
Rowland, Tracey, 31, 38

sanctity of life
   arguments, artificial nutrition, 228–41
   Christian thinking, 240
   the *imago Dei*, 238–41
Sanders, Mark, 69, 96, 97
Sasson, Jack, 251
Savelescu, Julian, 200
Schiavo, Terri, 213, 214, 215, 222, 245
Schmitz, Anthony, 7
Schopenhauer, Arthur, 243
Schüller, Bruno, 22
Scripture
   abortion, 152–4
   artificial nutrition, 228–41
   conscience, 42–4
   embryo, 141
   greater emphasis in moral theology, 27–9
   and natural law, 31
   politicians, virtues, 325
   suicide and euthanasia, 248–71
   transplantation, 189–91
sexual ethics
   Catholic, 5–6, 23–9, 34–7
   natural law, 29
   post-modernity, 14–16
   virtue and community, 31–4
Sgreccia, Cardinal Elio, 7, 147
Short, Roger, 105
Shuster, Evelyne, 168
Singer, Peter, 15, 117, 122, 129, 200, 215, 240
Stark, Rodney, 236
stem cells, 131–51
   adult, 132
   altered nuclear transfer or ANT cells, 134
   Alzheimer's, 135–6
   bone marrow, 132
   Catholic Church, 132
   cybrid, 134
   embryonic, 133, 134, 135
      ethical concerns, 138–48
      hybridization, 148

      incautious research, 148
      social concerns, 148–51
   induced pluripotent or iPS cells, 133
   placental, 133
   potential sources, 145
sterilization in Catholic hospitals, 74
Stout, Jeffrey, 34
Suaudeau, Jacques, 78
suicide and euthanasia
   Catechism of the Catholic Church, 270
   compassion, duty to keep caring, 269–70
   divine mercy, 270–1
   Jesus
      autonomy vs God's will, 267–8
   scriptural view, 248–65
      Abimelech, 255–6
      Ahithophel, 261–2
      Jesus, 253–5
      Job, 251–2
      Jonah, 250–1
      Judas, 262–3
      Paul, 252–3
      Samson, 256–8
      Saul, 258–61
      Zimri, 264
Sullivan, Francis, 53, 55, 58, 59, 63
Synod of Bishops, 27, 327

Tabor, James, 248–71
Taylor, Charles, 63, 195, 218
Teo, Bernard, 195
Terrien, Samuel, 251
Tertullian, 142
Thomist revival, 29
Tollefsen, Christopher, 8, 112, 129, 130
Tonti-Filippini, Nicholas, 103, 121, 129, 221,
   312, 318
transplantation, 185–212
   allocation of organs, 208
   Benedict XVI, Pope, 208
   body as personal, 189
   body as property, 187
   body as trust, 187
   brain death, 197–8, 204
   costs, 211
   John Paul II, Pope, 185, 188, 198, 203, 204,
      206, 207, 208, 211
   Pius XII, Pope, 200, 206, 207
   tissue procurement, 191
      communitarian approach, 195
      consent, 192, 211
      consequentialist approach, 200
      deontological approach, 196
      humanizing the practice of, 204–5
      liberal-individualist approach, 193

natural law approach, 202
tissue reception
ethical issues, 209–12
xenotransplantation, 186, 187, 190, 199, 208, 210
Trounson, Alan, 105
tube feeding, *see* artificial nutrition

United Nations
Declaration on Human Cloning, 150
US Catholic bishops
artificial nutrition, 230
Committee for Pro-Life Activities, 229
condoms against HIV, 77
Ethical Directives for Catholic Health Care, 75, 76, 89–90, 229, 296
healthcare, 230, 289, 293, 297
sterilization in Catholic hospitals, 75
US President's Council on Bioethics, 149
US Supreme Court, 21
Casey, 214
Roe v *Wade*, 214
Webster, 214

Vatican II, 21, 27, 29, 50, 53, 285

abortion, 141, 155
Christian politicians, 304, 306, 325
conscience, 46
Dei Verbum, 34, 52, 54
Dignitatis Humanæ, 46, 47, 48, 54
euthanasia, 226, 231
Gaudium et Spes, 22, 31, 39, 46, 47, 51, 55, 66, 156, 284, 285, 304, 305, 307, 326
Lumen Gentium, 35, 46, 54, 284, 285
Optatum Totius, 22, 34
Presbyterorum Ordinis, 34
renewal of moral theology, 34, 36
Veatch, Henry, 29
virtue ethics
contemporary, 32–3
revival, 31–2
vocations crisis, 17
Von Balthasar, Hans Urs, 34

Watt, Helen, 7, 70, 312
Wennberg, Robert, 120
Williams, Bernard, 214
Wojtyła, Karol, *see* John Paul II, Pope
Wolf, Zane, 197
World Health Organization, 20